A KODANSHA COMICS TRADE PAPERBACK ORIGINAL

UQ HOLDER! VOLUME 8 COPYRIGHT © 2015 KEN AKAMATSU
ENGLISH TRANSLATION COPYRIGHT © 2016 KEN AKAMATSU

ALL RIGHTS RESERVED.

PUBLISHED IN THE UNITED STATES BY KODANSHA COMICS, AN IMPRINT OF KODANSHA USA PUBLISHING, LLC, NEW YORK.

PUBLICATION RIGHTS FOR THIS ENGLISH EDITION ARRANGED THROUGH KODANSHA LTD., TOKYO.

FIRST PUBLISHED IN JAPAN IN 2015 BY KODANSHA LTD., TOKYO.

ISBN 978-1-63236-271-1

PRINTED IN THE UNITED STATES OF AMERICA.

WWW.KODANSHACOMICS.COM

9 8 7 6 5 4 3 2 1

TRANSLATION: ALETHEA NIBLEY AND ATHENA NIBLEY
LETTERING: JAMES DASHIELL
EDITING: LAUREN SCANLAN
KODANSHA COMICS EDITION COVER DESIGN: PHIL BALSMAN

UQ HOLDER!

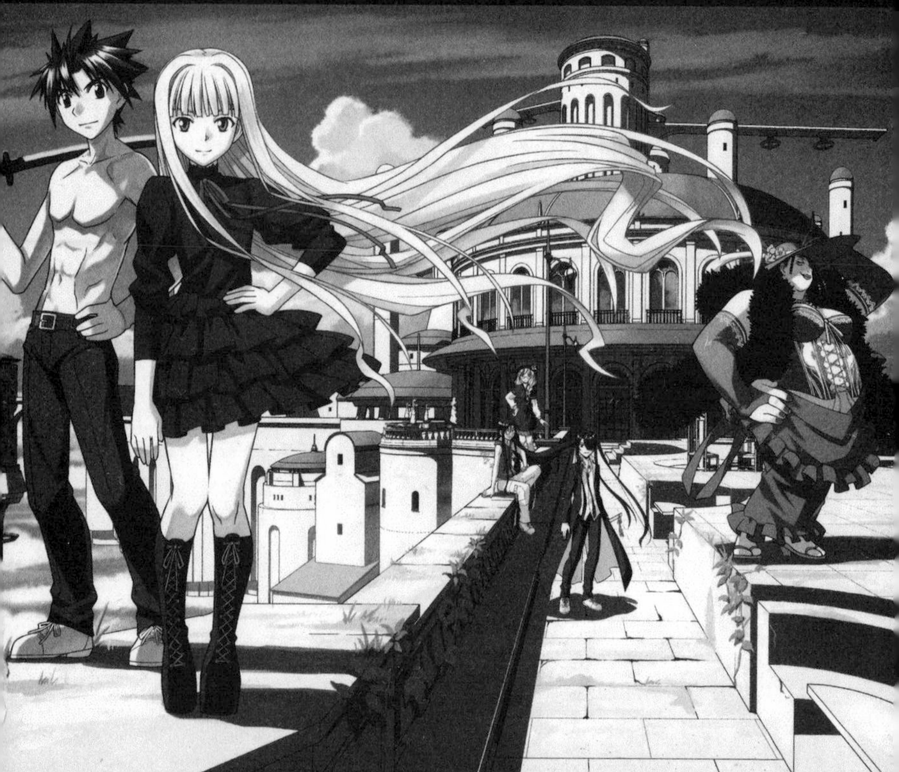

KEN AKAMATSU

vol. 8

CHARACTERS

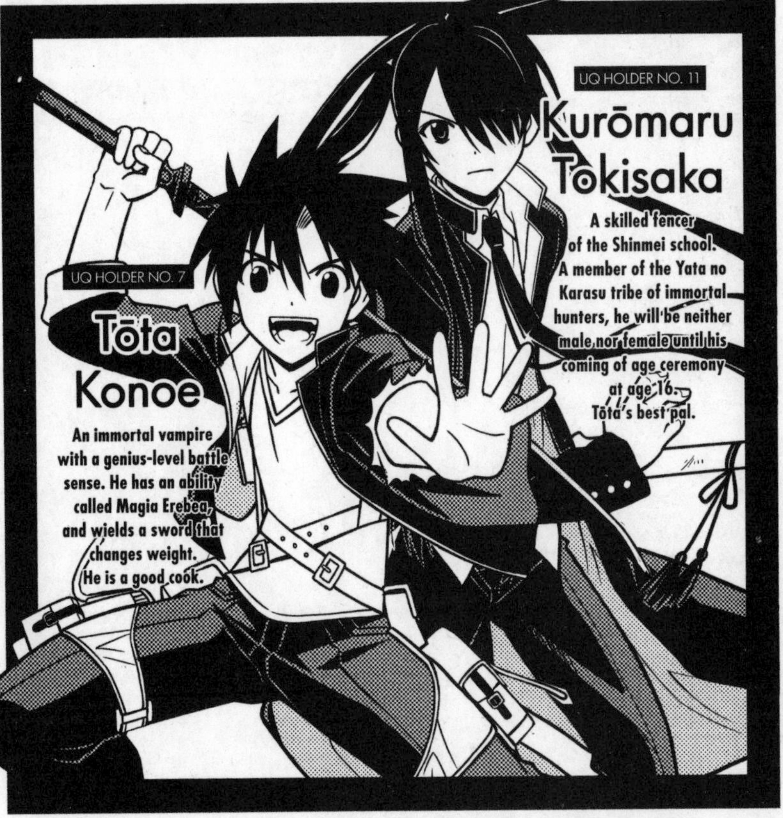
UQ HOLDER NO. 11
Kurōmaru Tokisaka
A skilled fencer of the Shinmei school. A member of the Yata no Karasu tribe of immortal hunters, he will be neither male nor female until his coming of age ceremony at age 16. Tōta's best pal.
UQ HOLDER NO. 7
Tōta Konoe
An immortal vampire with a genius-level battle sense. He has an ability called Magia Erebea, and wields a sword that changes weight. He is a good cook.

UQ HOLDER NUMBERS

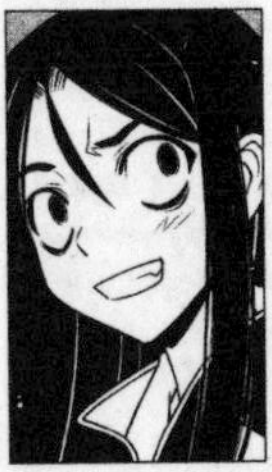

UQ HOLDER NO. 12

SANTA SASAKI

After a tormented past as the victim of bullying, he became a shut-in. He thought he was alive, but is actually a ghost. Because of that, he can use multiple abilities.

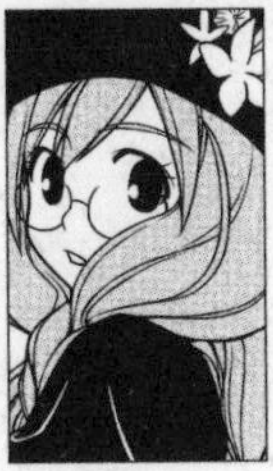

UQ HOLDER NO. 9

KIRIË SAKURAME

The greatest financial contributor to UQ Holder, and constantly calls Tōta incompetent. Her ability is called Reset & Restart.

UQ HOLDER!

Ken Akamatsu Presents

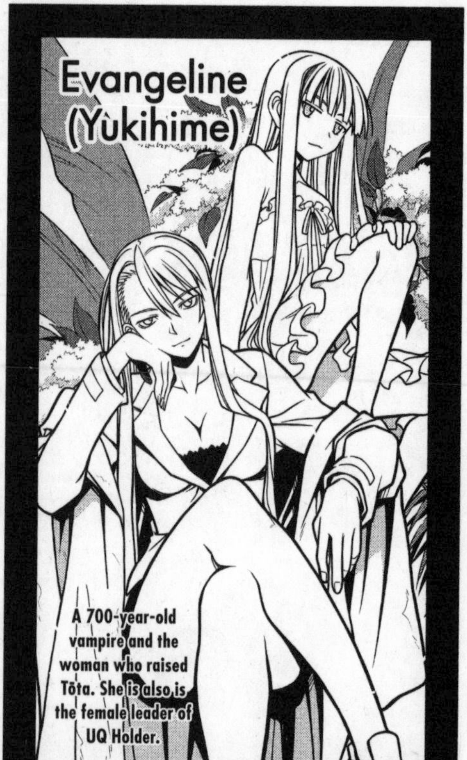

Evangeline (Yùkihime)
A 700-year-old vampire and the woman who raised Tōta. She is also is the female leader of UQ Holder.

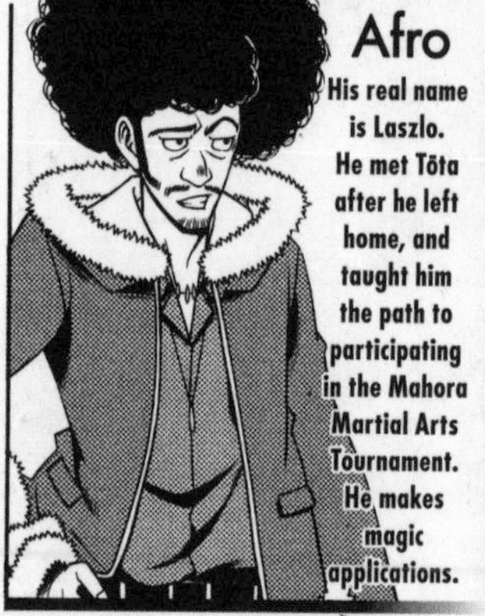

Afro
His real name is Laszlo. He met Tōta after he left home, and taught him the path to participating in the Mahora Martial Arts Tournament. He makes magic applications.

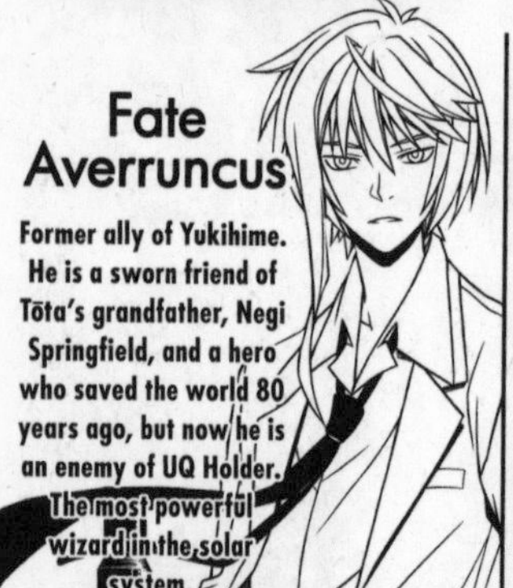

Fate Averruncus
Former ally of Yukihime. He is a sworn friend of Tōta's grandfather, Negi Springfield, and a hero who saved the world 80 years ago, but now he is an enemy of UQ Holder. The most powerful wizard in the solar system.

MAGE OF THE BEGINNING

Also known as "The Lifemaker," she is a fearsome wizard who is called the prime cause of all evil. Was once defeated by Tōta's great-grandfather, Nagi Springfield.

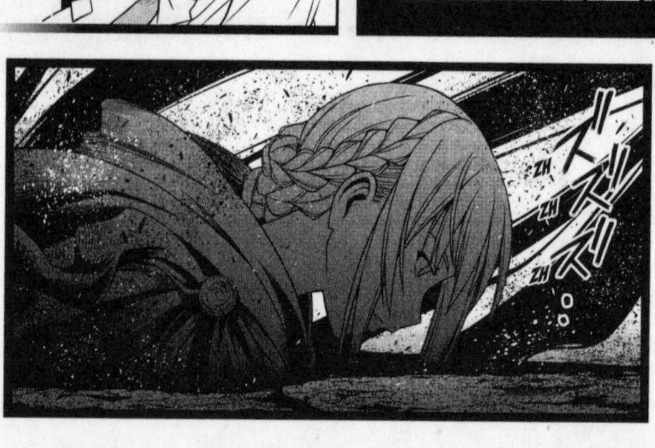

ZH
ZH
ZH

THE STORY SO FAR

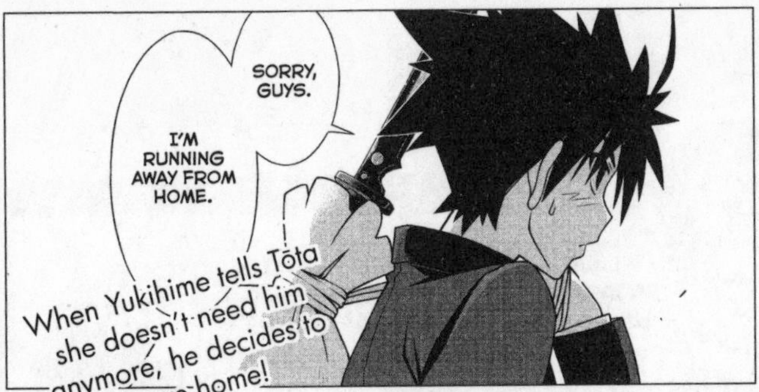
SORRY, GUYS.
I'M RUNNING AWAY FROM HOME.
When Yukihime tells Tōta she doesn't need him anymore, he decides to leave home!

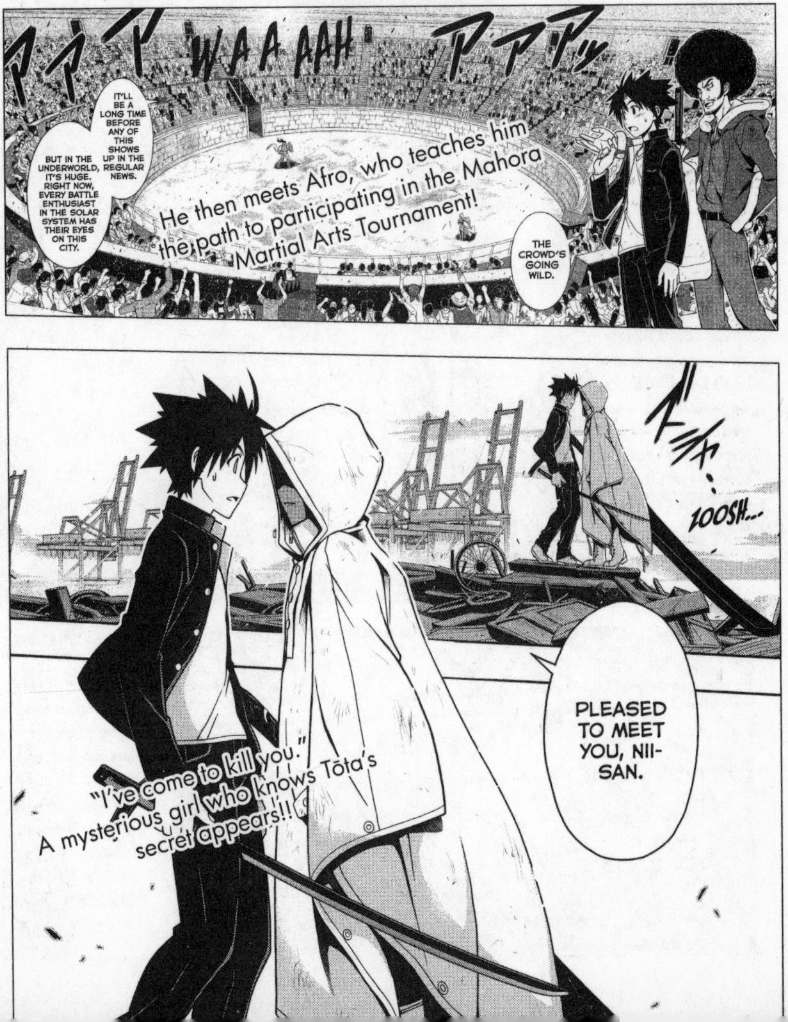
WAAAAH
THE CROWD'S GOING WILD.
IT'LL BE A LONG TIME BEFORE ANY OF THIS SHOWS UP IN THE REGULAR NEWS.
BUT IN THE UNDERWORLD, IT'S HUGE. RIGHT NOW, EVERY BATTLE ENTHUSIAST IN THE SOLAR SYSTEM HAS THEIR EYES ON THIS CITY.
He then meets Afro, who teaches him the path to participating in the Mahora Martial Arts Tournament!
ZOOSH...
PLEASED TO MEET YOU, NII-SAN.
"I've come to kill you." A mysterious girl who knows Tōta's secret appears!!

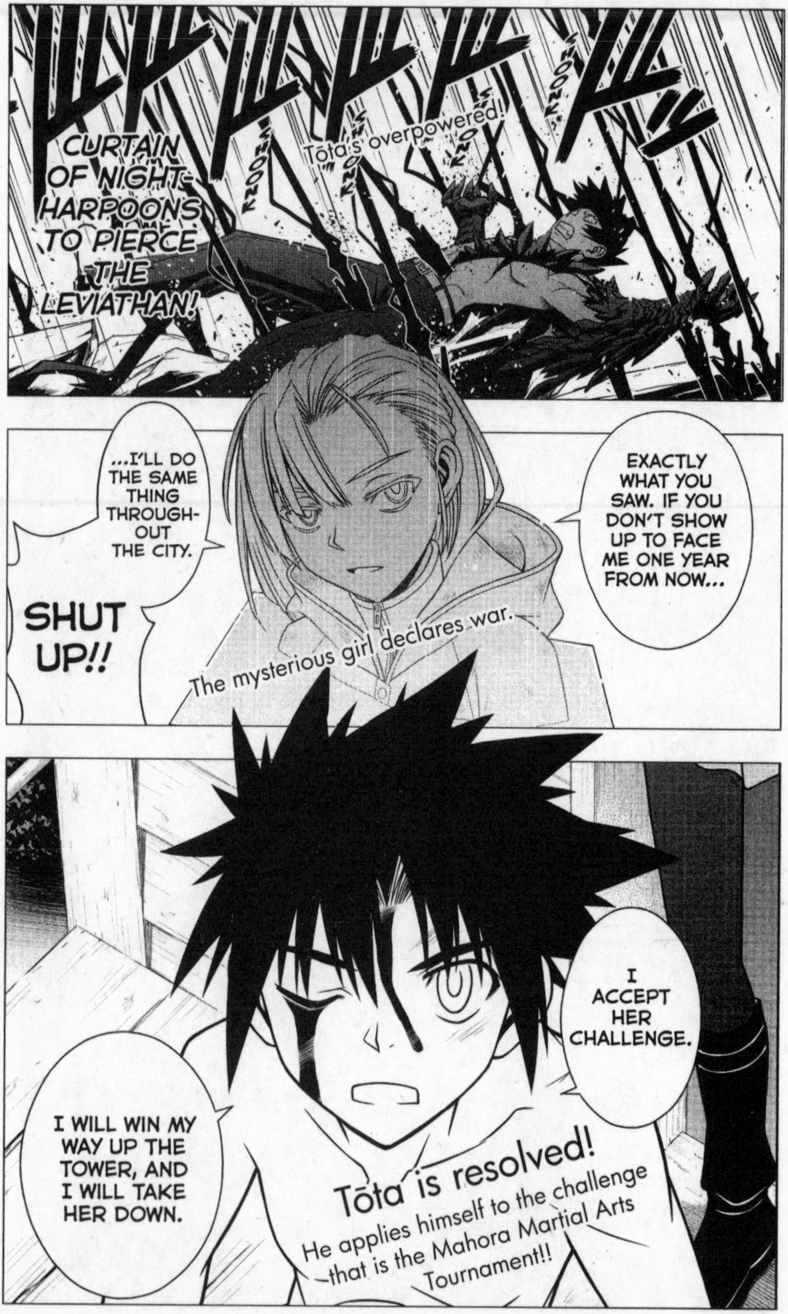
SHOONK
Tōta's overpowered!
SHOONK
SHOONK
SHOONK
CURTAIN OF NIGHT—HARPOONS TO PIERCE THE LEVIATHAN!
EXACTLY WHAT YOU SAW. IF YOU DON'T SHOW UP TO FACE ME ONE YEAR FROM NOW...
...I'LL DO THE SAME THING THROUGHOUT THE CITY.
SHUT UP!!
The mysterious girl declares war.
I ACCEPT HER CHALLENGE.
I WILL WIN MY WAY UP THE TOWER, AND I WILL TAKE HER DOWN.
Tōta is resolved!
He applies himself to the challenge that is the Mahora Martial Arts Tournament!!

CONTENTS

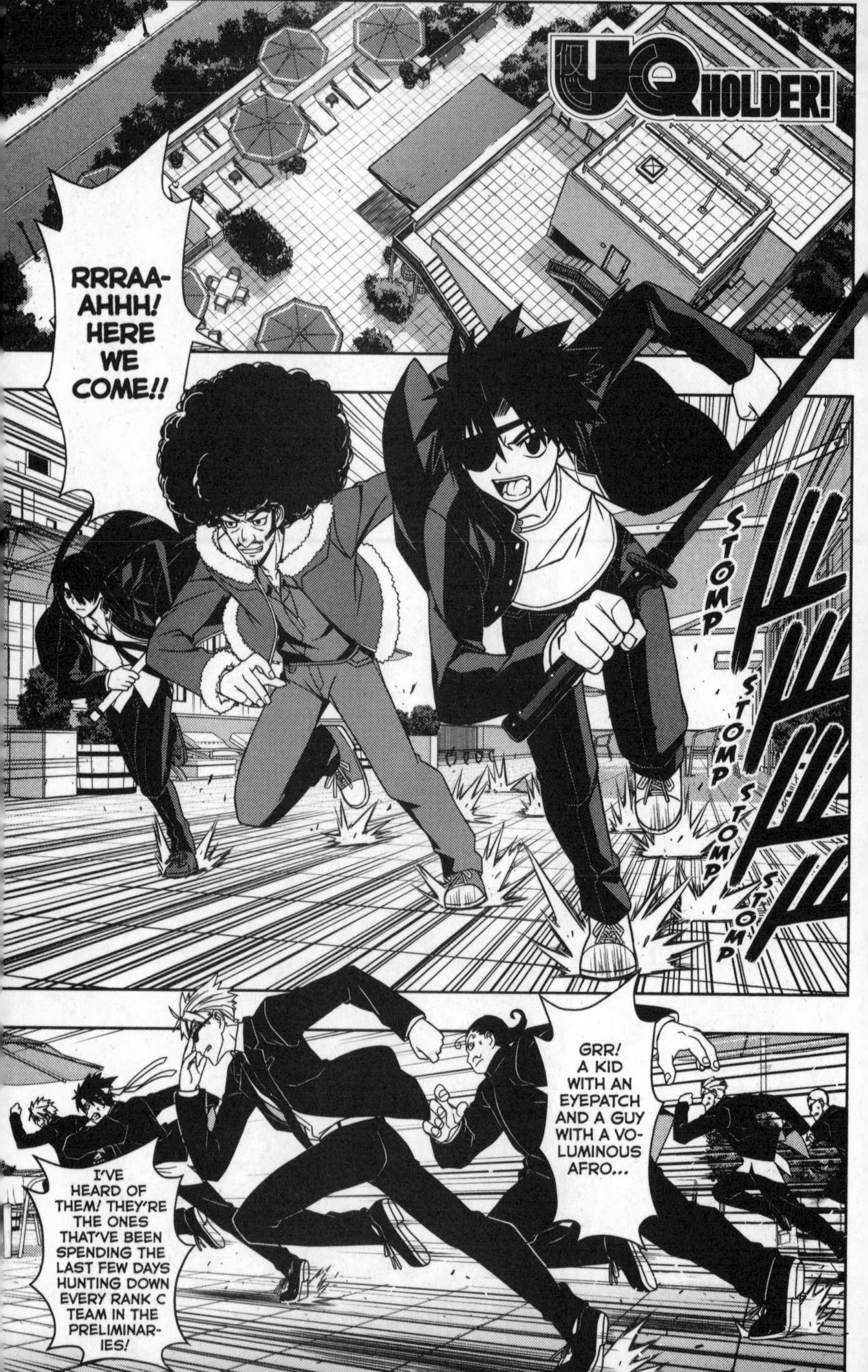
UQ HOLDER!
RRRAA-AHHH! HERE WE COME!!
STOMP
STOMP
STOMP
STOMP
GRR! A KID WITH AN EYEPATCH AND A GUY WITH A VOLUMINOUS AFRO...
I'VE HEARD OF THEM! THEY'RE THE ONES THAT'VE BEEN SPENDING THE LAST FEW DAYS HUNTING DOWN EVERY RANK C TEAM IN THE PRELIMINARIES!

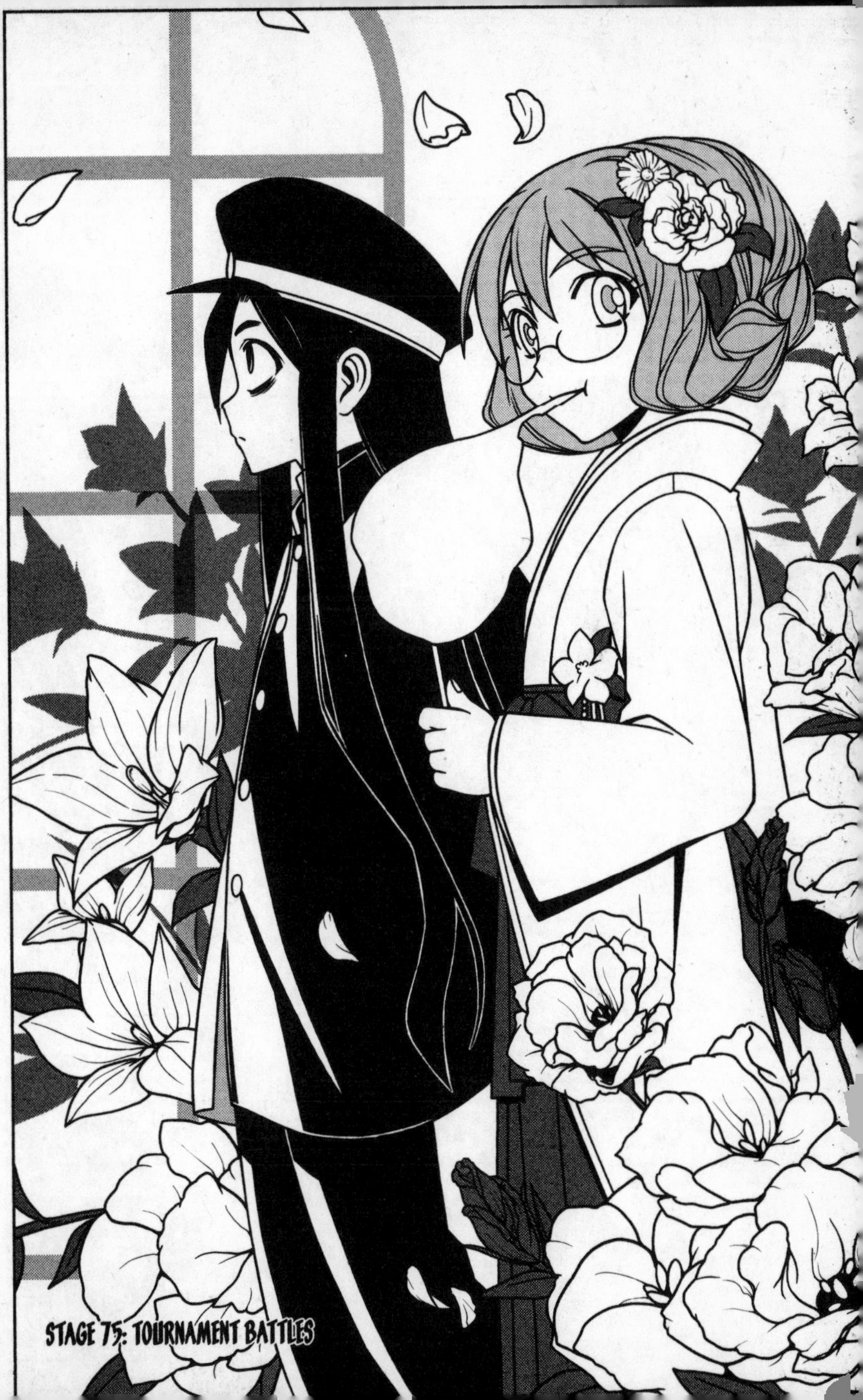
STAGE 75: TOURNAMENT BATTLES

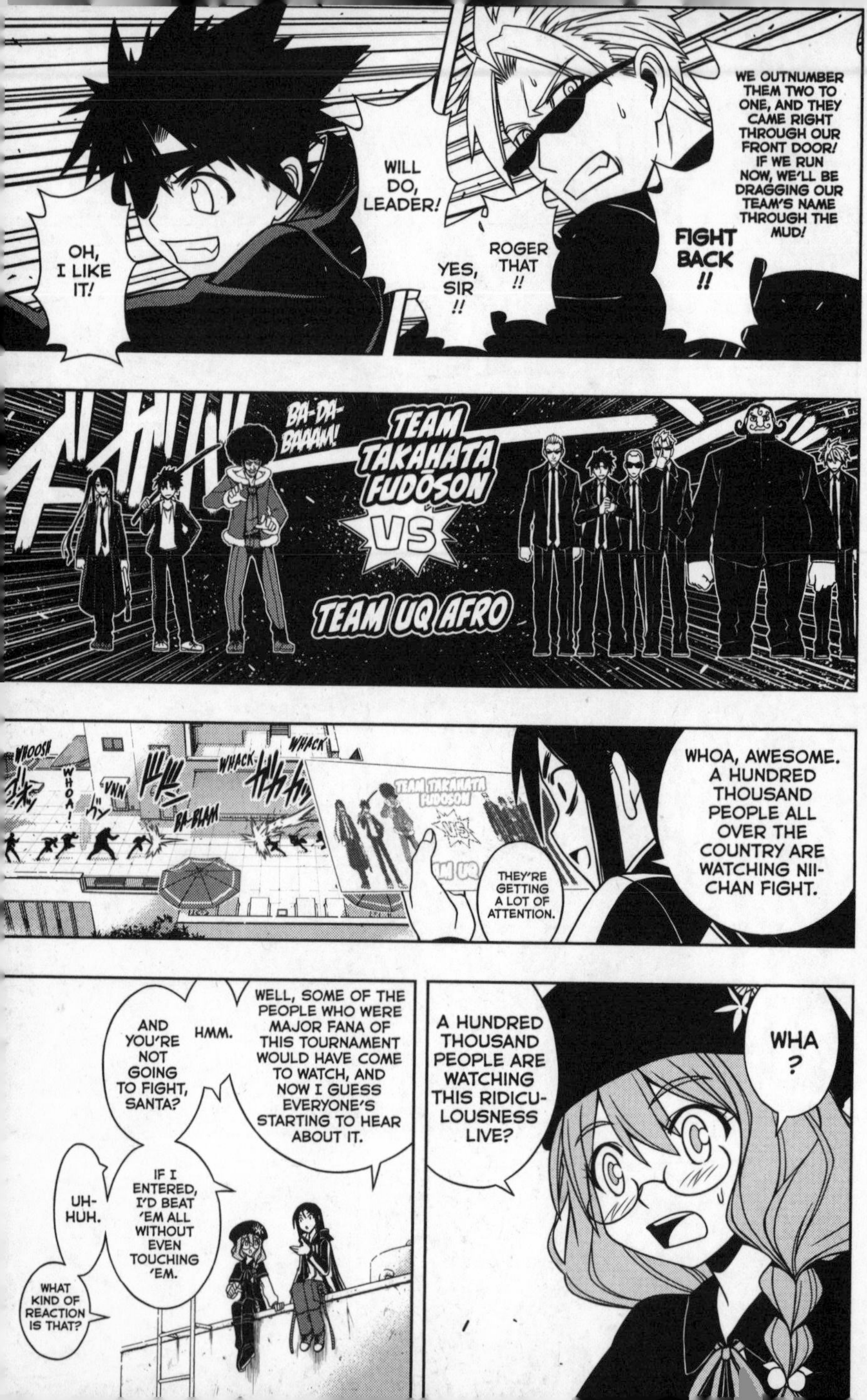
WE OUTNUMBER THEM TWO TO ONE, AND THEY CAME RIGHT THROUGH OUR FRONT DOOR! IF WE RUN NOW, WE'LL BE DRAGGING OUR TEAM'S NAME THROUGH THE MUD!
FIGHT BACK !!
ROGER THAT !!
YES, SIR !!
WILL DO, LEADER!
OH, I LIKE IT!
BA-DA-BAAAM!
TEAM TAKAHATA FUDŌSON
VS
TEAM UQ AFRO
WHOA, AWESOME. A HUNDRED THOUSAND PEOPLE ALL OVER THE COUNTRY ARE WATCHING NII-CHAN FIGHT.
THEY'RE GETTING A LOT OF ATTENTION.
WHACK
WHACK
BA-BLAM
VNN
WHOA!
WHOOSH
TEAM TAKAHATA FUDOSON
VS
WHA ?
A HUNDRED THOUSAND PEOPLE ARE WATCHING THIS RIDICU-LOUSNESS LIVE?
WELL, SOME OF THE PEOPLE WHO WERE MAJOR FANA OF THIS TOURNAMENT WOULD HAVE COME TO WATCH, AND NOW I GUESS EVERYONE'S STARTING TO HEAR ABOUT IT.
HMM.
AND YOU'RE NOT GOING TO FIGHT, SANTA?
IF I ENTERED, I'D BEAT 'EM ALL WITHOUT EVEN TOUCHING 'EM.
UH-HUH.
WHAT KIND OF REACTION IS THAT?

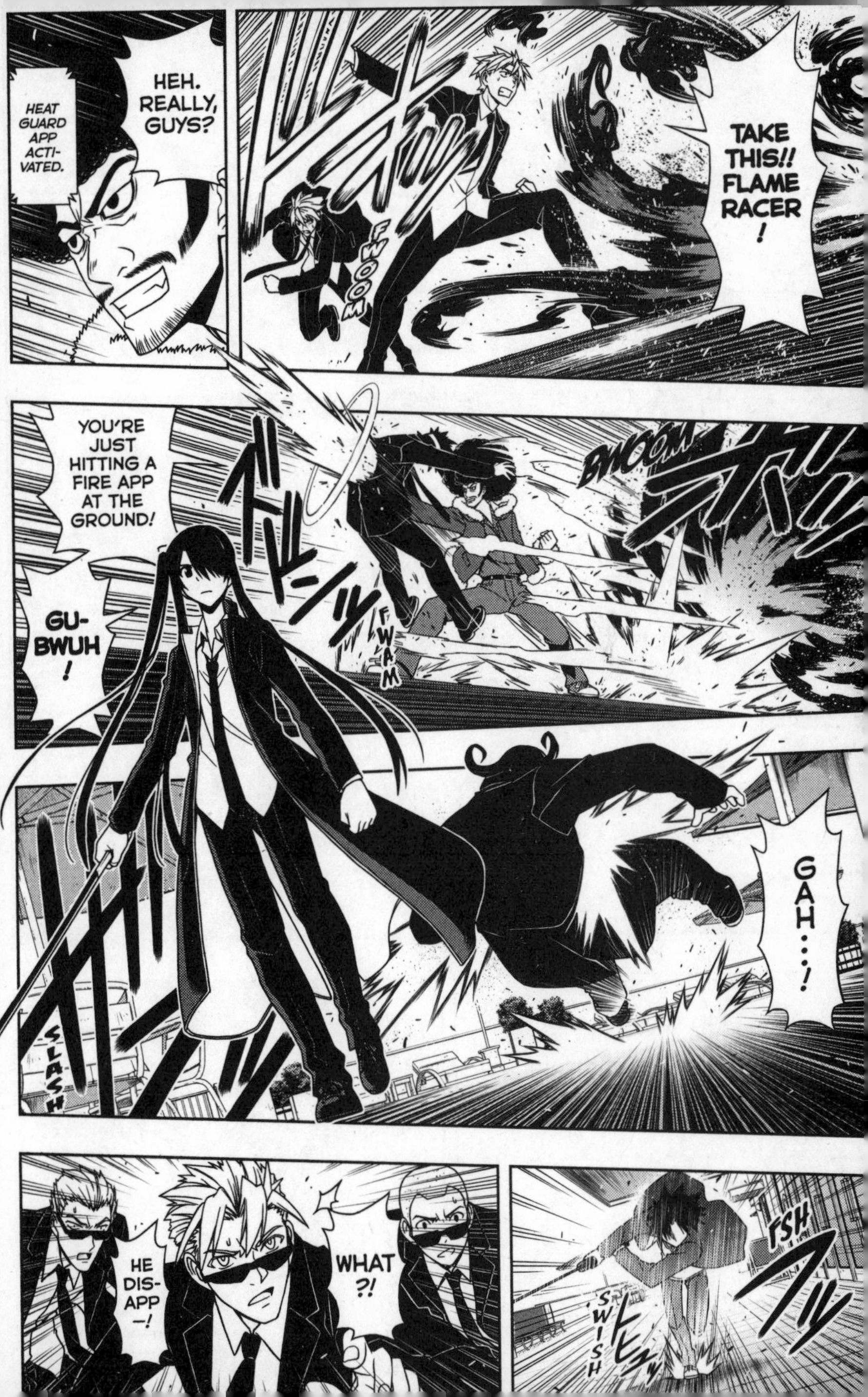
TAKE THIS!! FLAME RACER!
FWOOM
HEAT GUARD APP ACTI-VATED.
HEH. REALLY, GUYS?
BWOOM
YOU'RE JUST HITTING A FIRE APP AT THE GROUND!
FWAM
GU-BWUH!
GAH...!
SLASH
FSH
SWISH
WHAT?!
HE DIS-APP-!

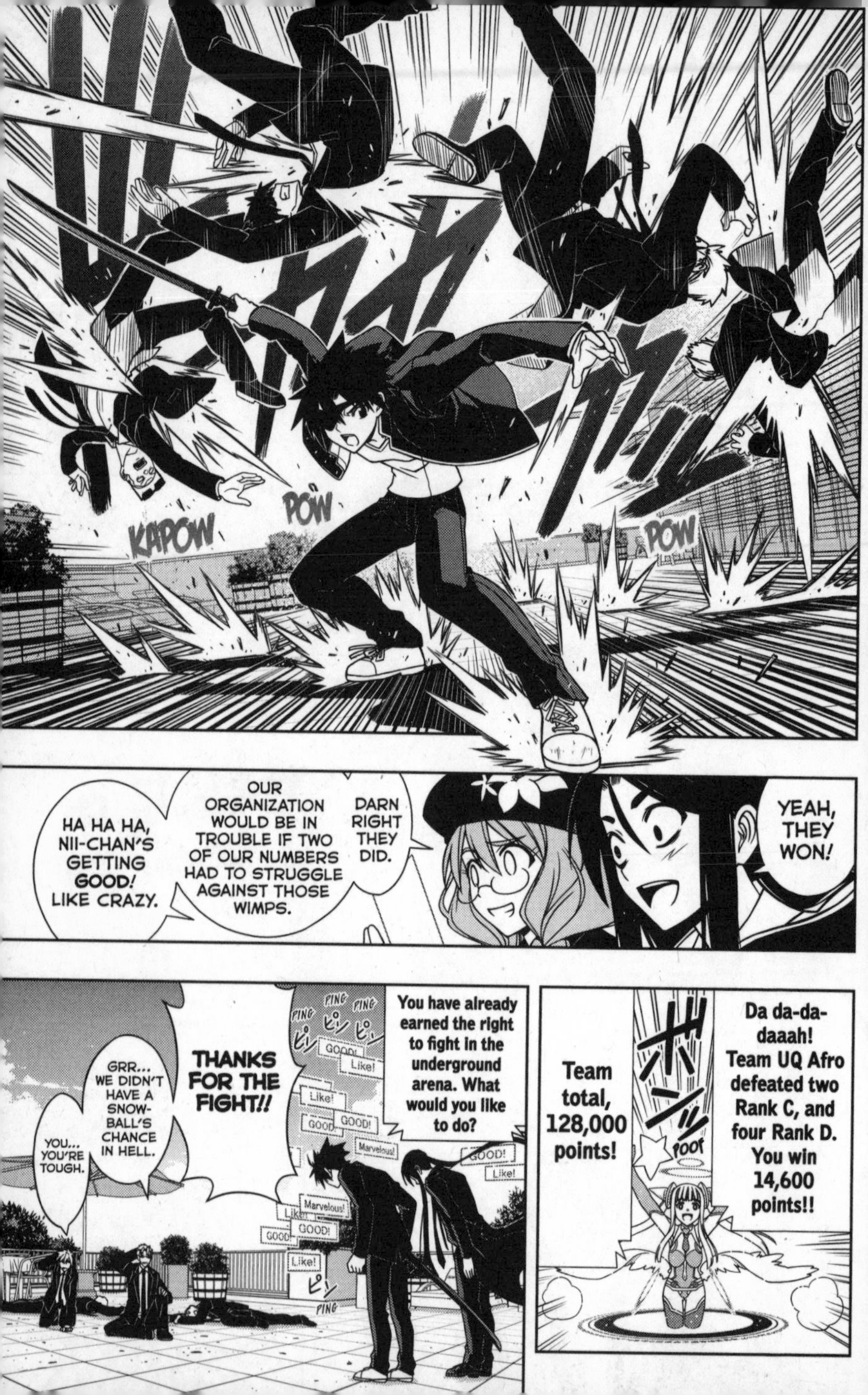
POW
POW
KAPOW
YEAH, THEY WON!
DARN RIGHT THEY DID.
OUR ORGANIZATION WOULD BE IN TROUBLE IF TWO OF OUR NUMBERS HAD TO STRUGGLE AGAINST THOSE WIMPS.
HA HA HA, NII-CHAN'S GETTING GOOD! LIKE CRAZY.
Da da-da-daaah! Team UQ Afro defeated two Rank C, and four Rank D. You win 14,600 points!!
Team total, 128,000 points!
POOF
You have already earned the right to fight in the underground arena. What would you like to do?
PING PING PING
GOOD! Like! Like! GOOD! GOOD! Marvelous! GOOD! Like! Marvelous! Like! GOOD! GOOD! Like!
PING
THANKS FOR THE FIGHT!!
GRR... WE DIDN'T HAVE A SNOW-BALL'S CHANCE IN HELL.
YOU... YOU'RE TOUGH.

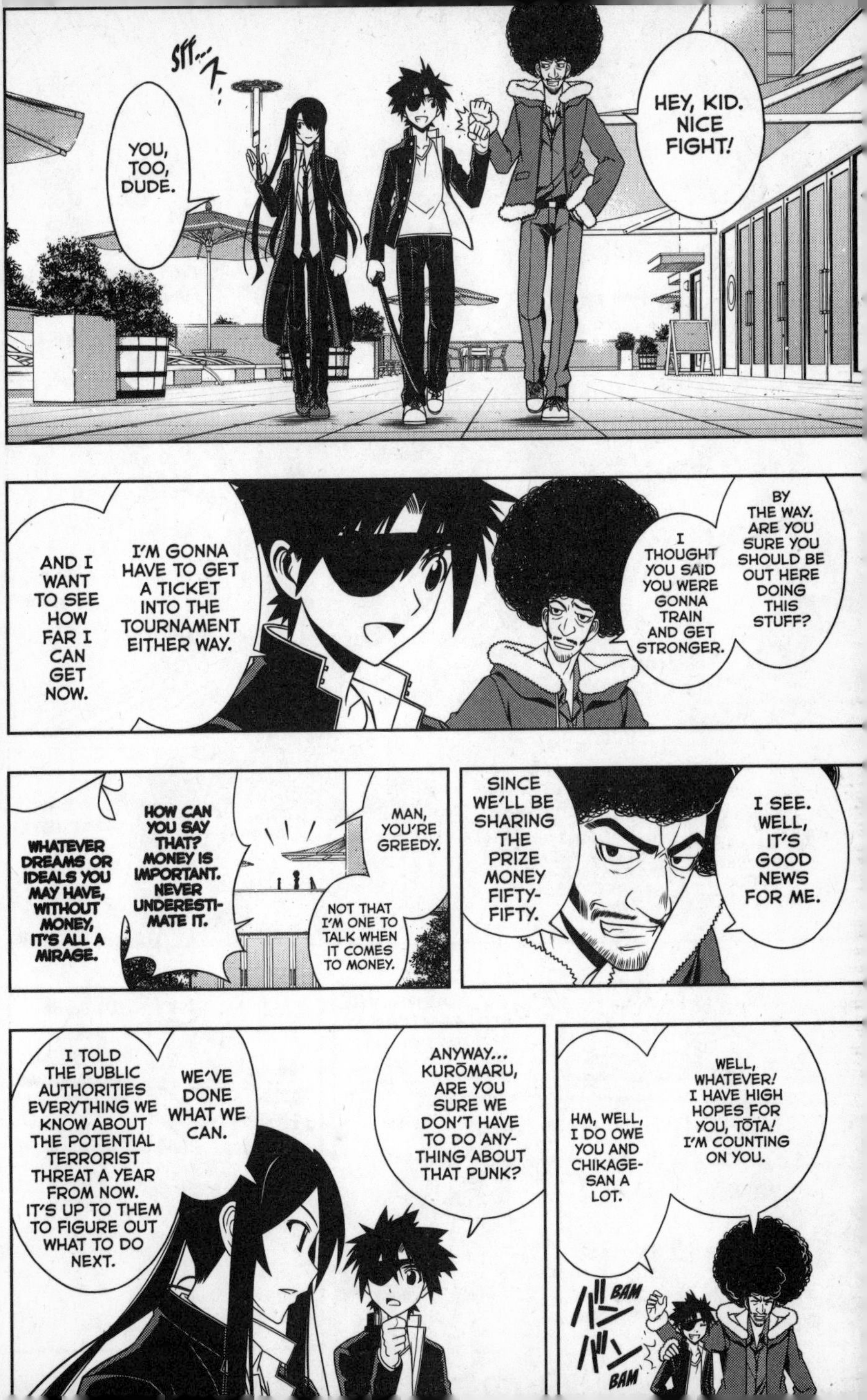
HEY, KID. NICE FIGHT!
SFF...
YOU, TOO, DUDE.
BY THE WAY. ARE YOU SURE YOU SHOULD BE OUT HERE DOING THIS STUFF?
I THOUGHT YOU SAID YOU WERE GONNA TRAIN AND GET STRONGER.
I'M GONNA HAVE TO GET A TICKET INTO THE TOURNAMENT EITHER WAY.
AND I WANT TO SEE HOW FAR I CAN GET NOW.
I SEE. WELL, IT'S GOOD NEWS FOR ME.
SINCE WE'LL BE SHARING THE PRIZE MONEY FIFTY-FIFTY.
MAN, YOU'RE GREEDY.
NOT THAT I'M ONE TO TALK WHEN IT COMES TO MONEY.
HOW CAN YOU SAY THAT? MONEY IS IMPORTANT. NEVER UNDERESTIMATE IT.
WHATEVER DREAMS OR IDEALS YOU MAY HAVE, WITHOUT MONEY, IT'S ALL A MIRAGE.
WELL, WHATEVER! I HAVE HIGH HOPES FOR YOU, TŌTA! I'M COUNTING ON YOU.
HM, WELL, I DO OWE YOU AND CHIKAGE-SAN A LOT.
BAM
BAM
ANYWAY... KURŌMARU, ARE YOU SURE WE DON'T HAVE TO DO ANYTHING ABOUT THAT PUNK?
WE'VE DONE WHAT WE CAN.
I TOLD THE PUBLIC AUTHORITIES EVERYTHING WE KNOW ABOUT THE POTENTIAL TERRORIST THREAT A YEAR FROM NOW. IT'S UP TO THEM TO FIGURE OUT WHAT TO DO NEXT.

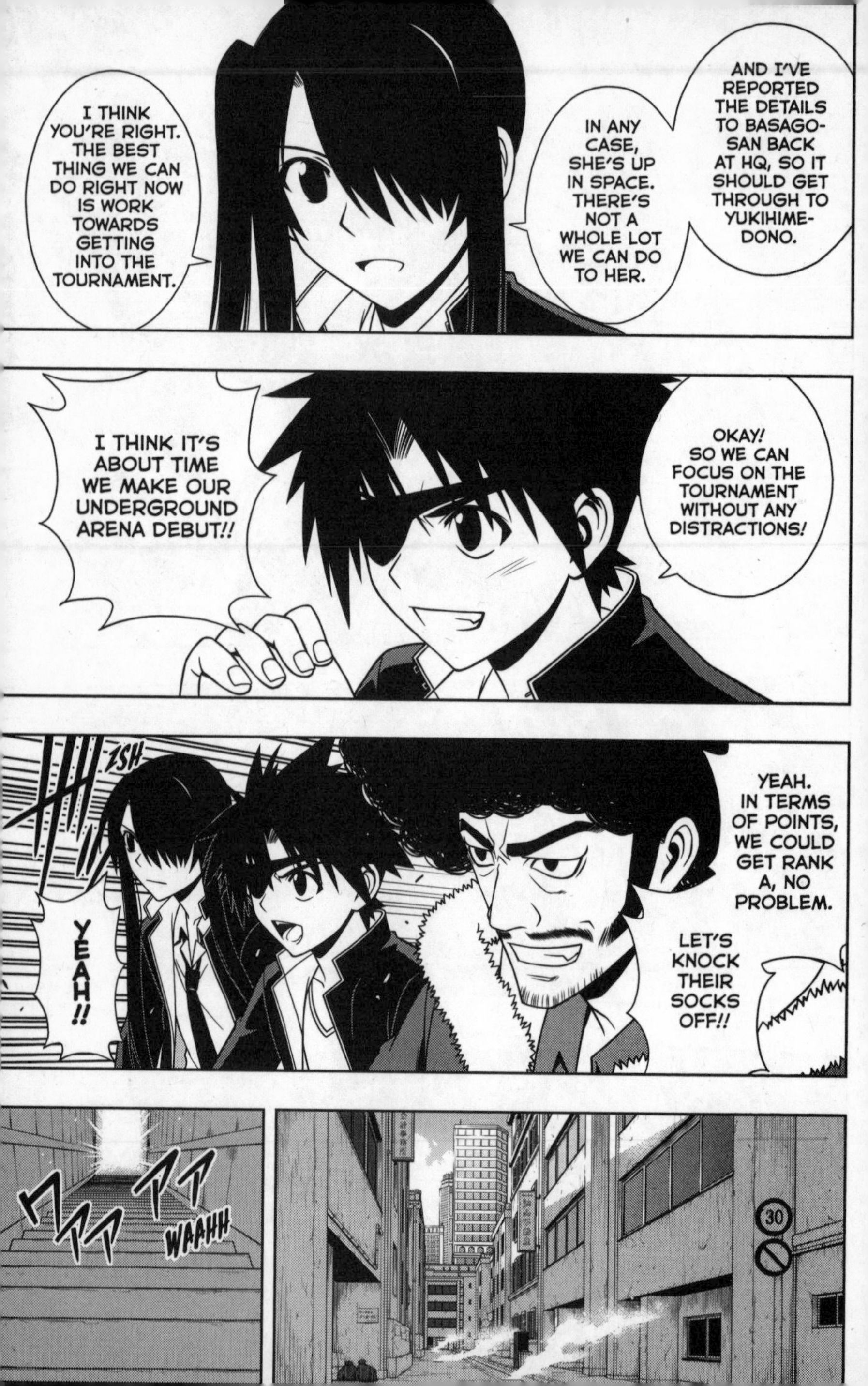
AND I'VE REPORTED THE DETAILS TO BASAGO-SAN BACK AT HQ, SO IT SHOULD GET THROUGH TO YUKIHIME-DONO.
IN ANY CASE, SHE'S UP IN SPACE. THERE'S NOT A WHOLE LOT WE CAN DO TO HER.
I THINK YOU'RE RIGHT. THE BEST THING WE CAN DO RIGHT NOW IS WORK TOWARDS GETTING INTO THE TOURNAMENT.
OKAY! SO WE CAN FOCUS ON THE TOURNAMENT WITHOUT ANY DISTRACTIONS!
I THINK IT'S ABOUT TIME WE MAKE OUR UNDERGROUND ARENA DEBUT!!
YEAH. IN TERMS OF POINTS, WE COULD GET RANK A, NO PROBLEM.
LET'S KNOCK THEIR SOCKS OFF!!
YEAH!!
ISH
30
WAAHH

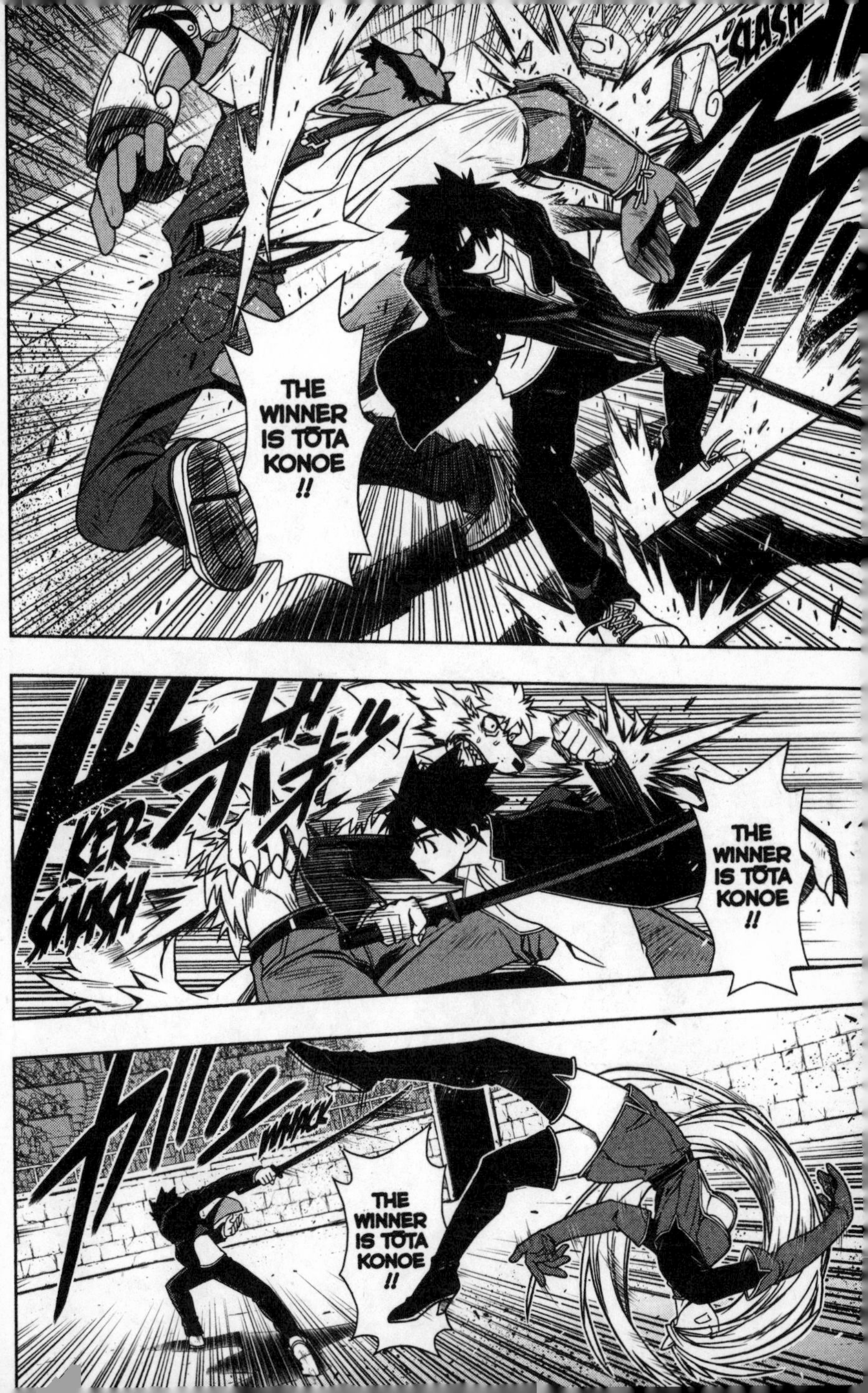
SLASH
THE WINNER IS TŌTA KONOE !!
THE WINNER IS TŌTA KONOE !!
KER-SMASH
WHACK
THE WINNER IS TŌTA KONOE !!

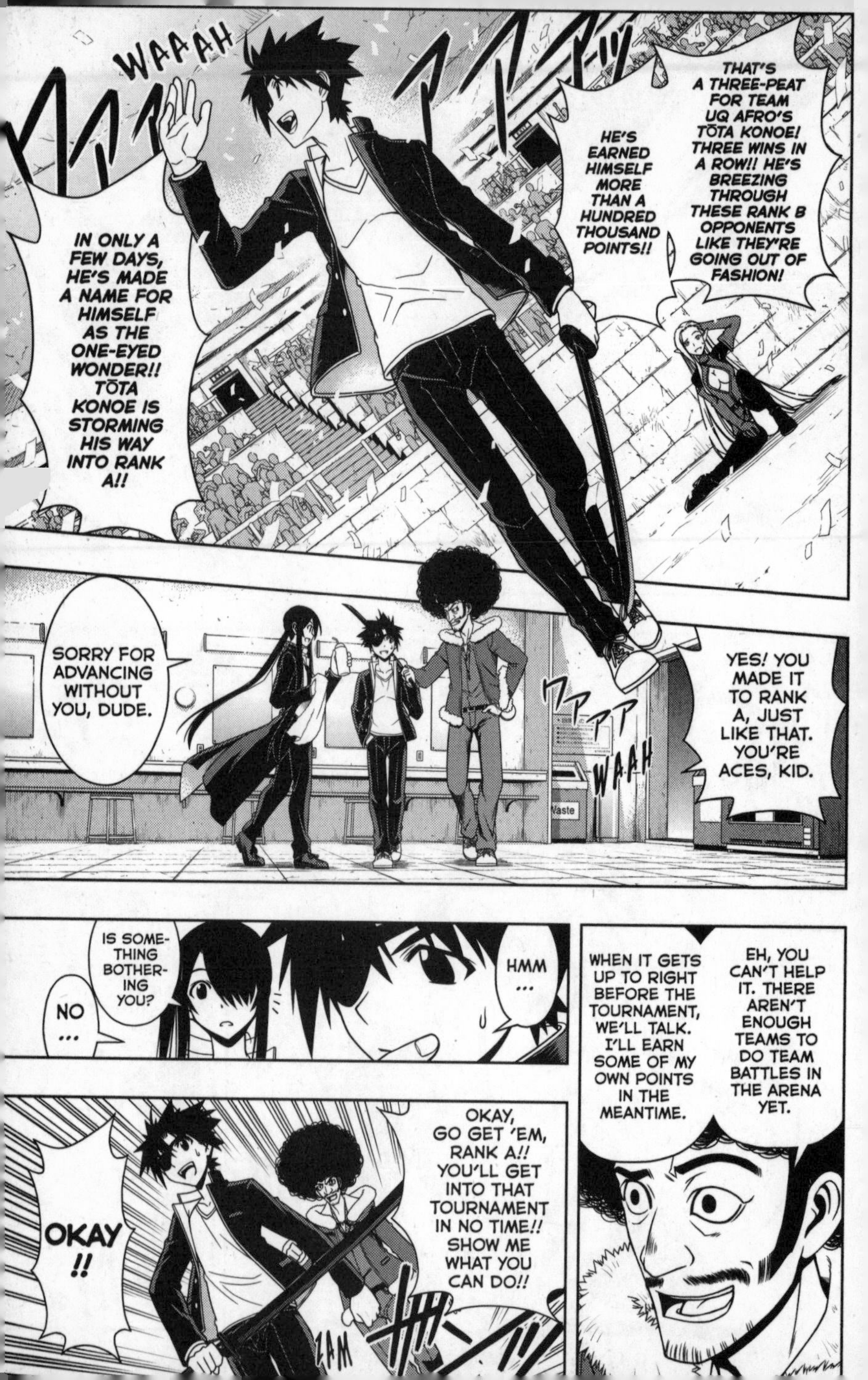
THAT'S A THREE-PEAT FOR TEAM UQ AFRO'S TŌTA KONOE! THREE WINS IN A ROW!! HE'S BREEZING THROUGH THESE RANK B OPPONENTS LIKE THEY'RE GOING OUT OF FASHION!
HE'S EARNED HIMSELF MORE THAN A HUNDRED THOUSAND POINTS!!
WAAAH
IN ONLY A FEW DAYS, HE'S MADE A NAME FOR HIMSELF AS THE ONE-EYED WONDER!! TŌTA KONOE IS STORMING HIS WAY INTO RANK A!!
YES! YOU MADE IT TO RANK A, JUST LIKE THAT. YOU'RE ACES, KID.
WAAH
Waste
SORRY FOR ADVANCING WITHOUT YOU, DUDE.
EH, YOU CAN'T HELP IT. THERE AREN'T ENOUGH TEAMS TO DO TEAM BATTLES IN THE ARENA YET.
WHEN IT GETS UP TO RIGHT BEFORE THE TOURNAMENT, WE'LL TALK. I'LL EARN SOME OF MY OWN POINTS IN THE MEANTIME.
HMM ...
IS SOME-THING BOTHER-ING YOU?
NO ...
OKAY, GO GET 'EM, RANK A!! YOU'LL GET INTO THAT TOURNAMENT IN NO TIME!! SHOW ME WHAT YOU CAN DO!!
OKAY !!
ZAM

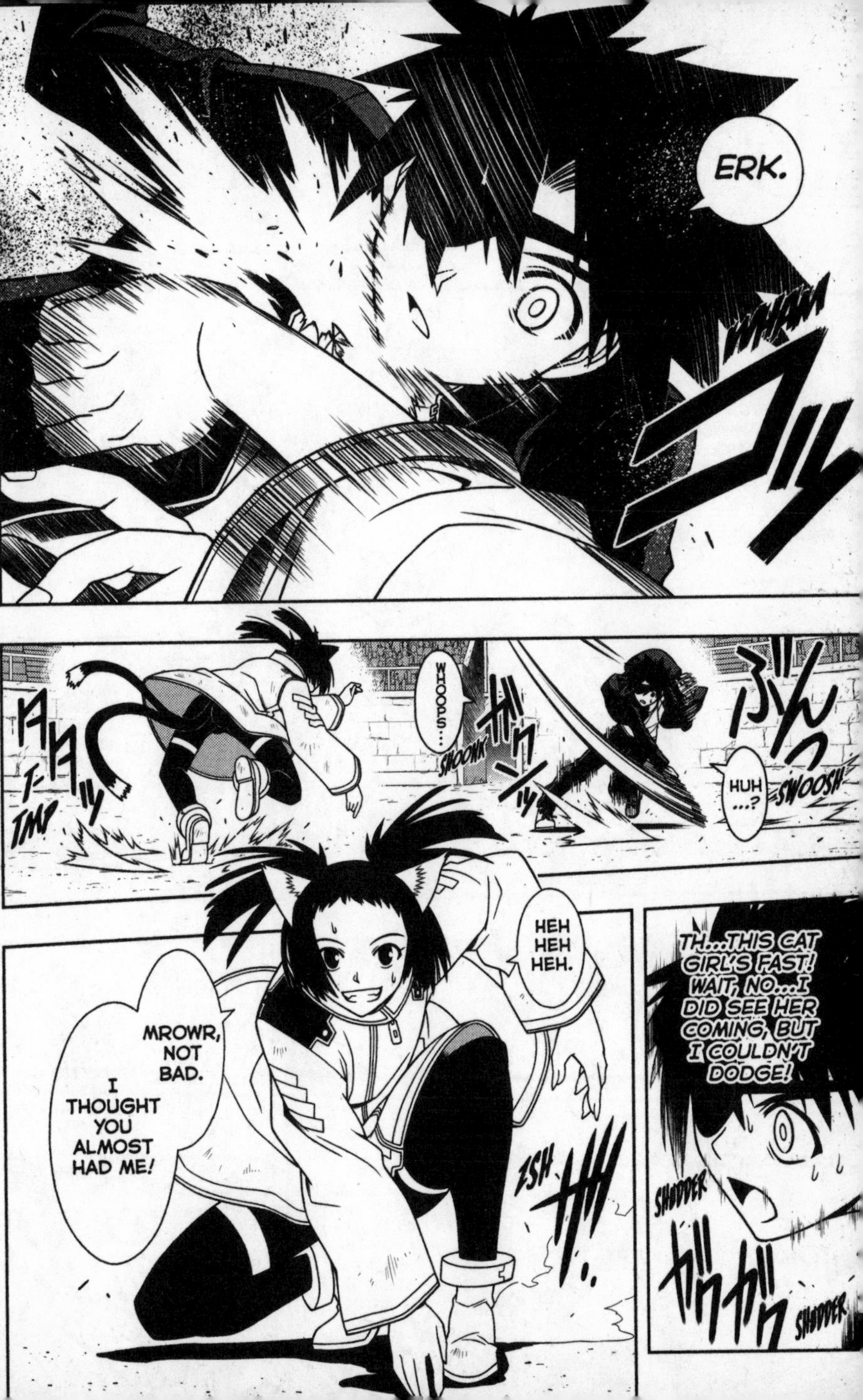
ERK.
WHAM
SWOOSH
HUH ...?
SHOONK
WHOOPS...
T-TMP
TH...THIS CAT GIRL'S FAST! WAIT, NO...I DID SEE HER COMING, BUT I COULDN'T DODGE!
SHUDDER
SHUDDER
HEH HEH HEH.
MROWR, NOT BAD.
I THOUGHT YOU ALMOST HAD ME!
ZSH

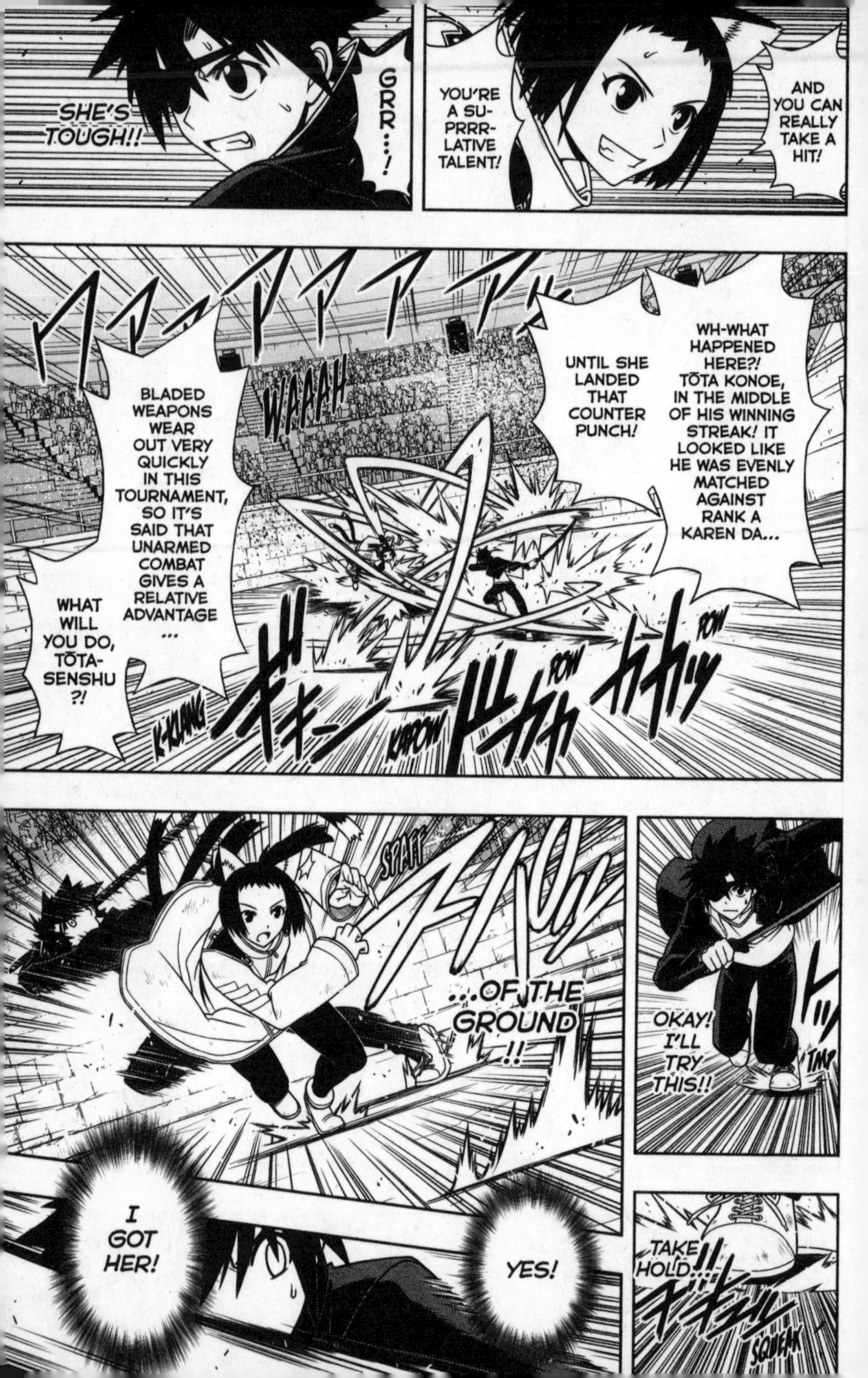
AND YOU CAN REALLY TAKE A HIT!
YOU'RE A SU-PRRR-LATIVE TALENT!
GRR...!
SHE'S TOUGH!!
WH-WHAT HAPPENED HERE?! TŌTA KONOE, IN THE MIDDLE OF HIS WINNING STREAK! IT LOOKED LIKE HE WAS EVENLY MATCHED AGAINST RANK A KAREN DA...
UNTIL SHE LANDED THAT COUNTER PUNCH!
WAAAH
BLADED WEAPONS WEAR OUT VERY QUICKLY IN THIS TOURNAMENT, SO IT'S SAID THAT UNARMED COMBAT GIVES A RELATIVE ADVANTAGE ...
WHAT WILL YOU DO, TŌTA-SENSHU?!
POW
POW
KAPOW
K-KLANG
OKAY! I'LL TRY THIS!!
TMP
SPAFF
...OF THE GROUND!!
TAKE HOLD!!
SQUEAK
YES!
I GOT HER!

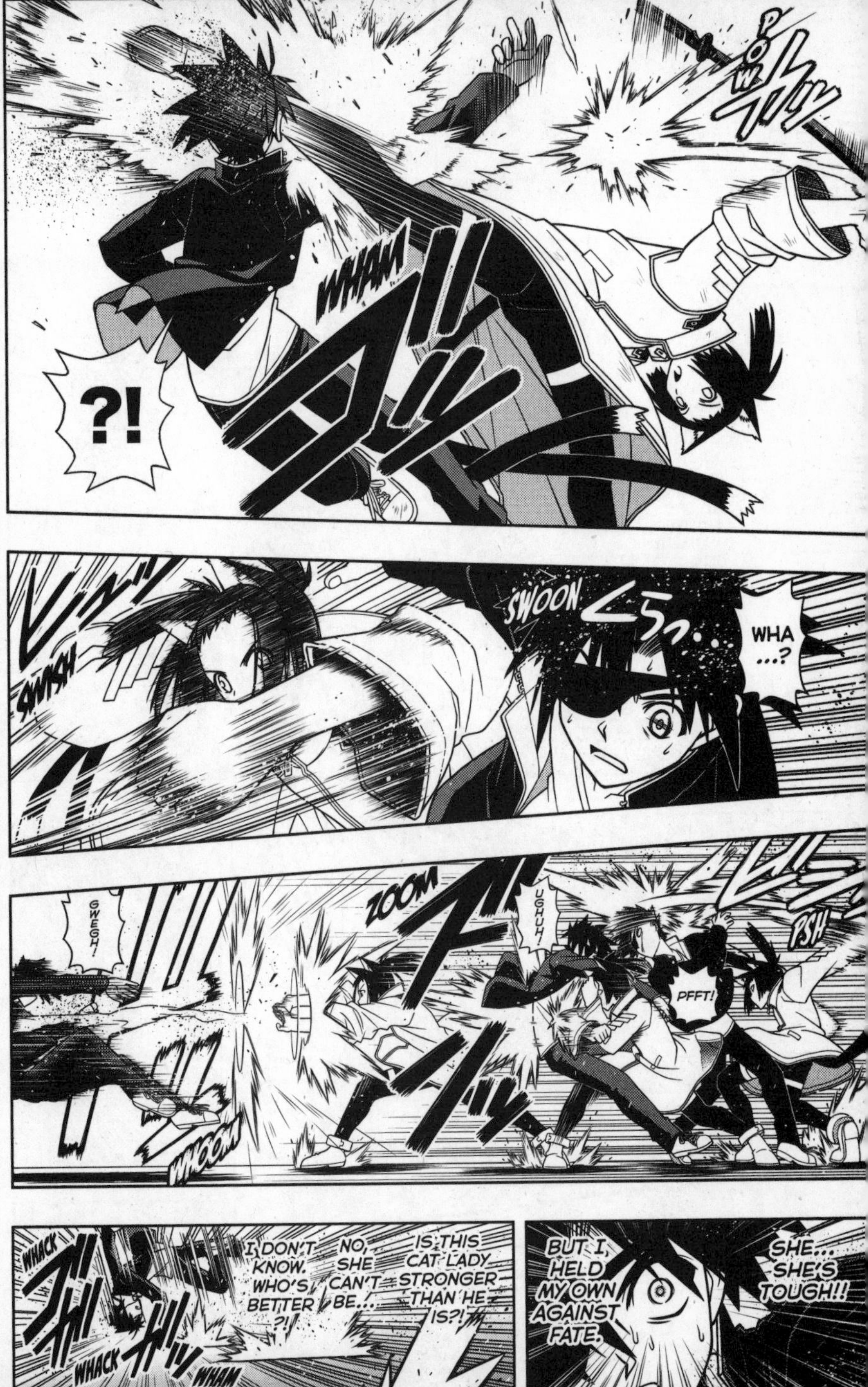
POW
WHAAM
?!
WHA ...?
SWOON
SWISH
PSH
UGHUH!
PFFT!
ZOOM
GWEGH!
WHOOM
SHE... SHE'S TOUGH!!
BUT I, HELD MY OWN AGAINST FATE.
IS THIS CAT LADY STRONGER THAN HE IS?!
NO, SHE CAN'T BE...
I DON'T KNOW. WHO'S BETTER?!
WHACK
WHACK
WHAM

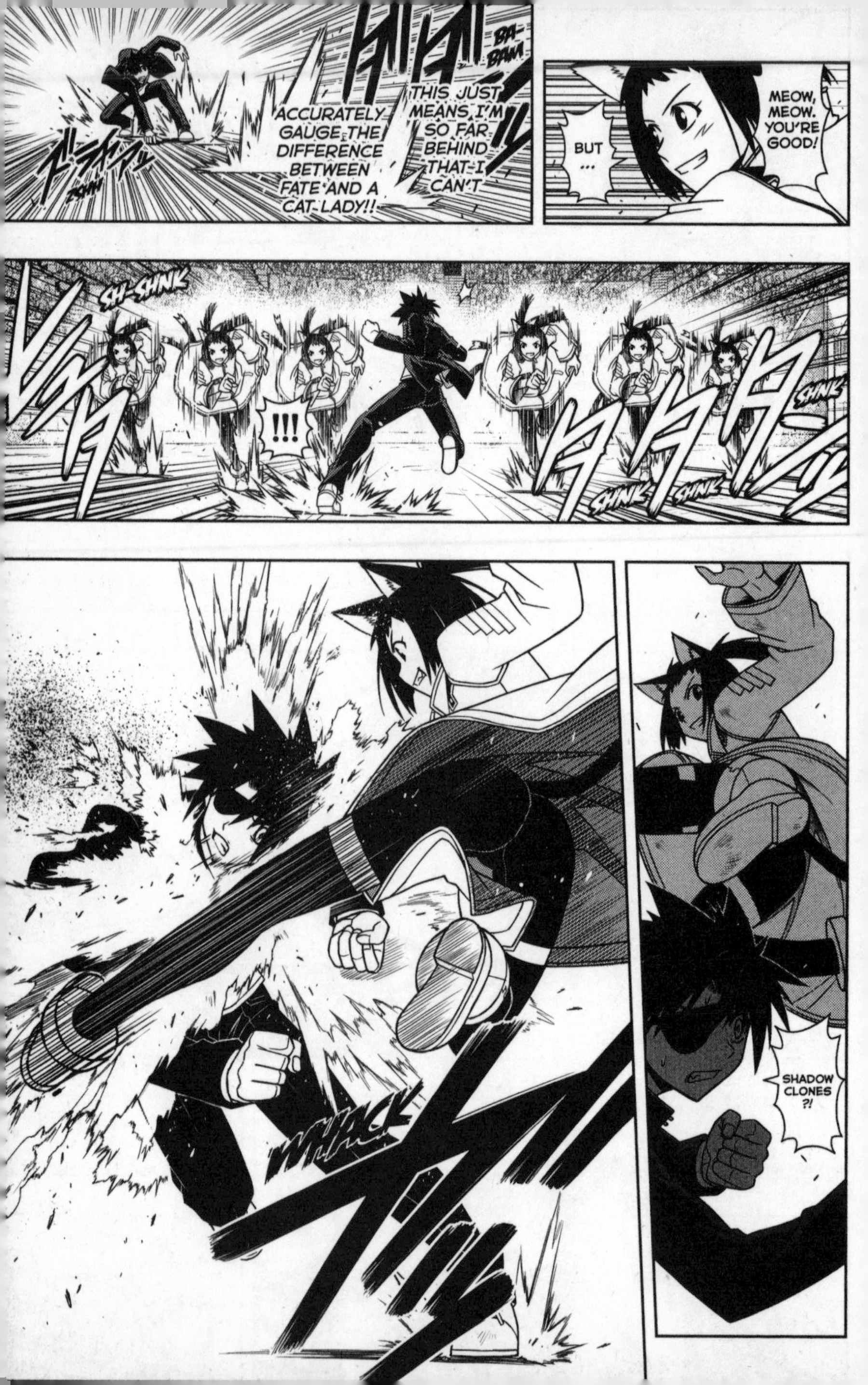
MEOW, MEOW. YOU'RE GOOD!
BUT ...
BA-BAM
THIS JUST MEANS I'M SO FAR BEHIND THAT I CAN'T
ACCURATELY GAUGE THE DIFFERENCE BETWEEN FATE AND A CAT LADY!!
SHNK
SHNK
SHNK
!!!
SH-SHNK
SHADOW CLONES ?!
WHACK

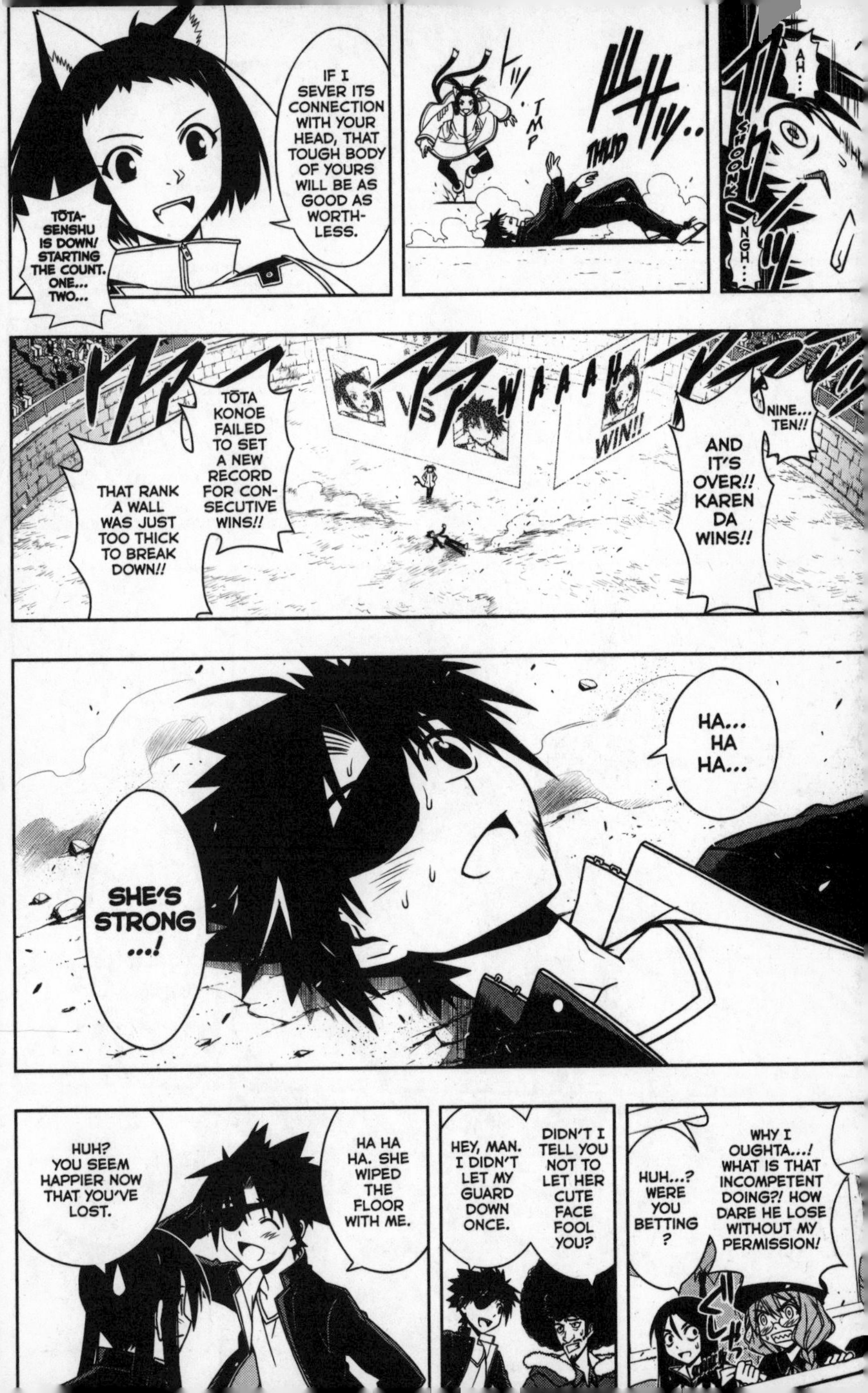
AH...
SHOOM
NGH...
TMP
THUD
IF I SEVER ITS CONNECTION WITH YOUR HEAD, THAT TOUGH BODY OF YOURS WILL BE AS GOOD AS WORTHLESS.
TŌTA-SENSHU IS DOWN! STARTING THE COUNT. ONE... TWO...
NINE... TEN!!
AND IT'S OVER!! KAREN DA WINS!!
WIN!!
WAAAAH
VS
TŌTA KONOE FAILED TO SET A NEW RECORD FOR CONSECUTIVE WINS!!
THAT RANK A WALL WAS JUST TOO THICK TO BREAK DOWN!!
HA... HA HA...
SHE'S STRONG ...!
WHY I OUGHTA...! WHAT IS THAT INCOMPETENT DOING?! HOW DARE HE LOSE WITHOUT MY PERMISSION!
HUH...? WERE YOU BETTING?
DIDN'T I TELL YOU NOT TO LET HER CUTE FACE FOOL YOU?
HEY, MAN. I DIDN'T LET MY GUARD DOWN ONCE.
HA HA HA. SHE WIPED THE FLOOR WITH ME.
HUH? YOU SEEM HAPPIER NOW THAT YOU'VE LOST.

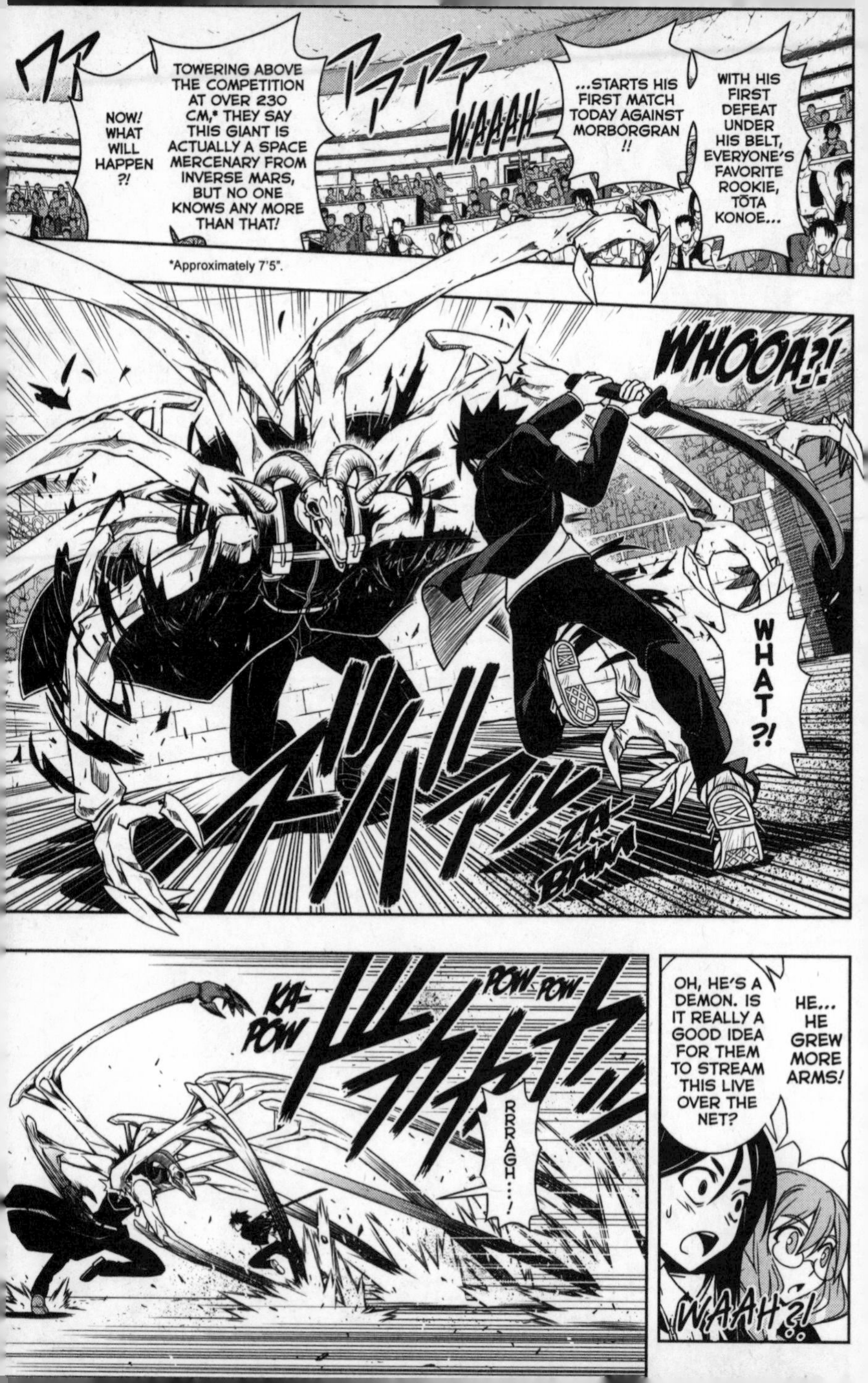
WITH HIS FIRST DEFEAT UNDER HIS BELT, EVERYONE'S FAVORITE ROOKIE, TŌTA KONOE...
...STARTS HIS FIRST MATCH TODAY AGAINST MORBORGRAN!!
WAAAH
TOWERING ABOVE THE COMPETITION AT OVER 230 CM,* THEY SAY THIS GIANT IS ACTUALLY A SPACE MERCENARY FROM INVERSE MARS, BUT NO ONE KNOWS ANY MORE THAN THAT!
NOW! WHAT WILL HAPPEN?!
WHOOA?!
WHAT?!
ZA-BAM
HE... HE GREW MORE ARMS!
OH, HE'S A DEMON. IS IT REALLY A GOOD IDEA FOR THEM TO STREAM THIS LIVE OVER THE NET?
WAAH?!
POW POW
KA-POW
RRRAGH...!
*Approximately 7'5".

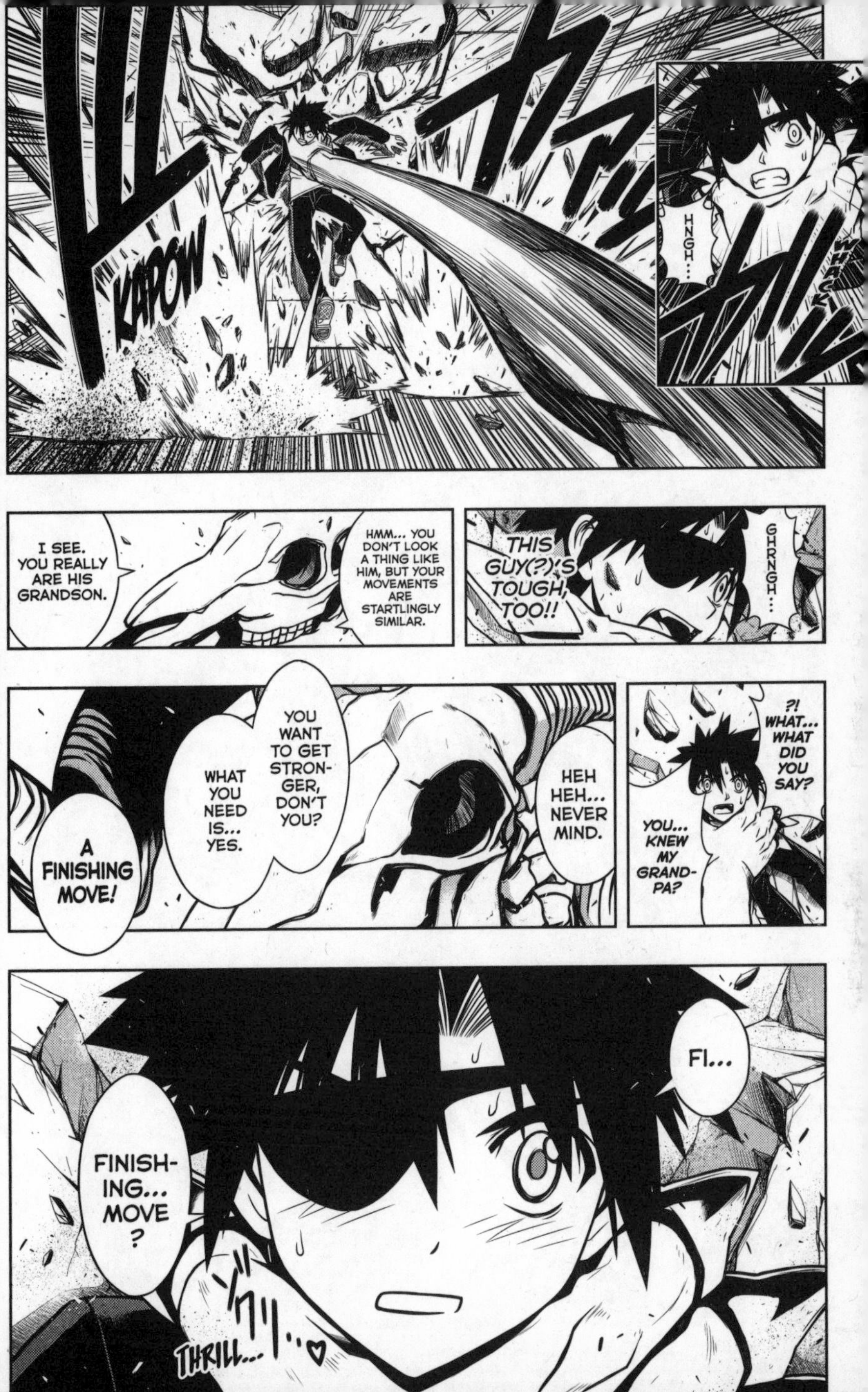
HNGH...
WHACK
KAPOW
GHRNGH...
THIS GUY(?)'S TOUGH, TOO!!
HMM... YOU DON'T LOOK A THING LIKE HIM, BUT YOUR MOVEMENTS ARE STARTLINGLY SIMILAR.
I SEE. YOU REALLY ARE HIS GRANDSON.
?! WHAT... WHAT DID YOU SAY?
YOU... KNEW MY GRAND-PA?
HEH HEH... NEVER MIND.
YOU WANT TO GET STRON-GER, DON'T YOU?
WHAT YOU NEED IS... YES.
A FINISHING MOVE!
FI...
FINISH-ING... MOVE ?
THRILL...

STAGE 76: YESTERDAY'S ENEMY IS TODAY'S TEACHE

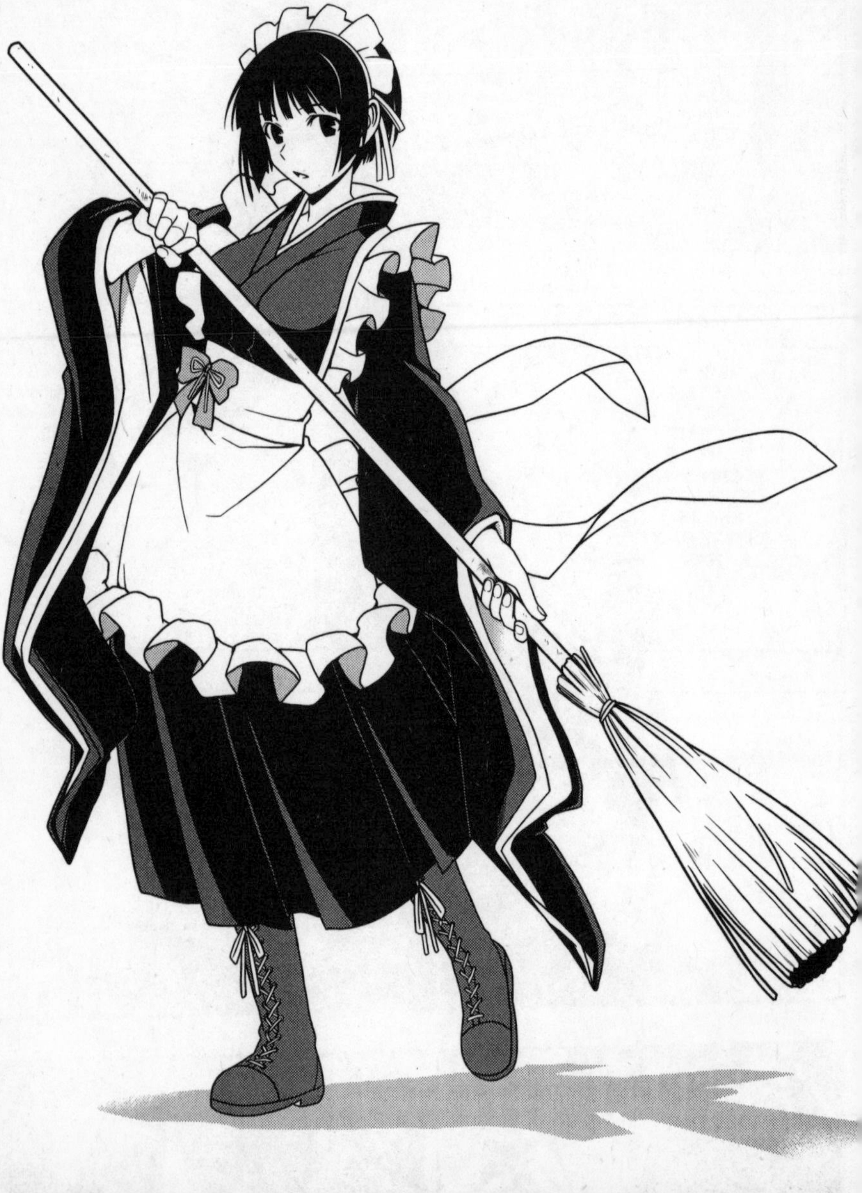

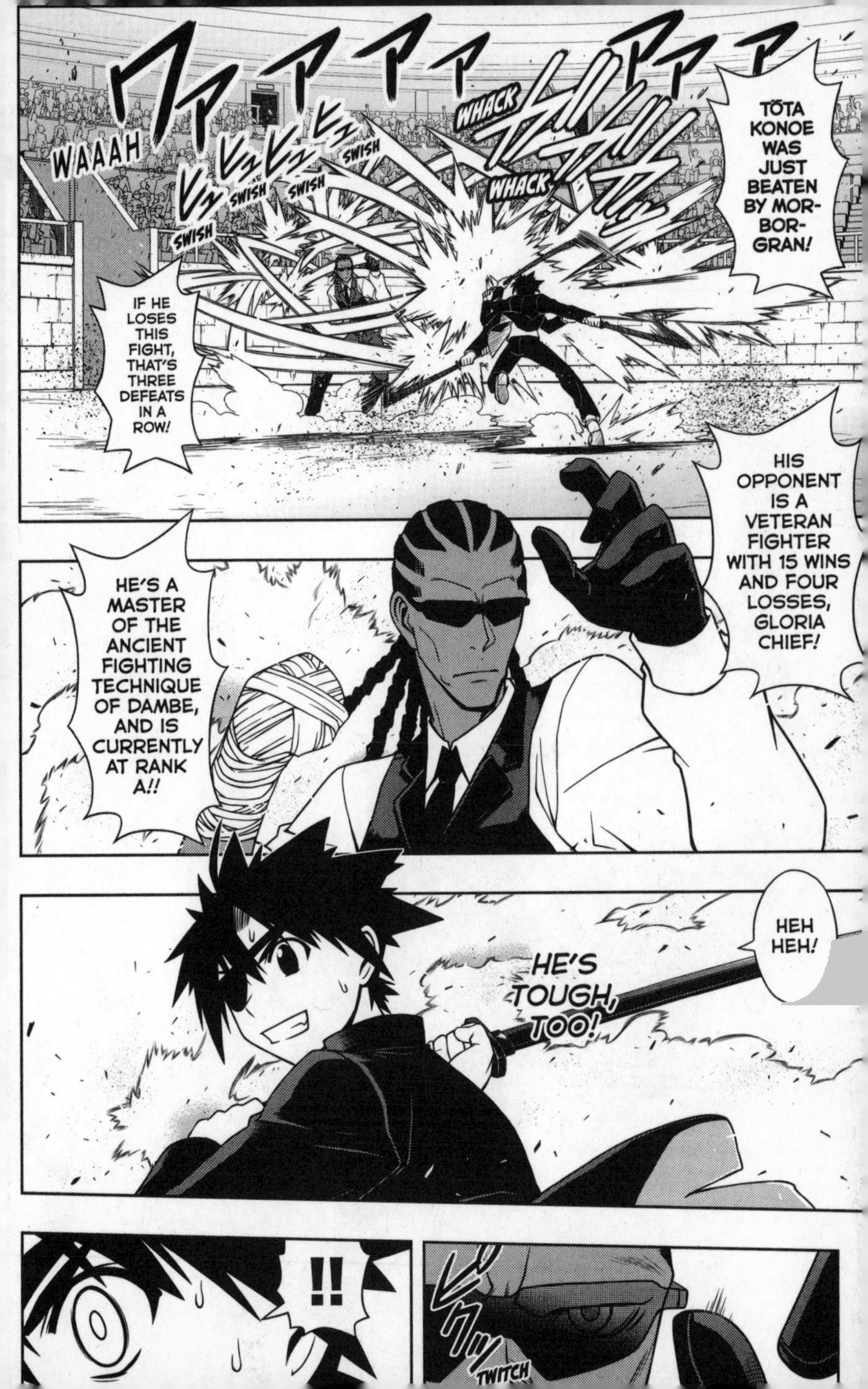
WAAAH
SWISH
SWISH
SWISH
SWISH
WHACK
WHACK
TŌTA KONOE WAS JUST BEATEN BY MOR-GRAN!
IF HE LOSES THIS FIGHT, THAT'S THREE DEFEATS IN A ROW!
HIS OPPONENT IS A VETERAN FIGHTER WITH 15 WINS AND FOUR LOSSES, GLORIA CHIEF!
HE'S A MASTER OF THE ANCIENT FIGHTING TECHNIQUE OF DAMBE, AND IS CURRENTLY AT RANK A!!
HEH HEH!
HE'S TOUGH, TOO!
TWITCH
!!

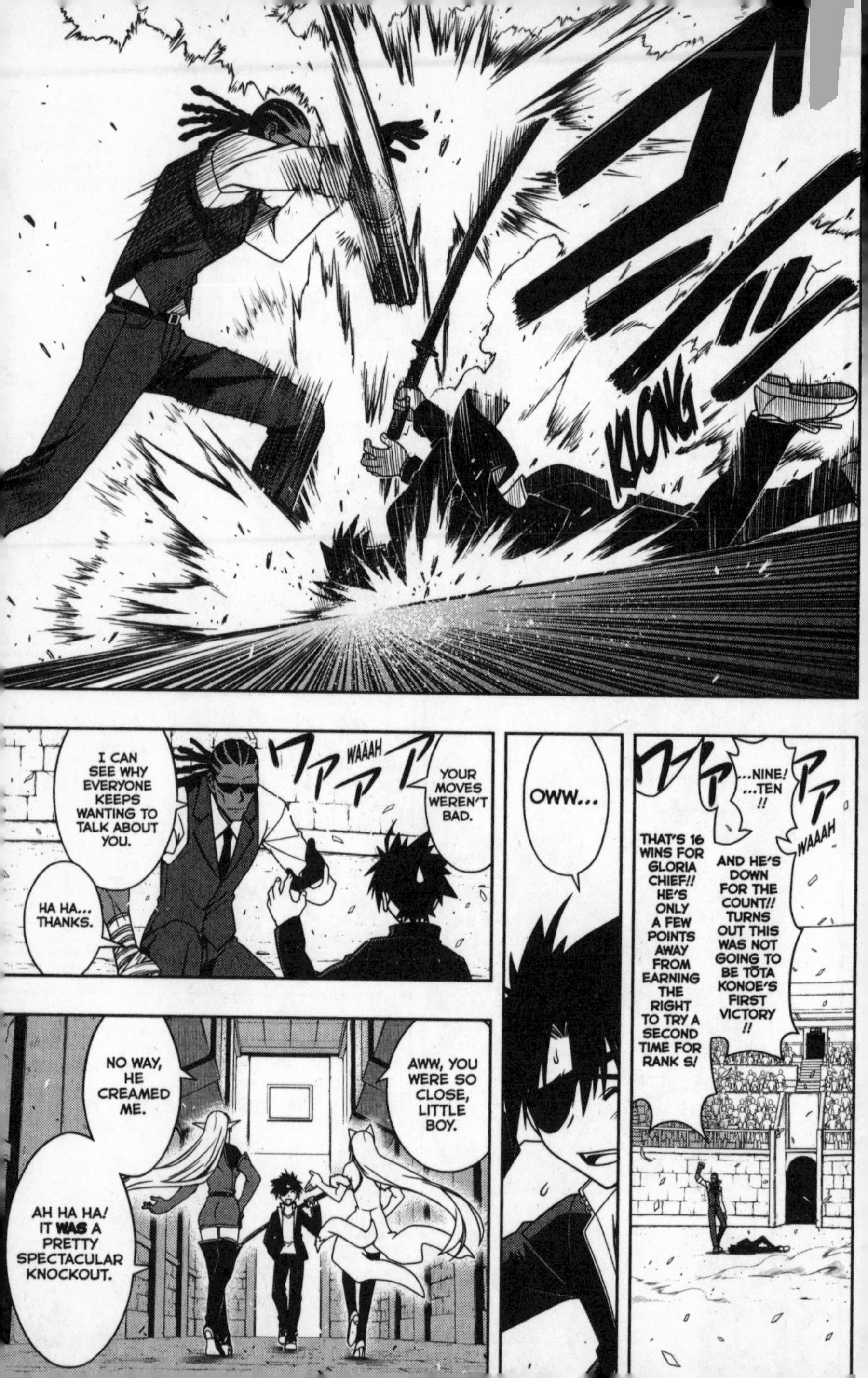
KLONG
...NINE! ...TEN!!
WAAAH
AND HE'S DOWN FOR THE COUNT!! TURNS OUT THIS WAS NOT GOING TO BE TŌTA KONOE'S FIRST VICTORY!!
THAT'S 16 WINS FOR GLORIA CHIEF!! HE'S ONLY A FEW POINTS AWAY FROM EARNING THE RIGHT TO TRY A SECOND TIME FOR RANK S!
OWW...
YOUR MOVES WEREN'T BAD.
WAAAH
I CAN SEE WHY EVERYONE KEEPS WANTING TO TALK ABOUT YOU.
HA HA... THANKS.
AWW, YOU WERE SO CLOSE, LITTLE BOY.
NO WAY, HE CREAMED ME.
AH HA HA! IT **WAS** A PRETTY SPECTACULAR KNOCKOUT.

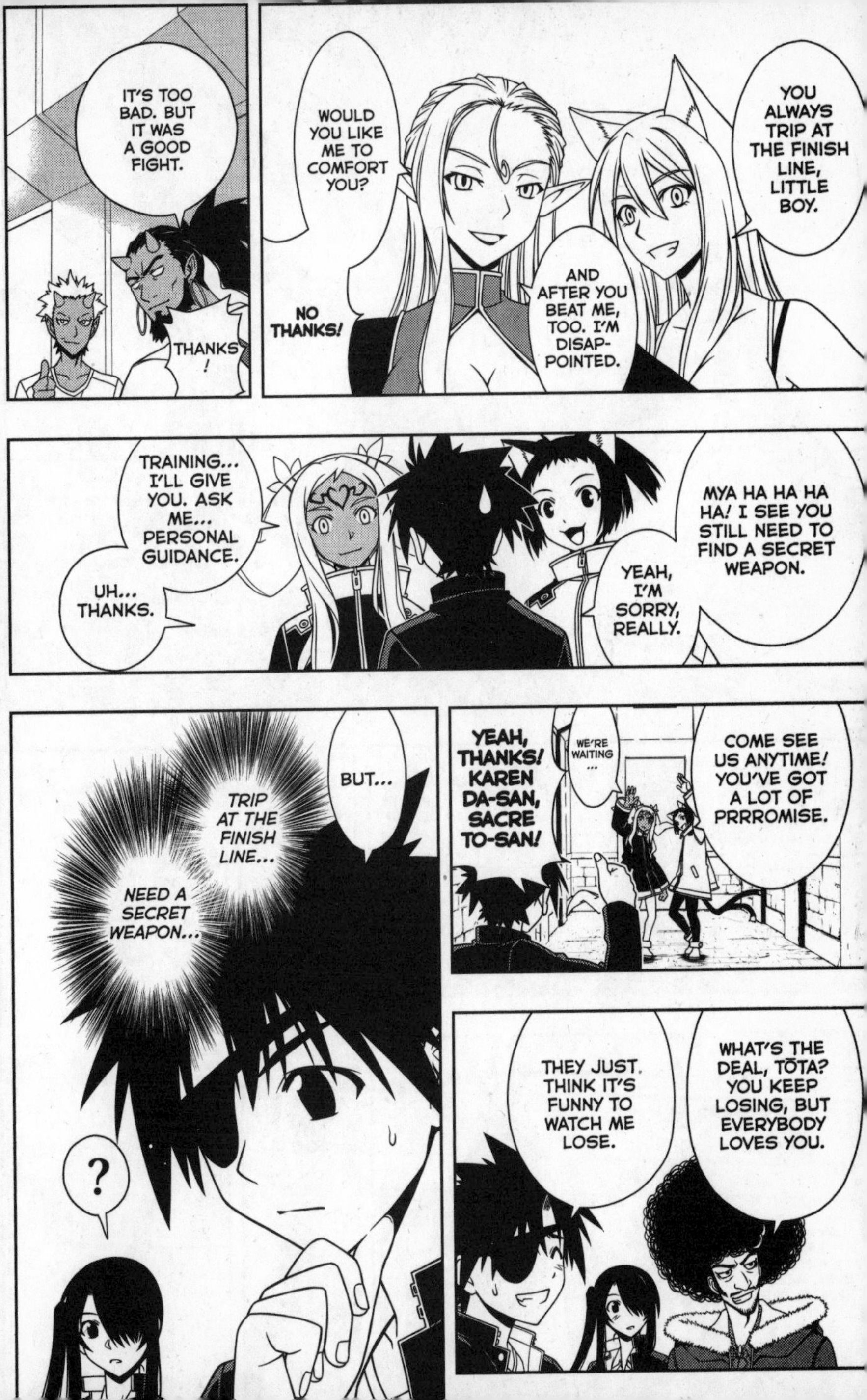
YOU ALWAYS TRIP AT THE FINISH LINE, LITTLE BOY.
WOULD YOU LIKE ME TO COMFORT YOU?
AND AFTER YOU BEAT ME, TOO. I'M DISAP-POINTED.
NO THANKS!
IT'S TOO BAD. BUT IT WAS A GOOD FIGHT.
THANKS!
MYA HA HA HA HA! I SEE YOU STILL NEED TO FIND A SECRET WEAPON.
YEAH, I'M SORRY, REALLY.
TRAINING... I'LL GIVE YOU. ASK ME... PERSONAL GUIDANCE.
UH... THANKS.
COME SEE US ANYTIME! YOU'VE GOT A LOT OF PRRROMISE.
WE'RE WAITING...
YEAH, THANKS! KAREN DA-SAN, SACRE TO-SAN!
WHAT'S THE DEAL, TŌTA? YOU KEEP LOSING, BUT EVERYBODY LOVES YOU.
THEY JUST THINK IT'S FUNNY TO WATCH ME LOSE.
BUT...
TRIP AT THE FINISH LINE...
NEED A SECRET WEAPON...
?

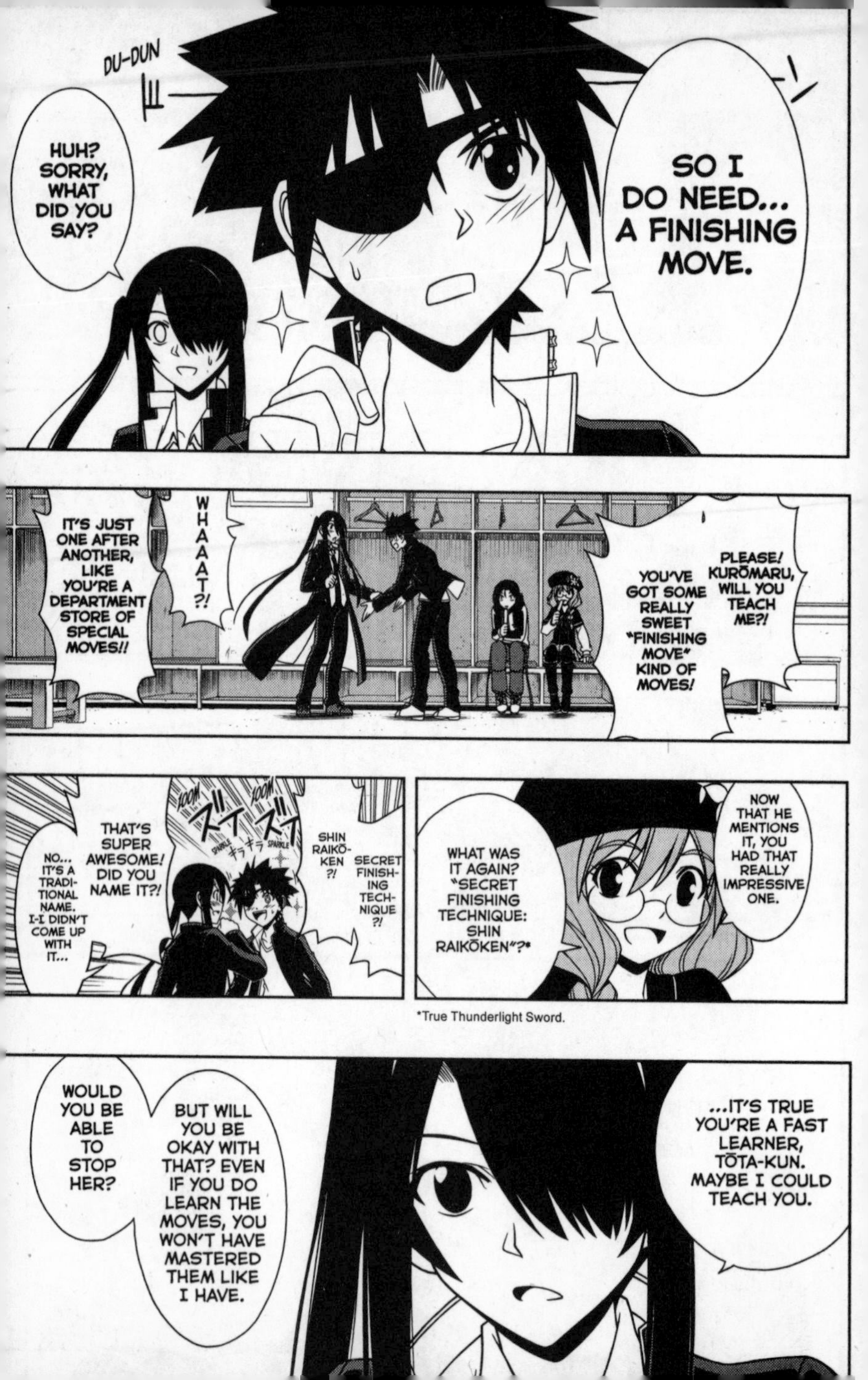
SO I DO NEED... A FINISHING MOVE.
DU-DUN
HUH? SORRY, WHAT DID YOU SAY?
PLEASE! KURŌMARU, WILL YOU TEACH ME?!
YOU'VE GOT SOME REALLY SWEET "FINISHING MOVE" KIND OF MOVES!
WHAAAAT?!
IT'S JUST ONE AFTER ANOTHER, LIKE YOU'RE A DEPARTMENT STORE OF SPECIAL MOVES!!
NOW THAT HE MENTIONS IT, YOU HAD THAT REALLY IMPRESSIVE ONE.
WHAT WAS IT AGAIN? "SECRET FINISHING TECHNIQUE: SHIN RAIKŌKEN"?*
SECRET FINISHING TECHNIQUE?!
SHIN RAIKŌKEN?!
ZOOM ZOOM
SPARKLE SPARKLE
THAT'S SUPER AWESOME! DID YOU NAME IT?!
NO... IT'S A TRADITIONAL NAME. I-I DIDN'T COME UP WITH IT...
...IT'S TRUE YOU'RE A FAST LEARNER, TŌTA-KUN. MAYBE I COULD TEACH YOU.
BUT WILL YOU BE OKAY WITH THAT? EVEN IF YOU DO LEARN THE MOVES, YOU WON'T HAVE MASTERED THEM LIKE I HAVE.
WOULD YOU BE ABLE TO STOP HER?
*True Thunderlight Sword.

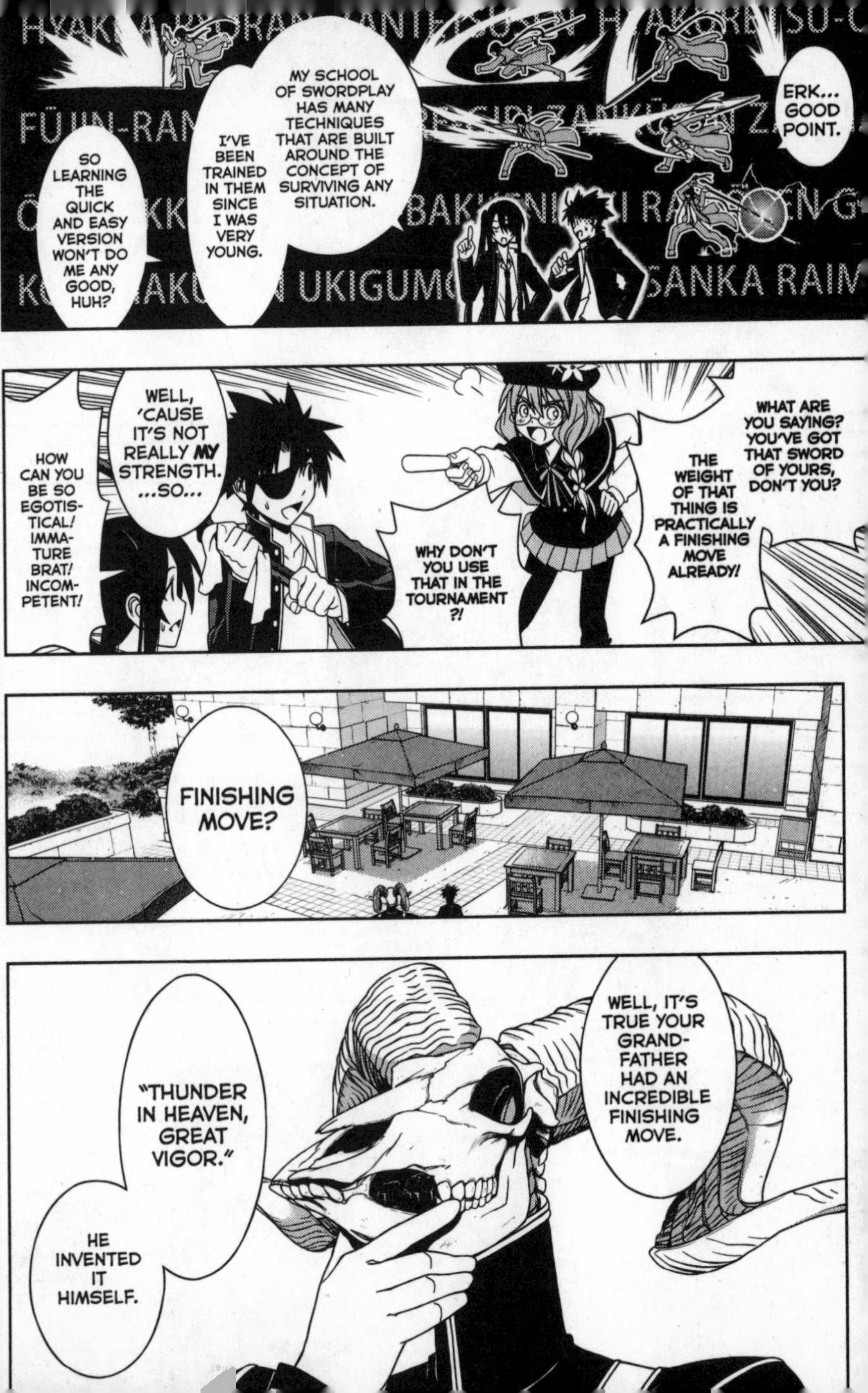
ERK... GOOD POINT.
MY SCHOOL OF SWORDPLAY HAS MANY TECHNIQUES THAT ARE BUILT AROUND THE CONCEPT OF SURVIVING ANY SITUATION.
I'VE BEEN TRAINED IN THEM SINCE I WAS VERY YOUNG.
SO LEARNING THE QUICK AND EASY VERSION WON'T DO ME ANY GOOD, HUH?
WHAT ARE YOU SAYING? YOU'VE GOT THAT SWORD OF YOURS, DON'T YOU?
THE WEIGHT OF THAT THING IS PRACTICALLY A FINISHING MOVE ALREADY!
WHY DON'T YOU USE THAT IN THE TOURNAMENT?!
WELL, 'CAUSE IT'S NOT REALLY **MY** STRENGTH. ...SO...
HOW CAN YOU BE SO EGOTISTICAL! IMMATURE BRAT! INCOMPETENT!
FINISHING MOVE?
WELL, IT'S TRUE YOUR GRANDFATHER HAD AN INCREDIBLE FINISHING MOVE.
"THUNDER IN HEAVEN, GREAT VIGOR."
HE INVENTED IT HIMSELF.

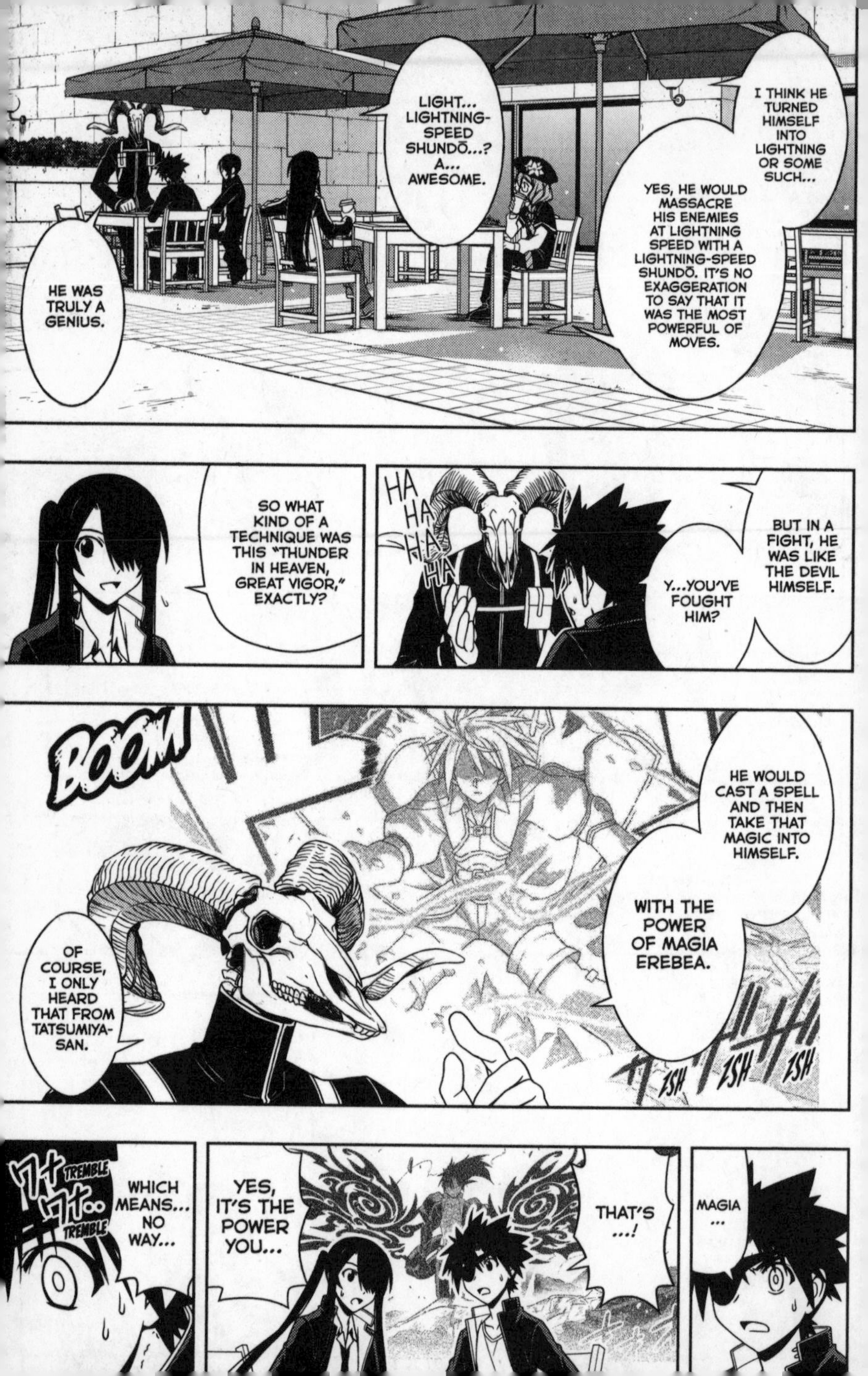
I THINK HE TURNED HIMSELF INTO LIGHTNING OR SOME SUCH...
LIGHT... LIGHTNING-SPEED SHUNDŌ...? A... AWESOME.
YES, HE WOULD MASSACRE HIS ENEMIES AT LIGHTNING SPEED WITH A LIGHTNING-SPEED SHUNDŌ. IT'S NO EXAGGERATION TO SAY THAT IT WAS THE MOST POWERFUL OF MOVES.
HE WAS TRULY A GENIUS.
BUT IN A FIGHT, HE WAS LIKE THE DEVIL HIMSELF.
Y...YOU'VE FOUGHT HIM?
HA HA HA HA
SO WHAT KIND OF A TECHNIQUE WAS THIS "THUNDER IN HEAVEN, GREAT VIGOR," EXACTLY?
HE WOULD CAST A SPELL AND THEN TAKE THAT MAGIC INTO HIMSELF.
BOOM
WITH THE POWER OF MAGIA EREBEA.
OF COURSE, I ONLY HEARD THAT FROM TATSUMIYA-SAN.
TSH TSH TSH
MAGIA ...
THAT'S ...!
YES, IT'S THE POWER YOU...
WHICH MEANS... NO WAY...
TREMBLE TREMBLE

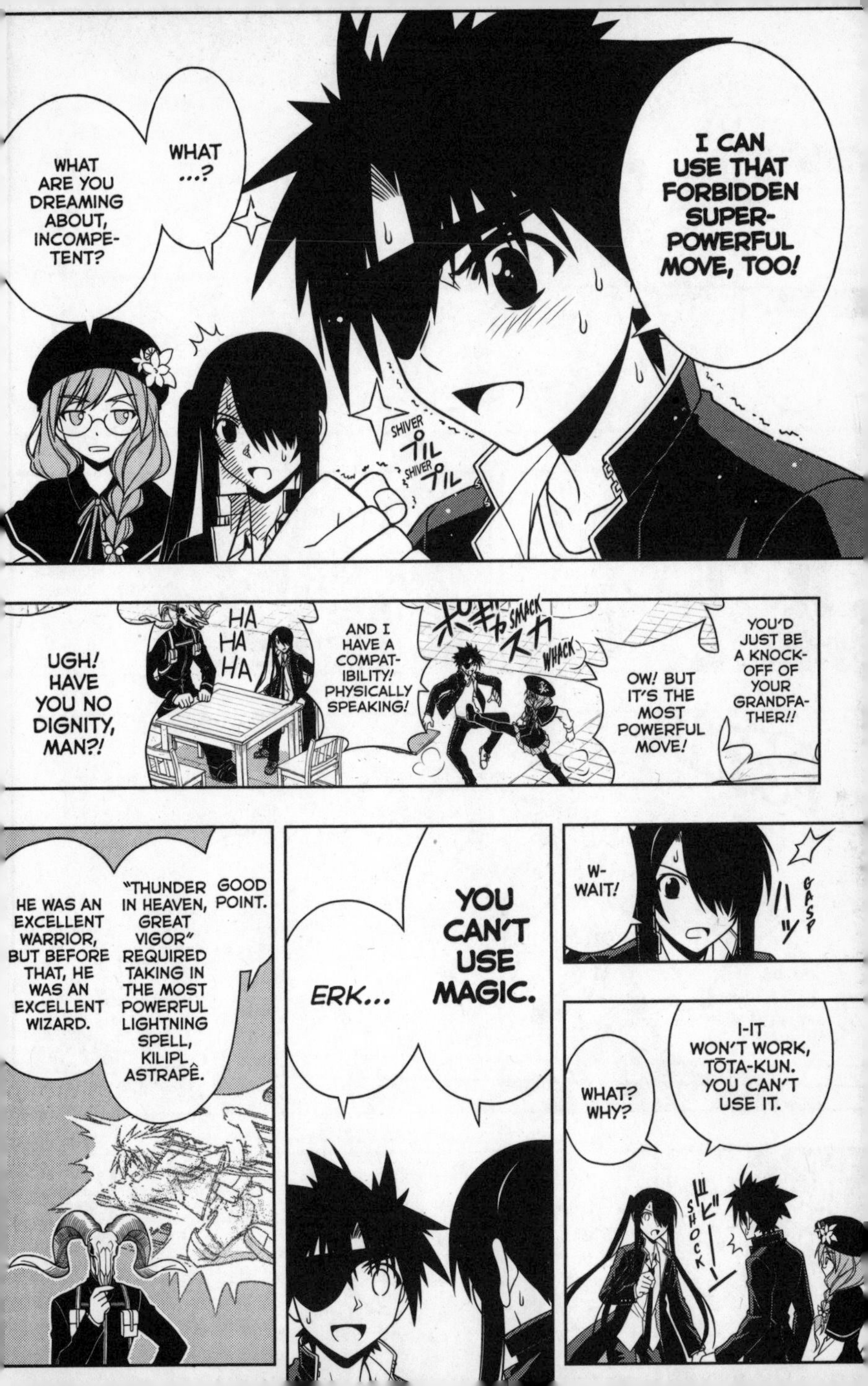
I CAN USE THAT FORBIDDEN SUPER-POWERFUL MOVE, TOO!
SHIVER プル
SHIVER プル
WHAT ...?
WHAT ARE YOU DREAMING ABOUT, INCOMPETENT?
YOU'D JUST BE A KNOCK-OFF OF YOUR GRANDFATHER!!
OW! BUT IT'S THE MOST POWERFUL MOVE!
SMACK
WHACK
AND I HAVE A COMPATIBILITY! PHYSICALLY SPEAKING!
HA HA HA
UGH! HAVE YOU NO DIGNITY, MAN?!
W-WAIT!
GASP
I-IT WON'T WORK, TŌTA-KUN. YOU CAN'T USE IT.
WHAT? WHY?
SHOCK
YOU CAN'T USE MAGIC.
ERK...
GOOD POINT.
"THUNDER IN HEAVEN, GREAT VIGOR" REQUIRED TAKING IN THE MOST POWERFUL LIGHTNING SPELL, KILIPL ASTRAPÊ.
HE WAS AN EXCELLENT WARRIOR, BUT BEFORE THAT, HE WAS AN EXCELLENT WIZARD.

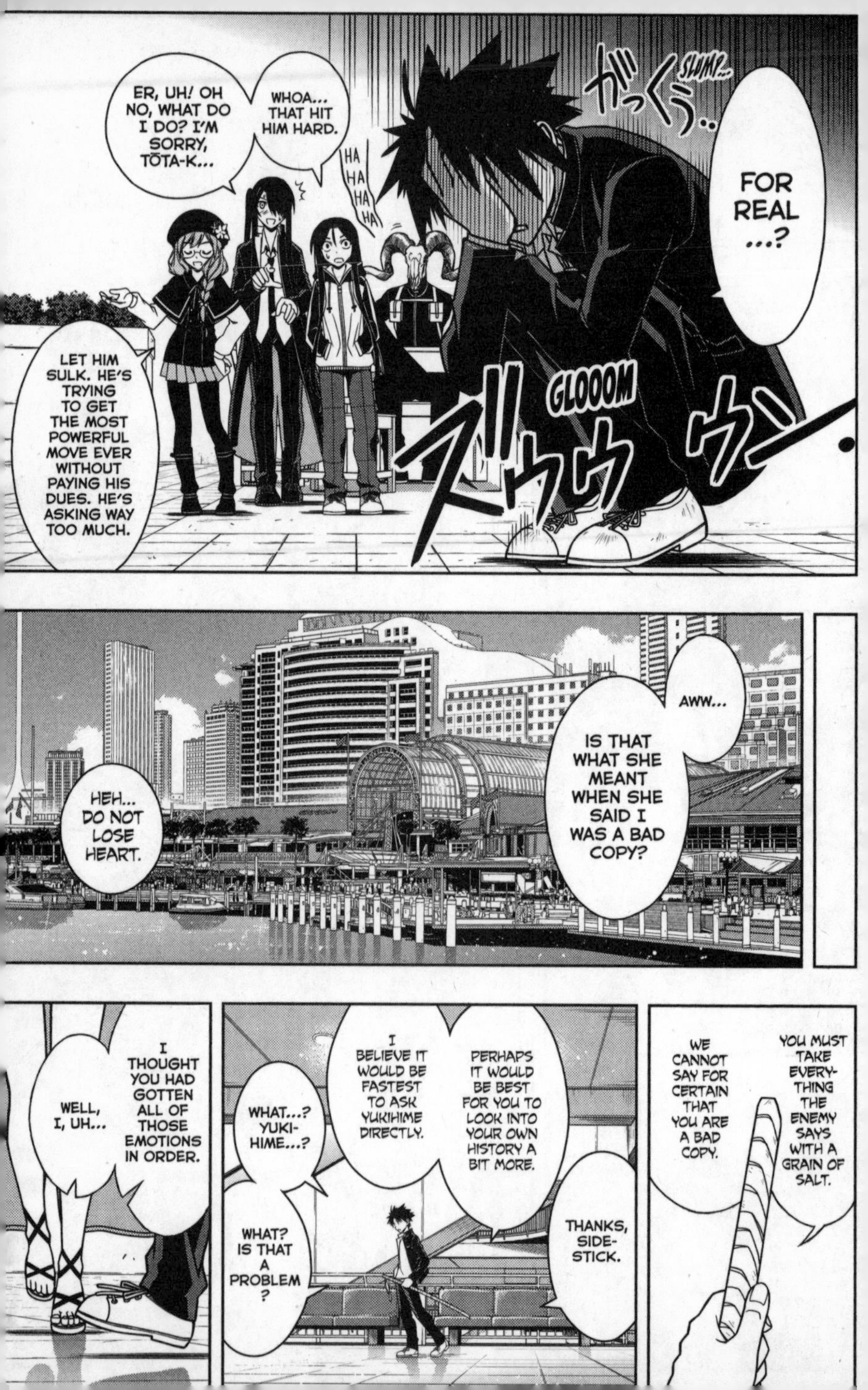
SLUMP...
FOR REAL ...?
GLOOOM
HA HA HA HA
WHOA... THAT HIT HIM HARD.
ER, UH! OH NO, WHAT DO I DO? I'M SORRY, TŌTA-K...
LET HIM SULK. HE'S TRYING TO GET THE MOST POWERFUL MOVE EVER WITHOUT PAYING HIS DUES. HE'S ASKING WAY TOO MUCH.
AWW...
IS THAT WHAT SHE MEANT WHEN SHE SAID I WAS A BAD COPY?
HEH... DO NOT LOSE HEART.
YOU MUST TAKE EVERY-THING THE ENEMY SAYS WITH A GRAIN OF SALT.
WE CANNOT SAY FOR CERTAIN THAT YOU ARE A BAD COPY.
PERHAPS IT WOULD BE BEST FOR YOU TO LOOK INTO YOUR OWN HISTORY A BIT MORE.
THANKS, SIDE-STICK.
I BELIEVE IT WOULD BE FASTEST TO ASK YUKIHIME DIRECTLY.
WHAT...? YUKI-HIME...?
WHAT? IS THAT A PROBLEM ?
I THOUGHT YOU HAD GOTTEN ALL OF THOSE EMOTIONS IN ORDER.
WELL, I, UH...

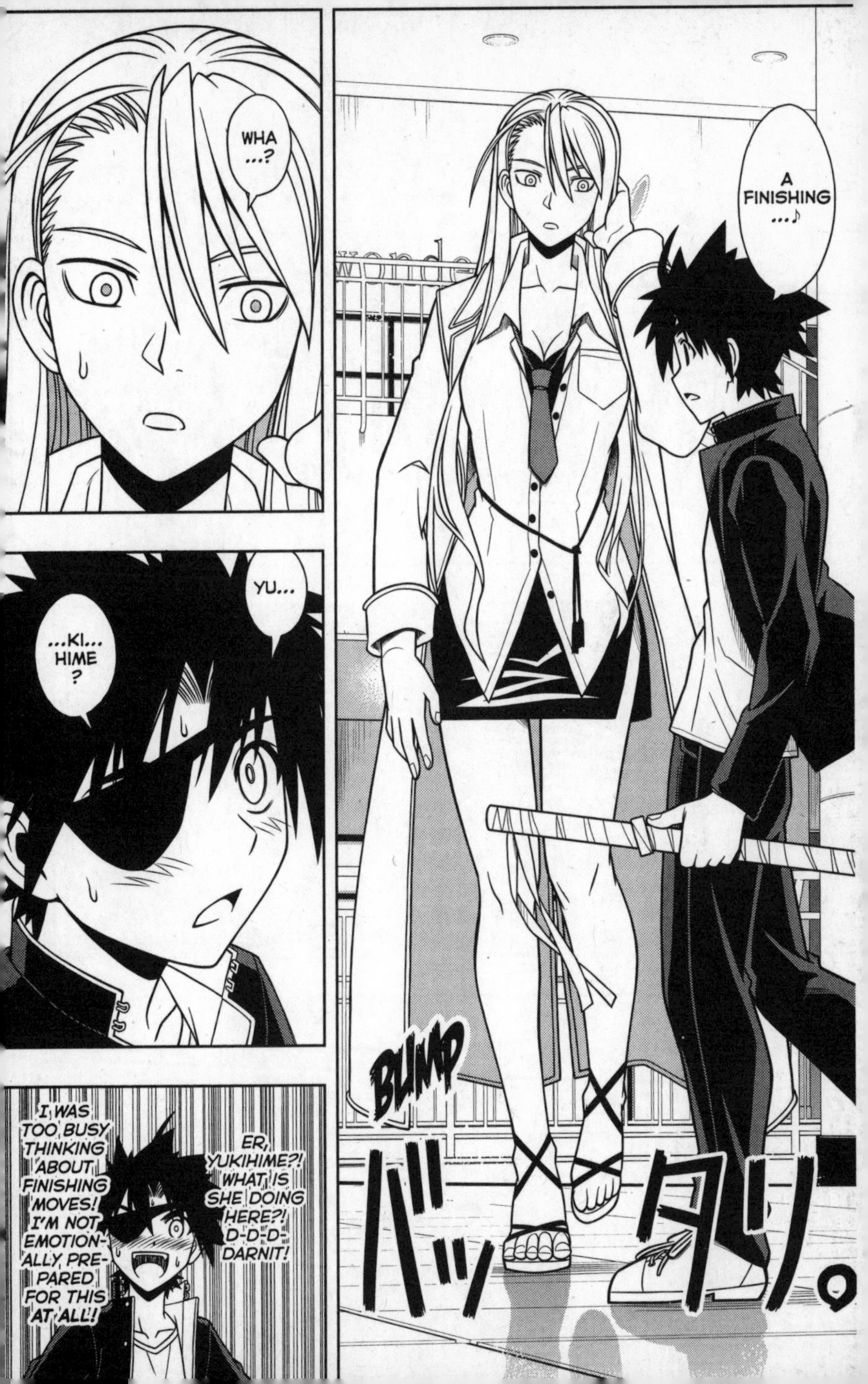
A FINISHING ...♪
BUMP
バッタリ。
WHA ...?
YU...
...KI... HIME ?
ER, YUKIHIME?! WHAT IS SHE DOING HERE?! D-D-D-DARNIT!
I WAS TOO BUSY THINKING ABOUT FINISHING MOVES! I'M NOT EMOTION-ALLY PRE-PARED FOR THIS AT ALL!

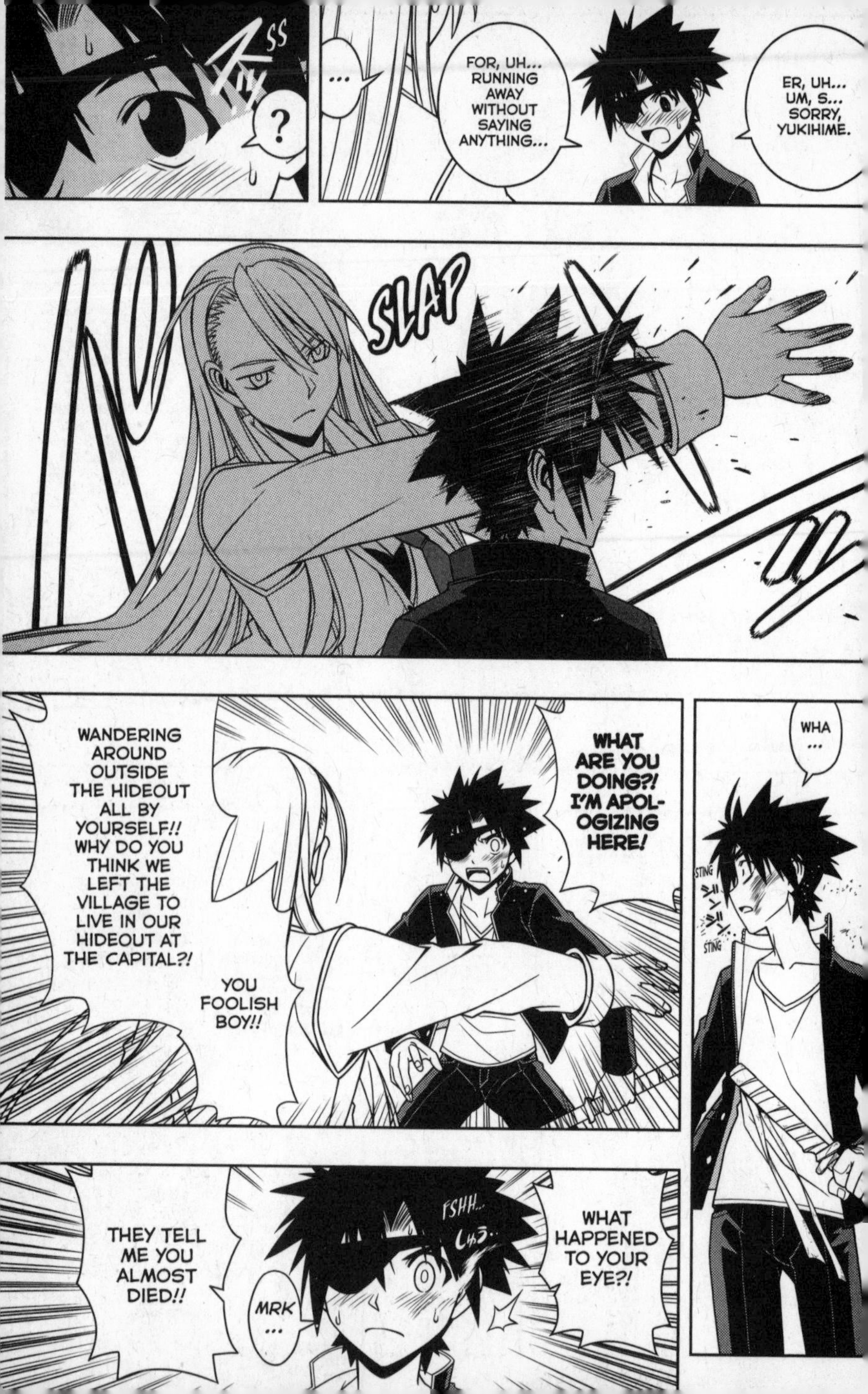
ER, UH... UM, S... SORRY, YUKIHIME.
FOR, UH... RUNNING AWAY WITHOUT SAYING ANYTHING...
...
?
SLAP
WHA...
STING
STING
WHAT ARE YOU DOING?! I'M APOLOGIZING HERE!
WANDERING AROUND OUTSIDE THE HIDEOUT ALL BY YOURSELF!! WHY DO YOU THINK WE LEFT THE VILLAGE TO LIVE IN OUR HIDEOUT AT THE CAPITAL?!
YOU FOOLISH BOY!!
WHAT HAPPENED TO YOUR EYE?!
FSHH...
THEY TELL ME YOU ALMOST DIED!!
MRK...

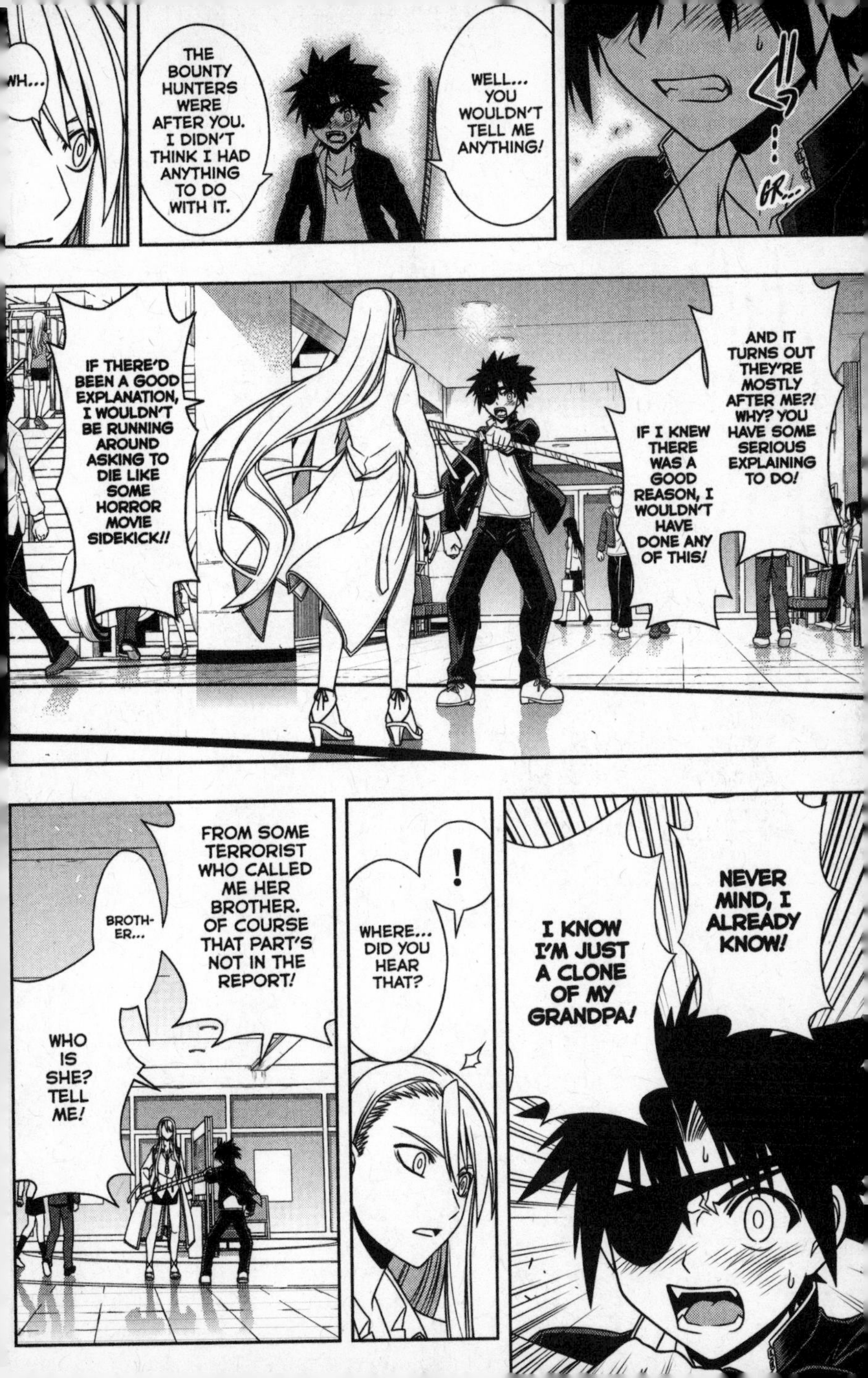
GR...
WELL... YOU WOULDN'T TELL ME ANYTHING!
THE BOUNTY HUNTERS WERE AFTER YOU. I DIDN'T THINK I HAD ANYTHING TO DO WITH IT.
WH...
AND IT TURNS OUT THEY'RE MOSTLY AFTER ME?! WHY? YOU HAVE SOME SERIOUS EXPLAINING TO DO!
IF I KNEW THERE WAS A GOOD REASON, I WOULDN'T HAVE DONE ANY OF THIS!
IF THERE'D BEEN A GOOD EXPLANATION, I WOULDN'T BE RUNNING AROUND ASKING TO DIE LIKE SOME HORROR MOVIE SIDEKICK!!
NEVER MIND, I ALREADY KNOW!
I KNOW I'M JUST A CLONE OF MY GRANDPA!
!
WHERE... DID YOU HEAR THAT?
FROM SOME TERRORIST WHO CALLED ME HER BROTHER. OF COURSE THAT PART'S NOT IN THE REPORT!
BROTH-ER...
WHO IS SHE? TELL ME!

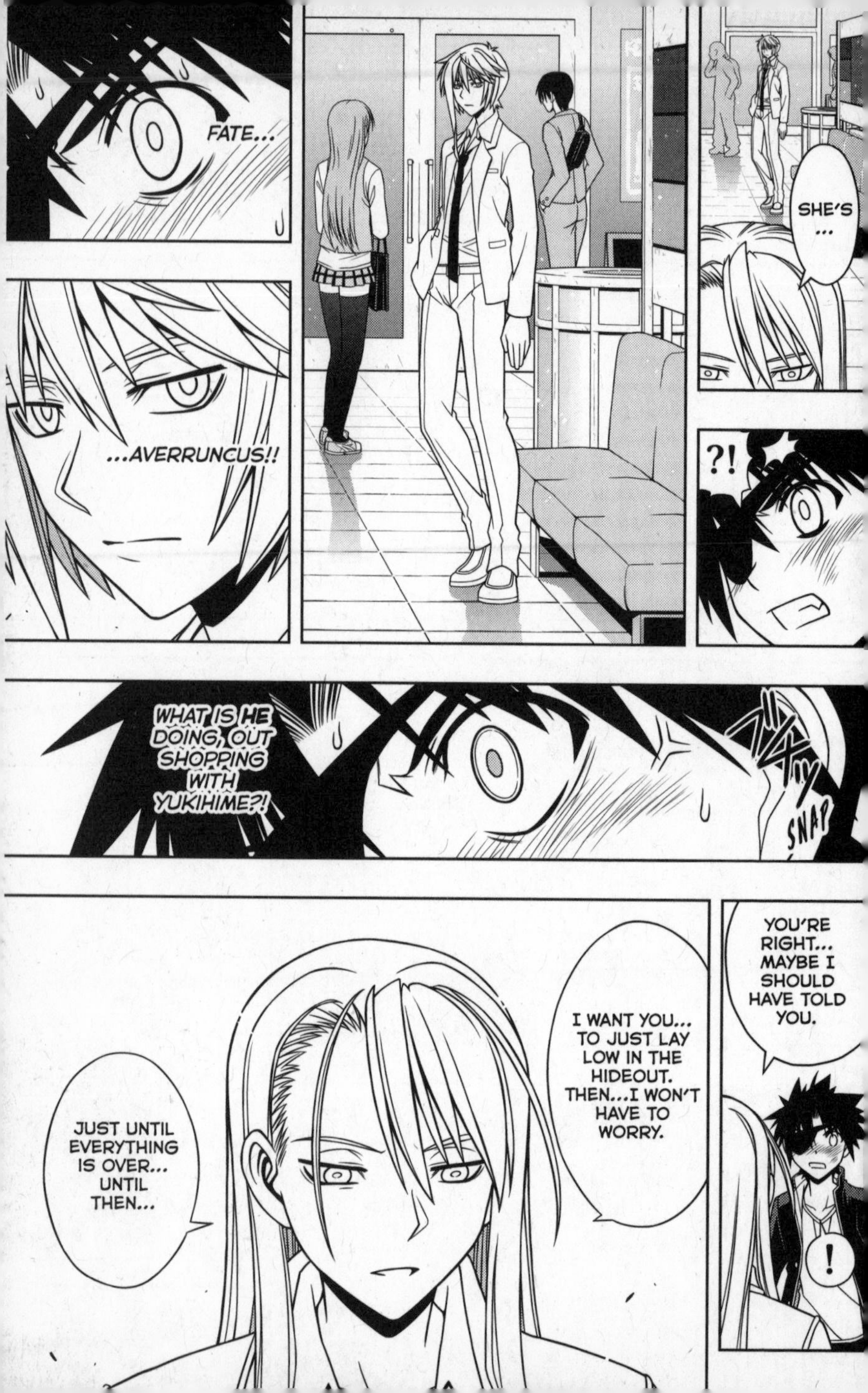
SHE'S ...
?!
FATE...
...AVERRUNCUS!!
SNAP
WHAT IS HE DOING, OUT SHOPPING WITH YUKIHIME?!
YOU'RE RIGHT... MAYBE I SHOULD HAVE TOLD YOU.
!
I WANT YOU... TO JUST LAY LOW IN THE HIDEOUT. THEN...I WON'T HAVE TO WORRY.
JUST UNTIL EVERYTHING IS OVER... UNTIL THEN...

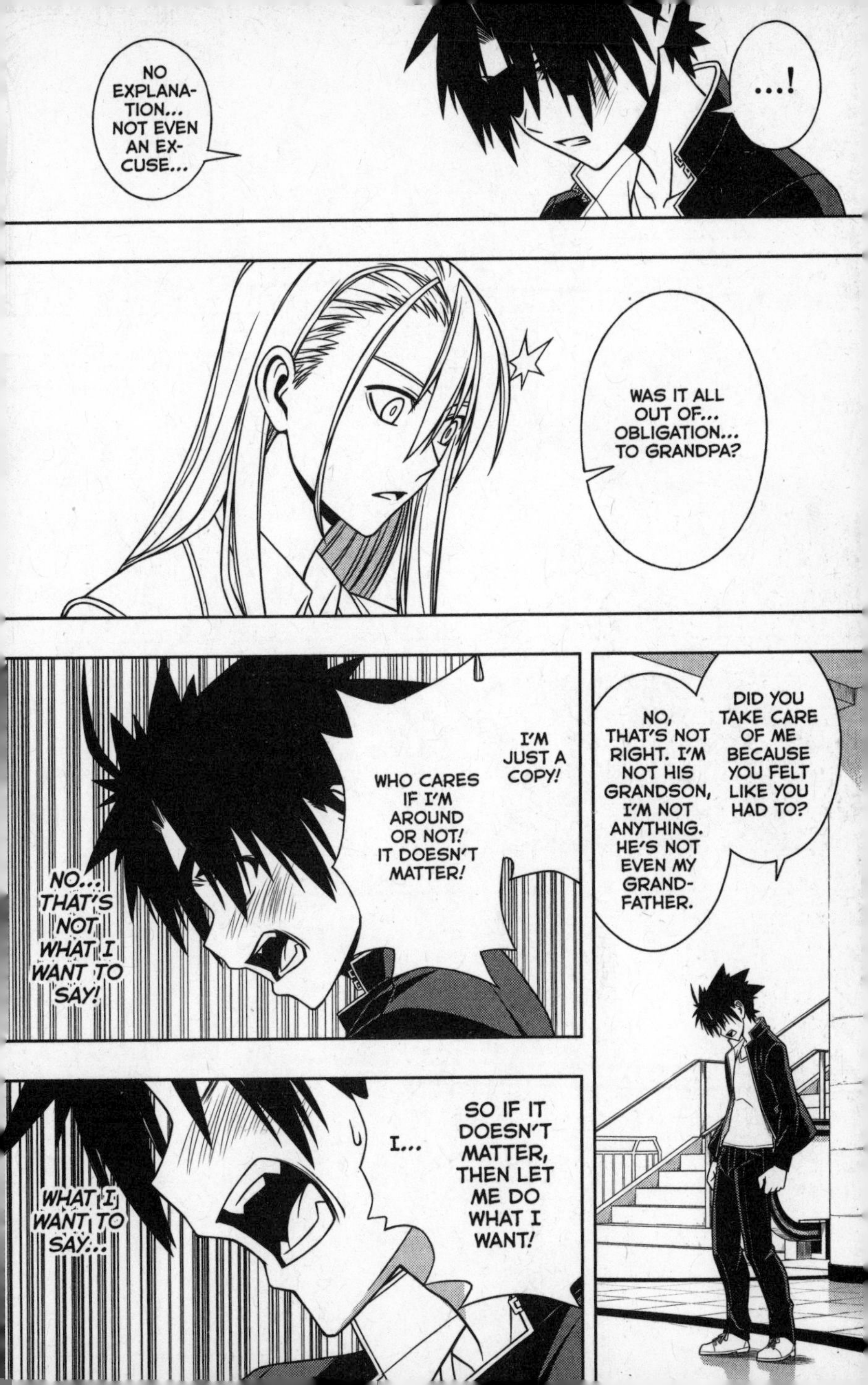
...!
NO EXPLANATION... NOT EVEN AN EXCUSE...
WAS IT ALL OUT OF... OBLIGATION... TO GRANDPA?
DID YOU TAKE CARE OF ME BECAUSE YOU FELT LIKE YOU HAD TO?
NO, THAT'S NOT RIGHT. I'M NOT HIS GRANDSON, I'M NOT ANYTHING. HE'S NOT EVEN MY GRAND-FATHER.
I'M JUST A COPY!
WHO CARES IF I'M AROUND OR NOT! IT DOESN'T MATTER!
NO... THAT'S NOT WHAT I WANT TO SAY!
SO IF IT DOESN'T MATTER, THEN LET ME DO WHAT I WANT!
I...
WHAT I WANT TO SAY...

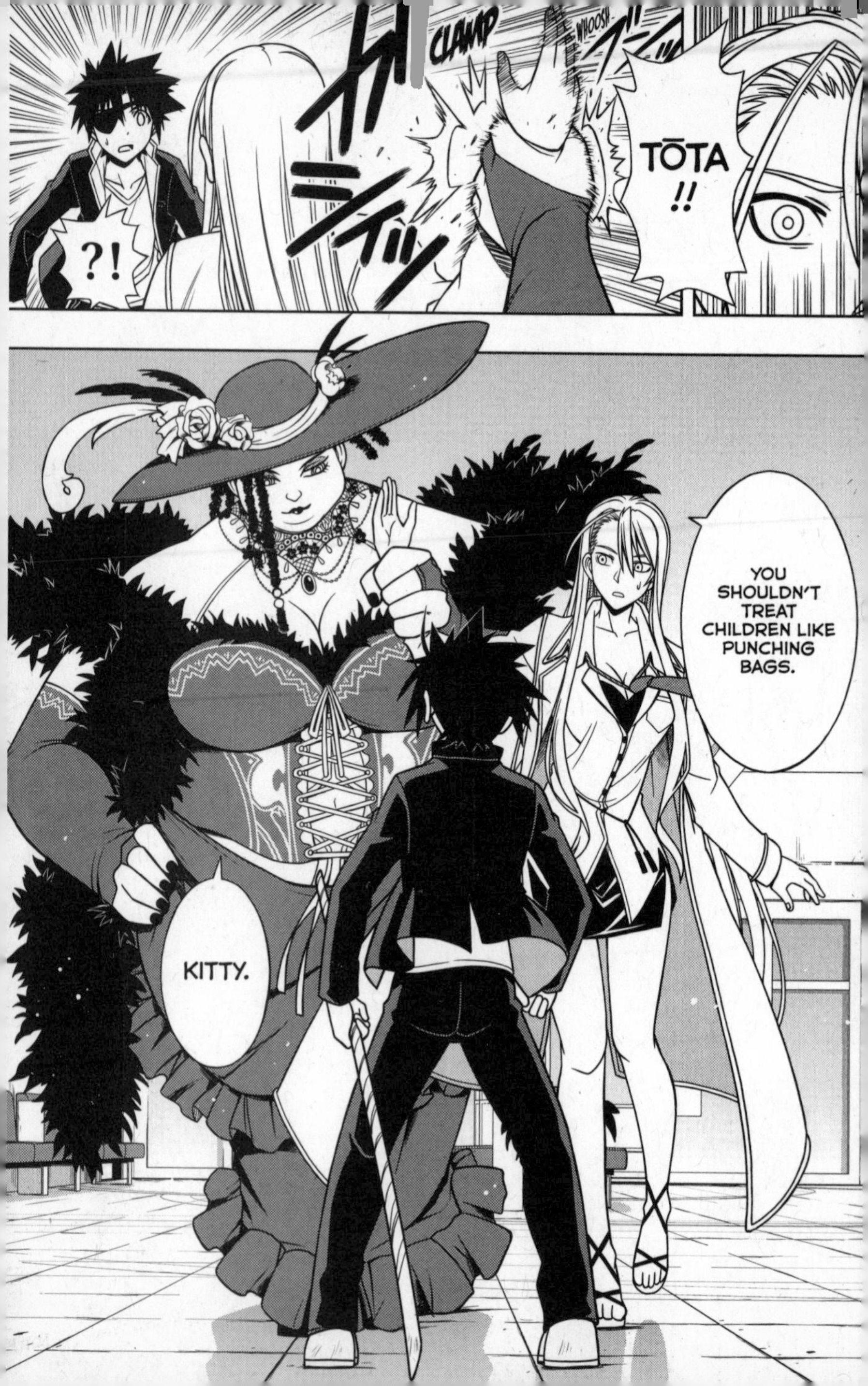
TŌTA !!
WHOOSH
CLAMP
?!
YOU SHOULDN'T TREAT CHILDREN LIKE PUNCHING BAGS.
KITTY.

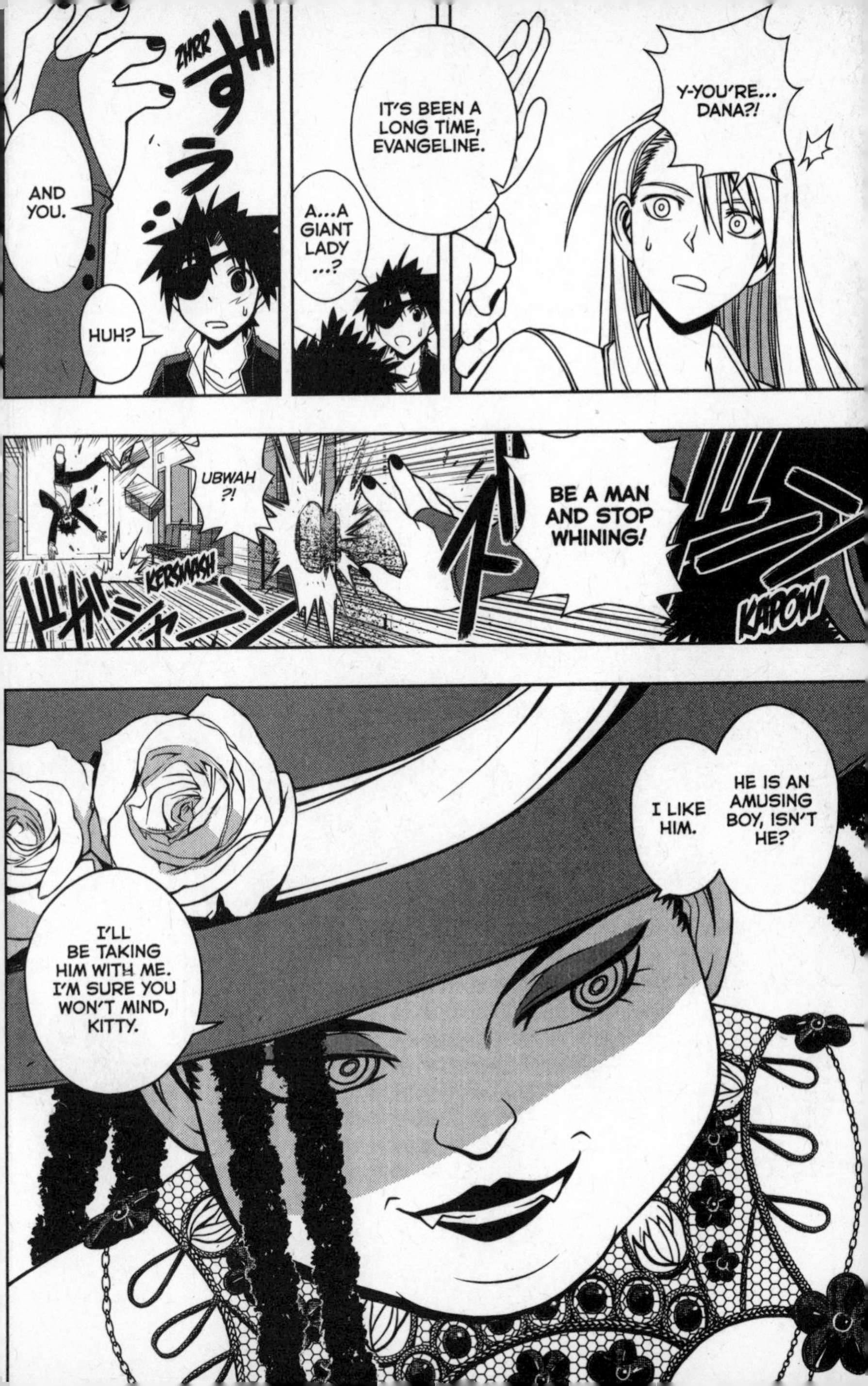
Y-YOU'RE... DANA?!
IT'S BEEN A LONG TIME, EVANGELINE.
A...A GIANT LADY ...?
ZHRR
AND YOU.
HUH?
KAPOW
BE A MAN AND STOP WHINING!
UBWAH ?!
KERSMASH
HE IS AN AMUSING BOY, ISN'T HE?
I LIKE HIM.
I'LL BE TAKING HIM WITH ME. I'M SURE YOU WON'T MIND, KITTY.

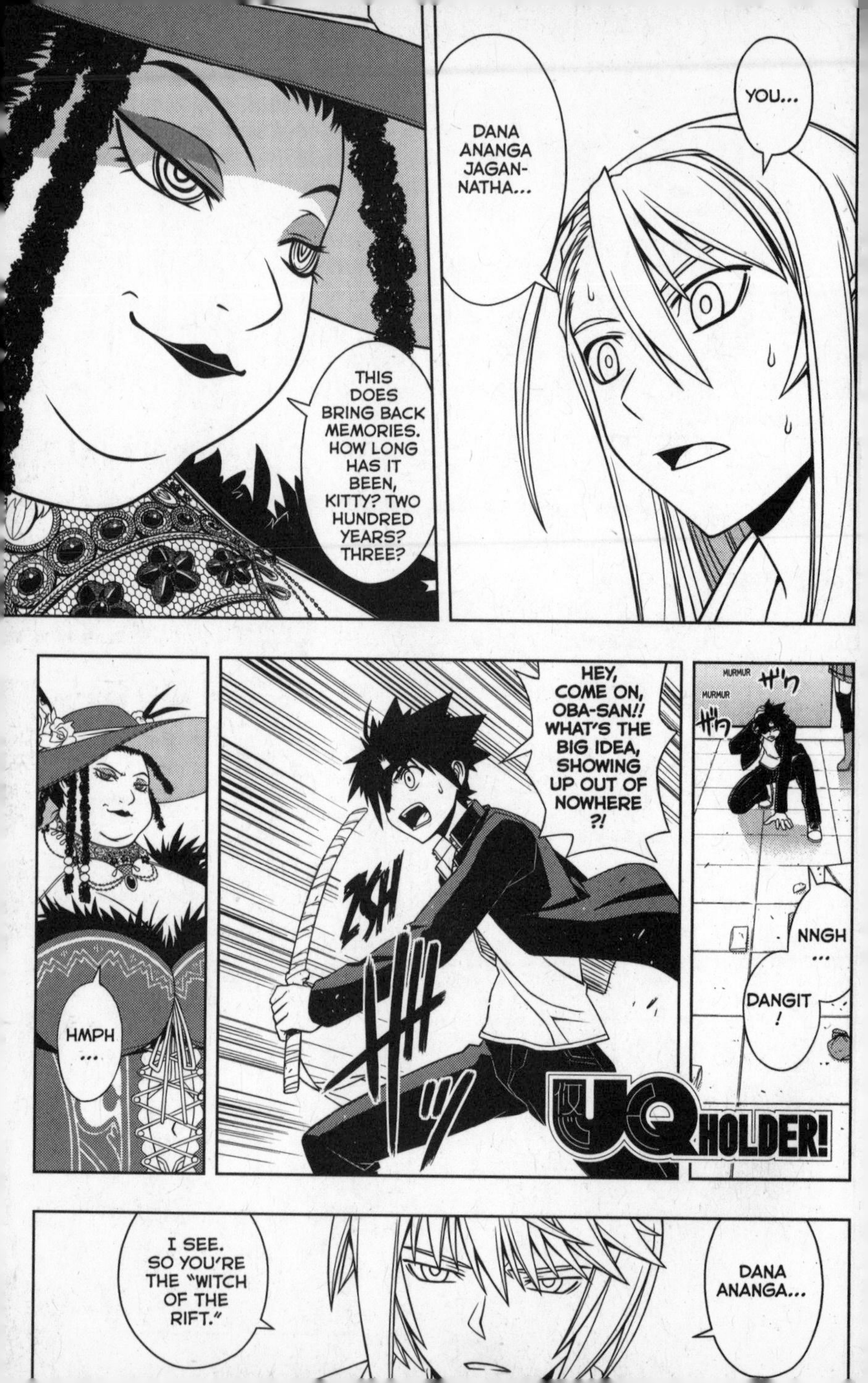
YOU...
DANA ANANGA JAGAN-NATHA...
THIS DOES BRING BACK MEMORIES. HOW LONG HAS IT BEEN, KITTY? TWO HUNDRED YEARS? THREE?
MURMUR
ザワ
MURMUR
ザワ
NNGH...
DANGIT!
UQ HOLDER!
HEY, COME ON, OBA-SAN!! WHAT'S THE BIG IDEA, SHOWING UP OUT OF NOWHERE?!
ZSH
HMPH...
DANA ANANGA...
I SEE. SO YOU'RE THE "WITCH OF THE RIFT."

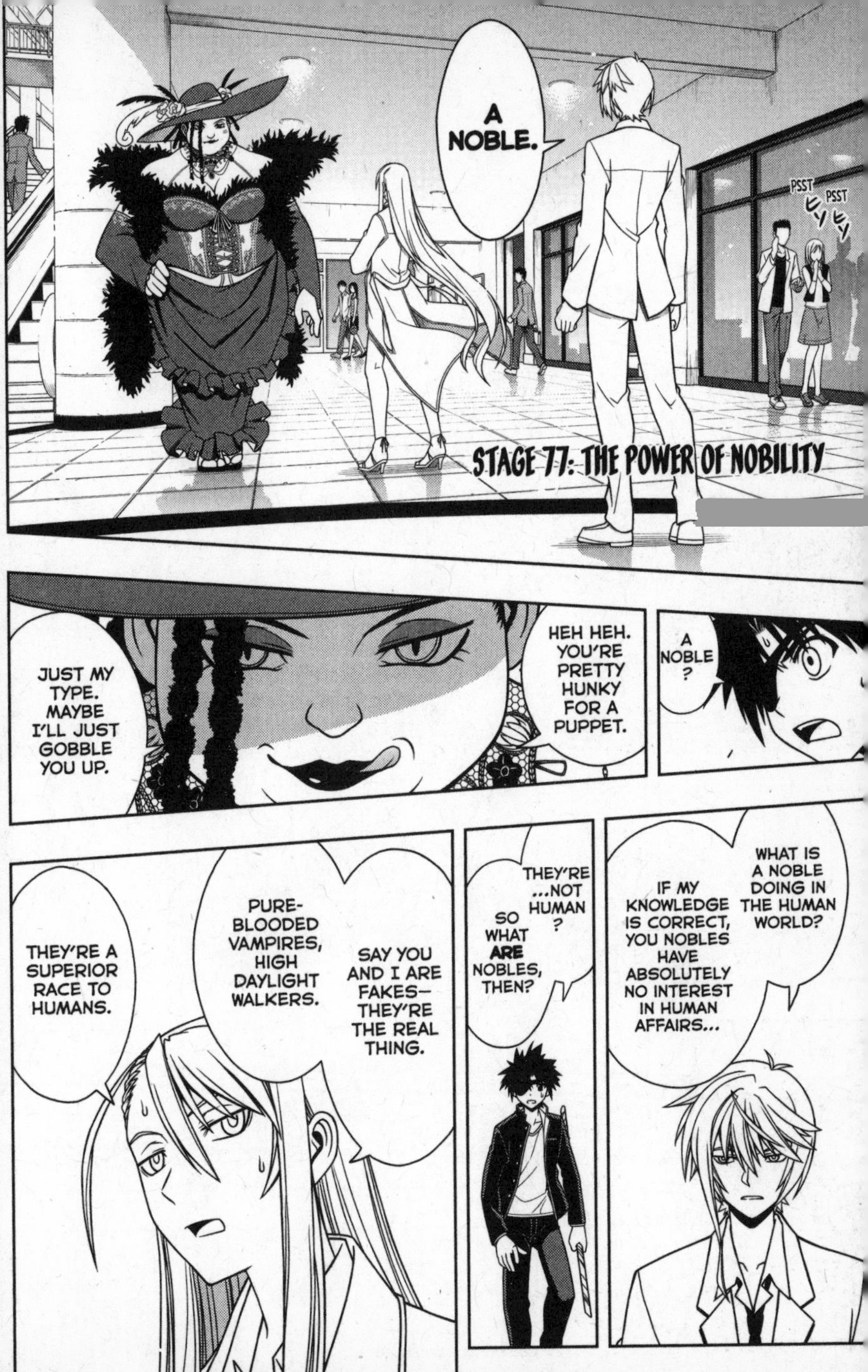
A NOBLE.
PSST PSST
ヒソヒソ
STAGE 77: THE POWER OF NOBILITY
A NOBLE?
HEH HEH. YOU'RE PRETTY HUNKY FOR A PUPPET.
JUST MY TYPE. MAYBE I'LL JUST GOBBLE YOU UP.
WHAT IS A NOBLE DOING IN THE HUMAN WORLD?
IF MY KNOWLEDGE IS CORRECT, YOU NOBLES HAVE ABSOLUTELY NO INTEREST IN HUMAN AFFAIRS...
THEY'RE ...NOT HUMAN?
SO WHAT **ARE** NOBLES, THEN?
PURE-BLOODED VAMPIRES, HIGH DAYLIGHT WALKERS.
SAY YOU AND I ARE FAKES— THEY'RE THE REAL THING.
THEY'RE A SUPERIOR RACE TO HUMANS.

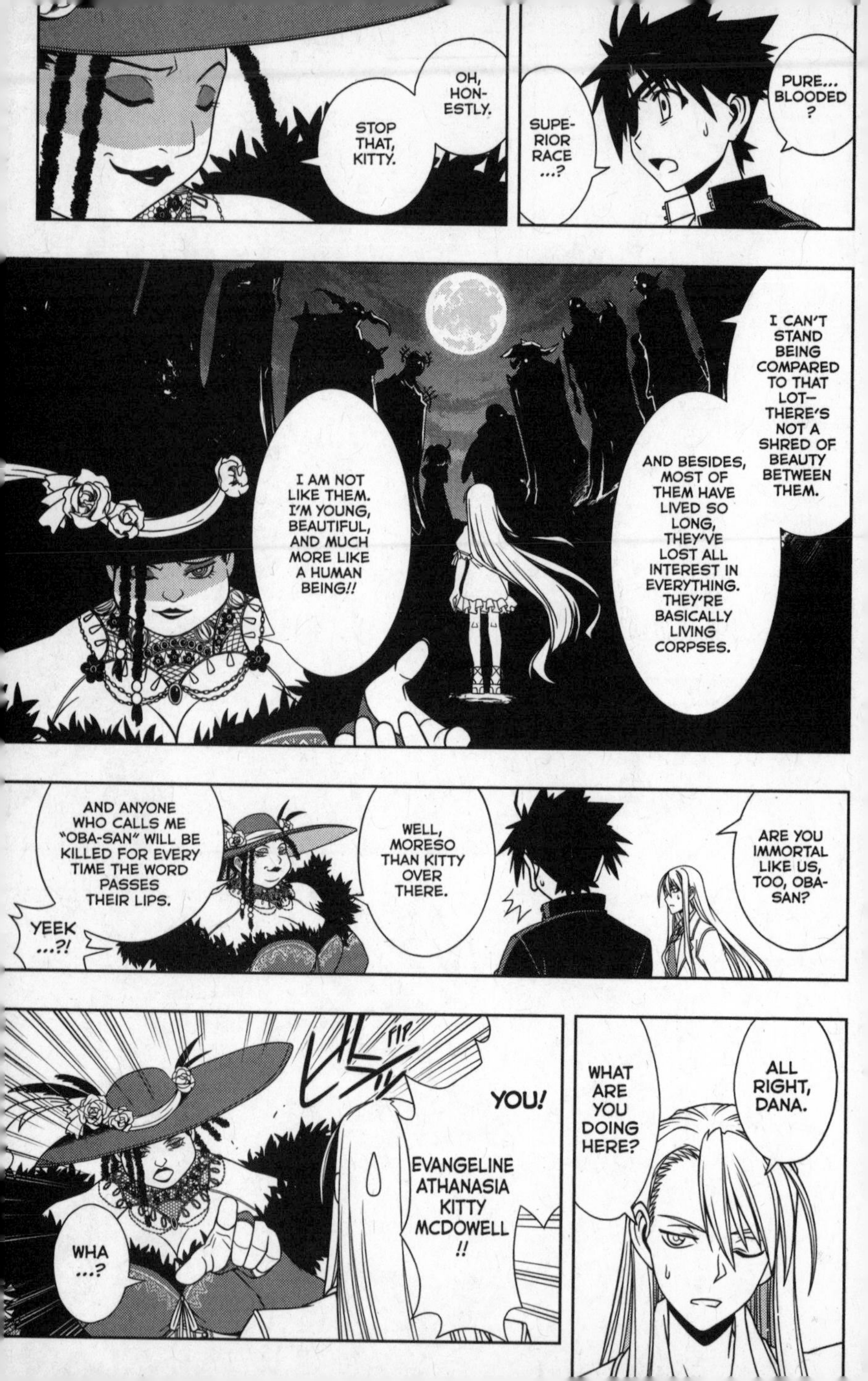
PURE... BLOODED?
SUPERIOR RACE ...?
OH, HONESTLY.
STOP THAT, KITTY.
I CAN'T STAND BEING COMPARED TO THAT LOT— THERE'S NOT A SHRED OF BEAUTY BETWEEN THEM.
AND BESIDES, MOST OF THEM HAVE LIVED SO LONG, THEY'VE LOST ALL INTEREST IN EVERYTHING. THEY'RE BASICALLY LIVING CORPSES.
I AM NOT LIKE THEM. I'M YOUNG, BEAUTIFUL, AND MUCH MORE LIKE A HUMAN BEING!!
ARE YOU IMMORTAL LIKE US, TOO, OBA-SAN?
WELL, MORESO THAN KITTY OVER THERE.
AND ANYONE WHO CALLS ME "OBA-SAN" WILL BE KILLED FOR EVERY TIME THE WORD PASSES THEIR LIPS.
YEEK ...?!
ALL RIGHT, DANA.
WHAT ARE YOU DOING HERE?
FIP
YOU!
EVANGELINE ATHANASIA KITTY MCDOWELL !!
WHA ...?

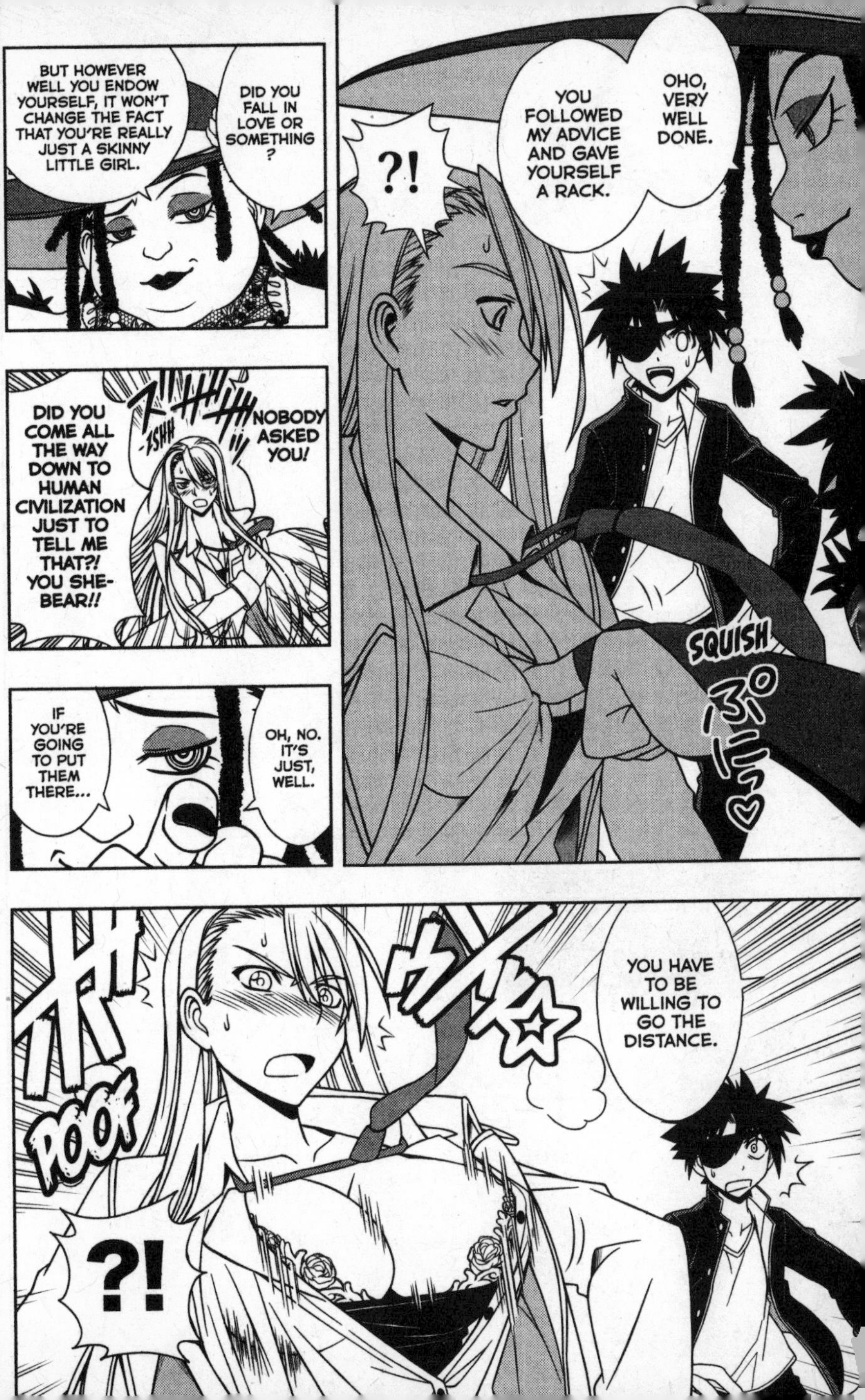
OHO, VERY WELL DONE.
YOU FOLLOWED MY ADVICE AND GAVE YOURSELF A RACK.
?!
SQUISH
DID YOU FALL IN LOVE OR SOMETHING?
BUT HOWEVER WELL YOU ENDOW YOURSELF, IT WON'T CHANGE THE FACT THAT YOU'RE REALLY JUST A SKINNY LITTLE GIRL.
NOBODY ASKED YOU!
-ZSHH
DID YOU COME ALL THE WAY DOWN TO HUMAN CIVILIZATION JUST TO TELL ME THAT?! YOU SHE-BEAR!!
OH, NO. IT'S JUST, WELL.
IF YOU'RE GOING TO PUT THEM THERE...
YOU HAVE TO BE WILLING TO GO THE DISTANCE.
POOF
?!

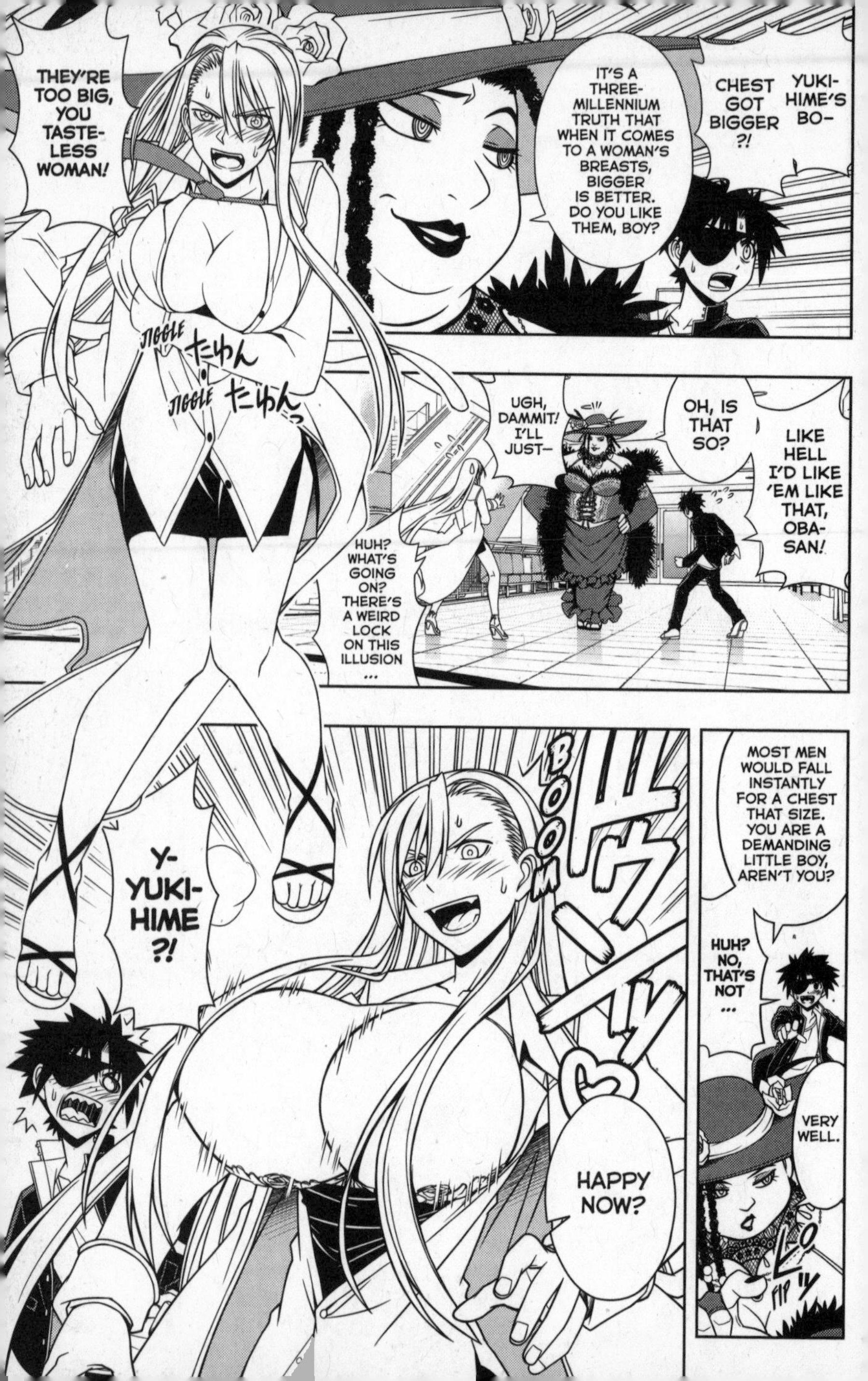
YUKI-HIME'S BO—
CHEST GOT BIGGER ?!
IT'S A THREE-MILLENNIUM TRUTH THAT WHEN IT COMES TO A WOMAN'S BREASTS, BIGGER IS BETTER. DO YOU LIKE THEM, BOY?
THEY'RE TOO BIG, YOU TASTE-LESS WOMAN!
JIGGLE たゆん
JIGGLE たゆん
LIKE HELL I'D LIKE 'EM LIKE THAT, OBA-SAN!
OH, IS THAT SO?
UGH, DAMMIT! I'LL JUST—
HUH? WHAT'S GOING ON? THERE'S A WEIRD LOCK ON THIS ILLUSION ...
MOST MEN WOULD FALL INSTANTLY FOR A CHEST THAT SIZE. YOU ARE A DEMANDING LITTLE BOY, AREN'T YOU?
HUH? NO, THAT'S NOT ...
VERY WELL.
FLIP
BOOM
HAPPY NOW?
Y-YUKI-HIME ?!

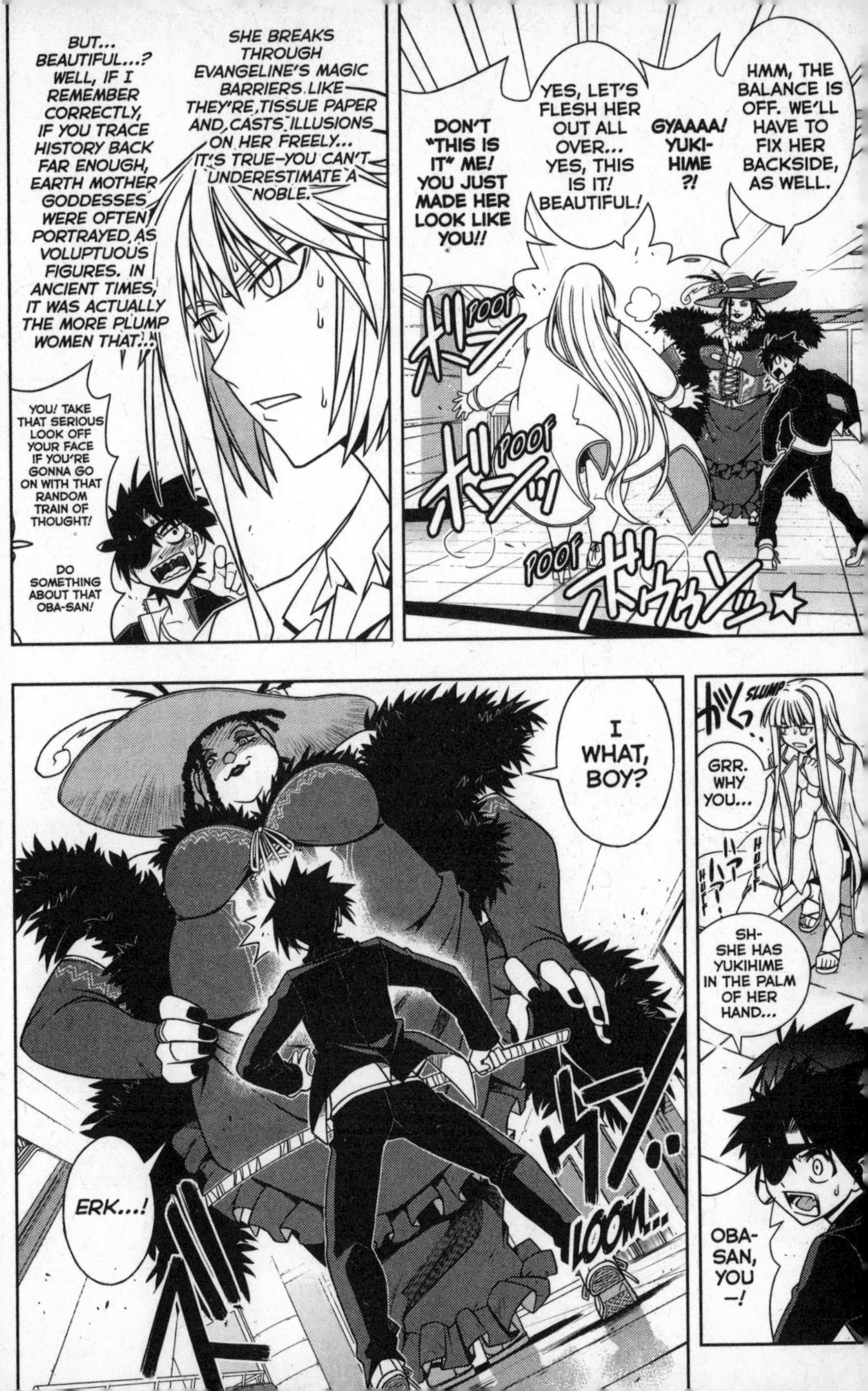
HMM, THE BALANCE IS OFF. WE'LL HAVE TO FIX HER BACKSIDE, AS WELL.
GYAAAA! YUKI-HIME ?!
YES, LET'S FLESH HER OUT ALL OVER... YES, THIS IS IT! BEAUTIFUL!
DON'T "THIS IS IT" ME! YOU JUST MADE HER LOOK LIKE YOU!!
POOF
POOF
POOF
SHE BREAKS THROUGH EVANGELINE'S MAGIC BARRIERS LIKE THEY'RE TISSUE PAPER AND CASTS ILLUSIONS ON HER FREELY... IT'S TRUE—YOU CAN'T UNDERESTIMATE A NOBLE.
BUT... BEAUTIFUL...? WELL, IF I REMEMBER CORRECTLY, IF YOU TRACE HISTORY BACK FAR ENOUGH, EARTH MOTHER GODDESSES WERE OFTEN PORTRAYED AS VOLUPTUOUS FIGURES. IN ANCIENT TIMES, IT WAS ACTUALLY THE MORE PLUMP WOMEN THAT...
YOU! TAKE THAT SERIOUS LOOK OFF YOUR FACE IF YOU'RE GONNA GO ON WITH THAT RANDOM TRAIN OF THOUGHT!
DO SOMETHING ABOUT THAT OBA-SAN!
SLUMP
GRR. WHY YOU...
HUFF
HUFF
SH-SHE HAS YUKIHIME IN THE PALM OF HER HAND...
OBA-SAN, YOU—!
I WHAT, BOY?
LOOM...
ERK...!

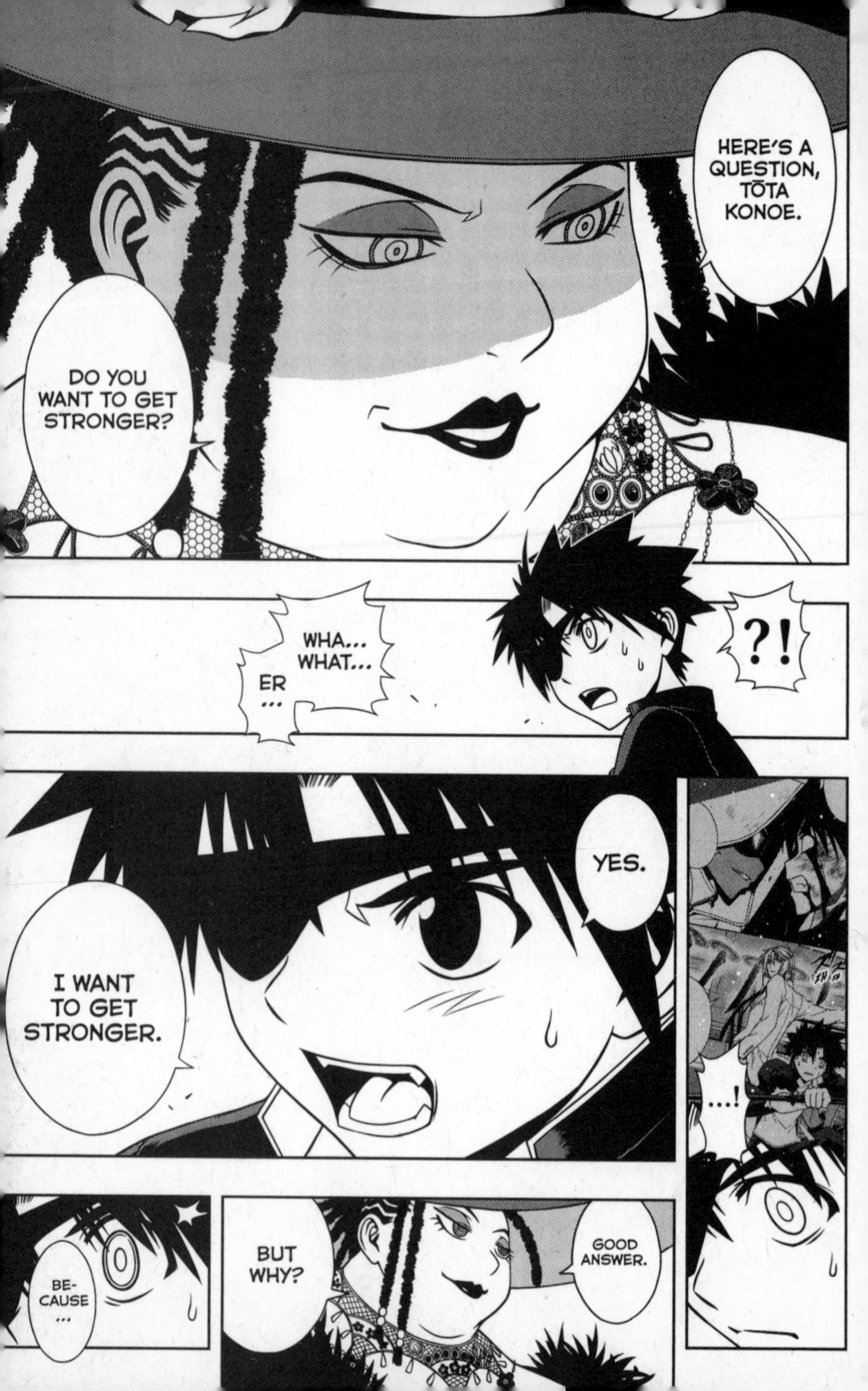
HERE'S A QUESTION, TŌTA KONOE.
DO YOU WANT TO GET STRONGER?
?!
WHA... WHAT...
ER...
...!
YES.
I WANT TO GET STRONGER.
GOOD ANSWER.
BUT WHY?
BE-CAUSE...

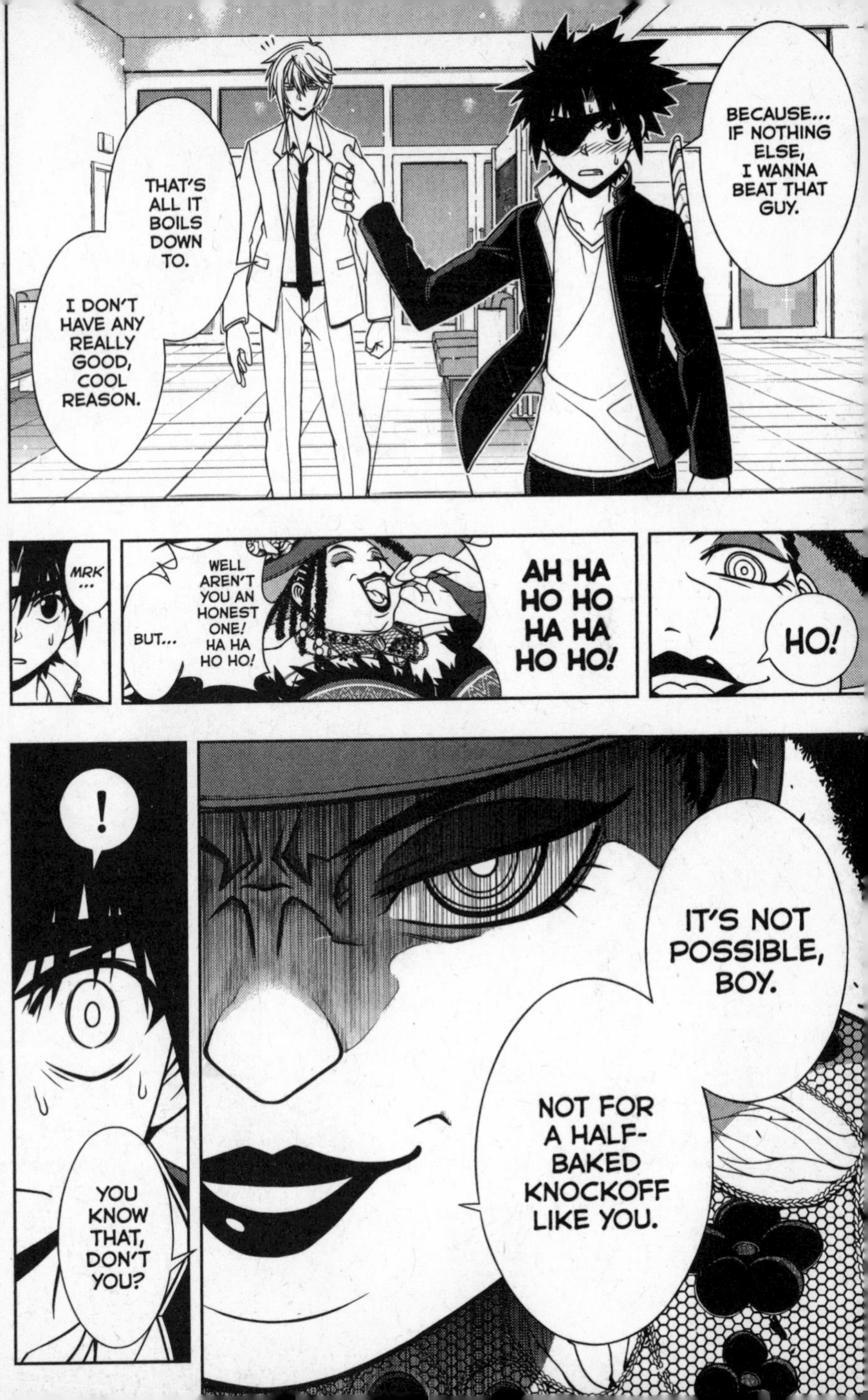
BECAUSE... IF NOTHING ELSE, I WANNA BEAT THAT GUY.
THAT'S ALL IT BOILS DOWN TO.
I DON'T HAVE ANY REALLY GOOD, COOL REASON.
HO!
AH HA HO HO HA HA HO HO!
WELL AREN'T YOU AN HONEST ONE! HA HA HO HO!
BUT...
MRK...
IT'S NOT POSSIBLE, BOY.
NOT FOR A HALF-BAKED KNOCKOFF LIKE YOU.
YOU KNOW THAT, DON'T YOU?
!

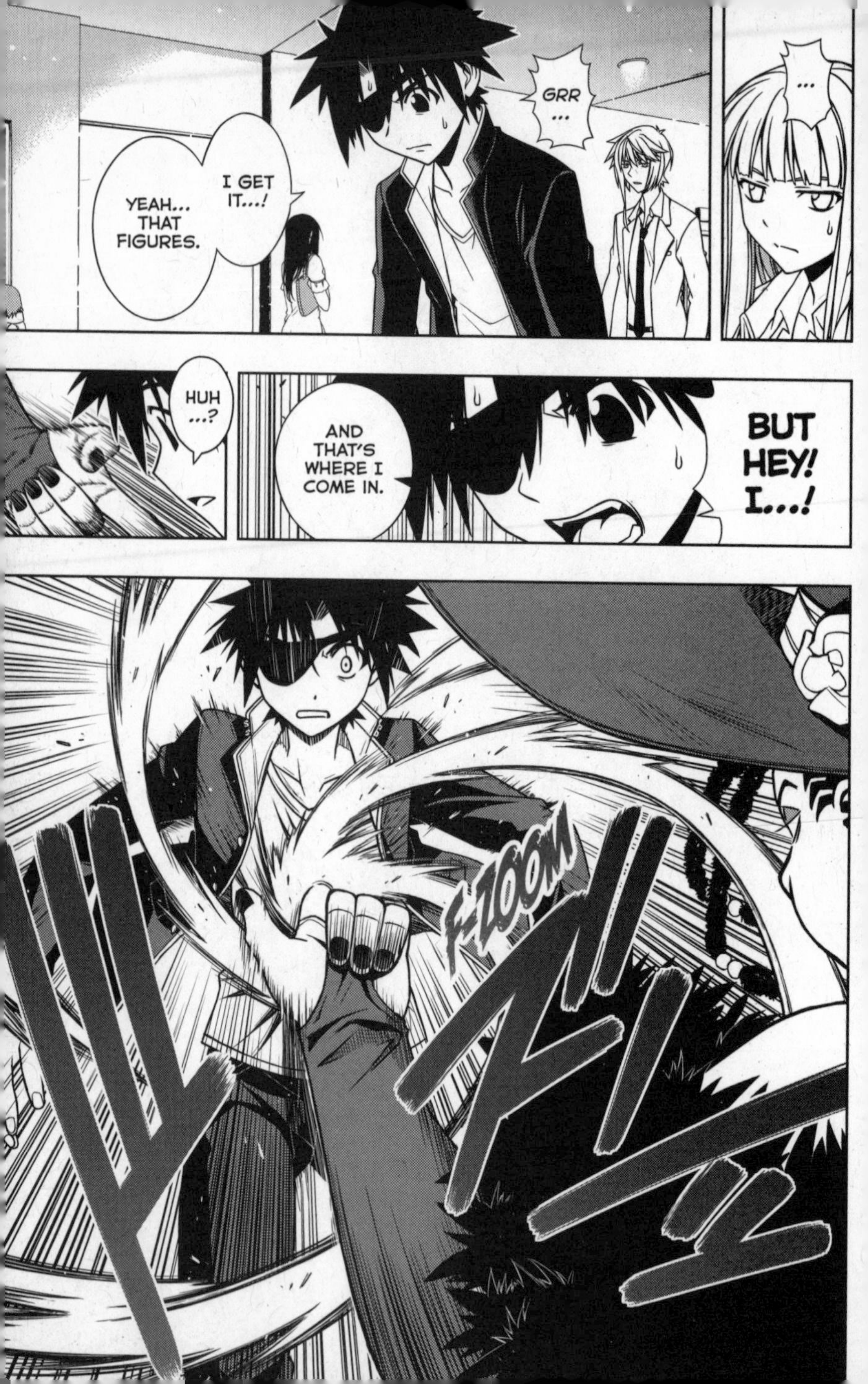
...
GRR ...
I GET IT...!
YEAH... THAT FIGURES.
BUT HEY! I...!
AND THAT'S WHERE I COME IN.
HUH ...?
F-ZOOM

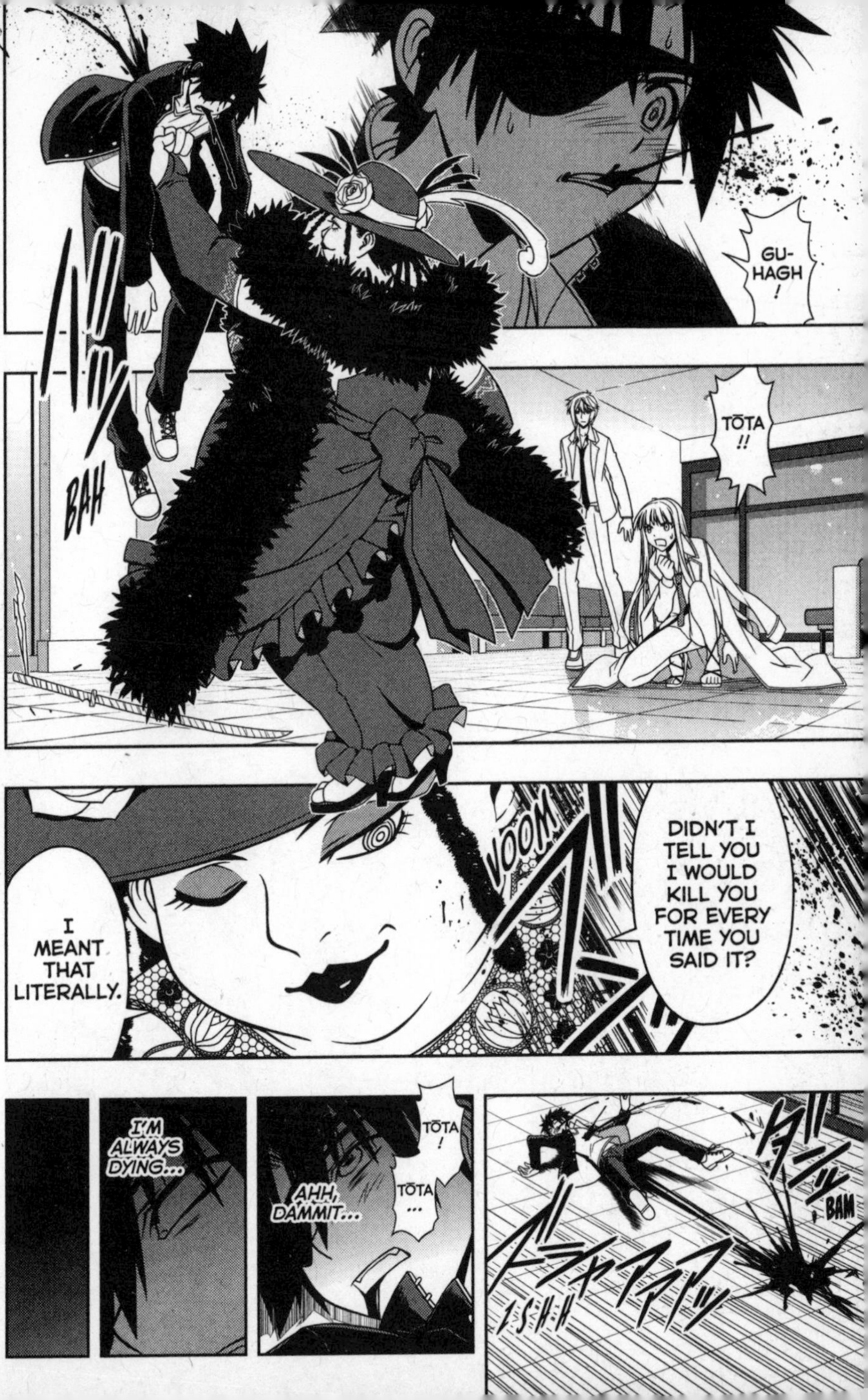
GU-HAGH!
TŌTA!!
BAH
VOOM
DIDN'T I TELL YOU I WOULD KILL YOU FOR EVERY TIME YOU SAID IT?
I MEANT THAT LITERALLY.
BAM
TŌTA!
TŌTA...
AHH, DAMMIT...
I'M ALWAYS DYING...

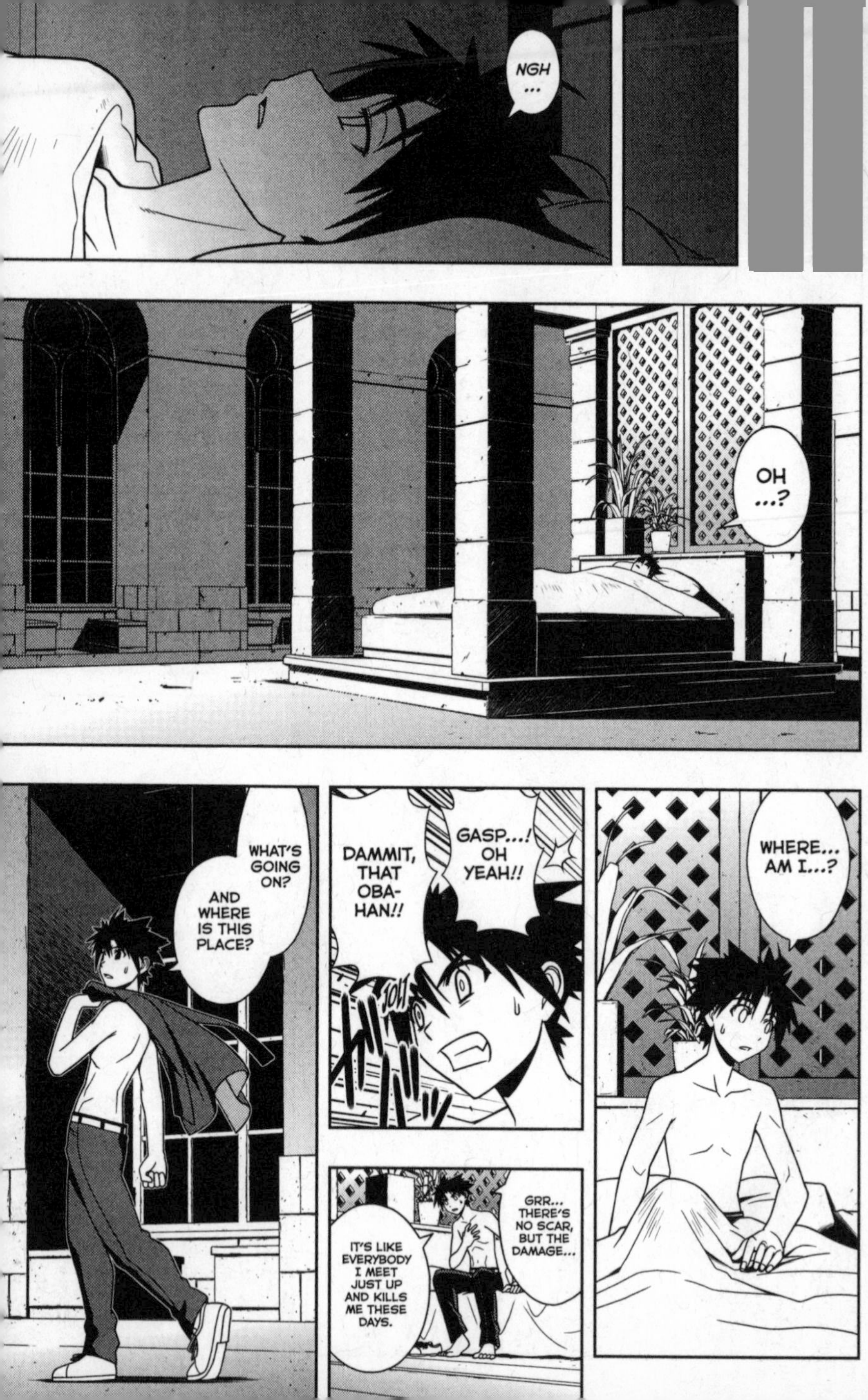
NGH ...
OH ...?
WHERE... AM I...?
GASP...! OH YEAH!!
DAMMIT, THAT OBA-HAN!!
JOLT
GRR... THERE'S NO SCAR, BUT THE DAMAGE...
IT'S LIKE EVERYBODY I MEET JUST UP AND KILLS ME THESE DAYS.
WHAT'S GOING ON?
AND WHERE IS THIS PLACE?

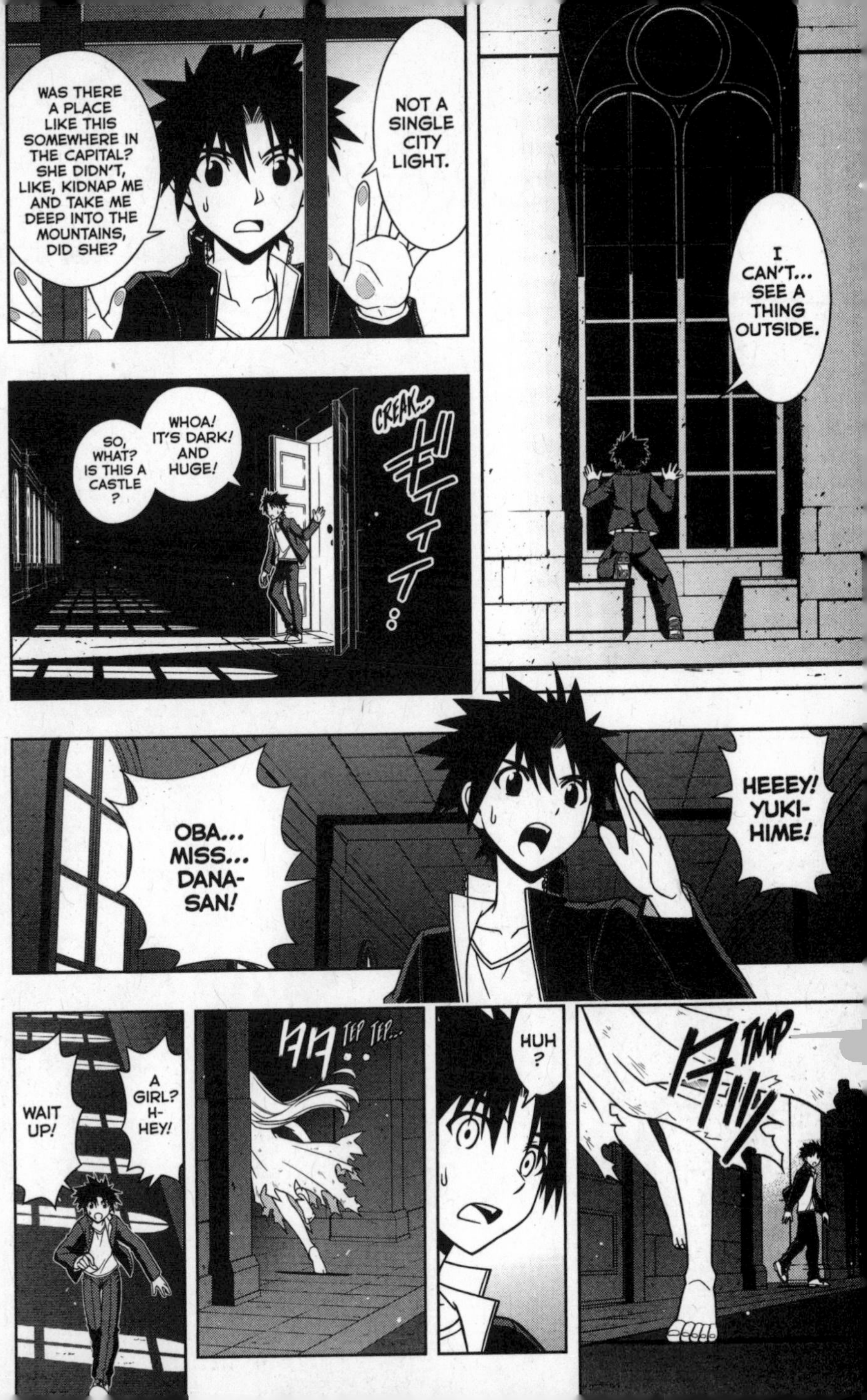

I CAN'T... SEE A THING OUTSIDE.
NOT A SINGLE CITY LIGHT.
WAS THERE A PLACE LIKE THIS SOMEWHERE IN THE CAPITAL? SHE DIDN'T, LIKE, KIDNAP ME AND TAKE ME DEEP INTO THE MOUNTAINS, DID SHE?
CREAK...
WHOA! IT'S DARK! AND HUGE!
SO, WHAT? IS THIS A CASTLE?
HEEEY! YUKI-HIME!
OBA... MISS... DANA-SAN!
TMP
HUH?
TEP TEP...
A GIRL? H-HEY!
WAIT UP!

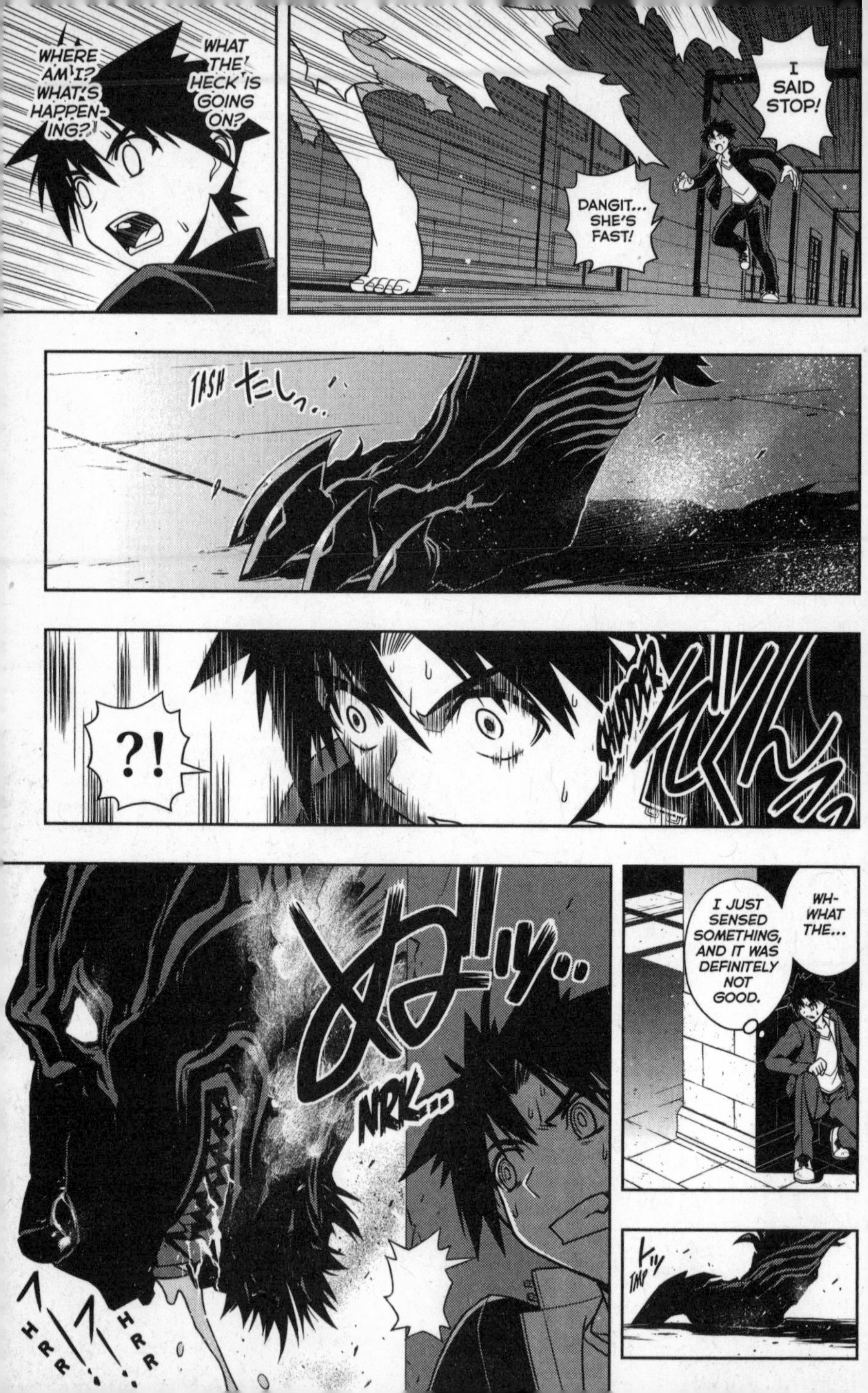

I SAID STOP!
DANGIT... SHE'S FAST!
WHAT THE HECK IS GOING ON?
WHERE AM I? WHAT'S HAPPENING?
TASH
SHUDDER
?!
WH-WHAT THE...
I JUST SENSED SOMETHING, AND IT WAS DEFINITELY NOT GOOD.
TMP
NRK...
HRR
HRR

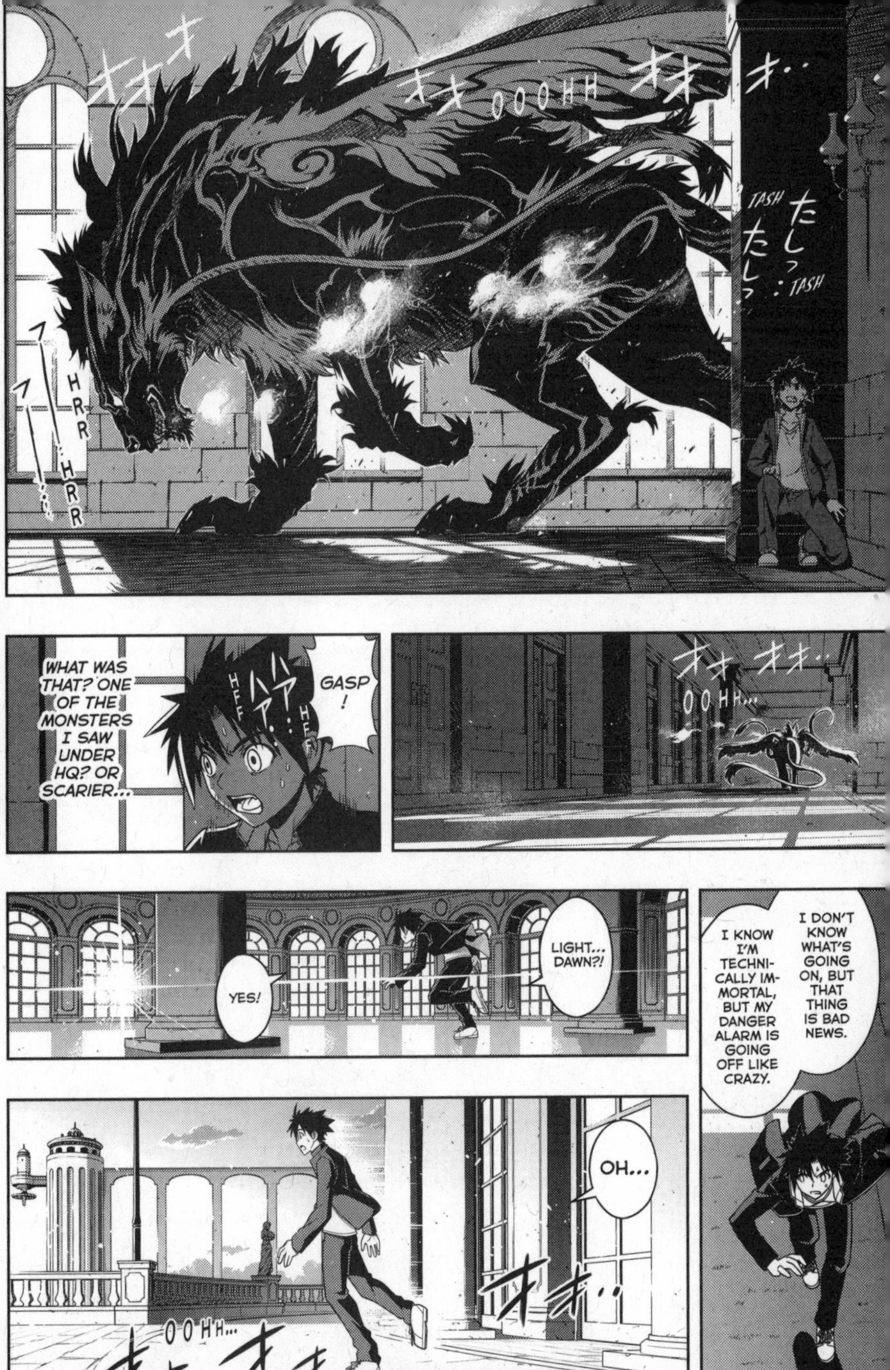

オオオ
オオ OOOHH オオ オ‥
たしっ たしっ
TASH TASH
フー… フー…
HRR HRR
オオ オオ‥
OOHH…
GASP!
ハァ ハァ
HFF HFF
WHAT WAS THAT? ONE OF THE MONSTERS I SAW UNDER HQ? OR SCARIER…
I DON'T KNOW WHAT'S GOING ON, BUT THAT THING IS BAD NEWS.
I KNOW I'M TECHNICALLY IMMORTAL, BUT MY DANGER ALARM IS GOING OFF LIKE CRAZY.
LIGHT… DAWN?!
YES!
OH…
オォ‥
OOHH…
オォ オォ

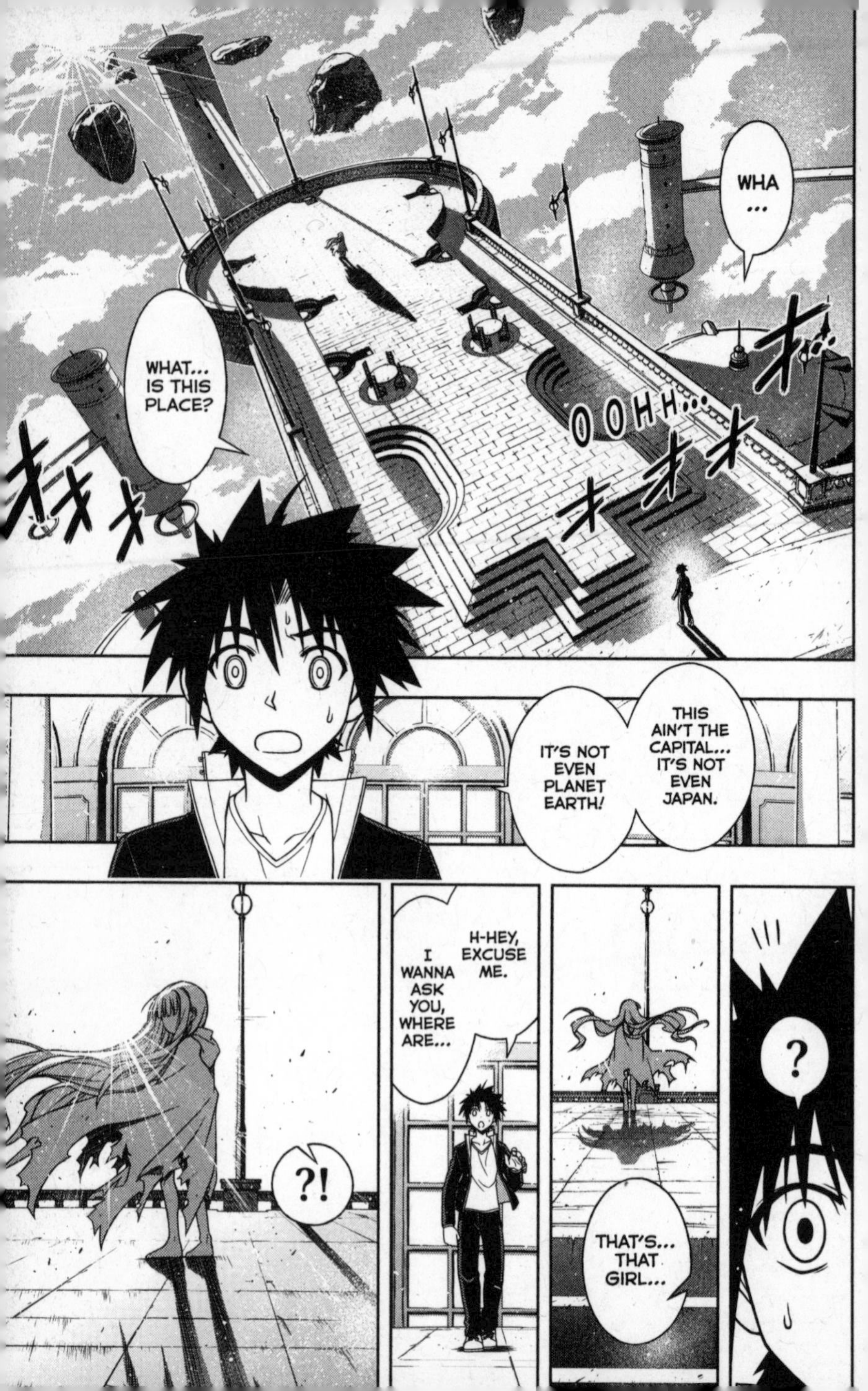
WHA...
OOHH...
WHAT... IS THIS PLACE?
THIS AIN'T THE CAPITAL... IT'S NOT EVEN JAPAN.
IT'S NOT EVEN PLANET EARTH!
?
THAT'S... THAT GIRL...
H-HEY, EXCUSE ME.
I WANNA ASK YOU, WHERE ARE...
?!

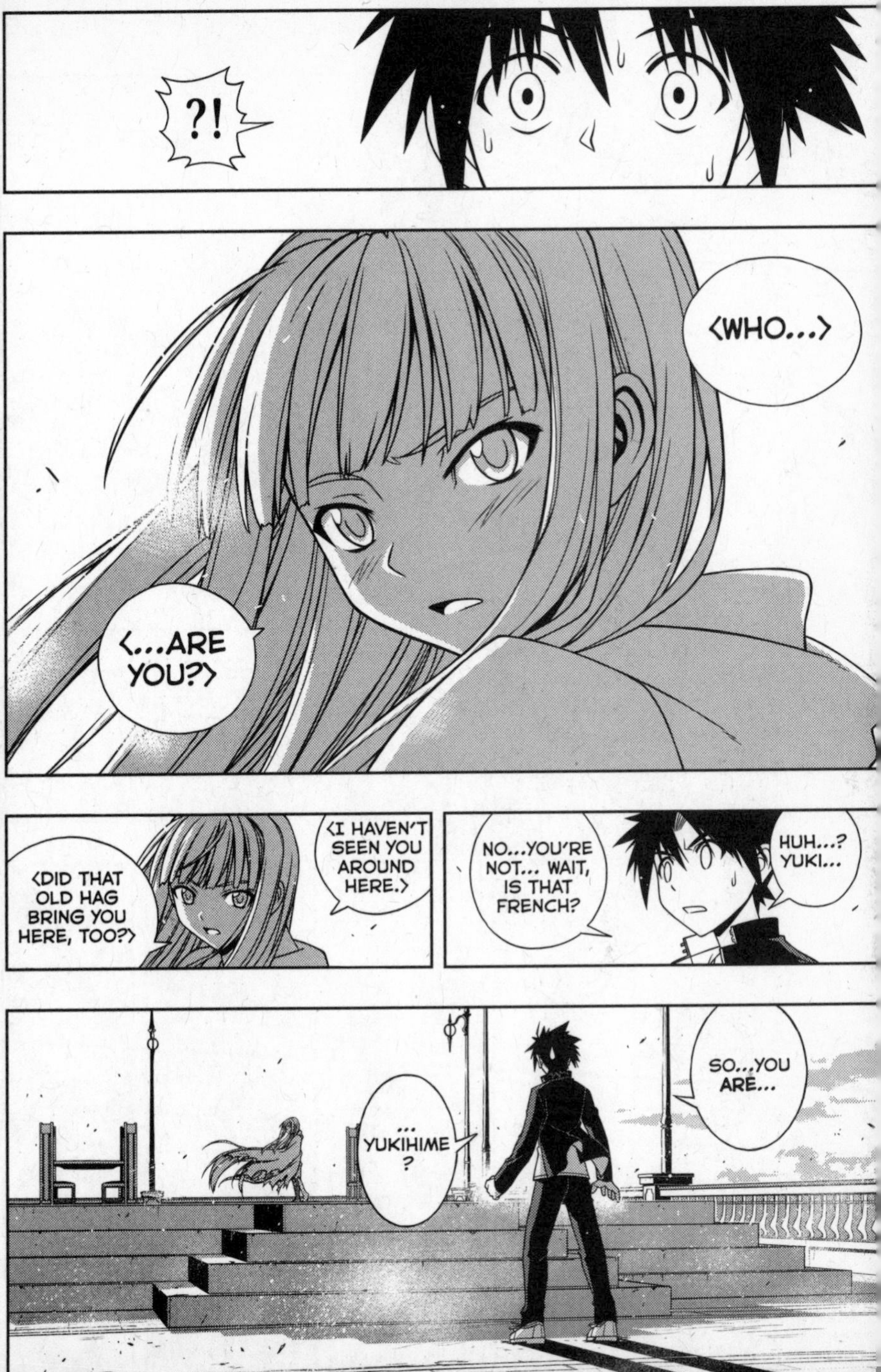
?!
⟨WHO...⟩
⟨...ARE YOU?⟩
HUH...? YUKI...
NO...YOU'RE NOT... WAIT, IS THAT FRENCH?
⟨I HAVEN'T SEEN YOU AROUND HERE.⟩
⟨DID THAT OLD HAG BRING YOU HERE, TOO?⟩
SO...YOU ARE...
...YUKIHIME?

STAGE 78: YUKIHIME AND THE WITCH OF THE RIFT

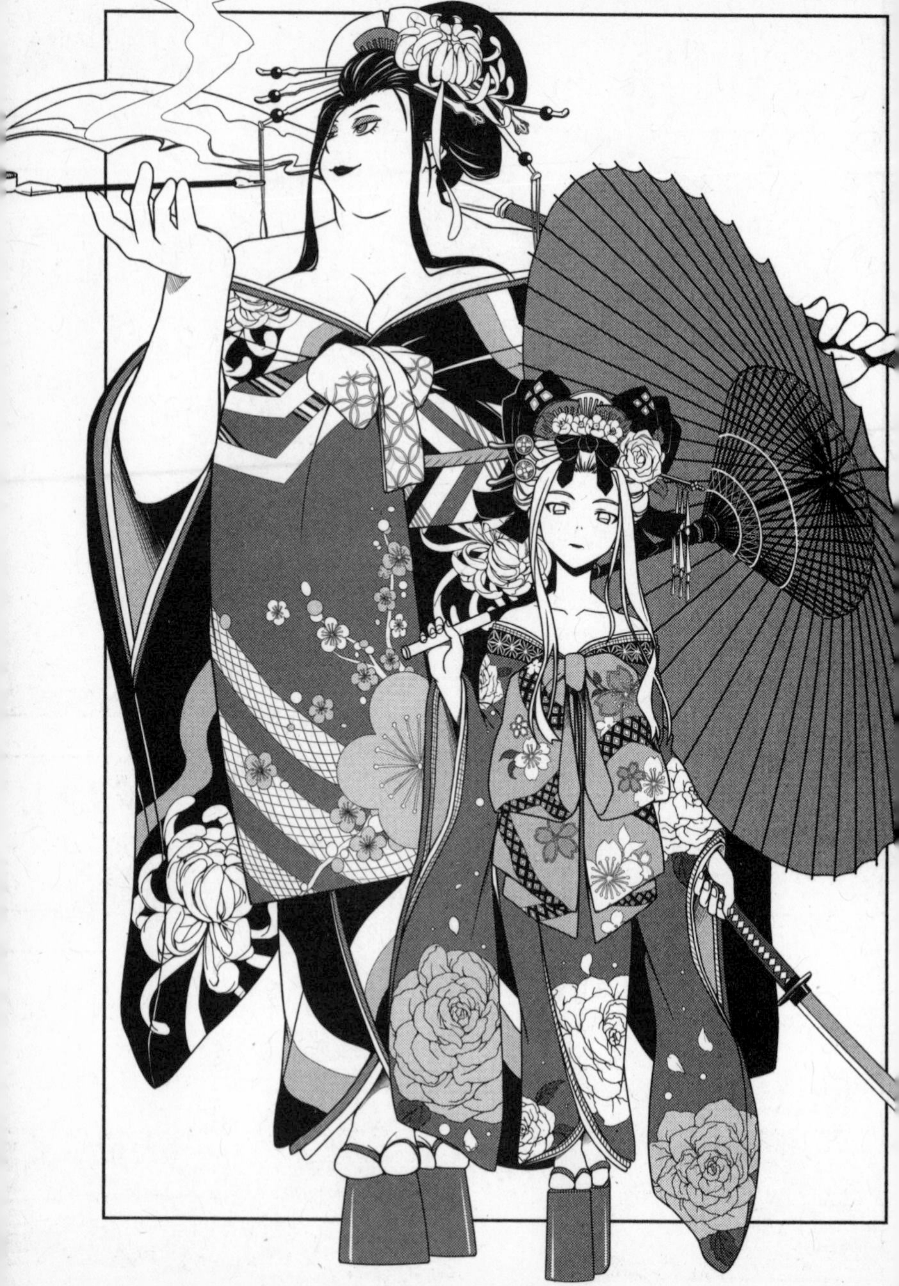

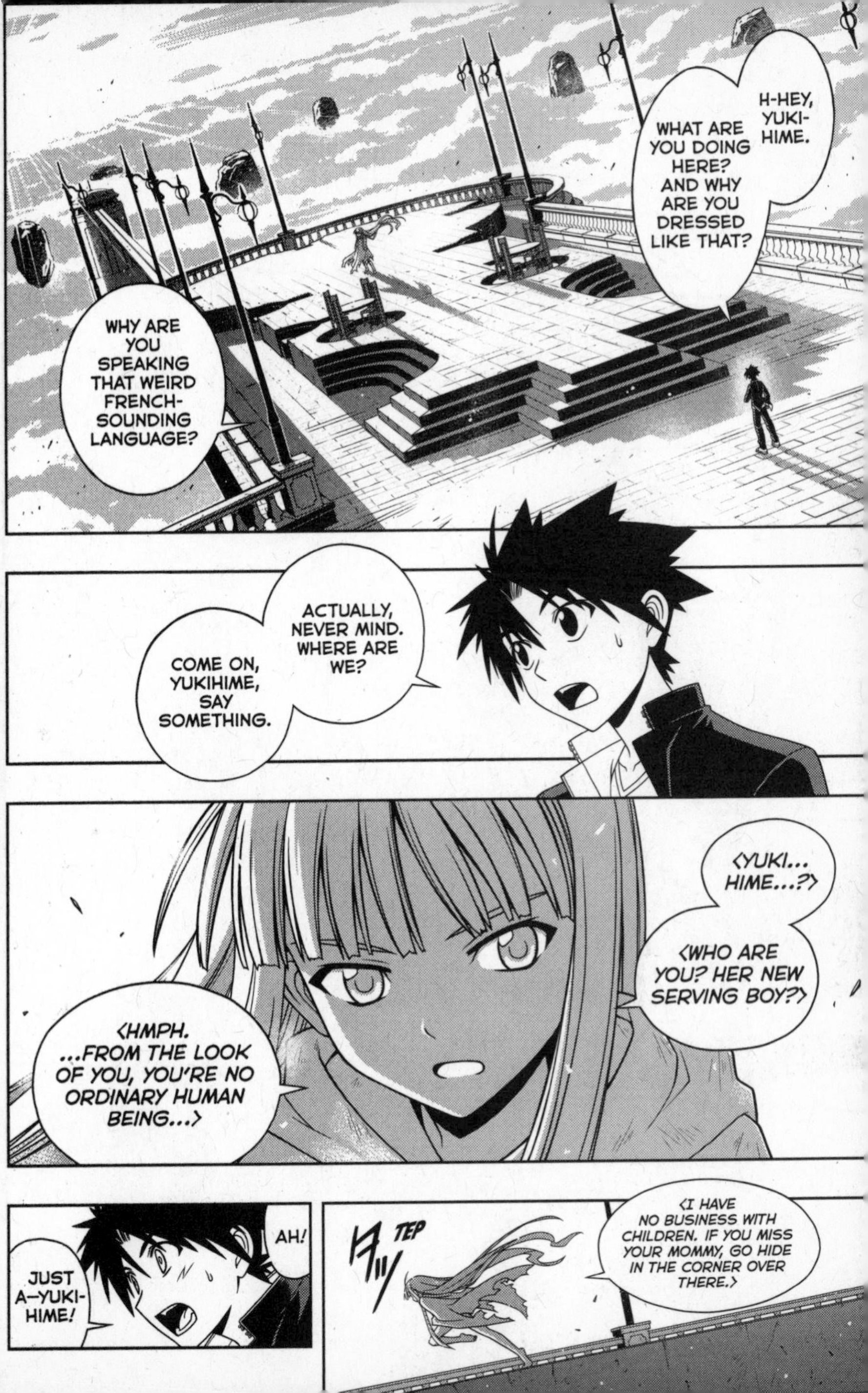
H-HEY, YUKI-HIME.
WHAT ARE YOU DOING HERE? AND WHY ARE YOU DRESSED LIKE THAT?
WHY ARE YOU SPEAKING THAT WEIRD FRENCH-SOUNDING LANGUAGE?
ACTUALLY, NEVER MIND. WHERE ARE WE?
COME ON, YUKIHIME, SAY SOMETHING.
<YUKI... HIME...?>
<WHO ARE YOU? HER NEW SERVING BOY?>
<HMPH. ...FROM THE LOOK OF YOU, YOU'RE NO ORDINARY HUMAN BEING...>
TEP
<I HAVE NO BUSINESS WITH CHILDREN. IF YOU MISS YOUR MOMMY, GO HIDE IN THE CORNER OVER THERE.>
AH!
JUST A—YUKI-HIME!

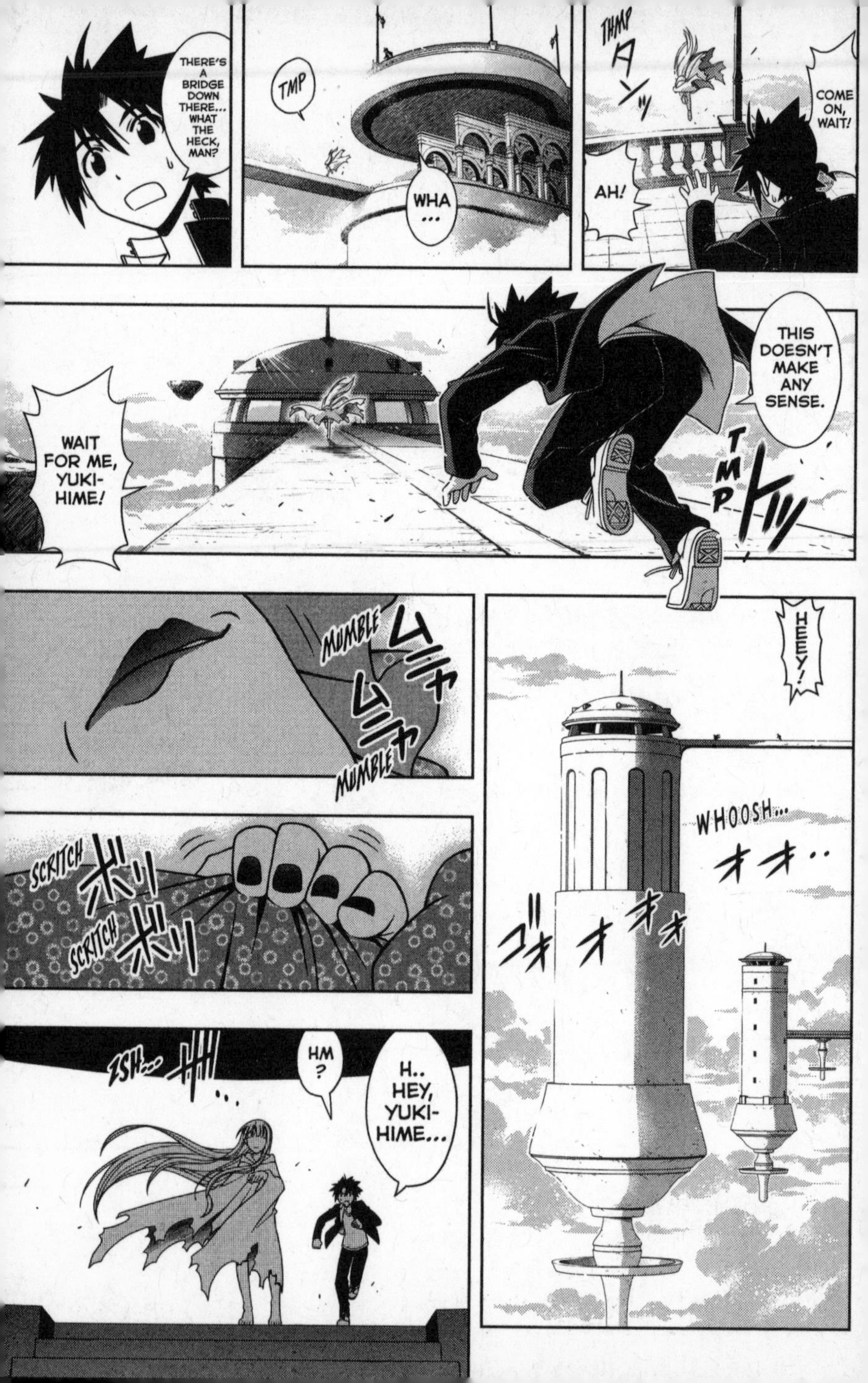

COME ON, WAIT!
THMP タンッ
AH!
TMP
WHA...
THERE'S A BRIDGE DOWN THERE... WHAT THE HECK, MAN?
THIS DOESN'T MAKE ANY SENSE.
TMP トッ
WAIT FOR ME, YUKI-HIME!
HEEY!
WHOOSH... オオ..
ゴォオオオ
MUMBLE ムニャ
ムニャ MUMBLE
SCRITCH ボリ
SCRITCH ボリ
H.. HEY, YUKI-HIME...
HM?
ZSH...
...

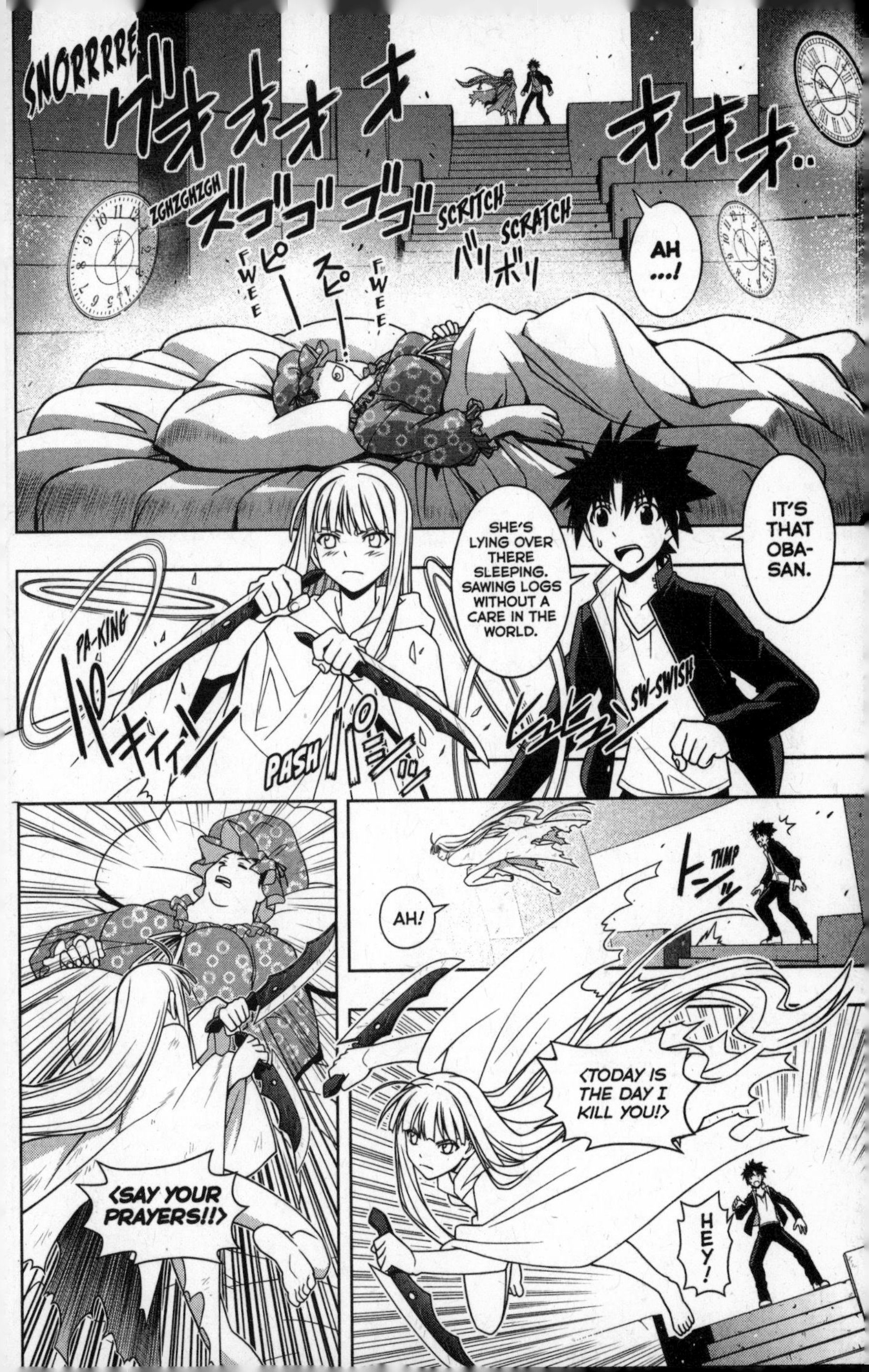
SNORRRRE
グオオオオオオオオ..
ZGHZGHZGH
ズゴゴゴゴ
SCRITCH SCRATCH
バリボリ
FWEE
ピー
FWEE
スピー
AH ...!
IT'S THAT OBA-SAN.
SHE'S LYING OVER THERE SLEEPING. SAWING LOGS WITHOUT A CARE IN THE WORLD.
SW-SWISH
PA-KING
PASH
THMP
AH!
HEY!
<TODAY IS THE DAY I KILL YOU!>
<SAY YOUR PRAYERS!!>

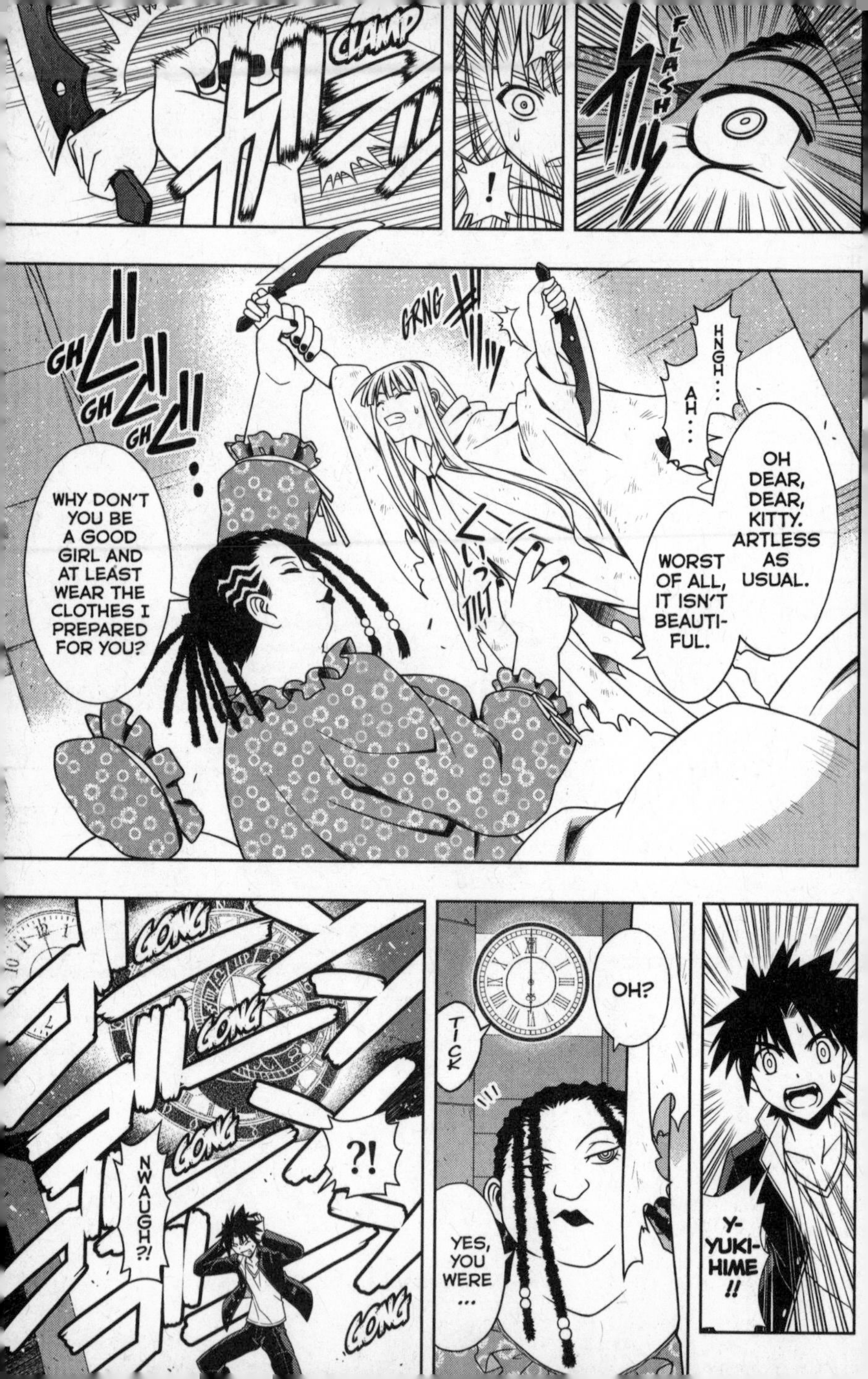
FLASH
!
CLAMP
HNGH... AH...
GRNG
OH DEAR, DEAR, KITTY. ARTLESS AS USUAL.
WORST OF ALL, IT ISN'T BEAUTI-FUL.
GH GH GH
WHY DON'T YOU BE A GOOD GIRL AND AT LEAST WEAR THE CLOTHES I PREPARED FOR YOU?
TILT
Y-YUKI-HIME!!
OH?
TICK
!!!
YES, YOU WERE...
GONG
GONG
GONG
GONG
?!
NWAUGH?!

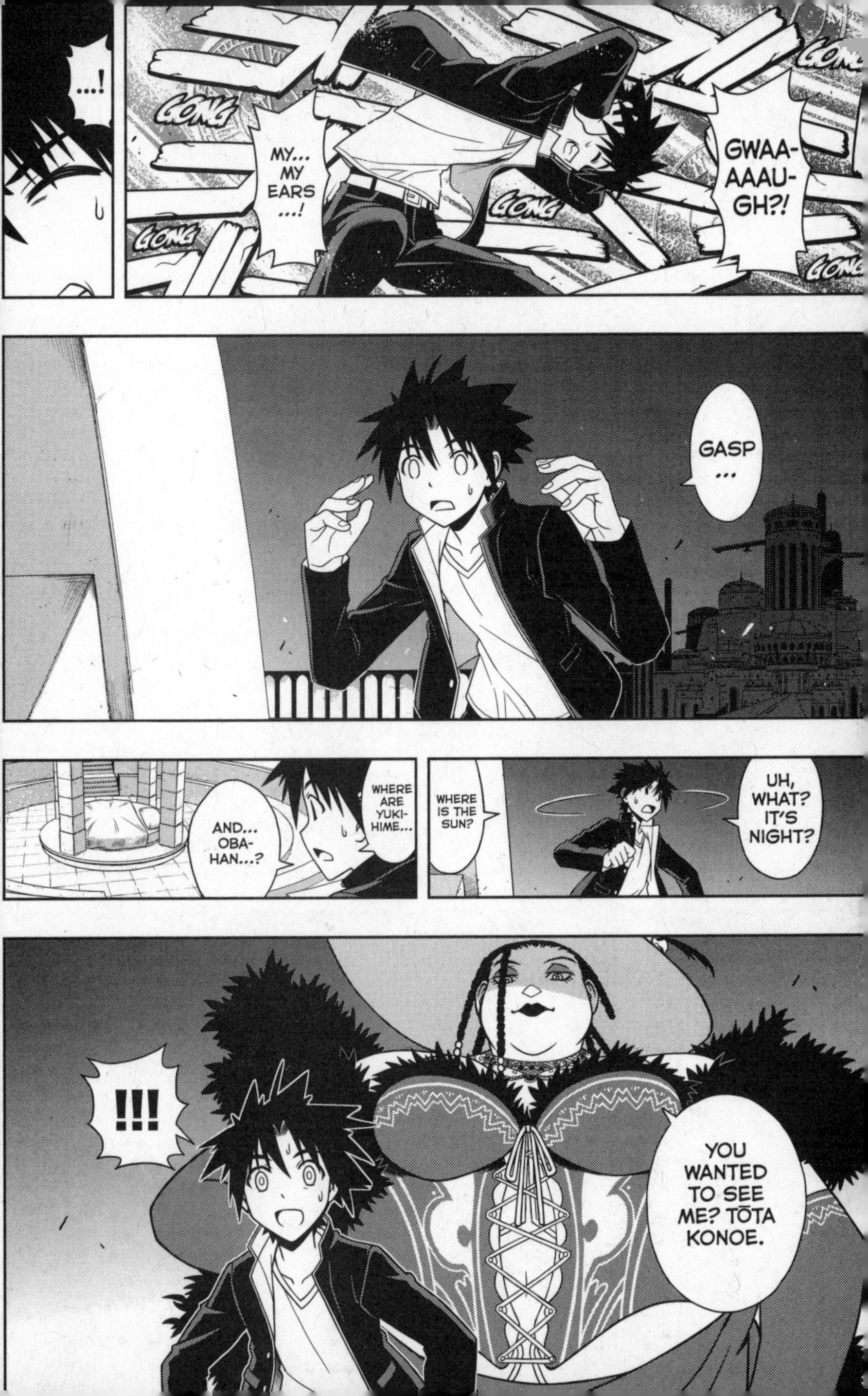
GONG
GWAA-AAAU-GH?!
GONG
MY... MY EARS ...!
GONG
GONG
GONG
...!
GASP ...
UH, WHAT? IT'S NIGHT?
WHERE IS THE SUN?
WHERE ARE YUKI-HIME...
AND... OBA-HAN...?
YOU WANTED TO SEE ME? TŌTA KONOE.
!!!

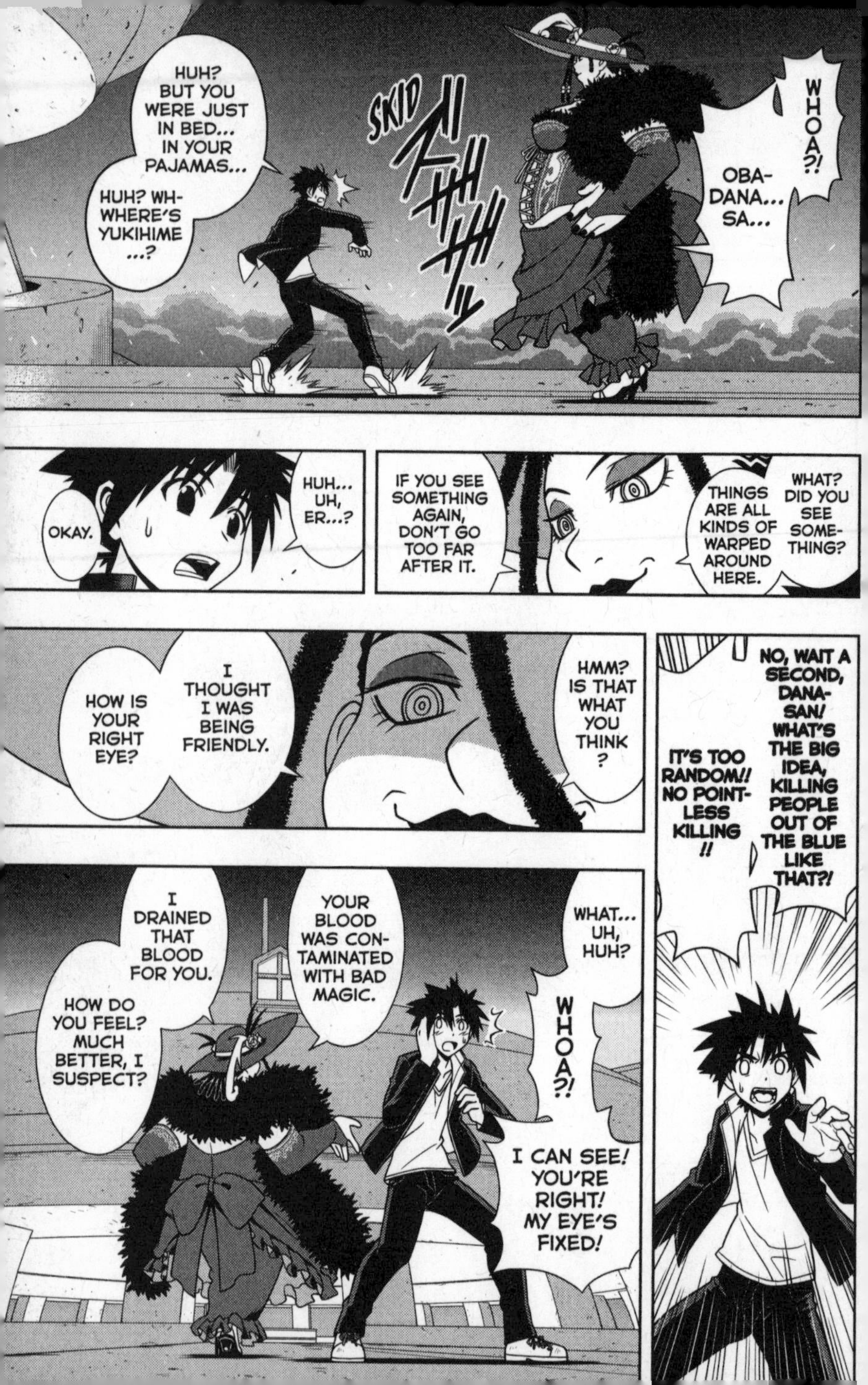
WHOA?!
OBA-DANA... SA...
SKID
HUH? BUT YOU WERE JUST IN BED... IN YOUR PAJAMAS...
HUH? WH-WHERE'S YUKIHIME ...?
WHAT? DID YOU SEE SOME-THING?
THINGS ARE ALL KINDS OF WARPED AROUND HERE.
IF YOU SEE SOMETHING AGAIN, DON'T GO TOO FAR AFTER IT.
HUH... UH, ER...?
OKAY.
NO, WAIT A SECOND, DANA-SAN! WHAT'S THE BIG IDEA, KILLING PEOPLE OUT OF THE BLUE LIKE THAT?!
IT'S TOO RANDOM!! NO POINT-LESS KILLING !!
HMM? IS THAT WHAT YOU THINK ?
I THOUGHT I WAS BEING FRIENDLY.
HOW IS YOUR RIGHT EYE?
WHAT... UH, HUH?
WHOA?!
YOUR BLOOD WAS CON-TAMINATED WITH BAD MAGIC.
I DRAINED THAT BLOOD FOR YOU.
HOW DO YOU FEEL? MUCH BETTER, I SUSPECT?
I CAN SEE! YOU'RE RIGHT! MY EYE'S FIXED!

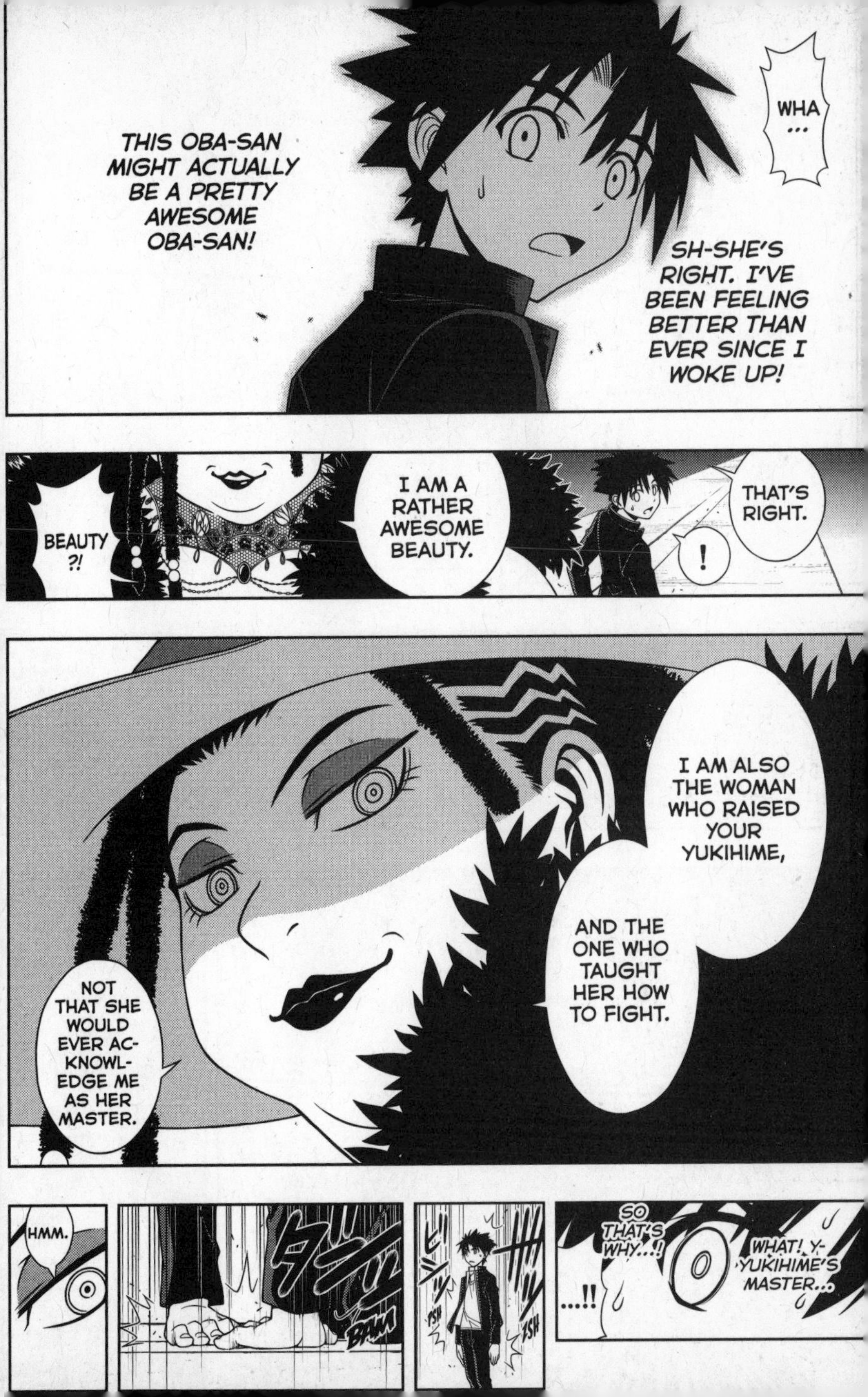
WHA ...
SH-SHE'S RIGHT. I'VE BEEN FEELING BETTER THAN EVER SINCE I WOKE UP!
THIS OBA-SAN MIGHT ACTUALLY BE A PRETTY AWESOME OBA-SAN!
THAT'S RIGHT.
!
I AM A RATHER AWESOME BEAUTY.
BEAUTY ?!
I AM ALSO THE WOMAN WHO RAISED YOUR YUKIHIME,
AND THE ONE WHO TAUGHT HER HOW TO FIGHT.
NOT THAT SHE WOULD EVER AC-KNOWL-EDGE ME AS HER MASTER.
WHAT! Y-YUKIHIME'S MASTER...
SO THAT'S WHY...!
...!!
PSH
BAM
HMM.

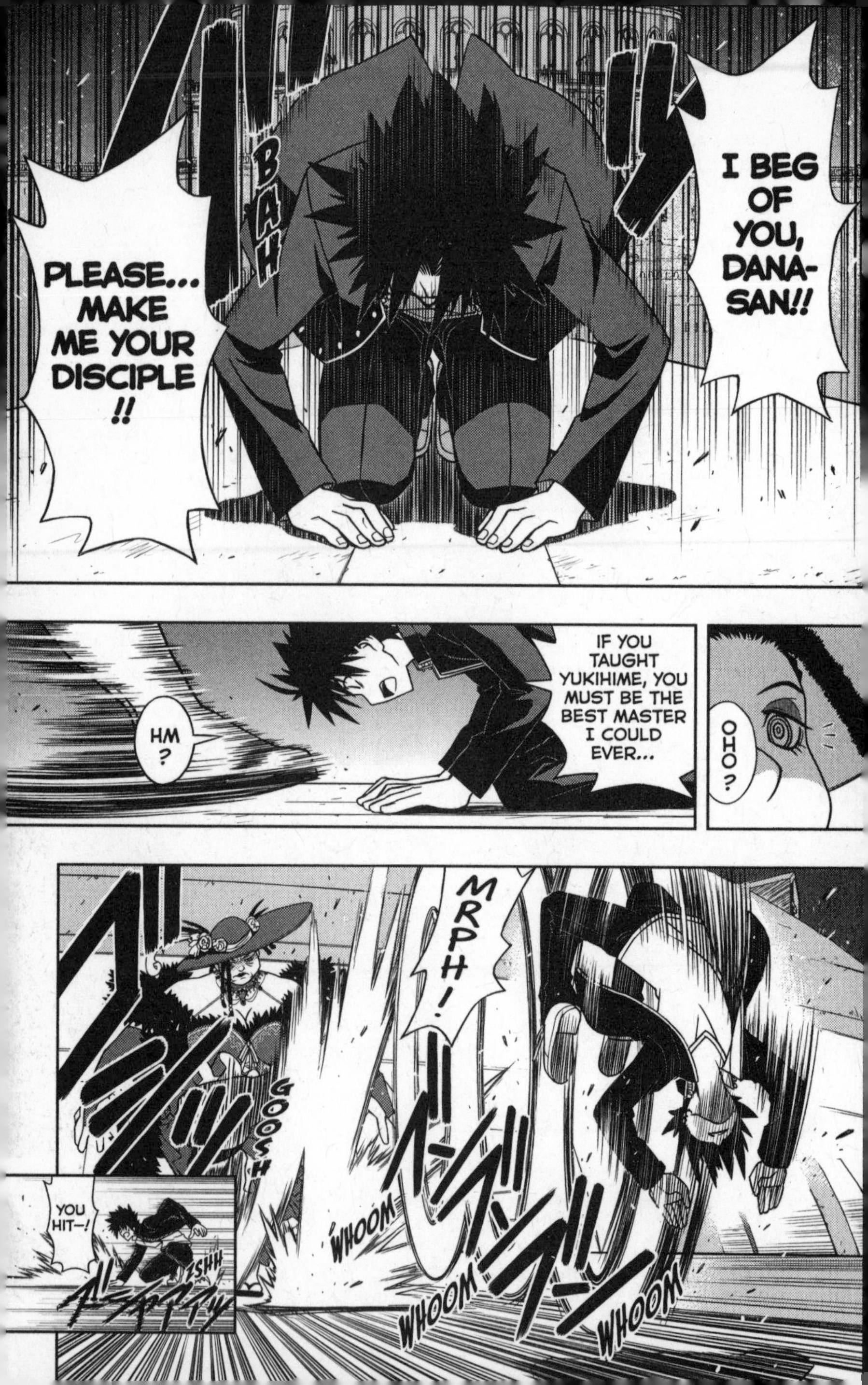
I BEG OF YOU, DANA-SAN!!
BAH
PLEASE... MAKE ME YOUR DISCIPLE!!
OHO?
IF YOU TAUGHT YUKIHIME, YOU MUST BE THE BEST MASTER I COULD EVER...
HM?
MRPH!
GOOSH
WHOOM
WHOOM
WHOOM
YOU HIT—!
ZSHH

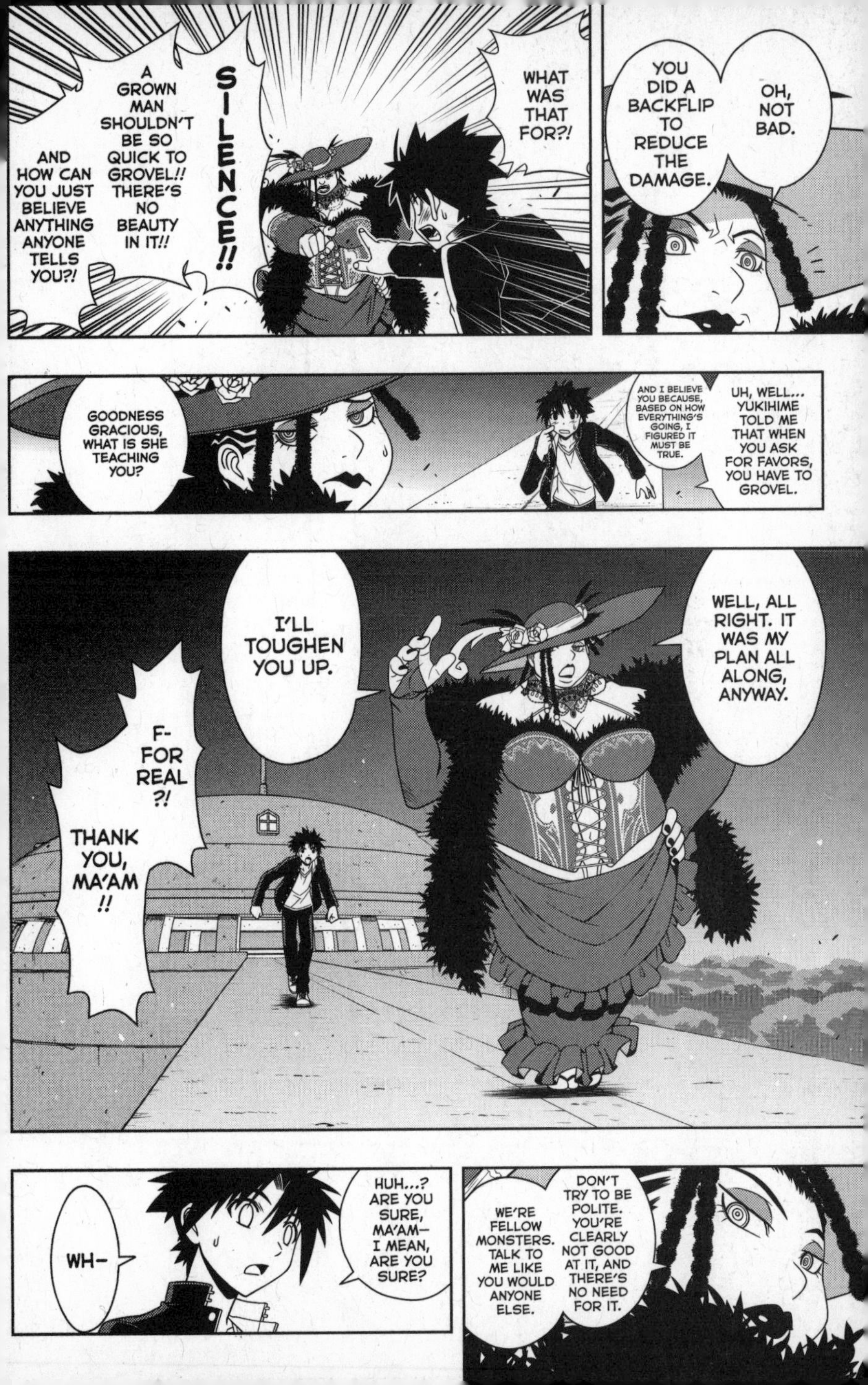
OH, NOT BAD.
YOU DID A BACKFLIP TO REDUCE THE DAMAGE.
WHAT WAS THAT FOR?!
SILENCE!!
A GROWN MAN SHOULDN'T BE SO QUICK TO GROVEL!! THERE'S NO BEAUTY IN IT!!
AND HOW CAN YOU JUST BELIEVE ANYTHING ANYONE TELLS YOU?!
UH, WELL... YUKIHIME TOLD ME THAT WHEN YOU ASK FOR FAVORS, YOU HAVE TO GROVEL.
AND I BELIEVE YOU BECAUSE, BASED ON HOW EVERYTHING'S GOING, I FIGURED IT MUST BE TRUE.
GOODNESS GRACIOUS, WHAT IS SHE TEACHING YOU?
WELL, ALL RIGHT. IT WAS MY PLAN ALL ALONG, ANYWAY.
I'LL TOUGHEN YOU UP.
F-FOR REAL?!
THANK YOU, MA'AM!!
DON'T TRY TO BE POLITE. YOU'RE CLEARLY NOT GOOD AT IT, AND THERE'S NO NEED FOR IT.
WE'RE FELLOW MONSTERS. TALK TO ME LIKE YOU WOULD ANYONE ELSE.
HUH...? ARE YOU SURE, MA'AM— I MEAN, ARE YOU SURE?
WH-

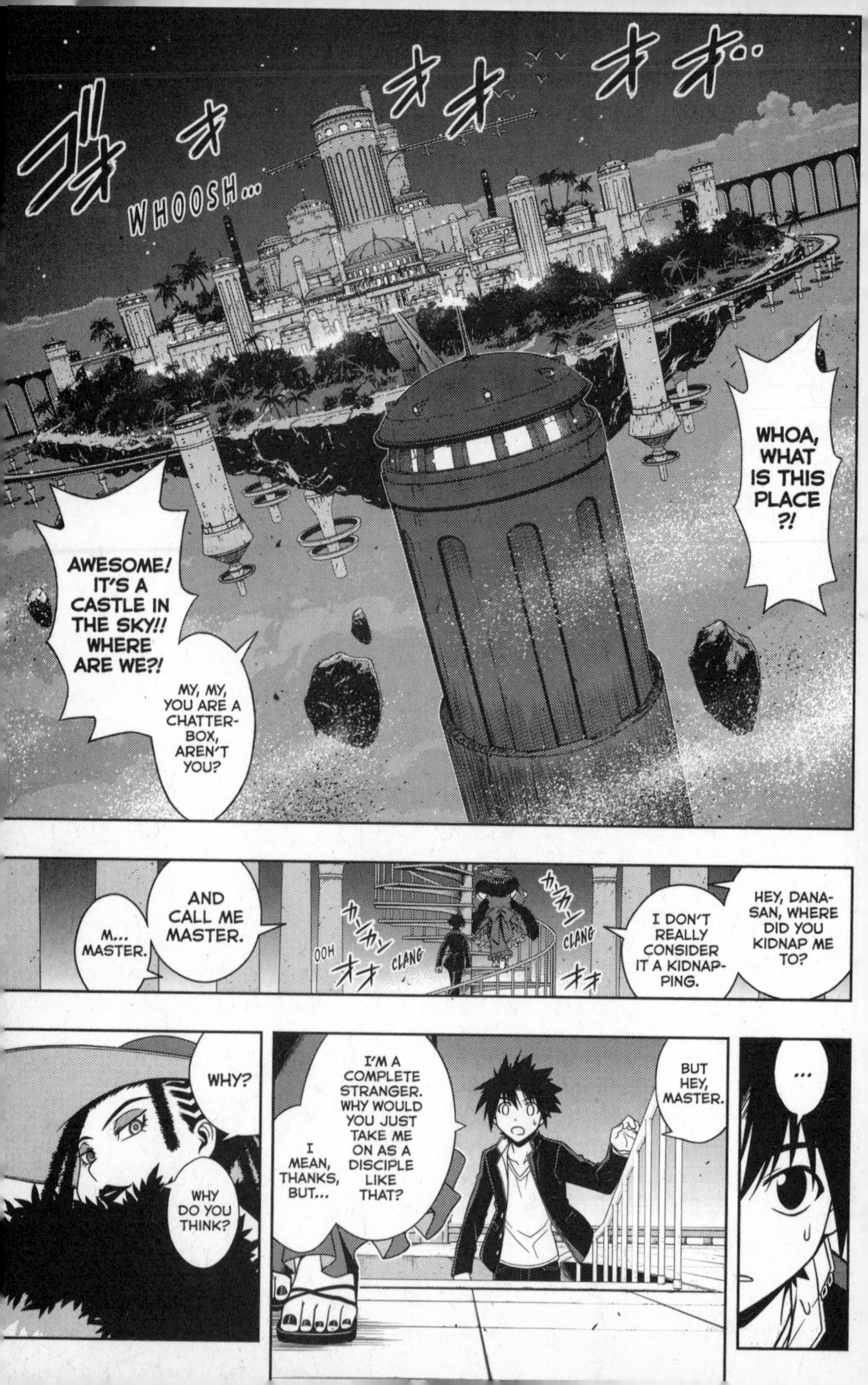
WHOOSH...
WHOA, WHAT IS THIS PLACE?!
AWESOME! IT'S A CASTLE IN THE SKY!! WHERE ARE WE?!
MY, MY, YOU ARE A CHATTER-BOX, AREN'T YOU?
HEY, DANA-SAN, WHERE DID YOU KIDNAP ME TO?
I DON'T REALLY CONSIDER IT A KIDNAP-PING.
CLANG
CLANG
OOH
AND CALL ME MASTER.
M... MASTER.
...
BUT HEY, MASTER.
I'M A COMPLETE STRANGER. WHY WOULD YOU JUST TAKE ME ON AS A DISCIPLE LIKE THAT?
I MEAN, THANKS, BUT...
WHY?
WHY DO YOU THINK?

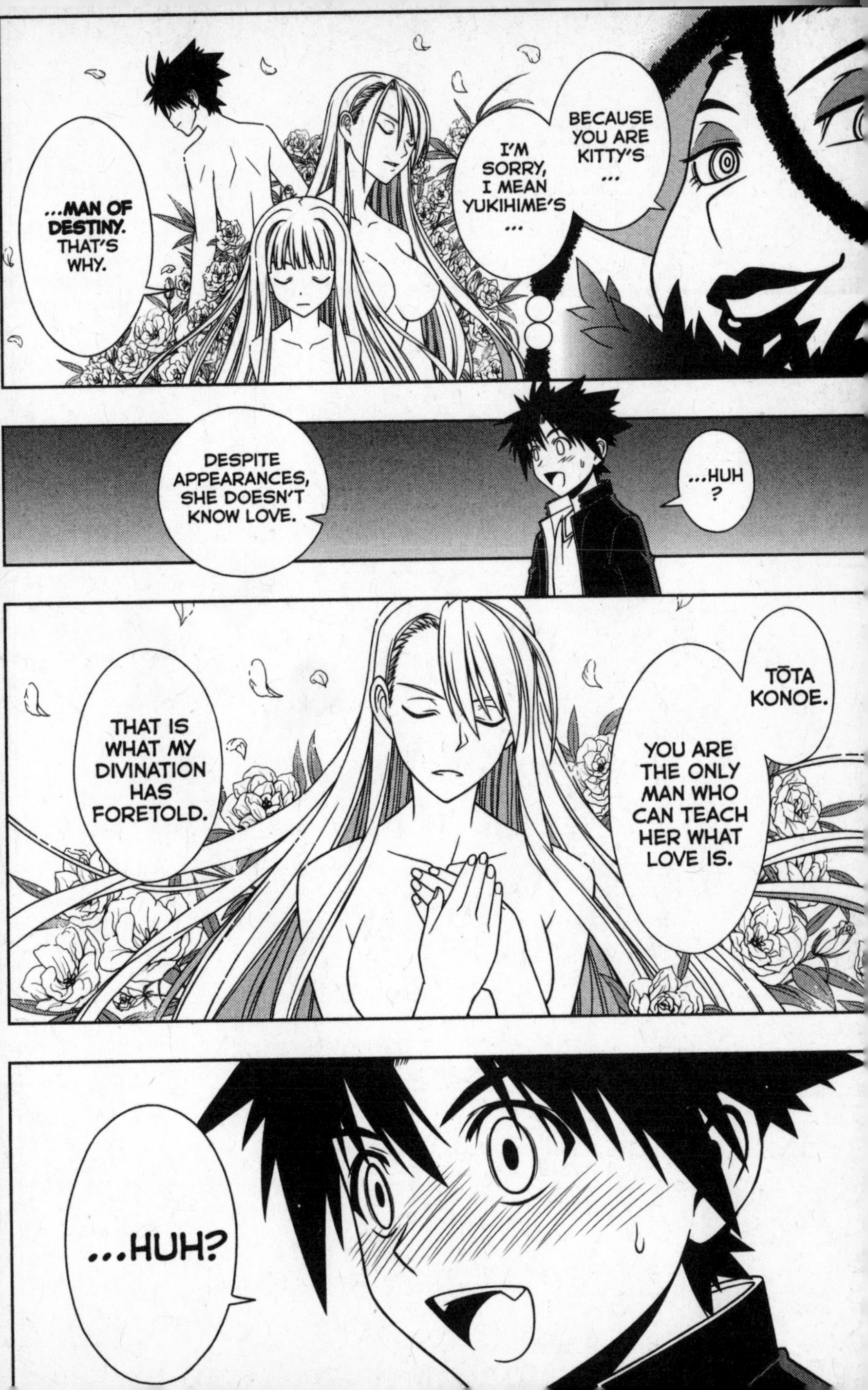
BECAUSE YOU ARE KITTY'S ...
I'M SORRY, I MEAN YUKIHIME'S ...
...MAN OF DESTINY. THAT'S WHY.
...HUH ?
DESPITE APPEARANCES, SHE DOESN'T KNOW LOVE.
TŌTA KONOE.
YOU ARE THE ONLY MAN WHO CAN TEACH HER WHAT LOVE IS.
THAT IS WHAT MY DIVINATION HAS FORETOLD.
...HUH?

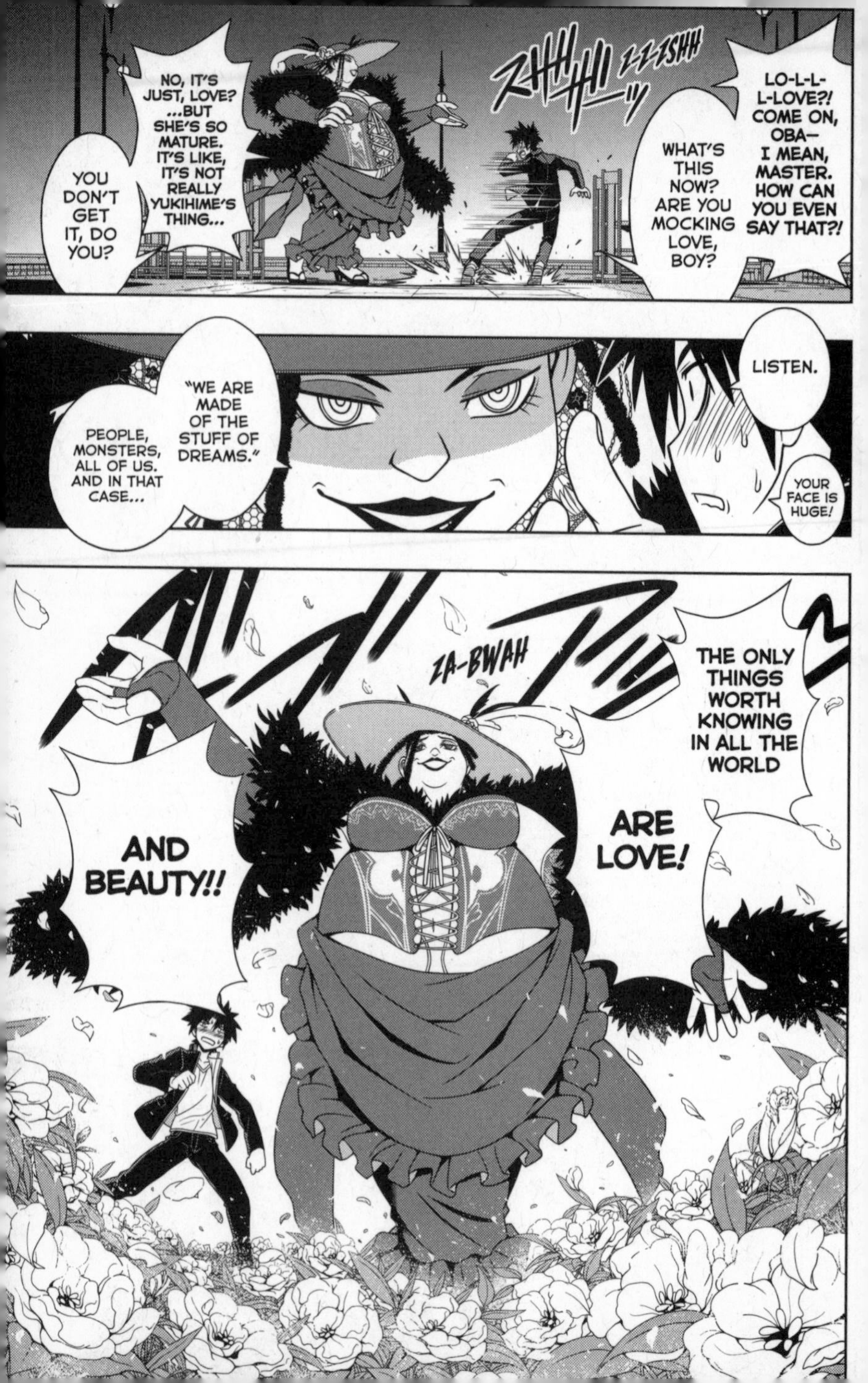

LO-L-L-L-LOVE?! COME ON, OBA— I MEAN, MASTER. HOW CAN YOU EVEN SAY THAT?!
Z-Z-ZSHH
WHAT'S THIS NOW? ARE YOU MOCKING LOVE, BOY?
NO, IT'S JUST, LOVE? ...BUT SHE'S SO MATURE. IT'S LIKE, IT'S NOT REALLY YUKIHIME'S THING...
YOU DON'T GET IT, DO YOU?
LISTEN.
YOUR FACE IS HUGE!
"WE ARE MADE OF THE STUFF OF DREAMS."
PEOPLE, MONSTERS, ALL OF US. AND IN THAT CASE...
ZA-BWAH
THE ONLY THINGS WORTH KNOWING IN ALL THE WORLD
ARE LOVE!
AND BEAUTY!!

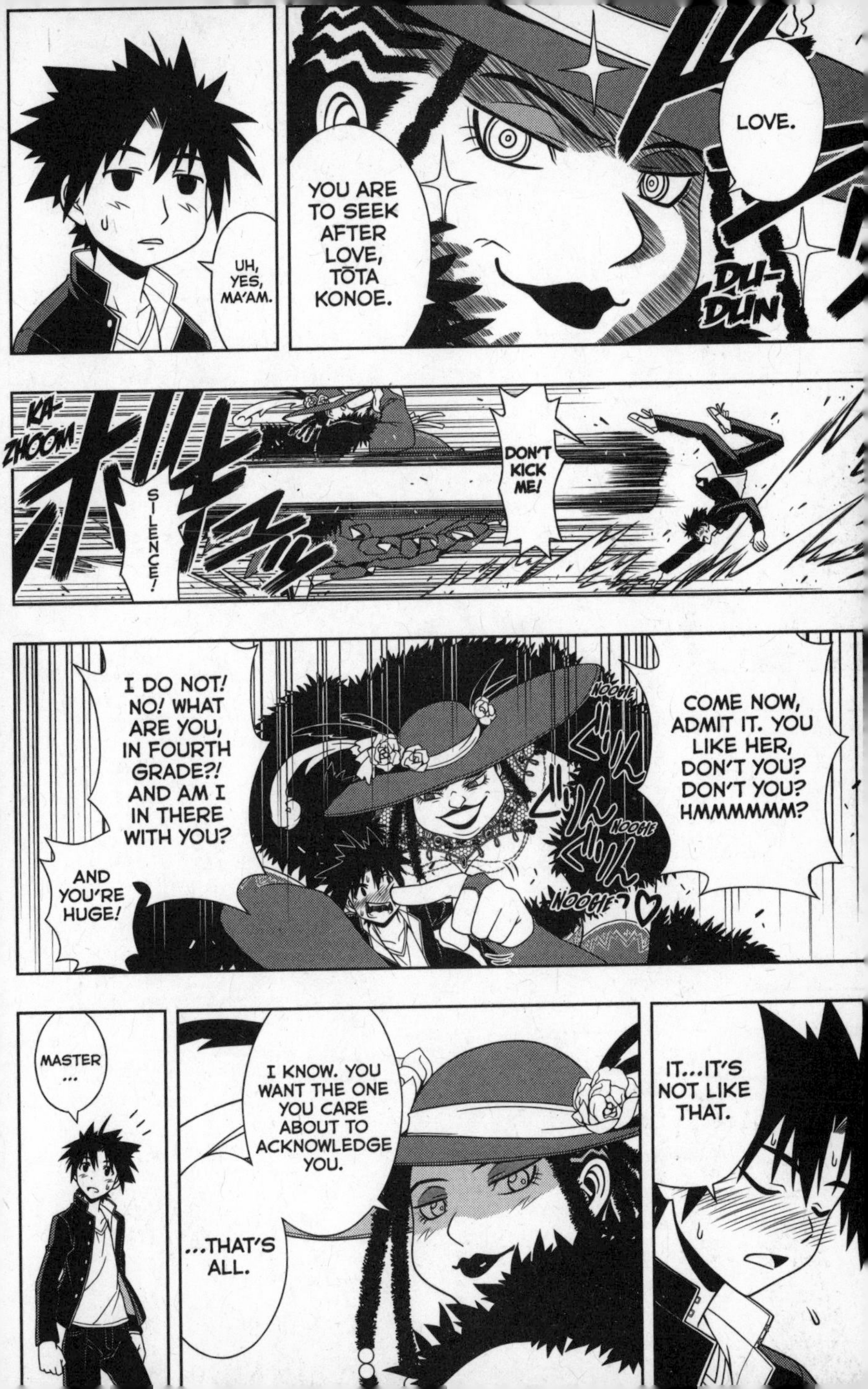
LOVE.
DU-DUN
YOU ARE TO SEEK AFTER LOVE, TŌTA KONOE.
UH, YES, MA'AM.
DON'T KICK ME!
SILENCE!
KA-ZHOOM
COME NOW, ADMIT IT. YOU LIKE HER, DON'T YOU? DON'T YOU? HMMMMMM?
NOOGIE
NOOGIE
NOOGIE
I DO NOT! NO! WHAT ARE YOU, IN FOURTH GRADE?! AND AM I IN THERE WITH YOU?
AND YOU'RE HUGE!
IT...IT'S NOT LIKE THAT.
I KNOW. YOU WANT THE ONE YOU CARE ABOUT TO ACKNOWLEDGE YOU.
...THAT'S ALL.
MASTER...

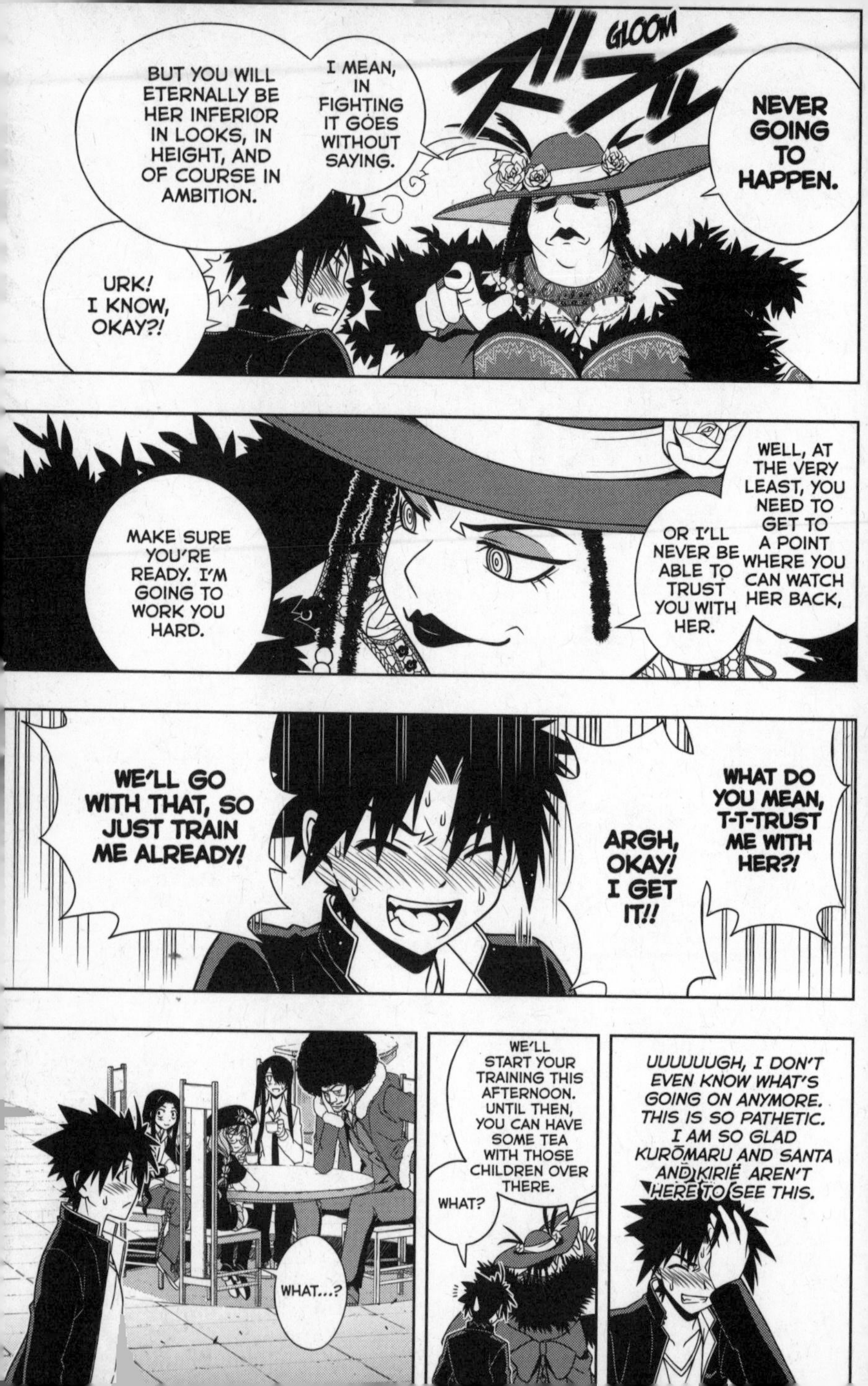
GLOOM
NEVER GOING TO HAPPEN.
I MEAN, IN FIGHTING IT GOES WITHOUT SAYING.
BUT YOU WILL ETERNALLY BE HER INFERIOR IN LOOKS, IN HEIGHT, AND OF COURSE IN AMBITION.
URK! I KNOW, OKAY?!
WELL, AT THE VERY LEAST, YOU NEED TO GET TO A POINT WHERE YOU CAN WATCH HER BACK,
OR I'LL NEVER BE ABLE TO TRUST YOU WITH HER.
MAKE SURE YOU'RE READY. I'M GOING TO WORK YOU HARD.
WHAT DO YOU MEAN, T-T-TRUST ME WITH HER?!
ARGH, OKAY! I GET IT!!
WE'LL GO WITH THAT, SO JUST TRAIN ME ALREADY!
UUUUUUGH, I DON'T EVEN KNOW WHAT'S GOING ON ANYMORE. THIS IS SO PATHETIC. I AM SO GLAD KURŌMARU AND SANTA AND KIRIË AREN'T HERE TO SEE THIS.
WE'LL START YOUR TRAINING THIS AFTERNOON. UNTIL THEN, YOU CAN HAVE SOME TEA WITH THOSE CHILDREN OVER THERE.
WHAT?
WHAT...?

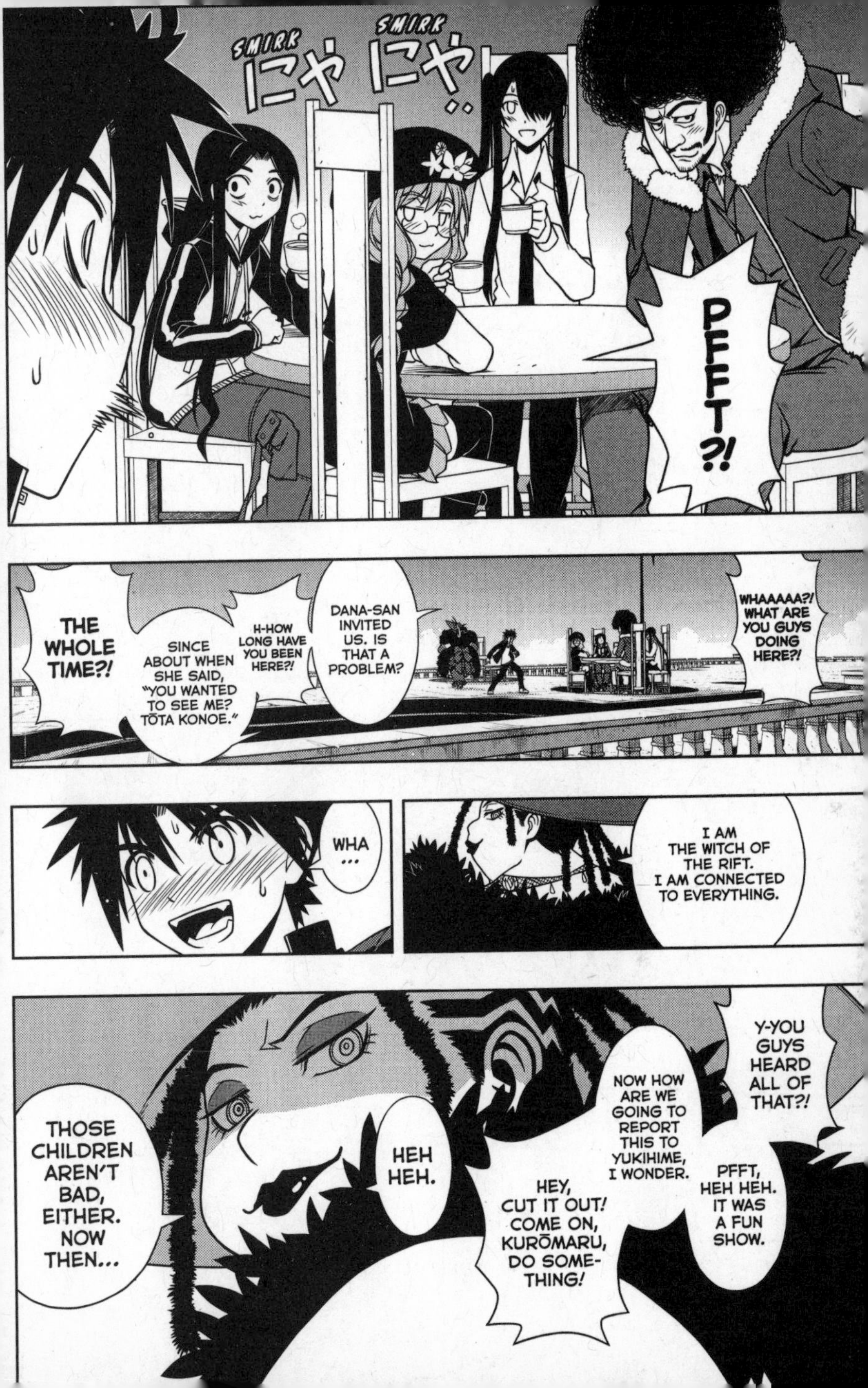
SMIRK SMIRK
にや にや
PFFT?!
WHAAAAA?! WHAT ARE YOU GUYS DOING HERE?!
DANA-SAN INVITED US. IS THAT A PROBLEM?
H-HOW LONG HAVE YOU BEEN HERE?!
SINCE ABOUT WHEN SHE SAID, "YOU WANTED TO SEE ME? TŌTA KONOE."
THE WHOLE TIME?!
I AM THE WITCH OF THE RIFT. I AM CONNECTED TO EVERYTHING.
WHA...
Y-YOU GUYS HEARD ALL OF THAT?!
PFFT, HEH HEH. IT WAS A FUN SHOW.
NOW HOW ARE WE GOING TO REPORT THIS TO YUKIHIME, I WONDER.
HEY, CUT IT OUT! COME ON, KURŌMARU, DO SOME-THING!
HEH HEH.
THOSE CHILDREN AREN'T BAD, EITHER. NOW THEN...

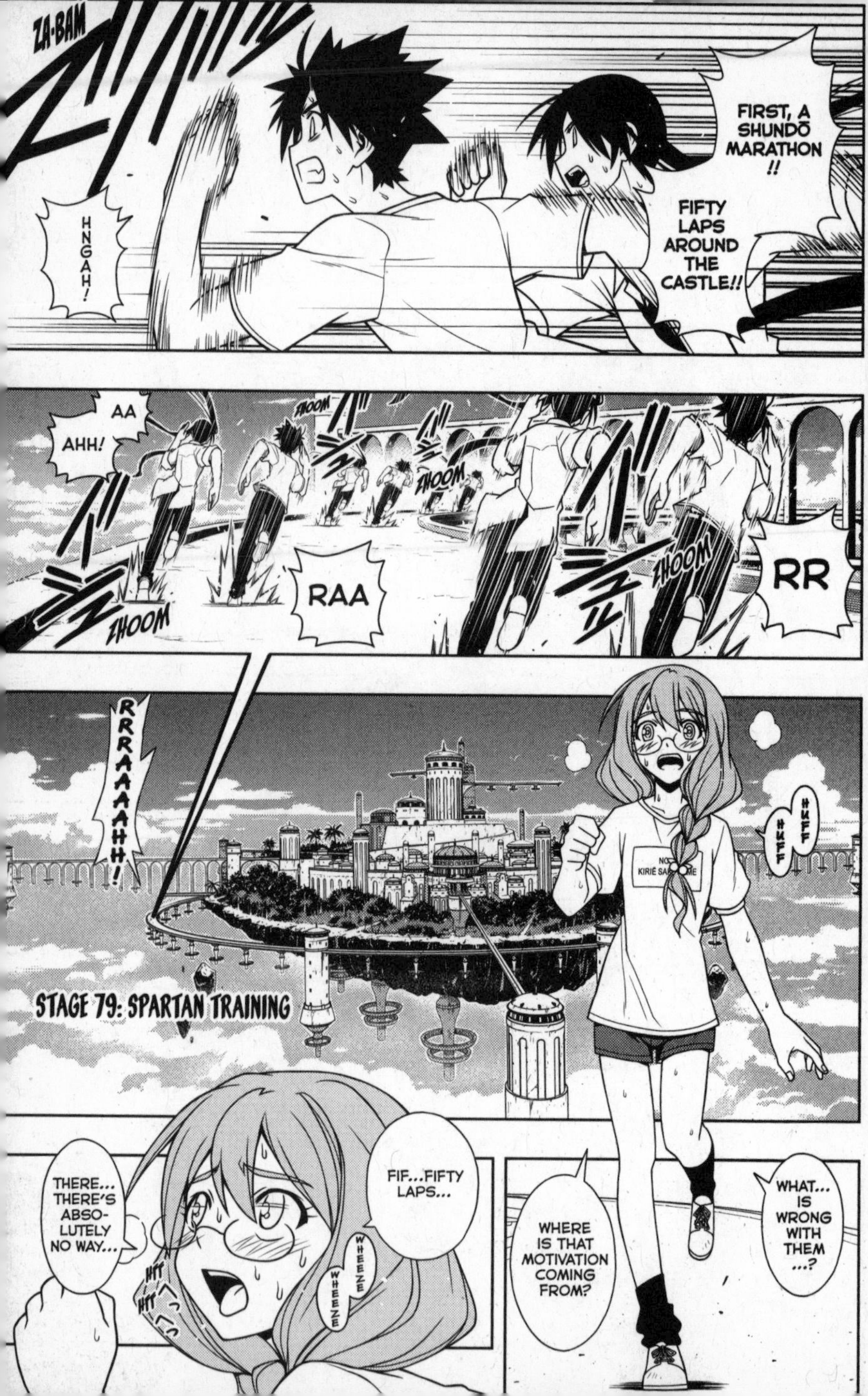
FIRST, A SHUNDŌ MARATHON !!
FIFTY LAPS AROUND THE CASTLE!!
ZA-BAM
HNGAH!
RR
ZHOOM
ZHOOM
ZHOOM
RAA
AA AHH!
ZHOOM
HUFF HUFF
RRRAAAAAHH!
STAGE 79: SPARTAN TRAINING
WHAT... IS WRONG WITH THEM ...?
WHERE IS THAT MOTIVATION COMING FROM?
FIF...FIFTY LAPS...
WHEEZE WHEEZE
THERE... THERE'S ABSO-LUTELY NO WAY...
HTT HTT

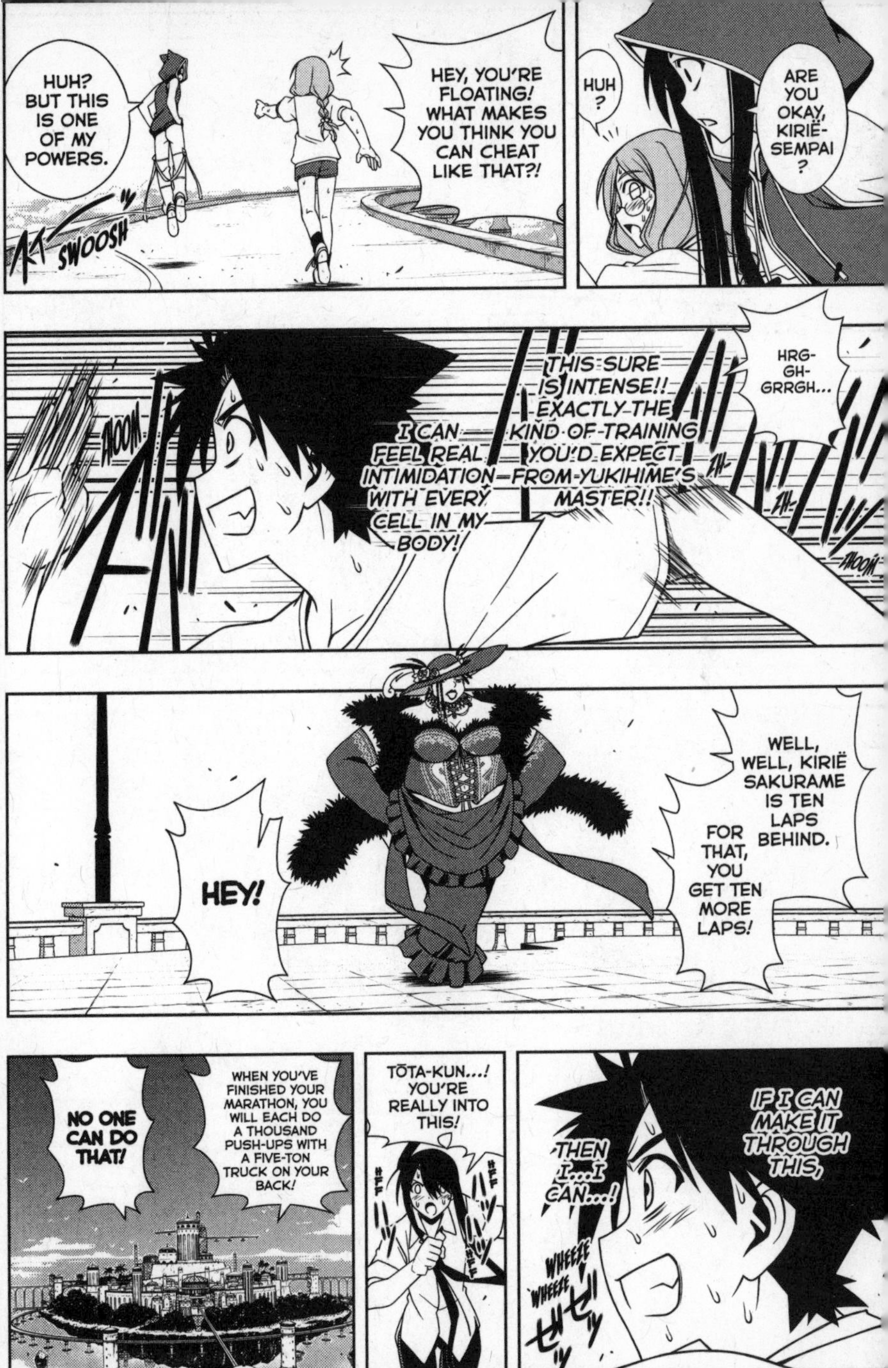
ARE YOU OKAY, KIRIË-SEMPAI?
HUH?
HEY, YOU'RE FLOATING! WHAT MAKES YOU THINK YOU CAN CHEAT LIKE THAT?!
HUH? BUT THIS IS ONE OF MY POWERS.
SWOOSH
HRG-GH-GRRGH...
THIS SURE IS INTENSE!! EXACTLY THE KIND OF TRAINING YOU'D EXPECT FROM YUKIHIME'S MASTER!!
I CAN FEEL REAL INTIMIDATION WITH EVERY CELL IN MY BODY!
FWOOM
WELL, WELL, KIRIË SAKURAME IS TEN LAPS BEHIND.
FOR THAT, YOU GET TEN MORE LAPS!
HEY!
IF I CAN MAKE IT THROUGH THIS,
THEN I...I CAN...!
WHEEZE
WHEEZE
TŌTA-KUN...! YOU'RE REALLY INTO THIS!
WHEN YOU'VE FINISHED YOUR MARATHON, YOU WILL EACH DO A THOUSAND PUSH-UPS WITH A FIVE-TON TRUCK ON YOUR BACK!
NO ONE CAN DO THAT!

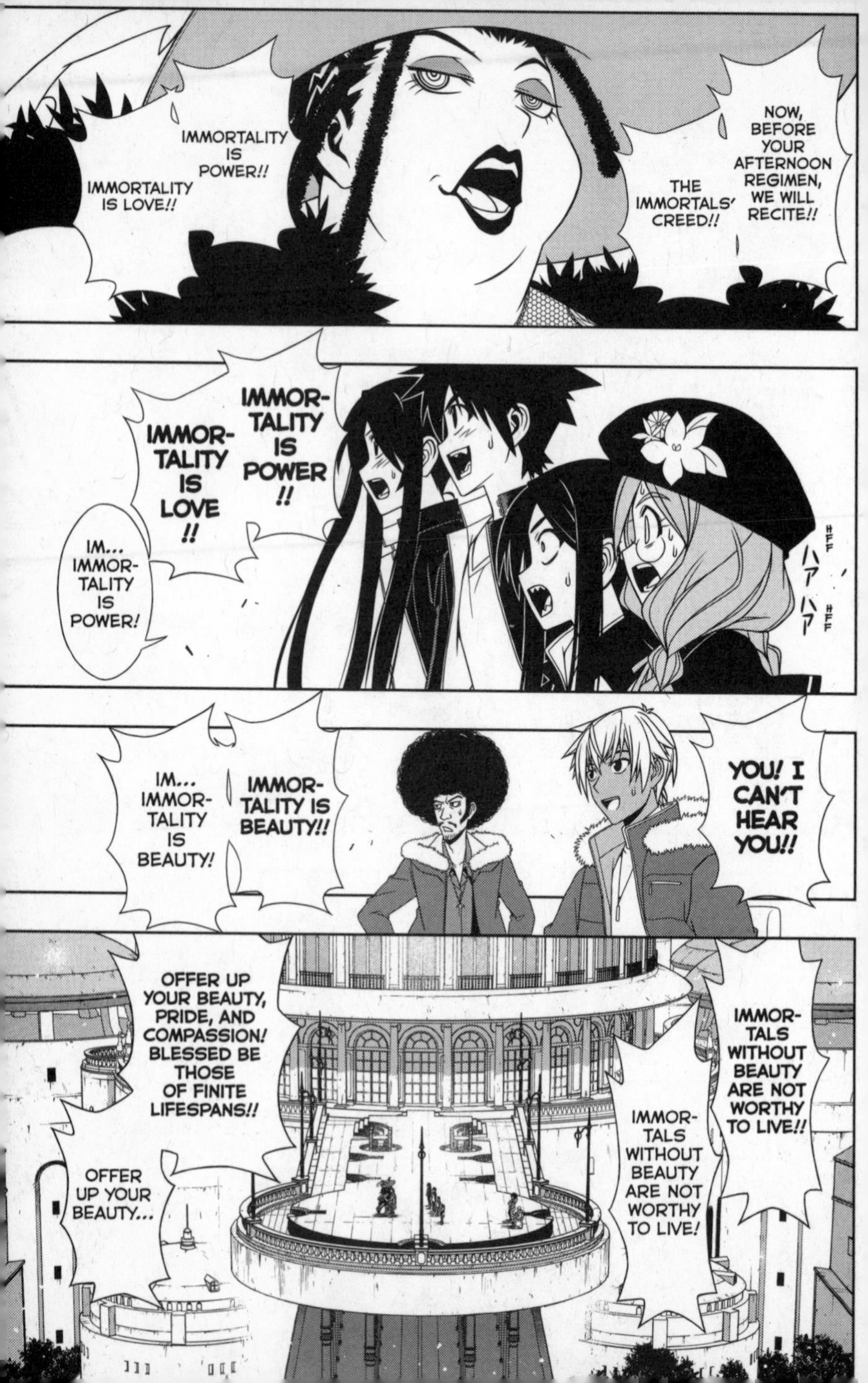
NOW, BEFORE YOUR AFTERNOON REGIMEN, WE WILL RECITE!!
THE IMMORTALS' CREED!!
IMMORTALITY IS POWER!!
IMMORTALITY IS LOVE!!
ハア ハア HFF HFF
IMMORTALITY IS POWER!!
IMMORTALITY IS LOVE!!
IM... IMMORTALITY IS POWER!
YOU! I CAN'T HEAR YOU!!
IMMORTALITY IS BEAUTY!!
IM... IMMORTALITY IS BEAUTY!
IMMORTALS WITHOUT BEAUTY ARE NOT WORTHY TO LIVE!!
IMMORTALS WITHOUT BEAUTY ARE NOT WORTHY TO LIVE!
OFFER UP YOUR BEAUTY, PRIDE, AND COMPASSION! BLESSED BE THOSE OF FINITE LIFESPANS!!
OFFER UP YOUR BEAUTY...

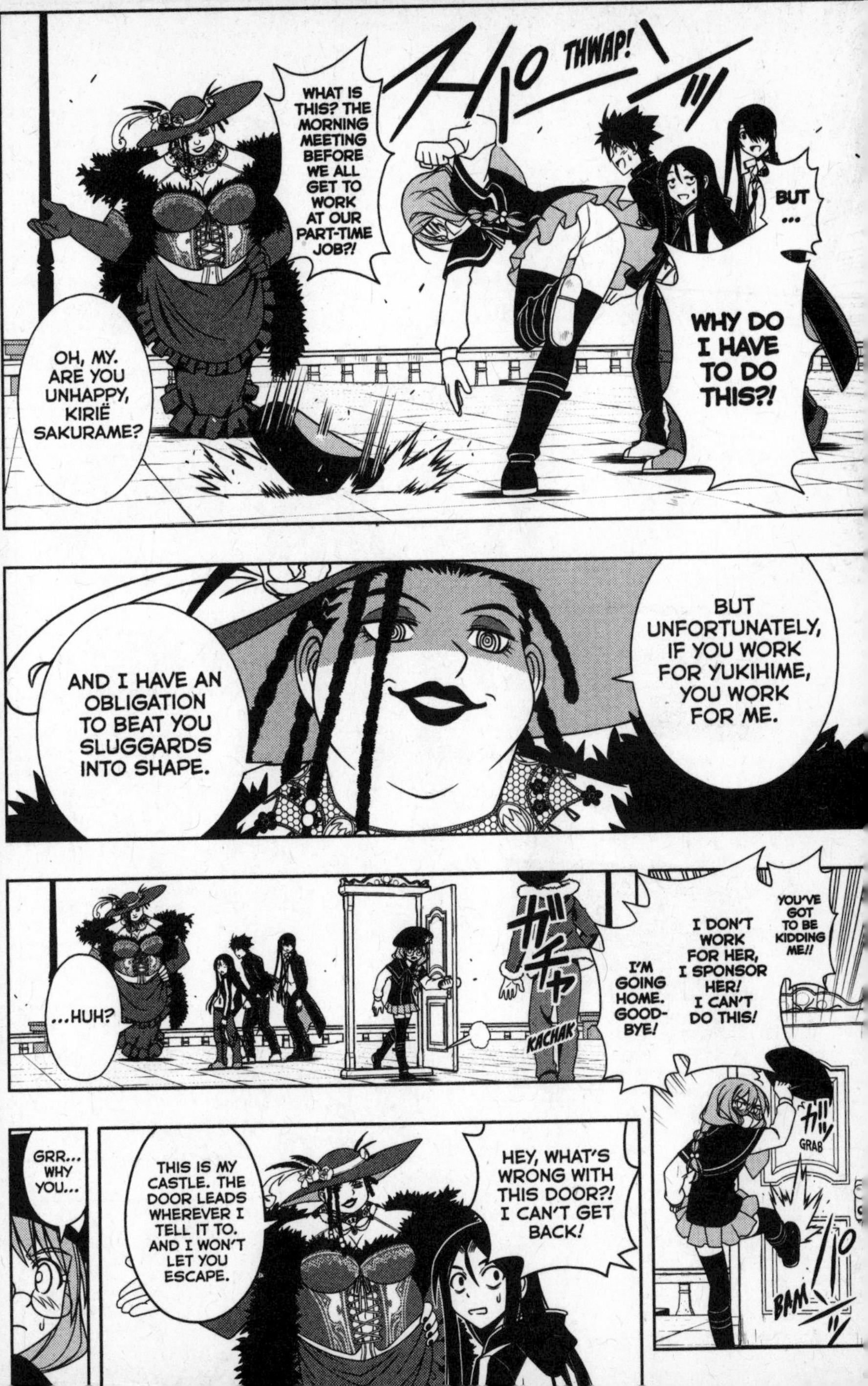
THWAP!
WHAT IS THIS? THE MORNING MEETING BEFORE WE ALL GET TO WORK AT OUR PART-TIME JOB?!
BUT ...
WHY DO I HAVE TO DO THIS?!
OH, MY. ARE YOU UNHAPPY, KIRIË SAKURAME?
BUT UNFORTUNATELY, IF YOU WORK FOR YUKIHIME, YOU WORK FOR ME.
AND I HAVE AN OBLIGATION TO BEAT YOU SLUGGARDS INTO SHAPE.
YOU'VE GOT TO BE KIDDING ME!!
I DON'T WORK FOR HER, I SPONSOR HER! I CAN'T DO THIS!
I'M GOING HOME. GOOD-BYE!
KACHAK
...HUH?
GRAB
BAM
HEY, WHAT'S WRONG WITH THIS DOOR?! I CAN'T GET BACK!
THIS IS MY CASTLE. THE DOOR LEADS WHEREVER I TELL IT TO. AND I WON'T LET YOU ESCAPE.
GRR... WHY YOU...

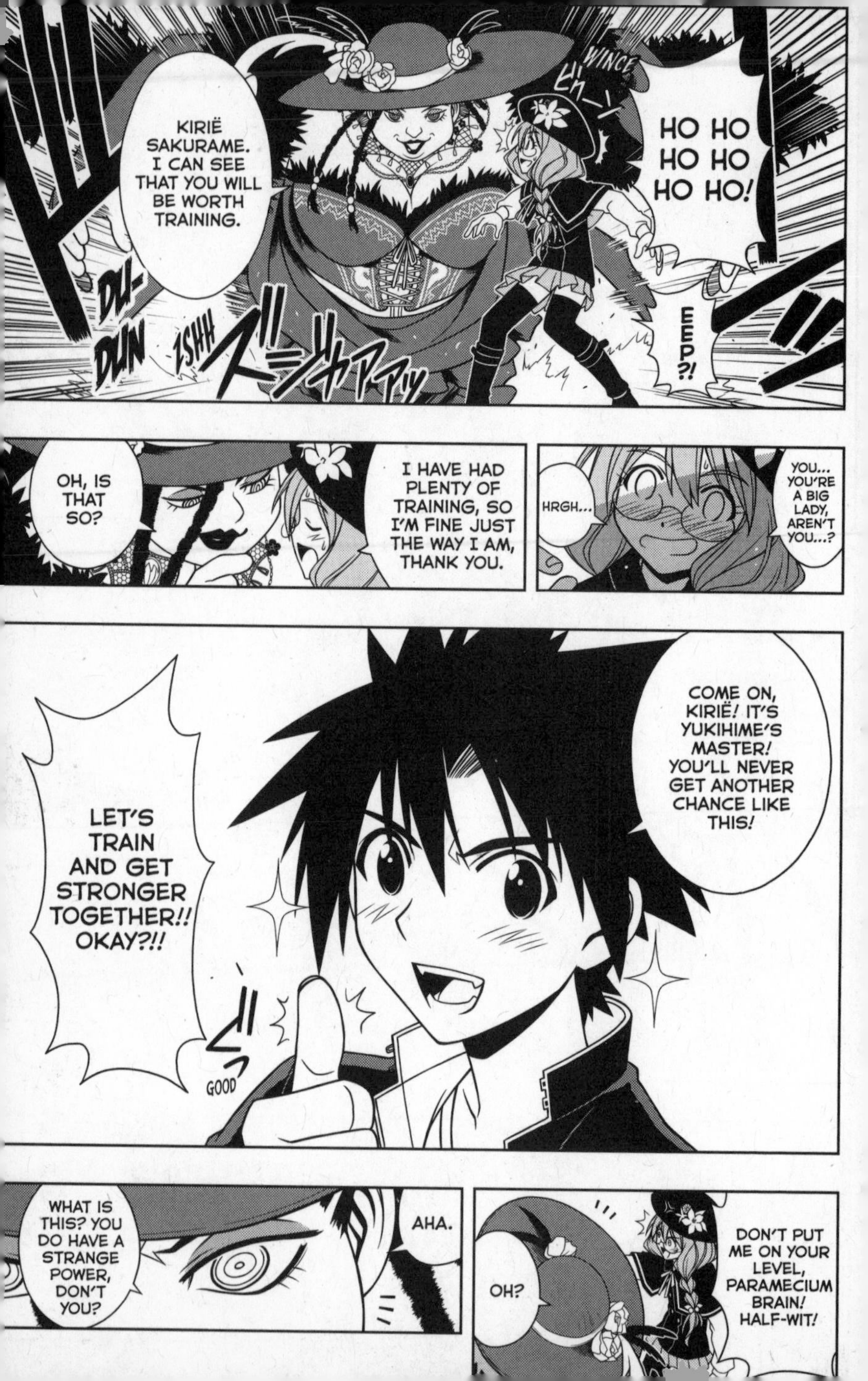
WINCE
HO HO HO HO HO HO!
KIRIË SAKURAME. I CAN SEE THAT YOU WILL BE WORTH TRAINING.
EEP?!
DU-DUN
ZSHH
YOU... YOU'RE A BIG LADY, AREN'T YOU...?
HRGH...
I HAVE HAD PLENTY OF TRAINING, SO I'M FINE JUST THE WAY I AM, THANK YOU.
OH, IS THAT SO?
COME ON, KIRIË! IT'S YUKIHIME'S MASTER! YOU'LL NEVER GET ANOTHER CHANCE LIKE THIS!
LET'S TRAIN AND GET STRONGER TOGETHER!! OKAY?!!
GOOD
DON'T PUT ME ON YOUR LEVEL, PARAMECIUM BRAIN! HALF-WIT!
OH?
AHA.
WHAT IS THIS? YOU DO HAVE A STRANGE POWER, DON'T YOU?

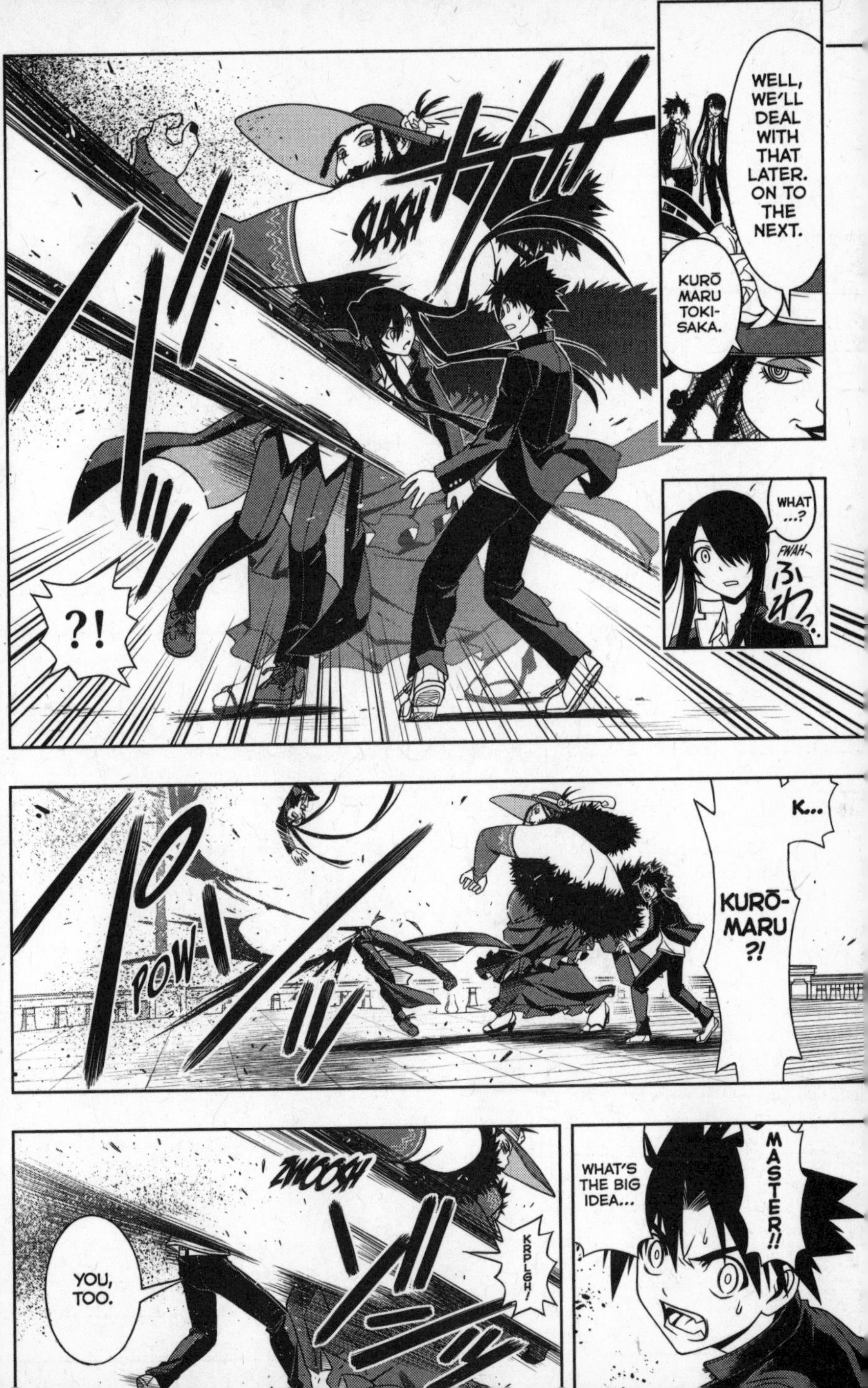
WELL, WE'LL DEAL WITH THAT LATER. ON TO THE NEXT.
KURŌ MARU TOKI-SAKA.
WHAT ...?
FWAH
ふわっ...
SLASH
?!
K...
KURŌ-MARU ?!
POW
MASTER!!
WHAT'S THE BIG IDEA...
ZWOOSH
KRPLGH!
YOU, TOO.

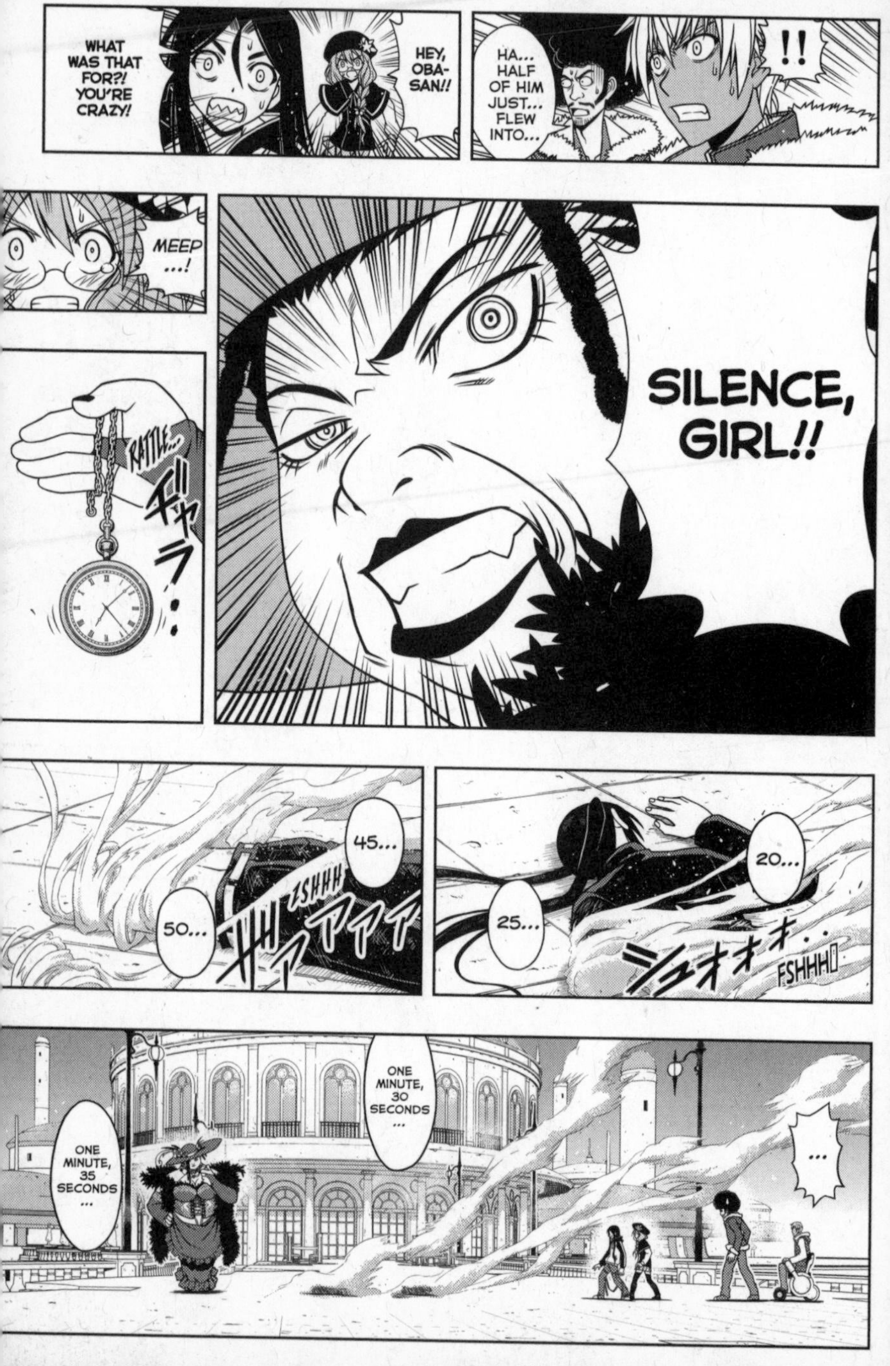
!!
HA... HALF OF HIM JUST... FLEW INTO...
HEY, OBA-SAN!!
WHAT WAS THAT FOR?! YOU'RE CRAZY!
SILENCE, GIRL!!
MEEP ...!
RATTLE...
20...
25...
FSHHH
45...
50...
FSHHH
...
ONE MINUTE, 30 SECONDS ...
ONE MINUTE, 35 SECONDS ...

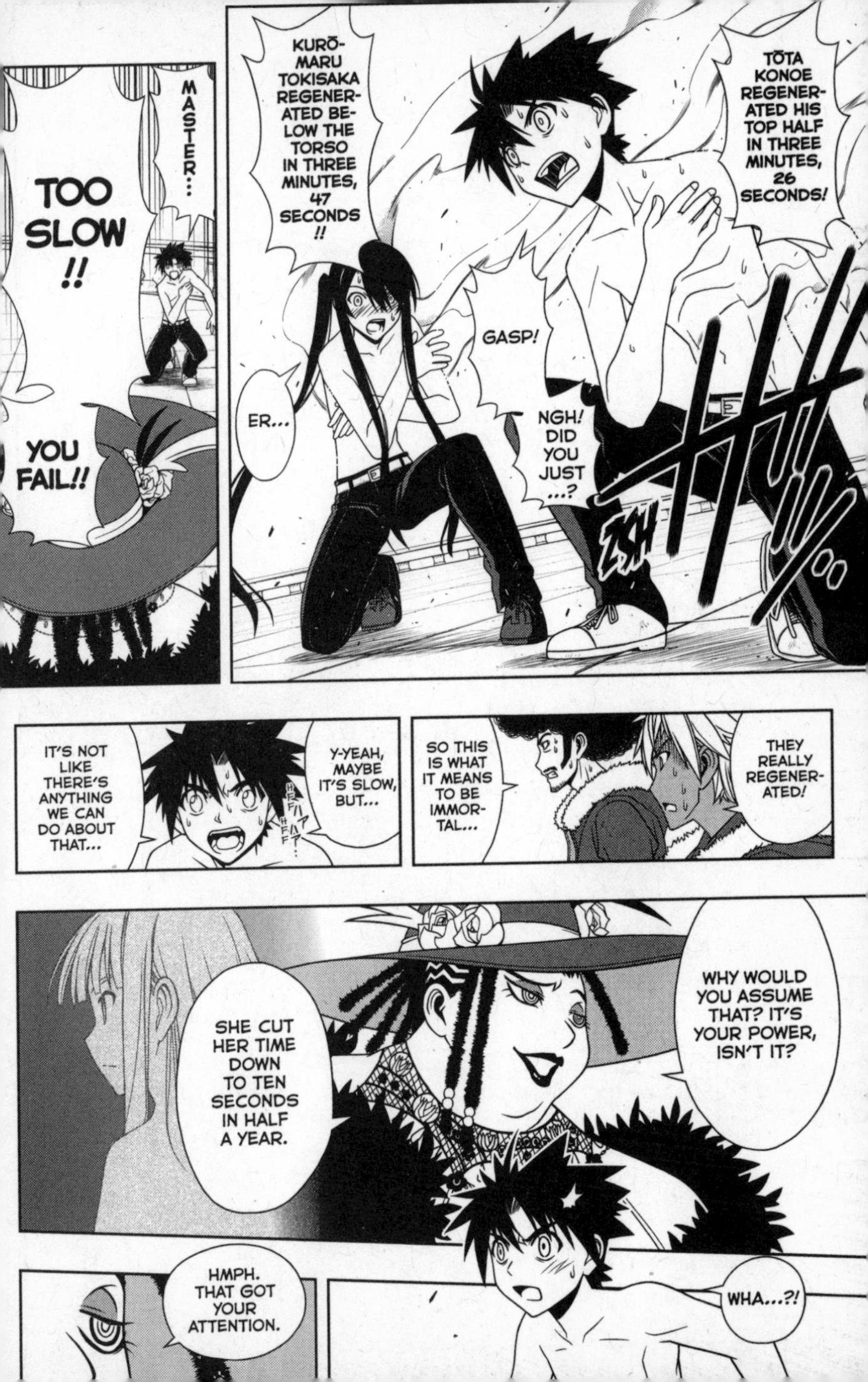
TŌTA KONOE REGENERATED HIS TOP HALF IN THREE MINUTES, 26 SECONDS!
KURŌMARU TOKISAKA REGENERATED BELOW THE TORSO IN THREE MINUTES, 47 SECONDS!!
GASP!
NGH! DID YOU JUST ...?
ER...
ZSH
MASTER...
TOO SLOW!!
YOU FAIL!!
THEY REALLY REGENERATED!
SO THIS IS WHAT IT MEANS TO BE IMMORTAL...
Y-YEAH, MAYBE IT'S SLOW, BUT...
IT'S NOT LIKE THERE'S ANYTHING WE CAN DO ABOUT THAT...
WHY WOULD YOU ASSUME THAT? IT'S YOUR POWER, ISN'T IT?
SHE CUT HER TIME DOWN TO TEN SECONDS IN HALF A YEAR.
WHA...?!
HMPH. THAT GOT YOUR ATTENTION.

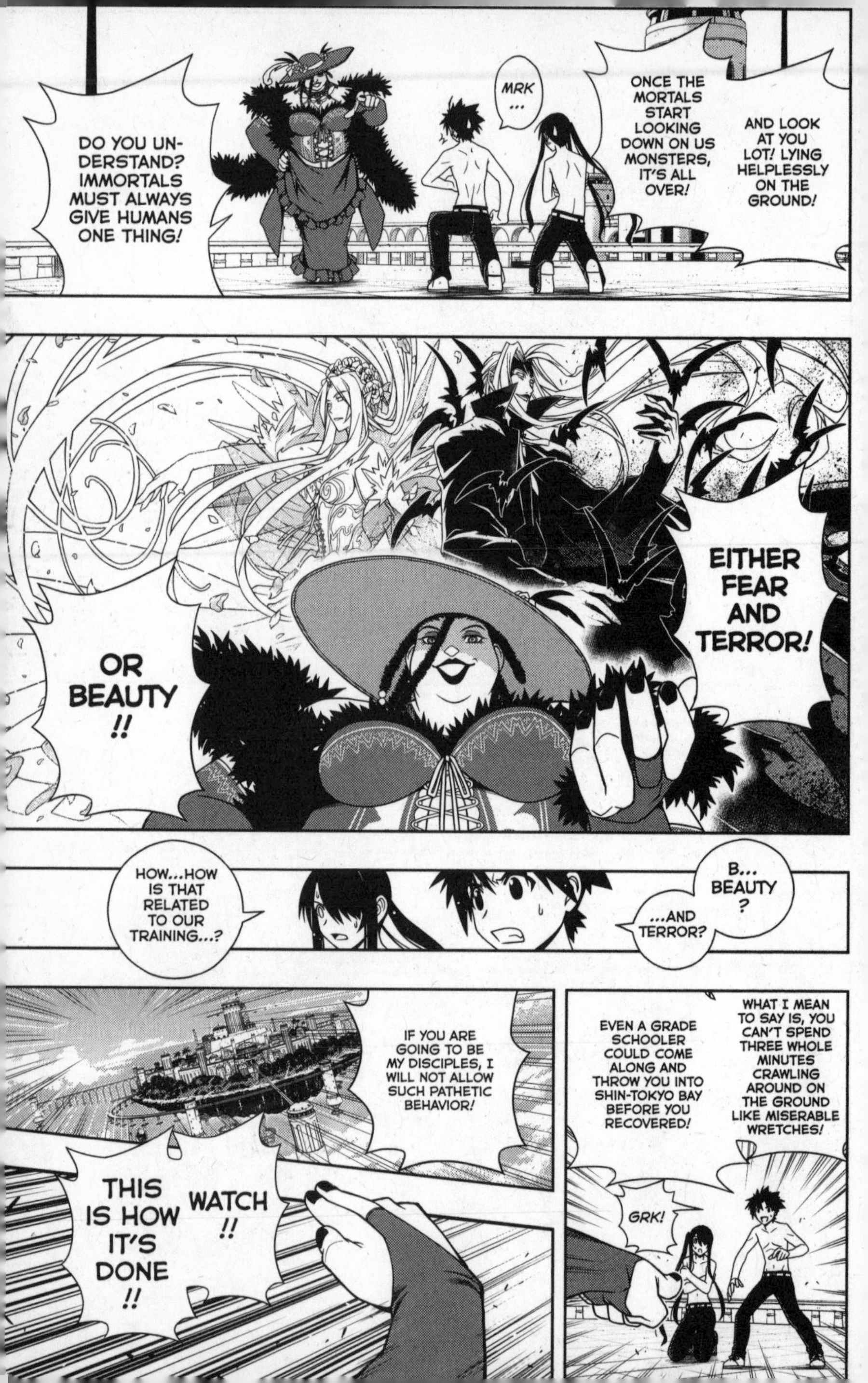
AND LOOK AT YOU LOT! LYING HELPLESSLY ON THE GROUND!
ONCE THE MORTALS START LOOKING DOWN ON US MONSTERS, IT'S ALL OVER!
MRK ...
DO YOU UNDERSTAND? IMMORTALS MUST ALWAYS GIVE HUMANS ONE THING!
EITHER FEAR AND TERROR!
OR BEAUTY !!
B... BEAUTY ?
...AND TERROR?
HOW...HOW IS THAT RELATED TO OUR TRAINING...?
WHAT I MEAN TO SAY IS, YOU CAN'T SPEND THREE WHOLE MINUTES CRAWLING AROUND ON THE GROUND LIKE MISERABLE WRETCHES!
EVEN A GRADE SCHOOLER COULD COME ALONG AND THROW YOU INTO SHIN-TOKYO BAY BEFORE YOU RECOVERED!
GRK!
IF YOU ARE GOING TO BE MY DISCIPLES, I WILL NOT ALLOW SUCH PATHETIC BEHAVIOR!
WATCH !!
THIS IS HOW IT'S DONE !!

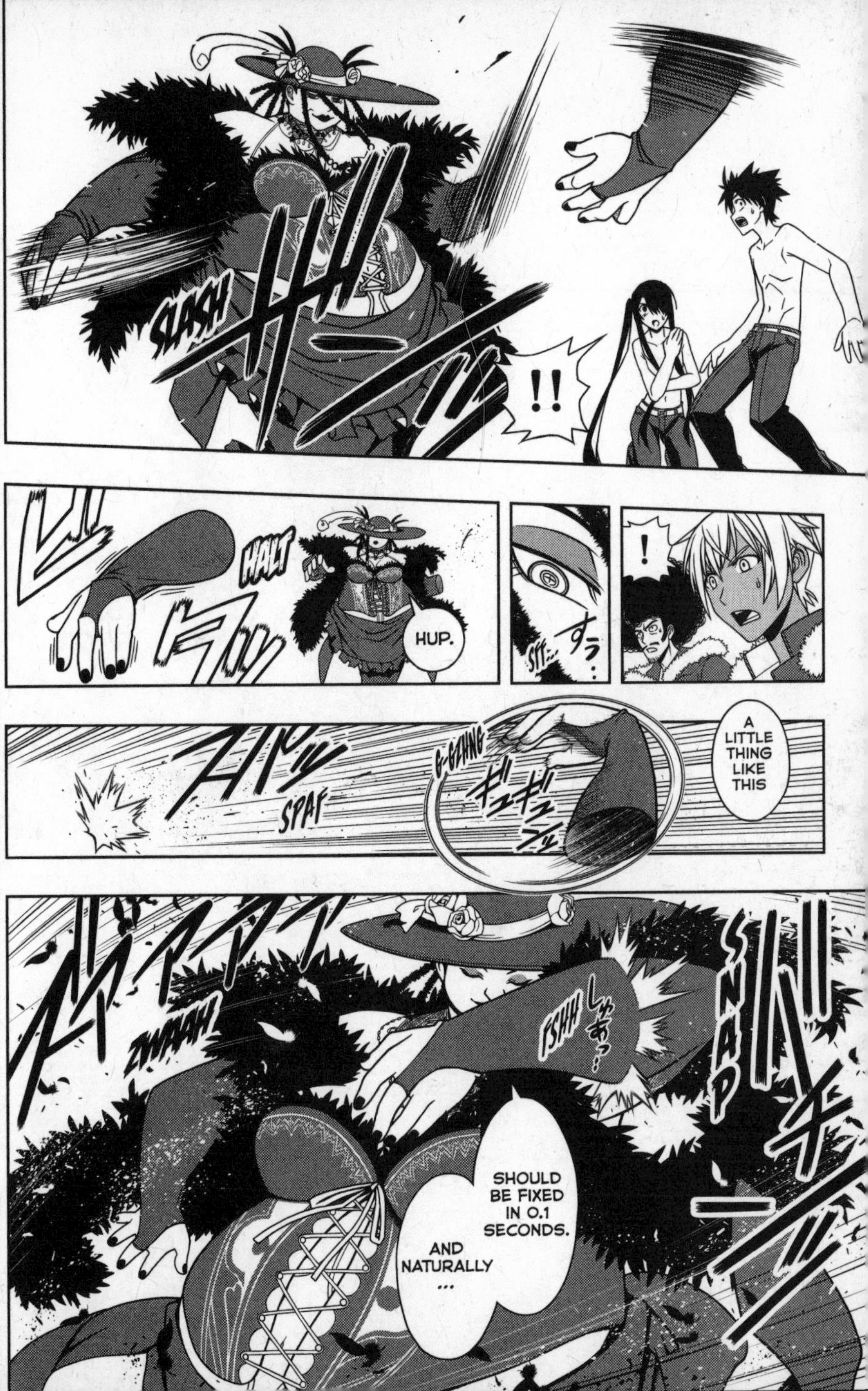
!!
SLASH
!
SFF...
すぅ‥
HALT
HUP.
A LITTLE THING LIKE THIS
G-GZHNG
SPAF
SNAP
FSHH
しゅあっ‥
SHOULD BE FIXED IN 0.1 SECONDS.
AND NATURALLY ...
ZWAAAH

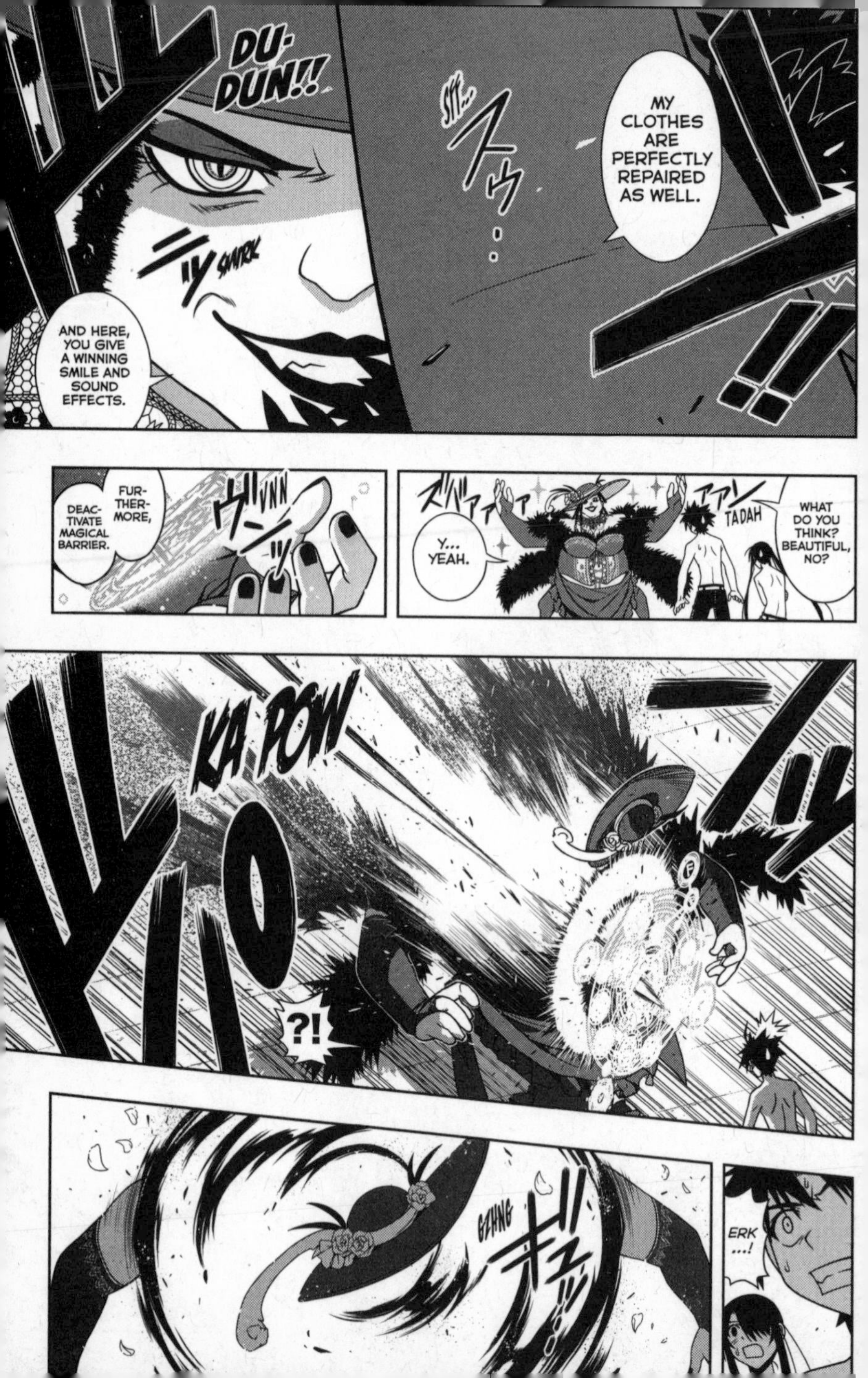
SFF..
MY CLOTHES ARE PERFECTLY REPAIRED AS WELL.
DU-DUN!!
SMIRK
AND HERE, YOU GIVE A WINNING SMILE AND SOUND EFFECTS.
WHAT DO YOU THINK? BEAUTIFUL, NO?
TADAH
Y... YEAH.
FURTHERMORE, DEACTIVATE MAGICAL BARRIER.
VNN
KA POW
?!
ERK ...!
GZHNG

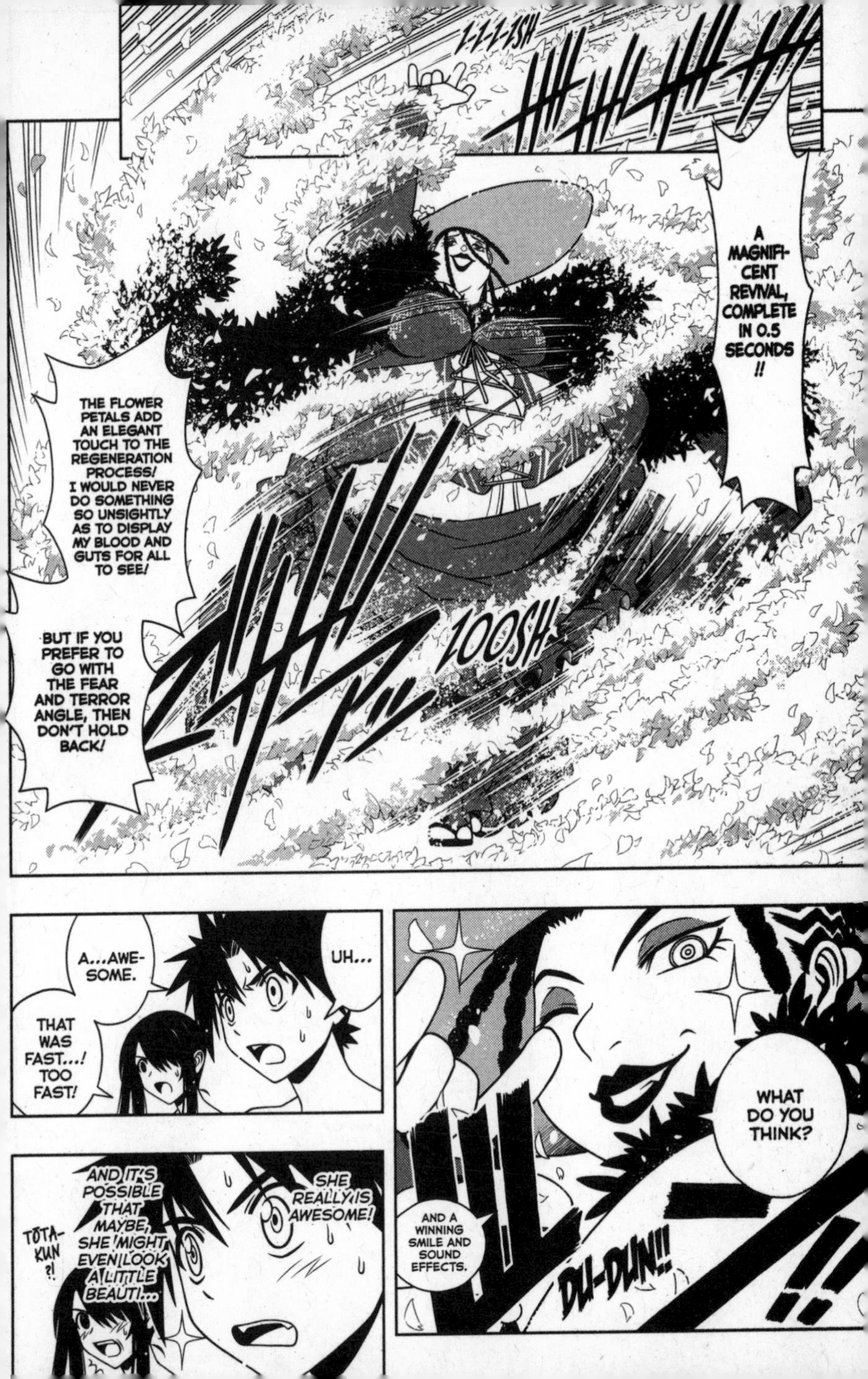
Z-Z-Z-ZSH
A MAGNIFICENT REVIVAL, COMPLETE IN 0.5 SECONDS!!
THE FLOWER PETALS ADD AN ELEGANT TOUCH TO THE REGENERATION PROCESS! I WOULD NEVER DO SOMETHING SO UNSIGHTLY AS TO DISPLAY MY BLOOD AND GUTS FOR ALL TO SEE!
BUT IF YOU PREFER TO GO WITH THE FEAR AND TERROR ANGLE, THEN DON'T HOLD BACK!
ZOOSH
WHAT DO YOU THINK?
AND A WINNING SMILE AND SOUND EFFECTS.
DU-DUN!!
UH...
A...AWESOME.
THAT WAS FAST...! TOO FAST!
SHE REALLY IS AWESOME!
AND IT'S POSSIBLE THAT MAYBE, SHE MIGHT EVEN LOOK A LITTLE BEAUTI...
TŌTA-KUN?!

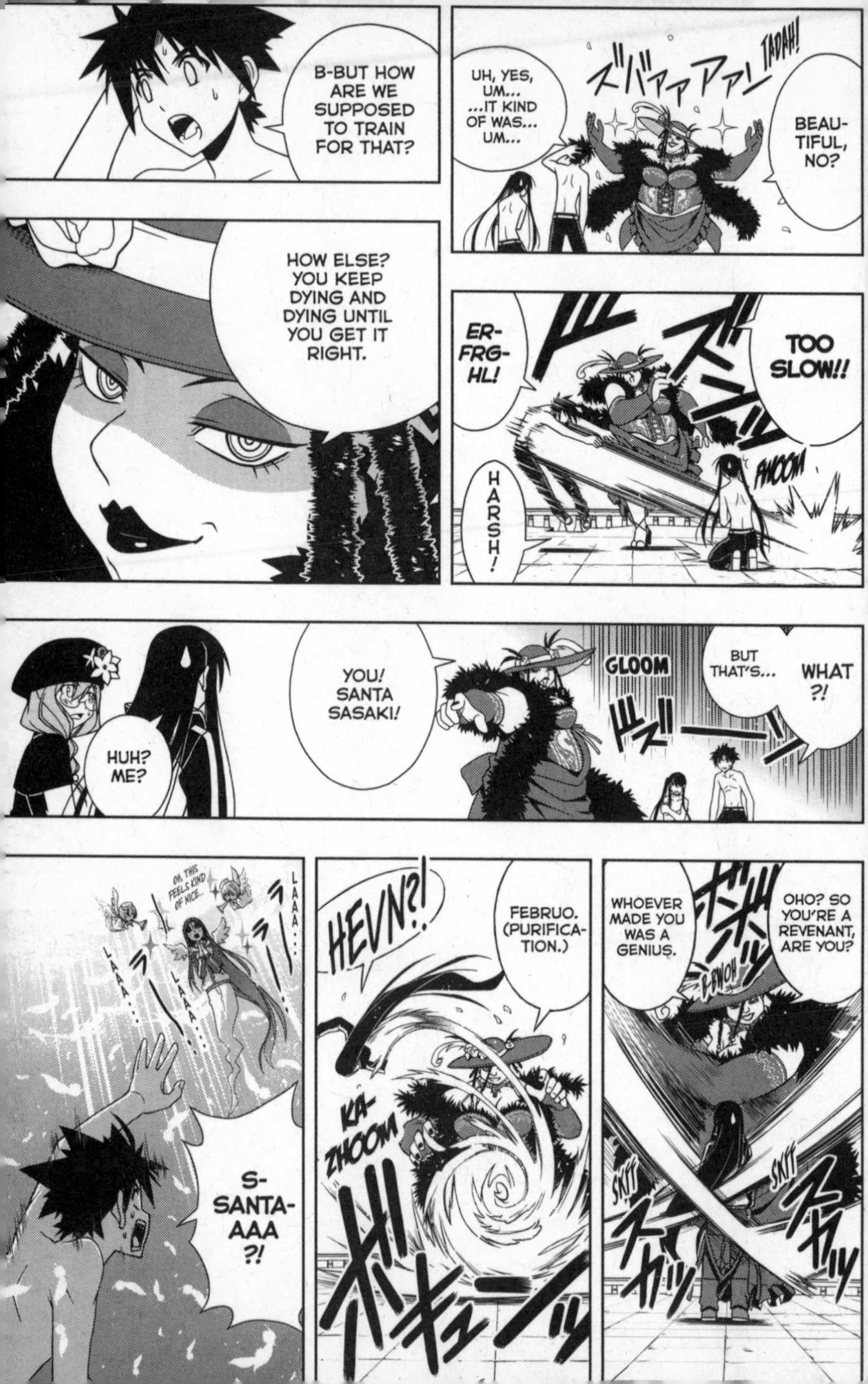
TADAH!
BEAU-TIFUL, NO?
UH, YES, UM... ...IT KIND OF WAS... UM...
B-BUT HOW ARE WE SUPPOSED TO TRAIN FOR THAT?
HOW ELSE? YOU KEEP DYING AND DYING UNTIL YOU GET IT RIGHT.
TOO SLOW!!
FWOOM
ER-FRG-HL!
HARSH!
WHAT?!
BUT THAT'S...
GLOOM
YOU! SANTA SASAKI!
HUH? ME?
OHO? SO YOU'RE A REVENANT, ARE YOU?
WHOEVER MADE YOU WAS A GENIUS.
FEBRUO. (PURIFICA-TION.)
HEVN?!
KA-ZHOOM
LAAA...
OH, THIS FEELS KIND OF NICE...
LAAA...
LAAA...
S-SANTA-AAA?!

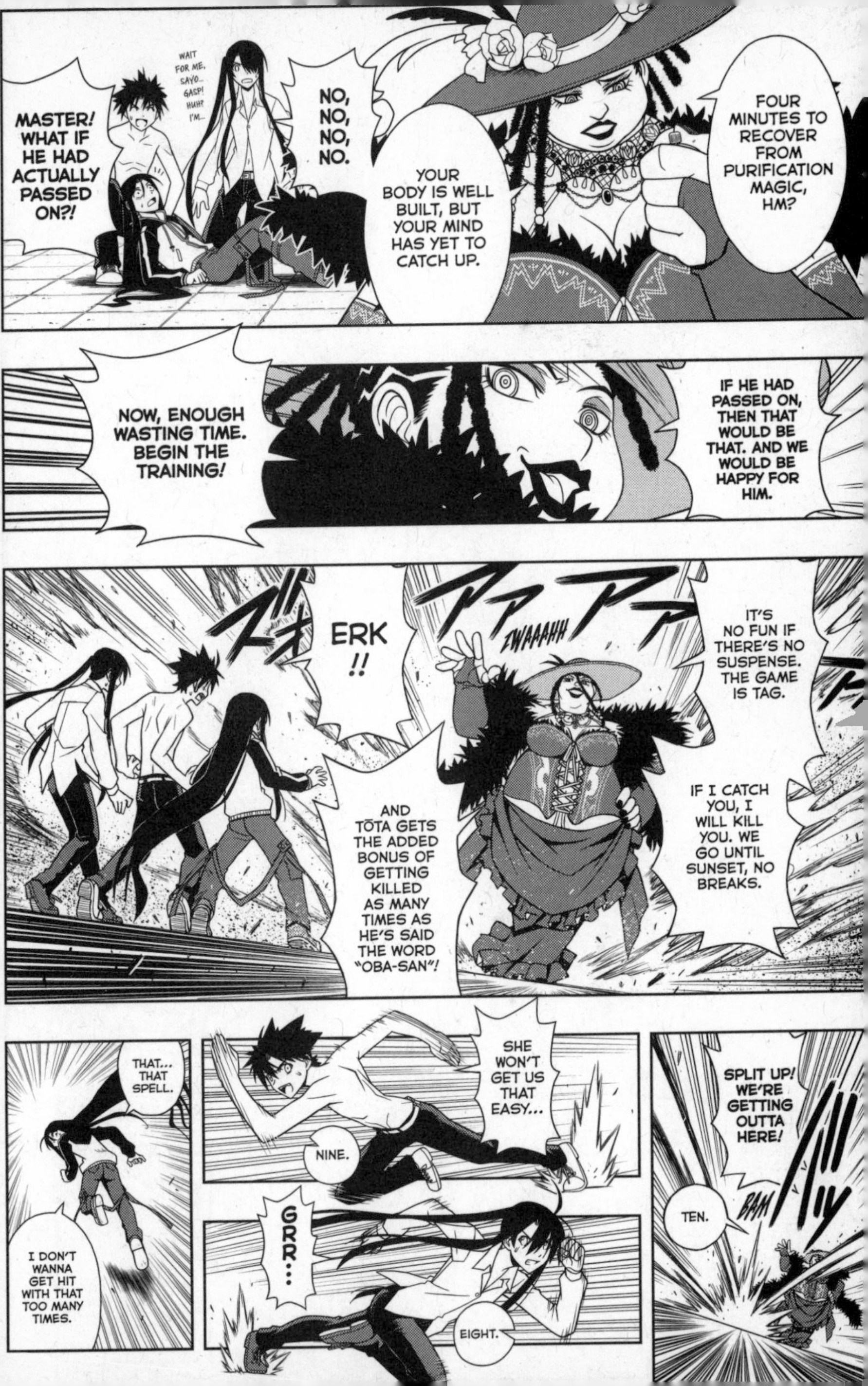
FOUR MINUTES TO RECOVER FROM PURIFICATION MAGIC, HM?
YOUR BODY IS WELL BUILT, BUT YOUR MIND HAS YET TO CATCH UP.
NO, NO, NO, NO.
WAIT FOR ME, SAYO... GASP! HUH? I'M...
MASTER! WHAT IF HE HAD ACTUALLY PASSED ON?!
IF HE HAD PASSED ON, THEN THAT WOULD BE THAT. AND WE WOULD BE HAPPY FOR HIM.
NOW, ENOUGH WASTING TIME. BEGIN THE TRAINING!
IT'S NO FUN IF THERE'S NO SUSPENSE. THE GAME IS TAG.
IF I CATCH YOU, I WILL KILL YOU. WE GO UNTIL SUNSET, NO BREAKS.
ZWAAAHH
AND TŌTA GETS THE ADDED BONUS OF GETTING KILLED AS MANY TIMES AS HE'S SAID THE WORD "OBA-SAN"!
ERK !!
SPLIT UP! WE'RE GETTING OUTTA HERE!
BAM
TEN.
SHE WON'T GET US THAT EASY...
NINE.
GRR...
EIGHT.
THAT... THAT SPELL.
I DON'T WANNA GET HIT WITH THAT TOO MANY TIMES.

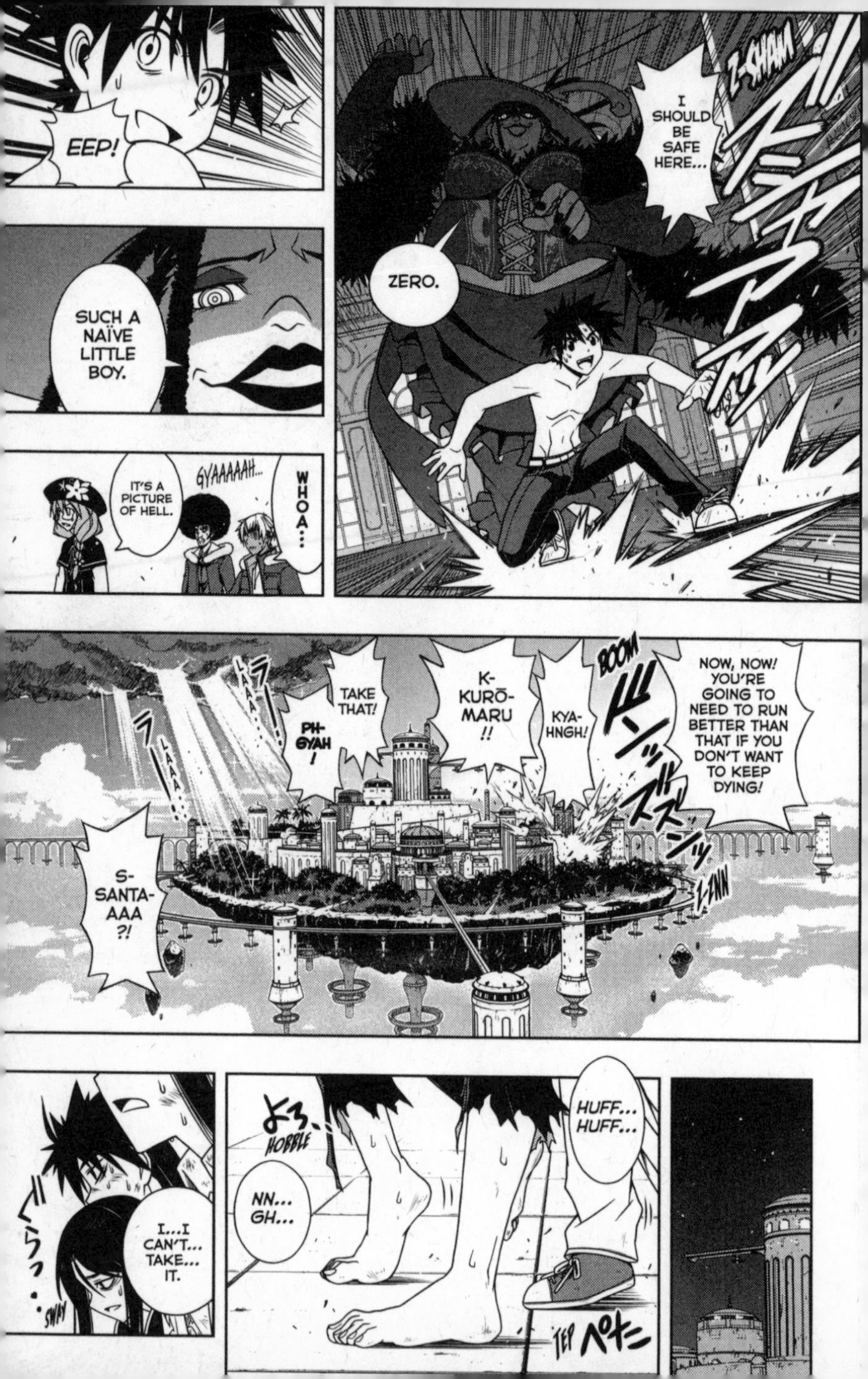
Z-SHAM
I SHOULD BE SAFE HERE...
ZERO.
EEP!
SUCH A NAÏVE LITTLE BOY.
WHOA...
GYAAAAAH...
IT'S A PICTURE OF HELL.
NOW, NOW! YOU'RE GOING TO NEED TO RUN BETTER THAN THAT IF YOU DON'T WANT TO KEEP DYING!
BOOM
Z-ZNN
KYA-HNGH!
K-KURŌMARU!!
TAKE THAT!
PH-GYAH!
LAAA...
LAAA...
S-SANTA-AAA?!
HUFF... HUFF...
HOBBLE
NN... GH...
TEP
I...I CAN'T... TAKE... IT.
SWAY

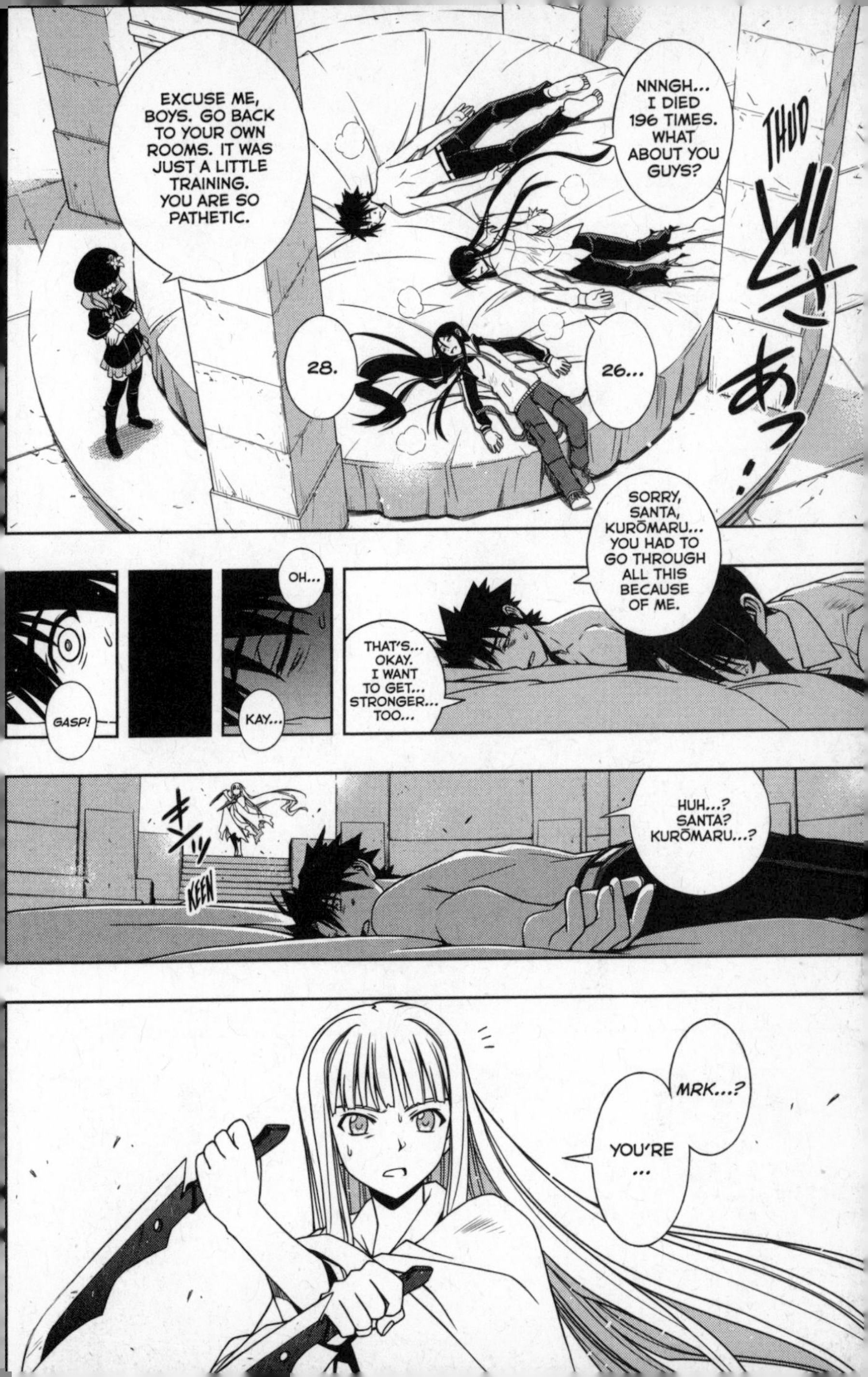
THUD
NNNGH... I DIED 196 TIMES. WHAT ABOUT YOU GUYS?
EXCUSE ME, BOYS. GO BACK TO YOUR OWN ROOMS. IT WAS JUST A LITTLE TRAINING. YOU ARE SO PATHETIC.
26...
28.
SORRY, SANTA, KURŌMARU... YOU HAD TO GO THROUGH ALL THIS BECAUSE OF ME.
THAT'S... OKAY. I WANT TO GET... STRONGER... TOO...
OH...
KAY...
GASP!
HUH...? SANTA? KURŌMARU...?
KEEN
MRK...?
YOU'RE ...

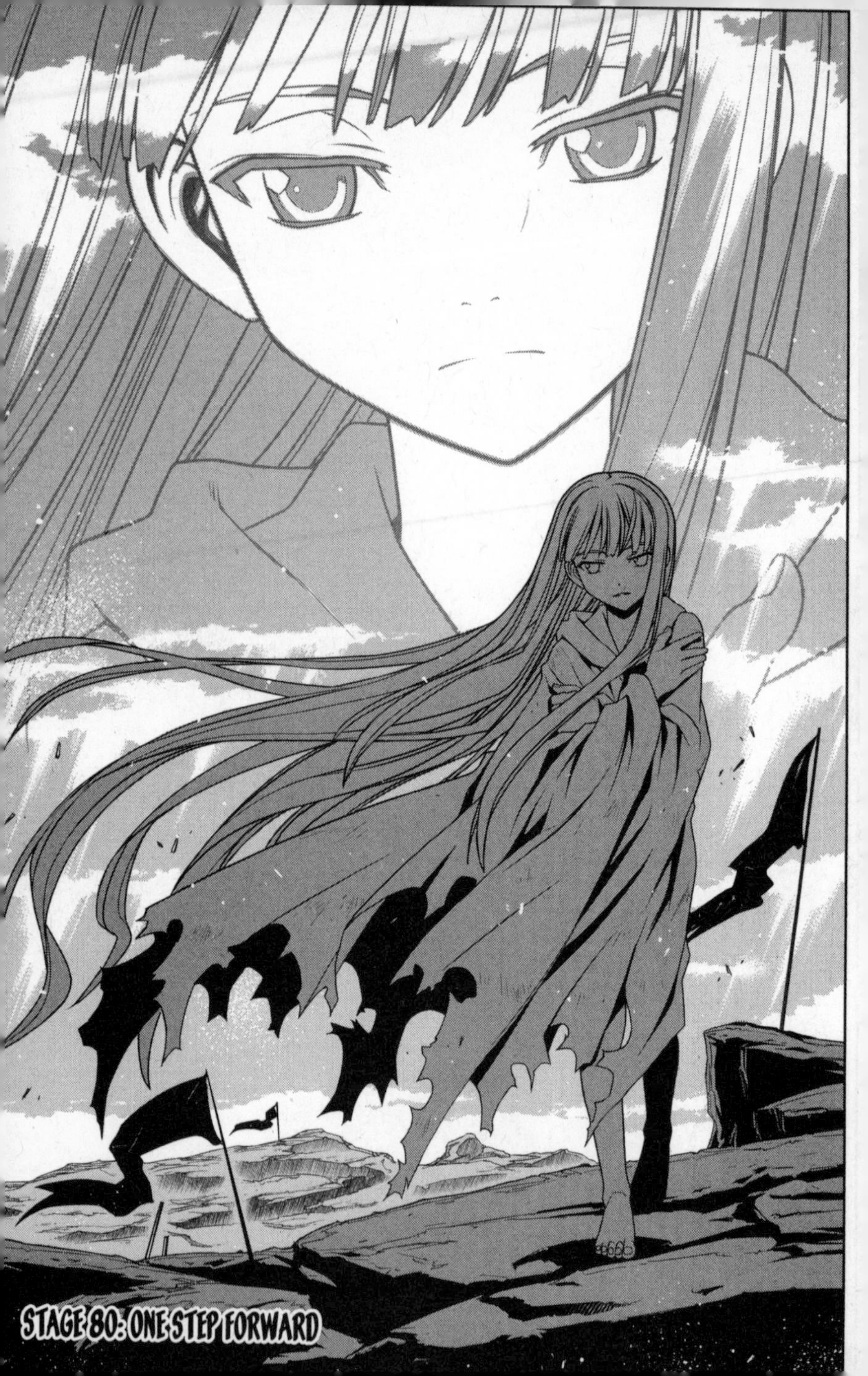
STAGE 80: ONE STEP FORWARD

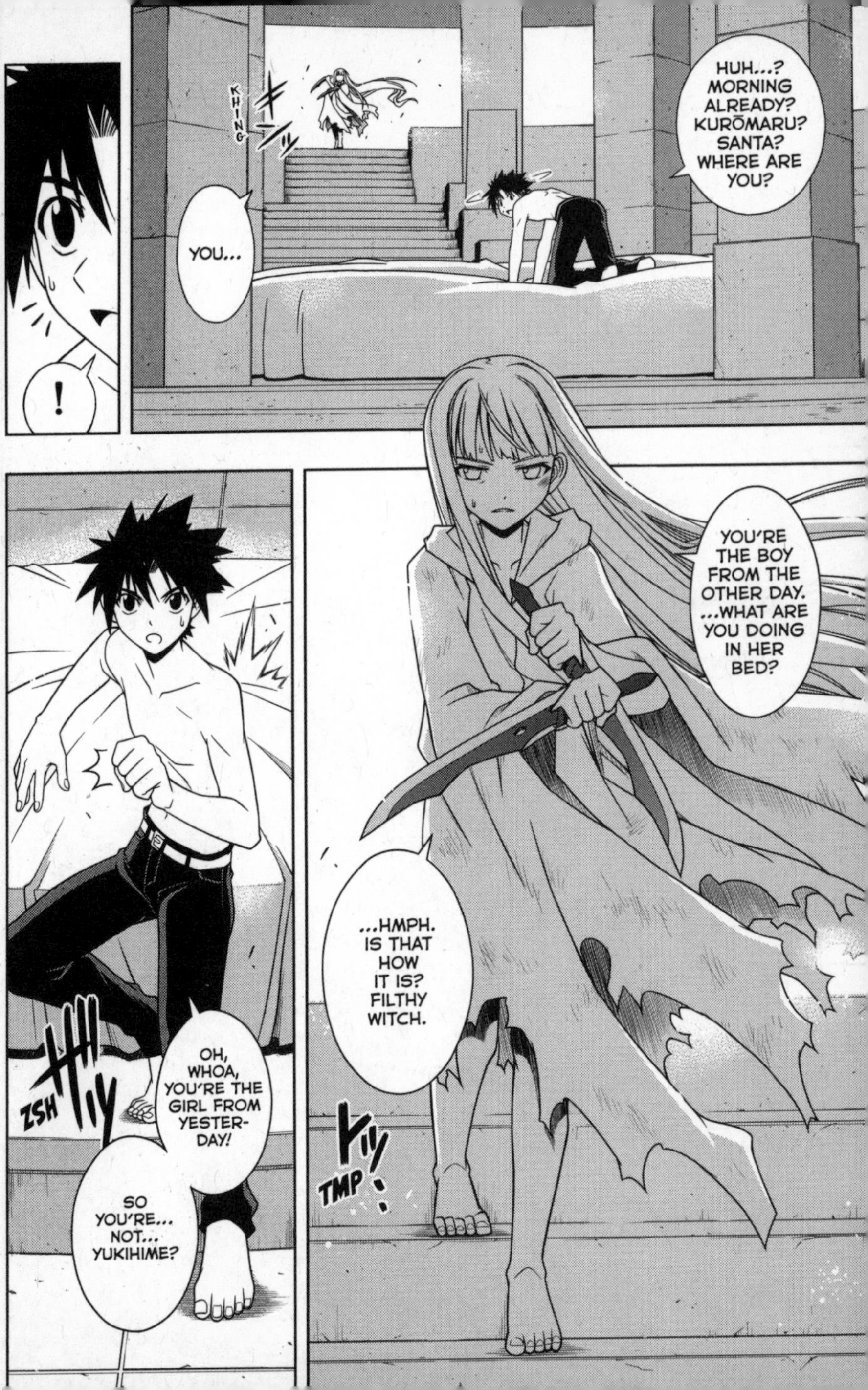
HUH...? MORNING ALREADY? KURŌMARU? SANTA? WHERE ARE YOU?
KHING
YOU...
!
YOU'RE THE BOY FROM THE OTHER DAY. ...WHAT ARE YOU DOING IN HER BED?
...HMPH. IS THAT HOW IT IS? FILTHY WITCH.
TMP
ZSH
OH, WHOA, YOU'RE THE GIRL FROM YESTER-DAY!
SO YOU'RE... NOT... YUKIHIME?

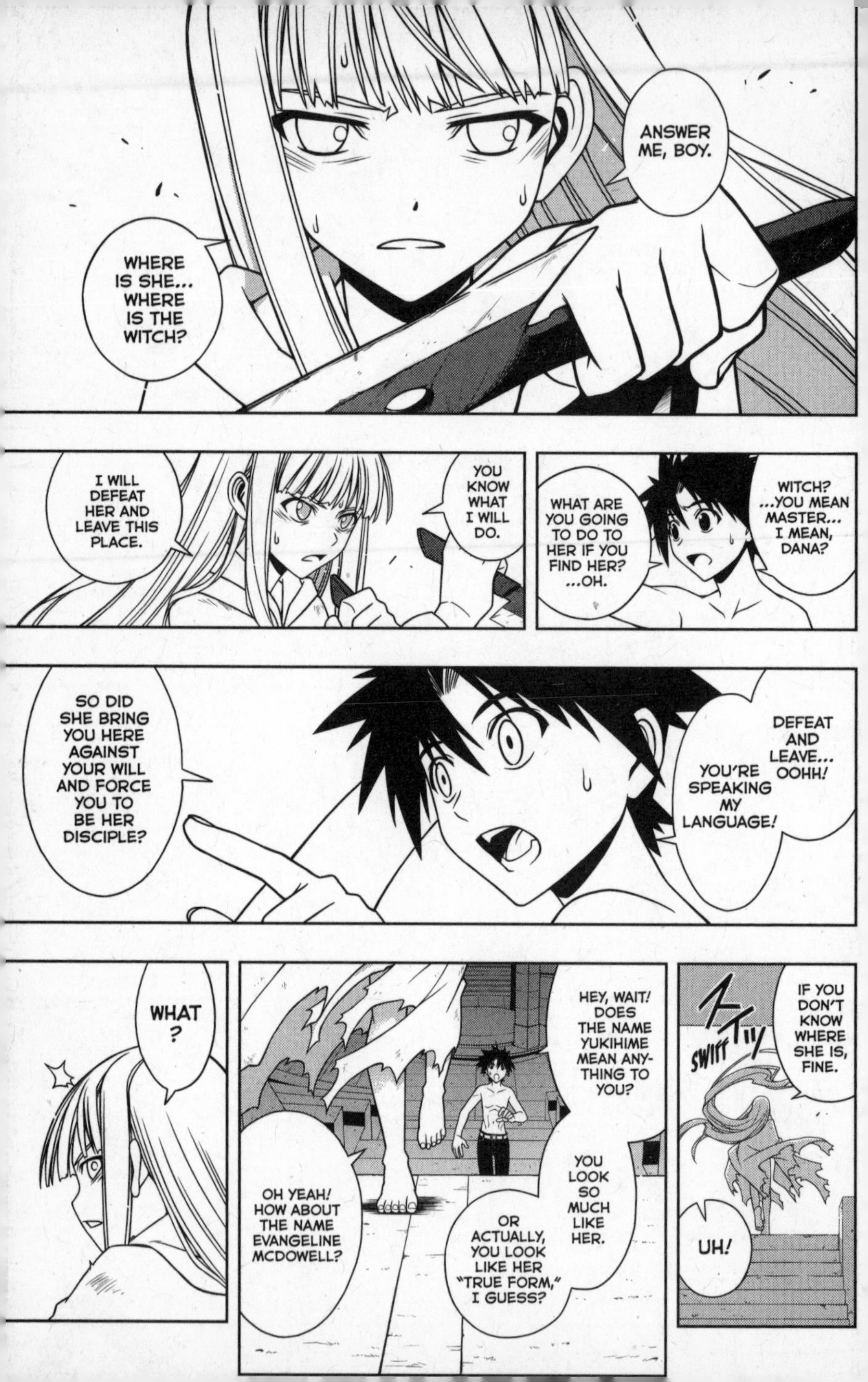
ANSWER ME, BOY.
WHERE IS SHE... WHERE IS THE WITCH?
WITCH? ...YOU MEAN MASTER... I MEAN, DANA?
WHAT ARE YOU GOING TO DO TO HER IF YOU FIND HER? ...OH.
YOU KNOW WHAT I WILL DO.
I WILL DEFEAT HER AND LEAVE THIS PLACE.
DEFEAT AND LEAVE... OOHH!
YOU'RE SPEAKING MY LANGUAGE!
SO DID SHE BRING YOU HERE AGAINST YOUR WILL AND FORCE YOU TO BE HER DISCIPLE?
IF YOU DON'T KNOW WHERE SHE IS, FINE.
SWIFF
UH!
HEY, WAIT! DOES THE NAME YUKIHIME MEAN ANY-THING TO YOU?
YOU LOOK SO MUCH LIKE HER.
OR ACTUALLY, YOU LOOK LIKE HER "TRUE FORM," I GUESS?
OH YEAH! HOW ABOUT THE NAME EVANGELINE MCDOWELL?
WHAT?

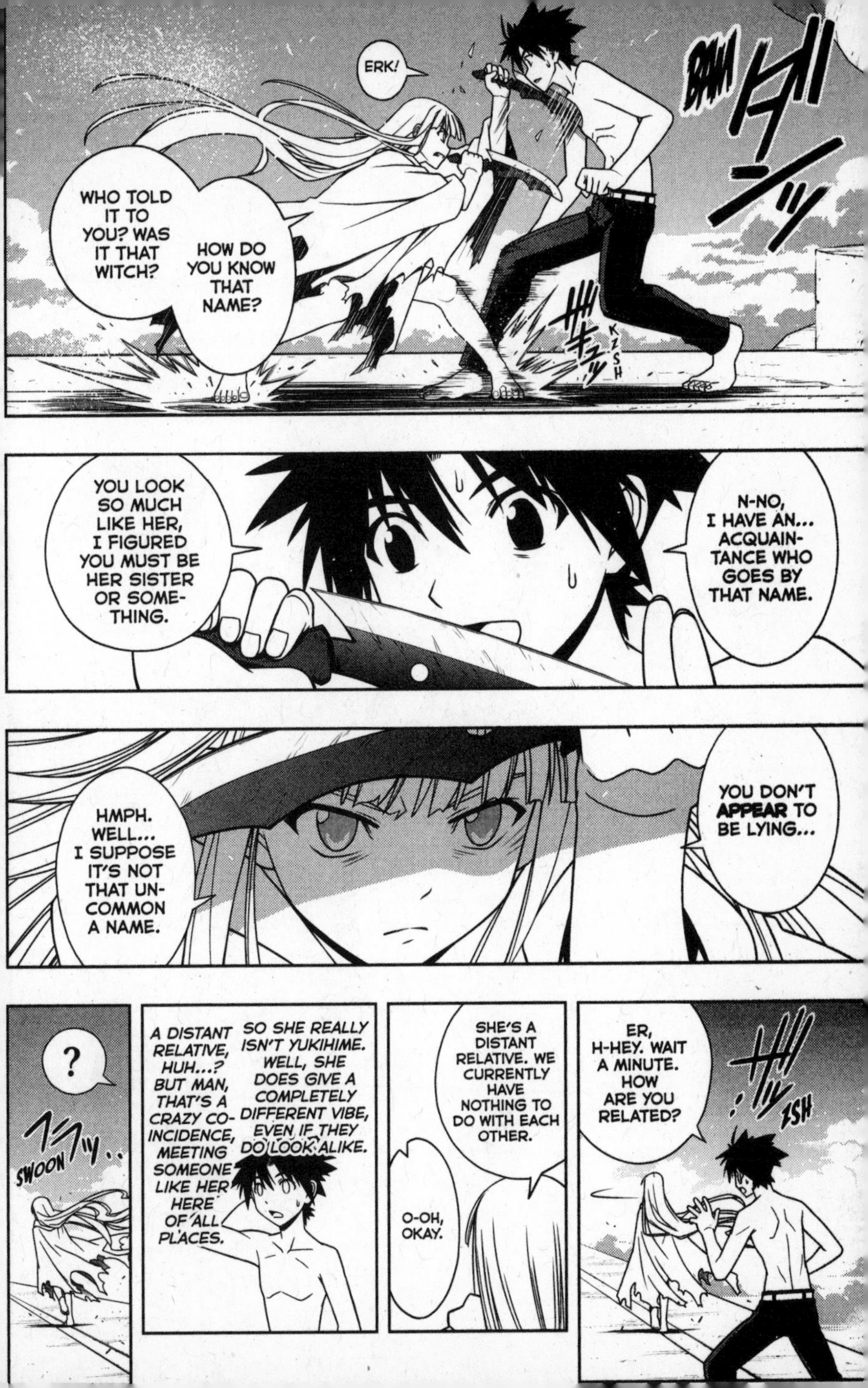
BAM
ERK!
HOW DO YOU KNOW THAT NAME?
WHO TOLD IT TO YOU? WAS IT THAT WITCH?
KZSH
N-NO, I HAVE AN... ACQUAINTANCE WHO GOES BY THAT NAME.
YOU LOOK SO MUCH LIKE HER, I FIGURED YOU MUST BE HER SISTER OR SOMETHING.
YOU DON'T **APPEAR** TO BE LYING...
HMPH. WELL... I SUPPOSE IT'S NOT THAT UNCOMMON A NAME.
ER, H-HEY. WAIT A MINUTE. HOW ARE YOU RELATED?
ISH
SHE'S A DISTANT RELATIVE. WE CURRENTLY HAVE NOTHING TO DO WITH EACH OTHER.
O-OH, OKAY.
SO SHE REALLY ISN'T YUKIHIME. WELL, SHE DOES GIVE A COMPLETELY DIFFERENT VIBE, EVEN IF THEY DO LOOK ALIKE.
A DISTANT RELATIVE, HUH...? BUT MAN, THAT'S A CRAZY COINCIDENCE, MEETING SOMEONE LIKE HER HERE OF ALL PLACES.
?
SWOON

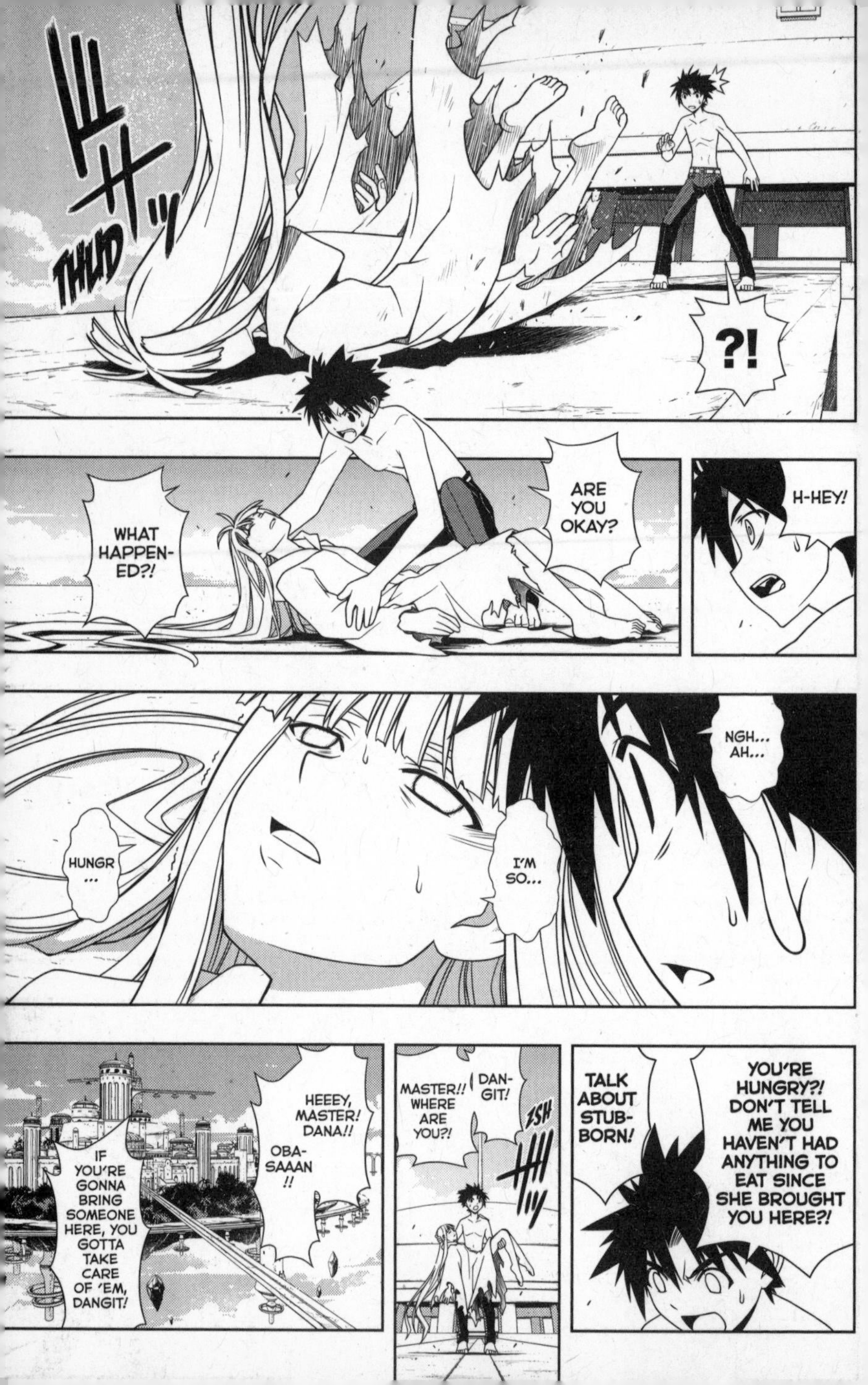
THUD
?!
H-HEY!
ARE YOU OKAY?
WHAT HAPPEN-ED?!
NGH... AH...
I'M SO...
HUNGR ...
YOU'RE HUNGRY?! DON'T TELL ME YOU HAVEN'T HAD ANYTHING TO EAT SINCE SHE BROUGHT YOU HERE?!
TALK ABOUT STUB-BORN!
DAN-GIT!
MASTER!! WHERE ARE YOU?!
ZSH
HEEEY, MASTER! DANA!!
OBA-SAAAN !!
IF YOU'RE GONNA BRING SOMEONE HERE, YOU GOTTA TAKE CARE OF 'EM, DANGIT!

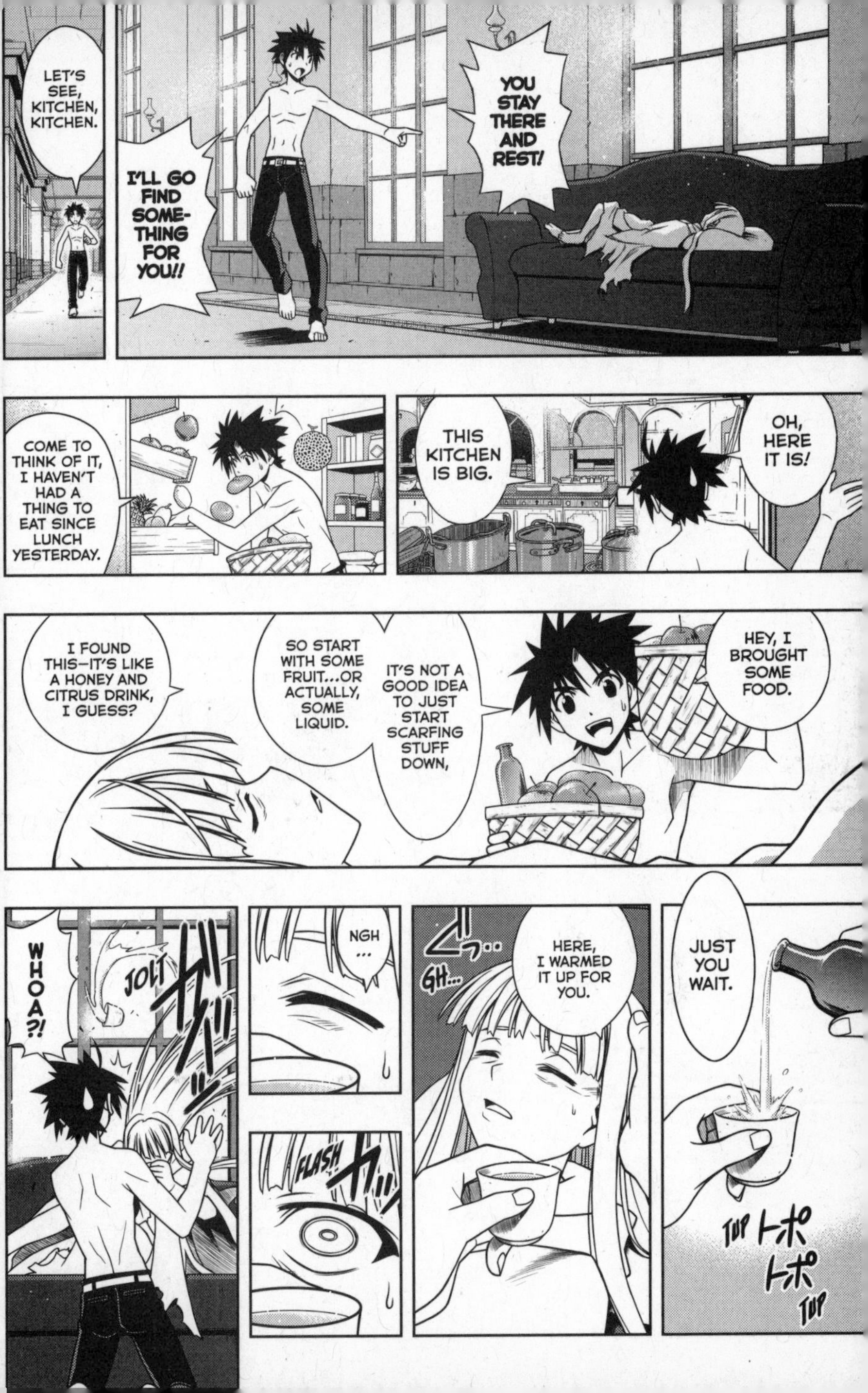
YOU STAY THERE AND REST!
I'LL GO FIND SOME-THING FOR YOU!!
LET'S SEE, KITCHEN, KITCHEN.
OH, HERE IT IS!
THIS KITCHEN IS BIG.
COME TO THINK OF IT, I HAVEN'T HAD A THING TO EAT SINCE LUNCH YESTERDAY.
HEY, I BROUGHT SOME FOOD.
IT'S NOT A GOOD IDEA TO JUST START SCARFING STUFF DOWN,
SO START WITH SOME FRUIT...OR ACTUALLY, SOME LIQUID.
I FOUND THIS—IT'S LIKE A HONEY AND CITRUS DRINK, I GUESS?
JUST YOU WAIT.
TUP トポ
トポ TUP
HERE, I WARMED IT UP FOR YOU.
GH...
NGH...
FLASH
JOLT
WHOA?!

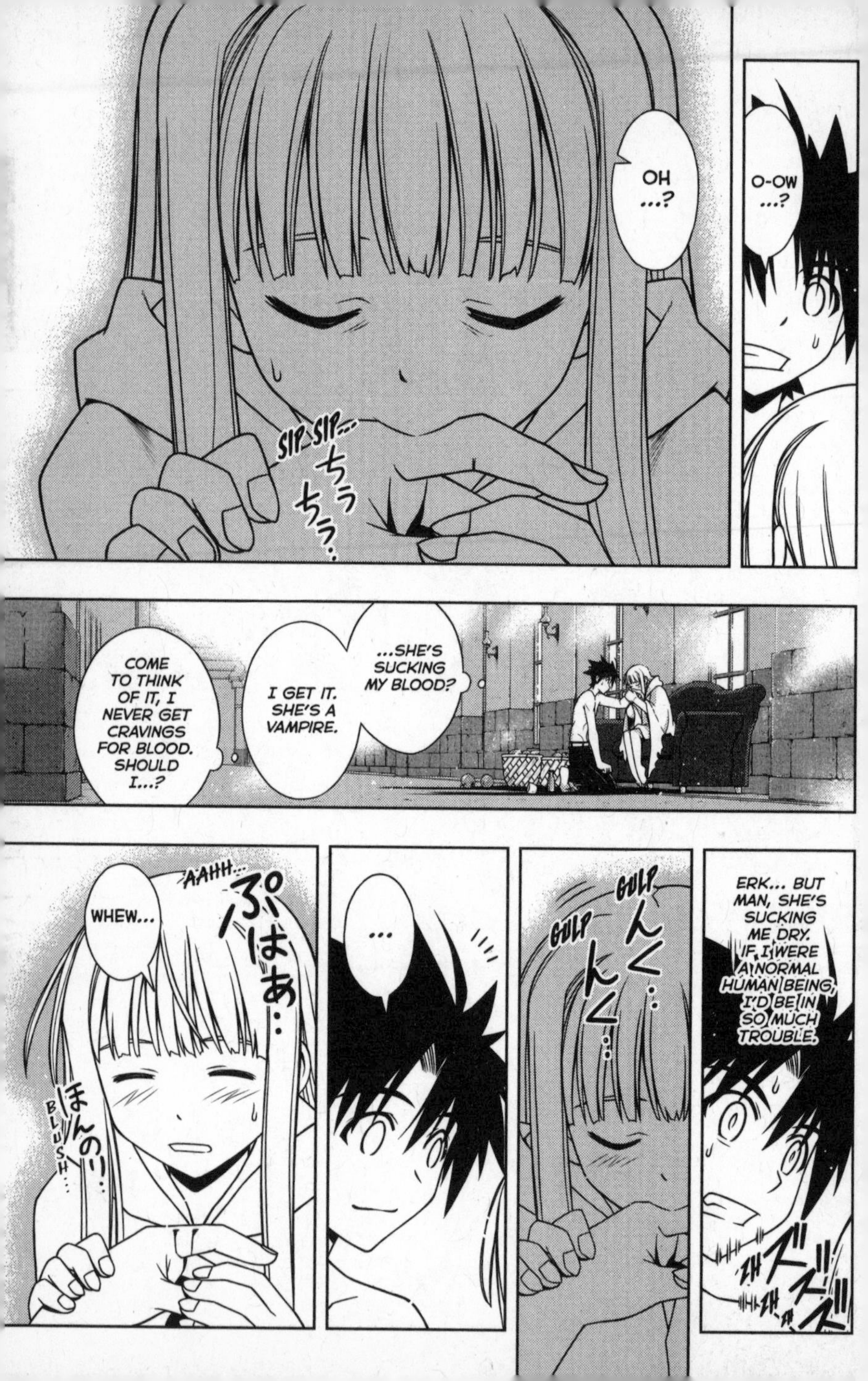
O-OW ...?
OH ...?
SIP SIP...
ちラ ちラ..
...SHE'S SUCKING MY BLOOD?
I GET IT. SHE'S A VAMPIRE.
COME TO THINK OF IT, I NEVER GET CRAVINGS FOR BLOOD. SHOULD I...?
ERK... BUT MAN, SHE'S SUCKING ME DRY. IF I WERE A NORMAL HUMAN BEING, I'D BE IN SO MUCH TROUBLE.
ZH ZH
ズズ
GULP GULP
んく.. んく..
...
WHEW...
AAHH...
ぷはあ..
BLUSH...
ほんのり..

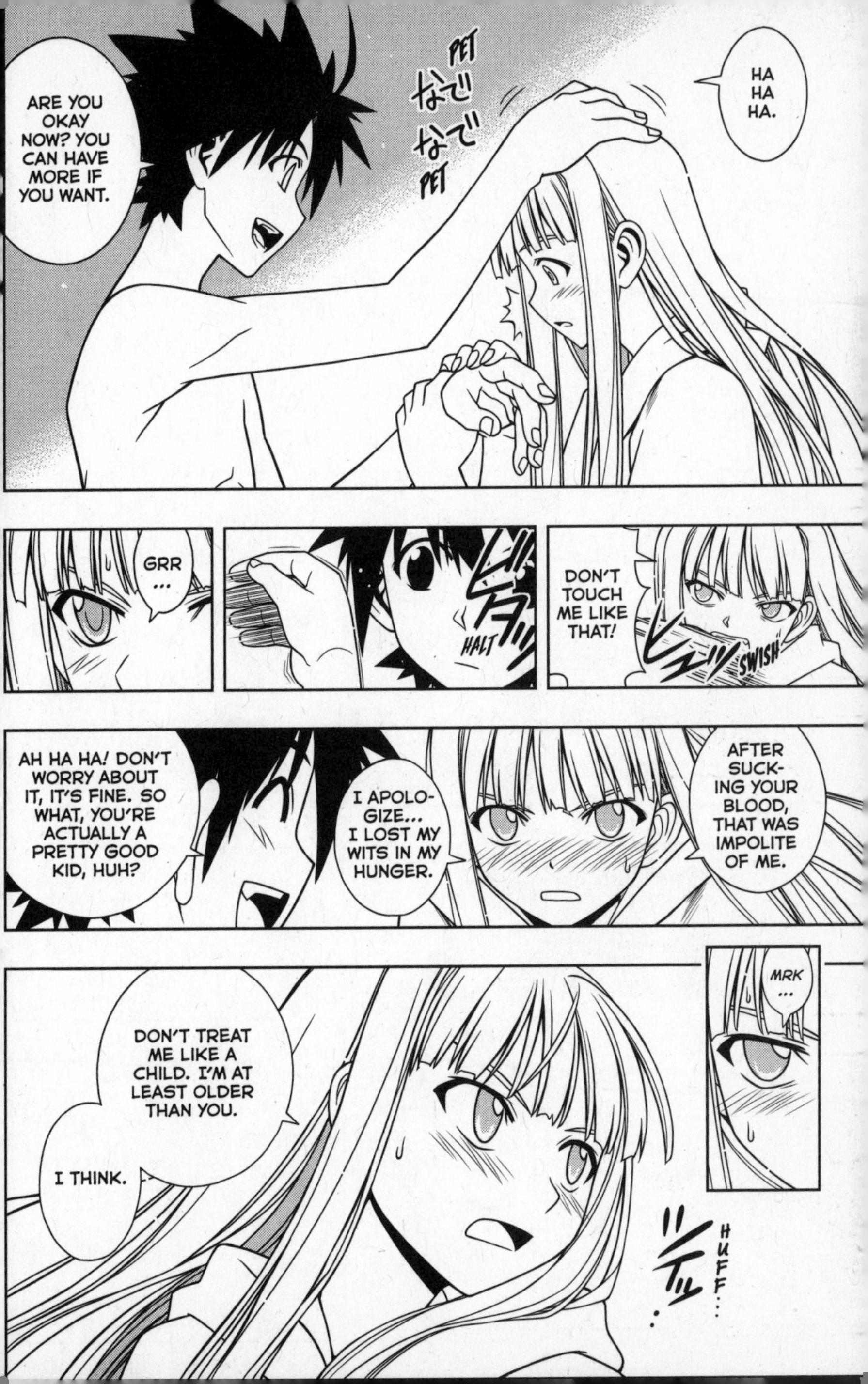
HA HA HA.
PET
なでなで
PET
ARE YOU OKAY NOW? YOU CAN HAVE MORE IF YOU WANT.
DON'T TOUCH ME LIKE THAT!
SWISH
HALT
GRR ...
AFTER SUCK-ING YOUR BLOOD, THAT WAS IMPOLITE OF ME.
I APOLO-GIZE... I LOST MY WITS IN MY HUNGER.
AH HA HA! DON'T WORRY ABOUT IT, IT'S FINE. SO WHAT, YOU'RE ACTUALLY A PRETTY GOOD KID, HUH?
MRK ...
HUFF...
DON'T TREAT ME LIKE A CHILD. I'M AT LEAST OLDER THAN YOU.
I THINK.

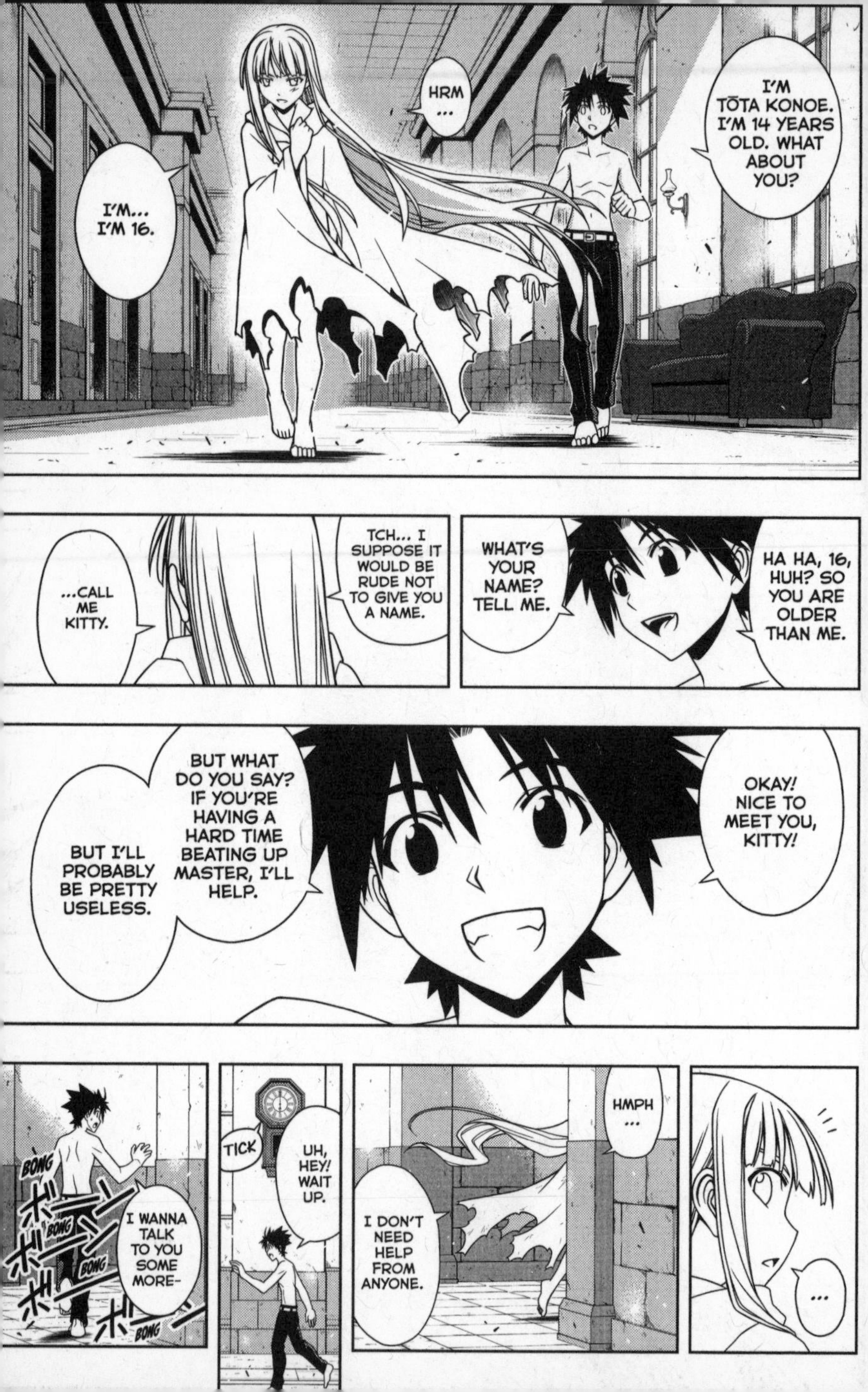
I'M TŌTA KONOE. I'M 14 YEARS OLD. WHAT ABOUT YOU?
HRM ...
I'M... I'M 16.
HA HA, 16, HUH? SO YOU ARE OLDER THAN ME.
WHAT'S YOUR NAME? TELL ME.
TCH... I SUPPOSE IT WOULD BE RUDE NOT TO GIVE YOU A NAME.
...CALL ME KITTY.
OKAY! NICE TO MEET YOU, KITTY!
BUT WHAT DO YOU SAY? IF YOU'RE HAVING A HARD TIME BEATING UP MASTER, I'LL HELP.
BUT I'LL PROBABLY BE PRETTY USELESS.
...
HMPH ...
I DON'T NEED HELP FROM ANYONE.
TICK
UH, HEY! WAIT UP.
BONG
BONG
BONG
BONG
I WANNA TALK TO YOU SOME MORE-

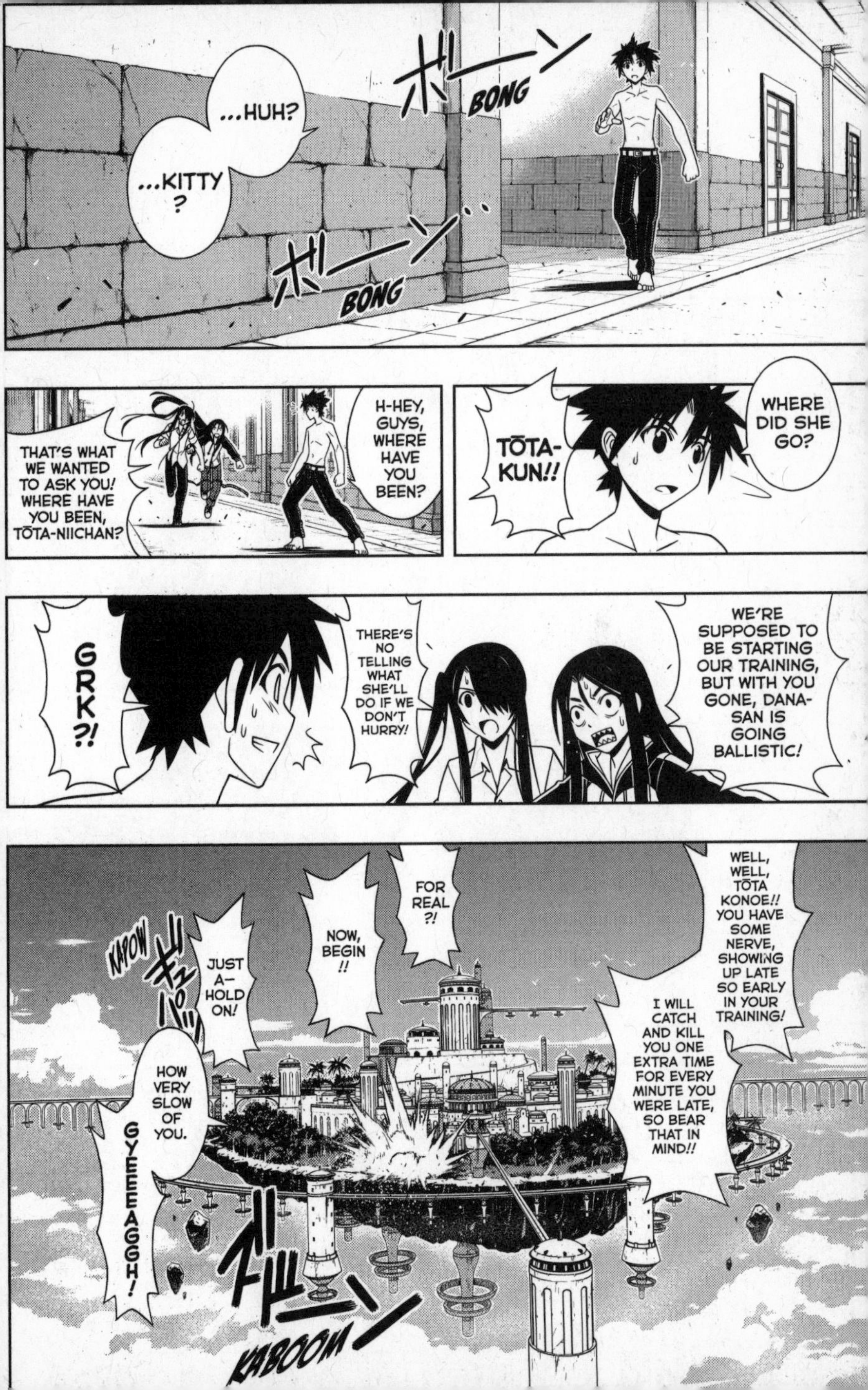
BONG
...HUH?
...KITTY ?
BONG
WHERE DID SHE GO?
TŌTA-KUN!!
H-HEY, GUYS, WHERE HAVE YOU BEEN?
THAT'S WHAT WE WANTED TO ASK YOU! WHERE HAVE YOU BEEN, TŌTA-NIICHAN?
WE'RE SUPPOSED TO BE STARTING OUR TRAINING, BUT WITH YOU GONE, DANA-SAN IS GOING BALLISTIC!
THERE'S NO TELLING WHAT SHE'LL DO IF WE DON'T HURRY!
GRK ?!
WELL, WELL, TŌTA KONOE!! YOU HAVE SOME NERVE, SHOWING UP LATE SO EARLY IN YOUR TRAINING!
FOR REAL ?!
I WILL CATCH AND KILL YOU ONE EXTRA TIME FOR EVERY MINUTE YOU WERE LATE, SO BEAR THAT IN MIND!!
NOW, BEGIN !!
KAPOW
JUST A-HOLD ON!
HOW VERY SLOW OF YOU.
GYEEEAGGH!
KABOOM

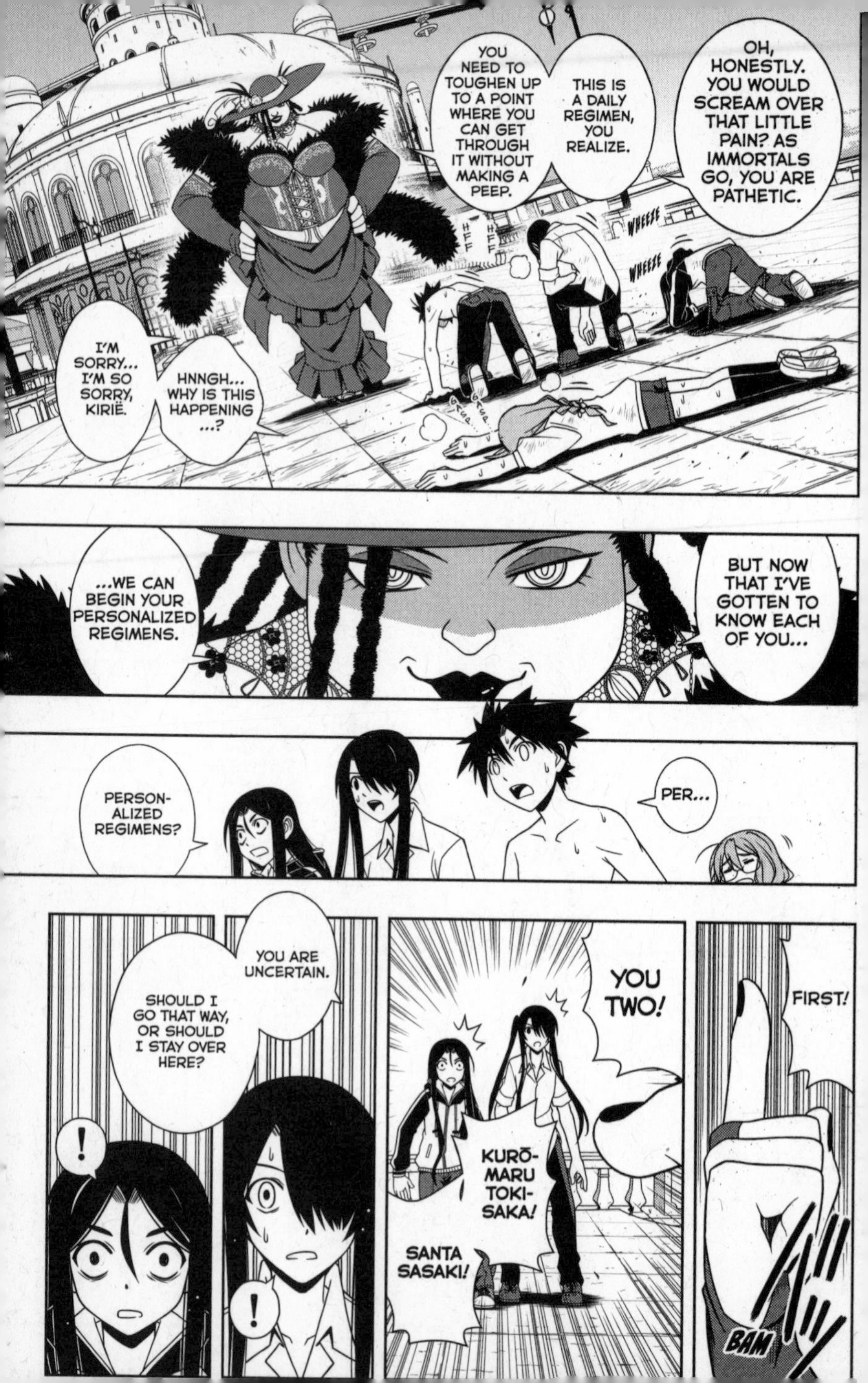
OH, HONESTLY. YOU WOULD SCREAM OVER THAT LITTLE PAIN? AS IMMORTALS GO, YOU ARE PATHETIC.
THIS IS A DAILY REGIMEN, YOU REALIZE.
YOU NEED TO TOUGHEN UP TO A POINT WHERE YOU CAN GET THROUGH IT WITHOUT MAKING A PEEP.
WHEEZE
WHEEZE
HFF
HFF
GASP
GASP
HNNGH... WHY IS THIS HAPPENING ...?
I'M SORRY... I'M SO SORRY, KIRIË.
BUT NOW THAT I'VE GOTTEN TO KNOW EACH OF YOU...
...WE CAN BEGIN YOUR PERSONALIZED REGIMENS.
PER...
PERSON-ALIZED REGIMENS?
FIRST!
BAM
YOU TWO!
KURŌ-MARU TOKI-SAKA!
SANTA SASAKI!
YOU ARE UNCERTAIN.
SHOULD I GO THAT WAY, OR SHOULD I STAY OVER HERE?
!
!

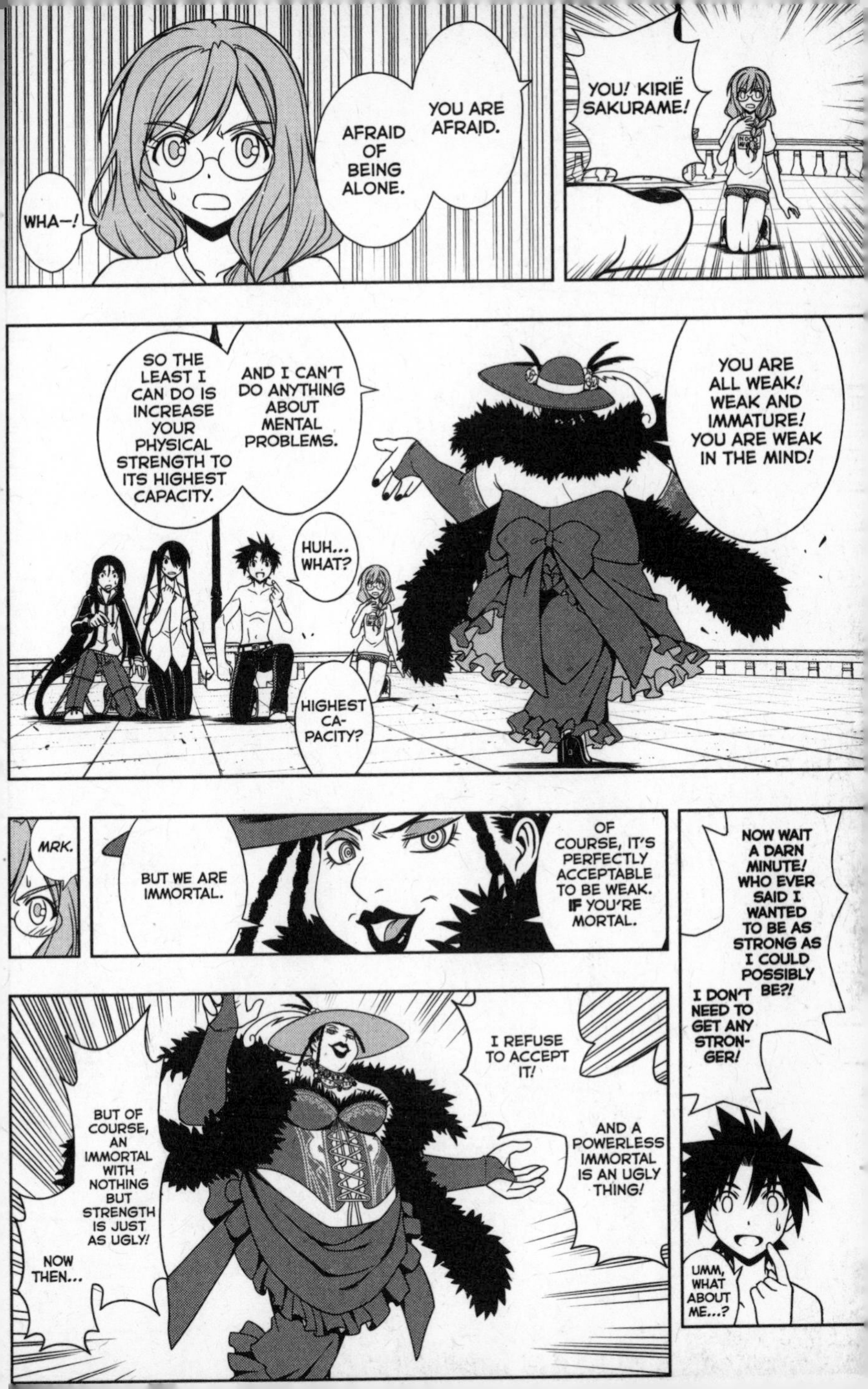
YOU! KIRIË SAKURAME!
YOU ARE AFRAID.
AFRAID OF BEING ALONE.
WHA—!
YOU ARE ALL WEAK! WEAK AND IMMATURE! YOU ARE WEAK IN THE MIND!
AND I CAN'T DO ANYTHING ABOUT MENTAL PROBLEMS.
SO THE LEAST I CAN DO IS INCREASE YOUR PHYSICAL STRENGTH TO ITS HIGHEST CAPACITY.
HUH... WHAT?
HIGHEST CA-PACITY?
NOW WAIT A DARN MINUTE! WHO EVER SAID I WANTED TO BE AS STRONG AS I COULD POSSIBLY BE?!
I DON'T NEED TO GET ANY STRON-GER!
UMM, WHAT ABOUT ME...?
OF COURSE, IT'S PERFECTLY ACCEPTABLE TO BE WEAK. IF YOU'RE MORTAL.
BUT WE ARE IMMORTAL.
MRK.
I REFUSE TO ACCEPT IT!
AND A POWERLESS IMMORTAL IS AN UGLY THING!
BUT OF COURSE, AN IMMORTAL WITH NOTHING BUT STRENGTH IS JUST AS UGLY!
NOW THEN...

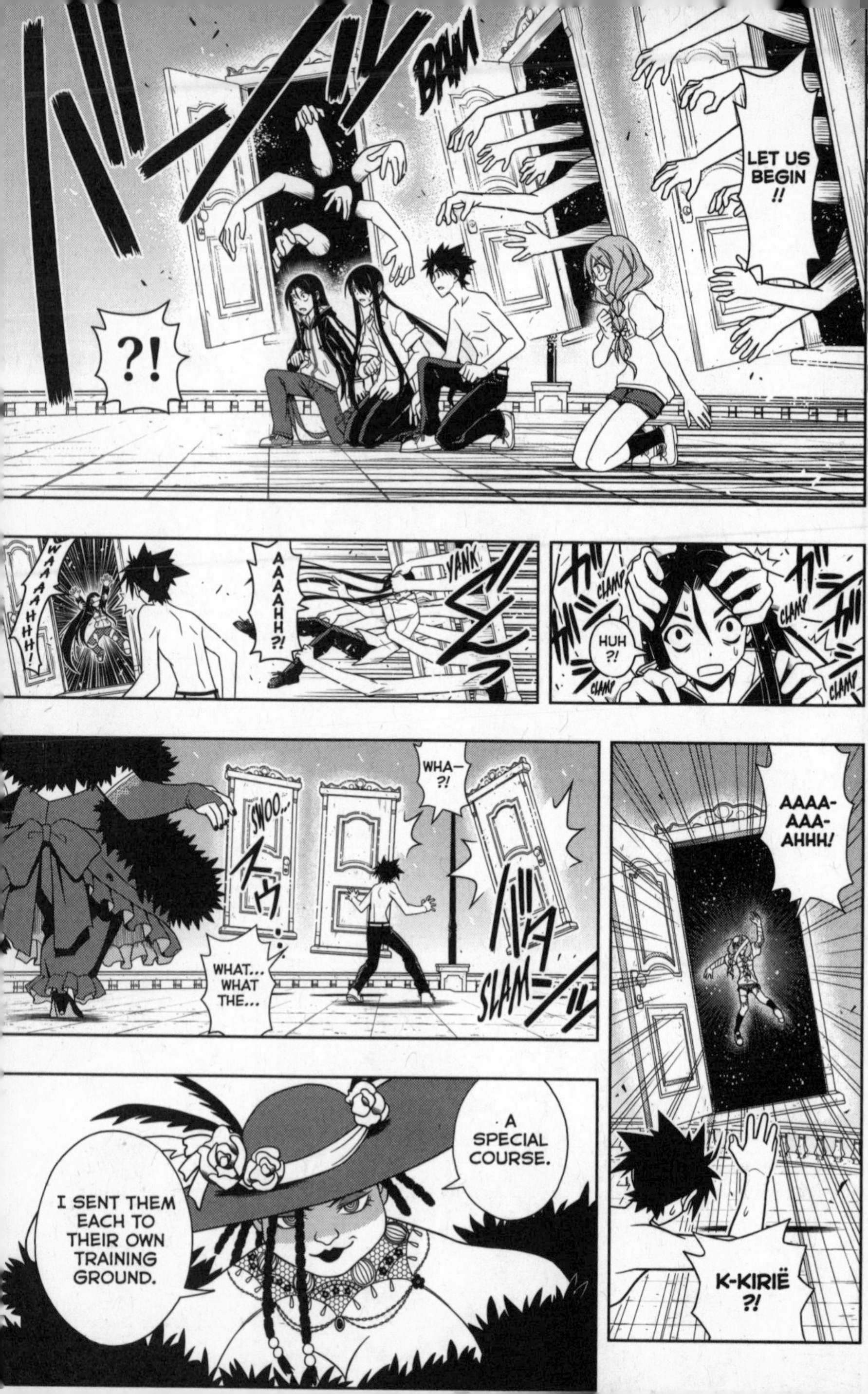
LET US BEGIN !!
BAM
?!
CLAMP
HUH ?!
CLAMP
CLAMP
CLAMP
YANK
AAAAAHH ?!
WAAAAAHHH!
AAAA-AAA-AHHH!
K-KIRIË ?!
WHA— ?!
SLAM
SWOO...
WHAT... WHAT THE...
A SPECIAL COURSE.
I SENT THEM EACH TO THEIR OWN TRAINING GROUND.

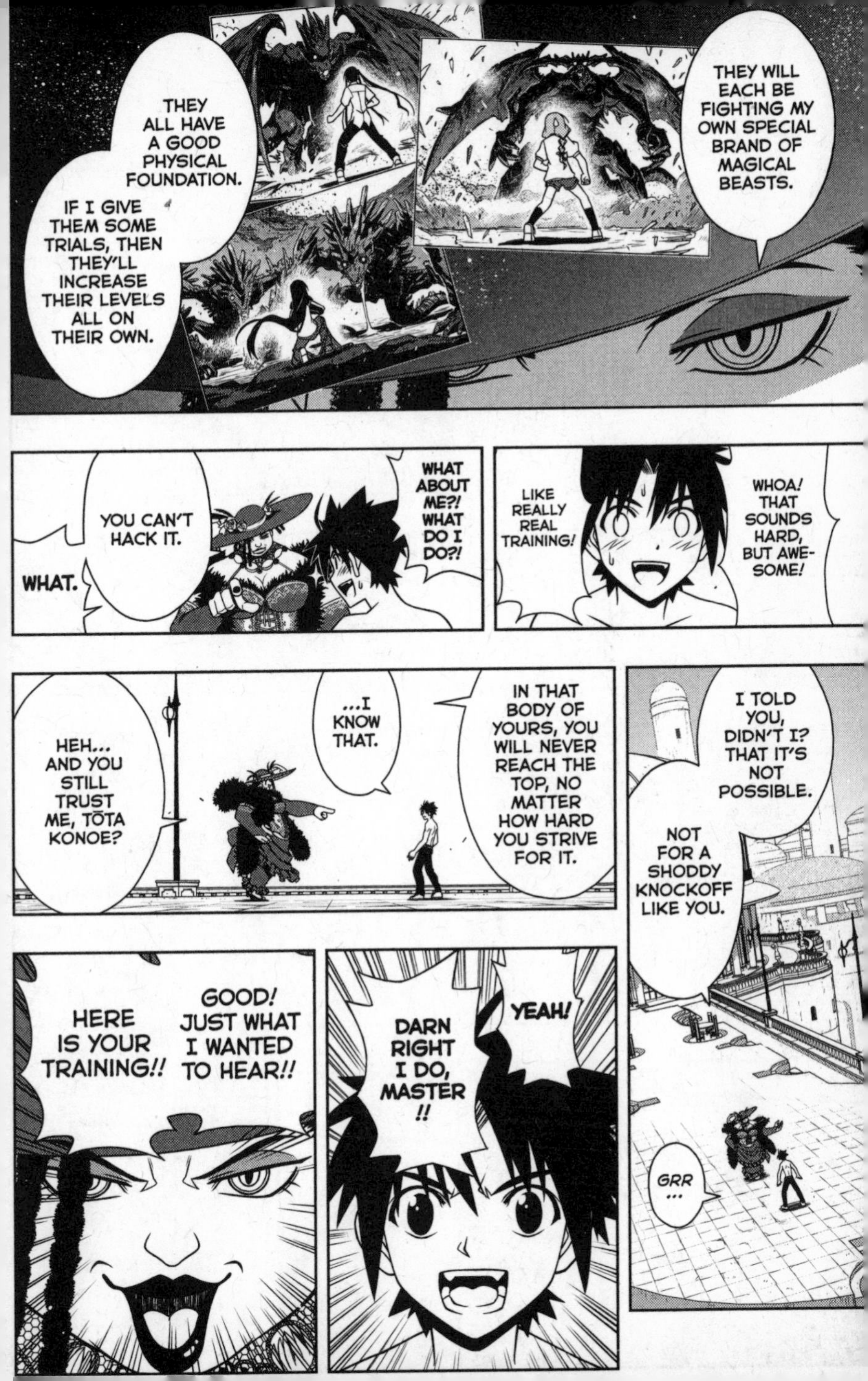
THEY WILL EACH BE FIGHTING MY OWN SPECIAL BRAND OF MAGICAL BEASTS.
THEY ALL HAVE A GOOD PHYSICAL FOUNDATION.
IF I GIVE THEM SOME TRIALS, THEN THEY'LL INCREASE THEIR LEVELS ALL ON THEIR OWN.
WHOA! THAT SOUNDS HARD, BUT AWE-SOME!
LIKE REALLY REAL TRAINING!
WHAT ABOUT ME?! WHAT DO I DO?!
YOU CAN'T HACK IT.
WHAT.
I TOLD YOU, DIDN'T I? THAT IT'S NOT POSSIBLE.
NOT FOR A SHODDY KNOCKOFF LIKE YOU.
GRR...
IN THAT BODY OF YOURS, YOU WILL NEVER REACH THE TOP, NO MATTER HOW HARD YOU STRIVE FOR IT.
...I KNOW THAT.
HEH... AND YOU STILL TRUST ME, TŌTA KONOE?
YEAH!
DARN RIGHT I DO, MASTER!!
GOOD! JUST WHAT I WANTED TO HEAR!!
HERE IS YOUR TRAINING!!

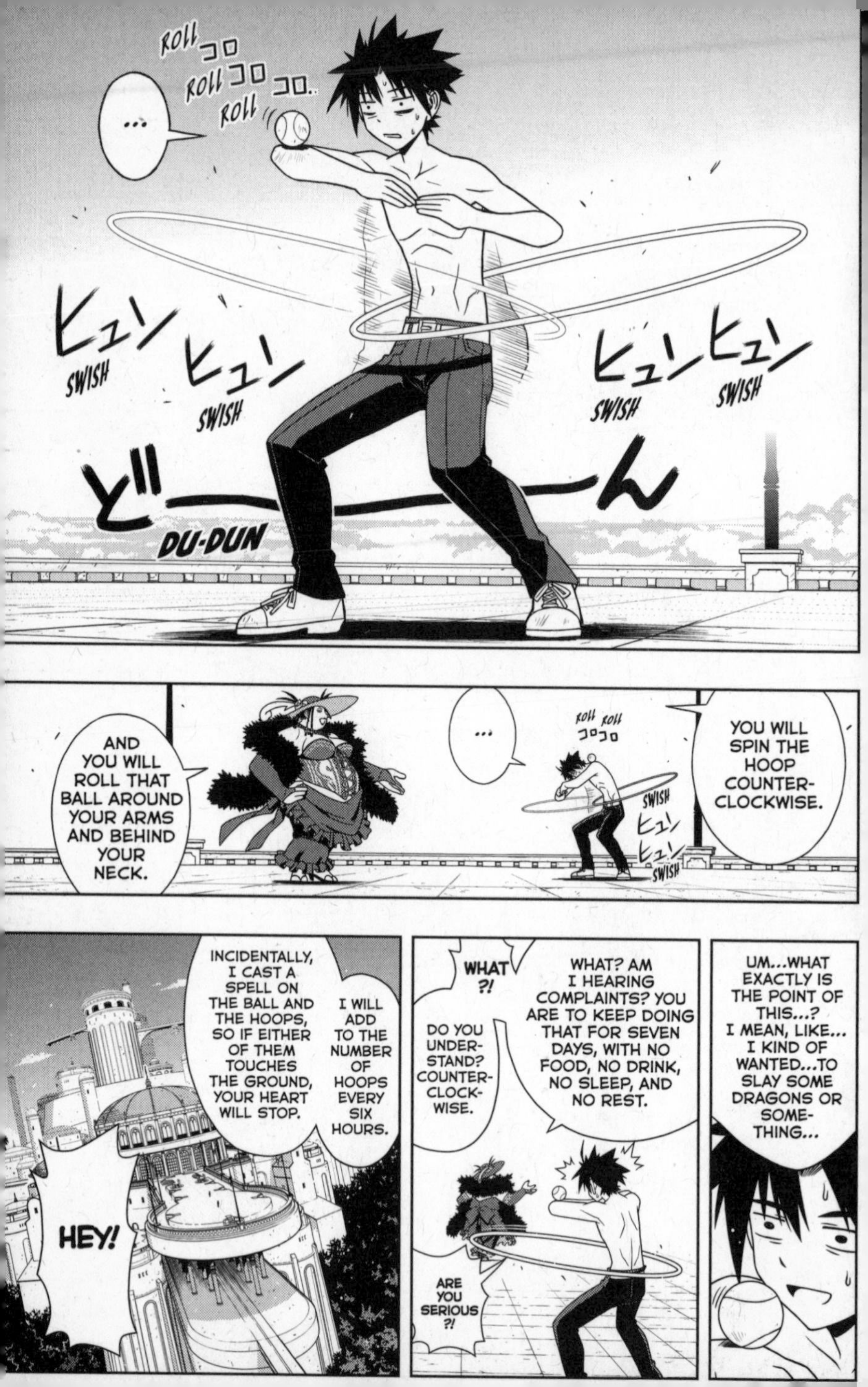
ROLL コロ
ROLL コロ
ROLL コロ..
...
ヒュン SWISH
ヒュン SWISH
ヒュン SWISH
ヒュン SWISH
どーーーん DU-DUN
YOU WILL SPIN THE HOOP COUNTER-CLOCKWISE.
ROLL ROLL コロコロ
ヒュン SWISH
ヒュン SWISH
...
AND YOU WILL ROLL THAT BALL AROUND YOUR ARMS AND BEHIND YOUR NECK.
UM...WHAT EXACTLY IS THE POINT OF THIS...? I MEAN, LIKE... I KIND OF WANTED...TO SLAY SOME DRAGONS OR SOME-THING...
WHAT? AM I HEARING COMPLAINTS? YOU ARE TO KEEP DOING THAT FOR SEVEN DAYS, WITH NO FOOD, NO DRINK, NO SLEEP, AND NO REST.
WHAT ?!
DO YOU UNDER-STAND? COUNTER-CLOCK-WISE.
ARE YOU SERIOUS ?!
I WILL ADD TO THE NUMBER OF HOOPS EVERY SIX HOURS.
INCIDENTALLY, I CAST A SPELL ON THE BALL AND THE HOOPS, SO IF EITHER OF THEM TOUCHES THE GROUND, YOUR HEART WILL STOP.
HEY!

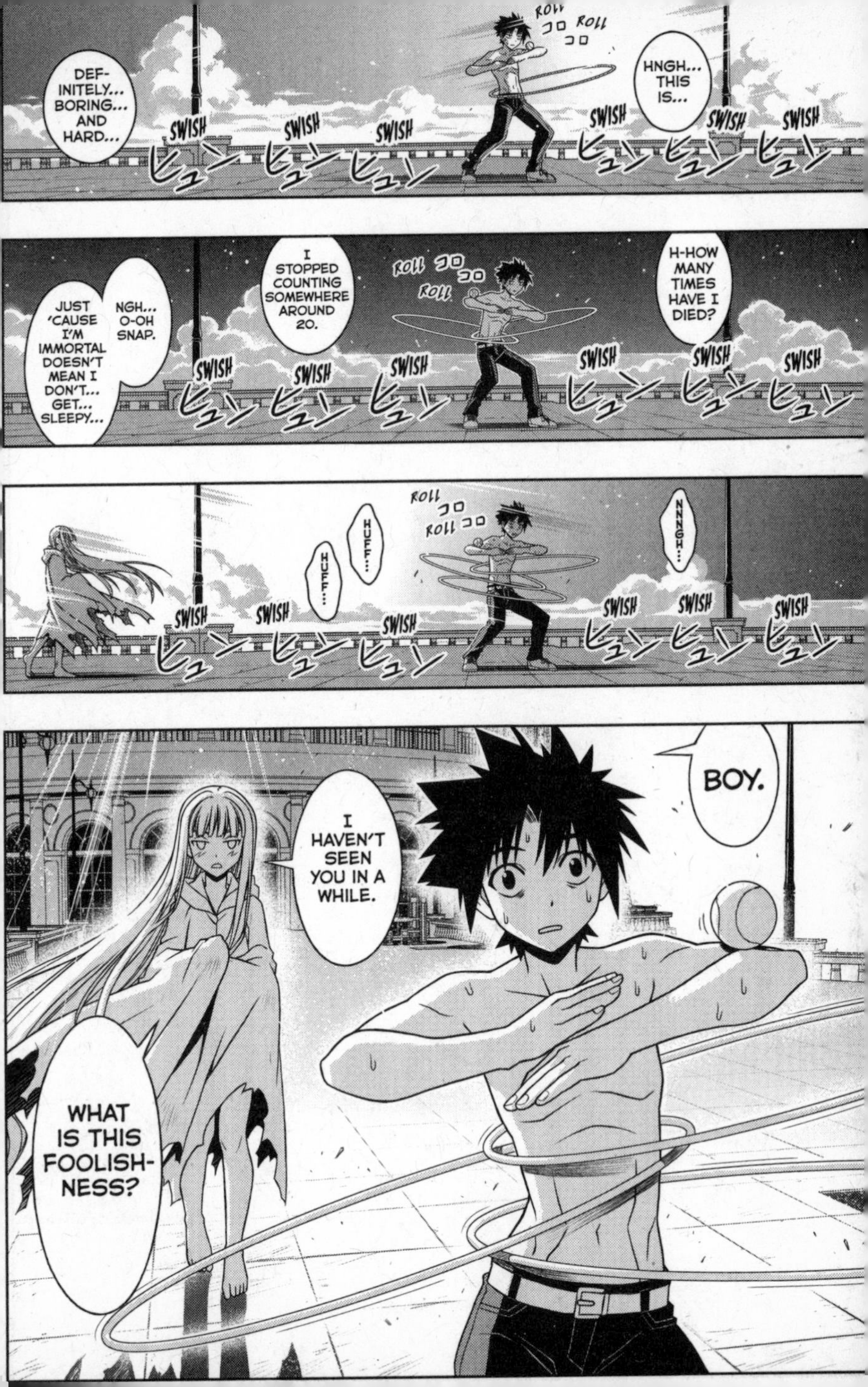
ROLL コロ ROLL コロ
HNGH... THIS IS...
SWISH ヒュン SWISH ヒュン SWISH ヒュン
SWISH ヒュン SWISH ヒュン SWISH ヒュン
DEF-INITELY... BORING... AND HARD...
H-HOW MANY TIMES HAVE I DIED?
ROLL コロ コロ ROLL
SWISH ヒュン SWISH ヒュン SWISH ヒュン
SWISH ヒュン SWISH ヒュン SWISH ヒュン
I STOPPED COUNTING SOMEWHERE AROUND 20.
NGH... O-OH SNAP.
JUST 'CAUSE I'M IMMORTAL DOESN'T MEAN I DON'T... GET... SLEEPY...
NNNGH...
ROLL コロ ROLL コロ
SWISH ヒュン SWISH ヒュン SWISH ヒュン
HUFF...
HUFF...
SWISH ヒュン SWISH ヒュン SWISH ヒュン
BOY.
I HAVEN'T SEEN YOU IN A WHILE.
WHAT IS THIS FOOLISH-NESS?

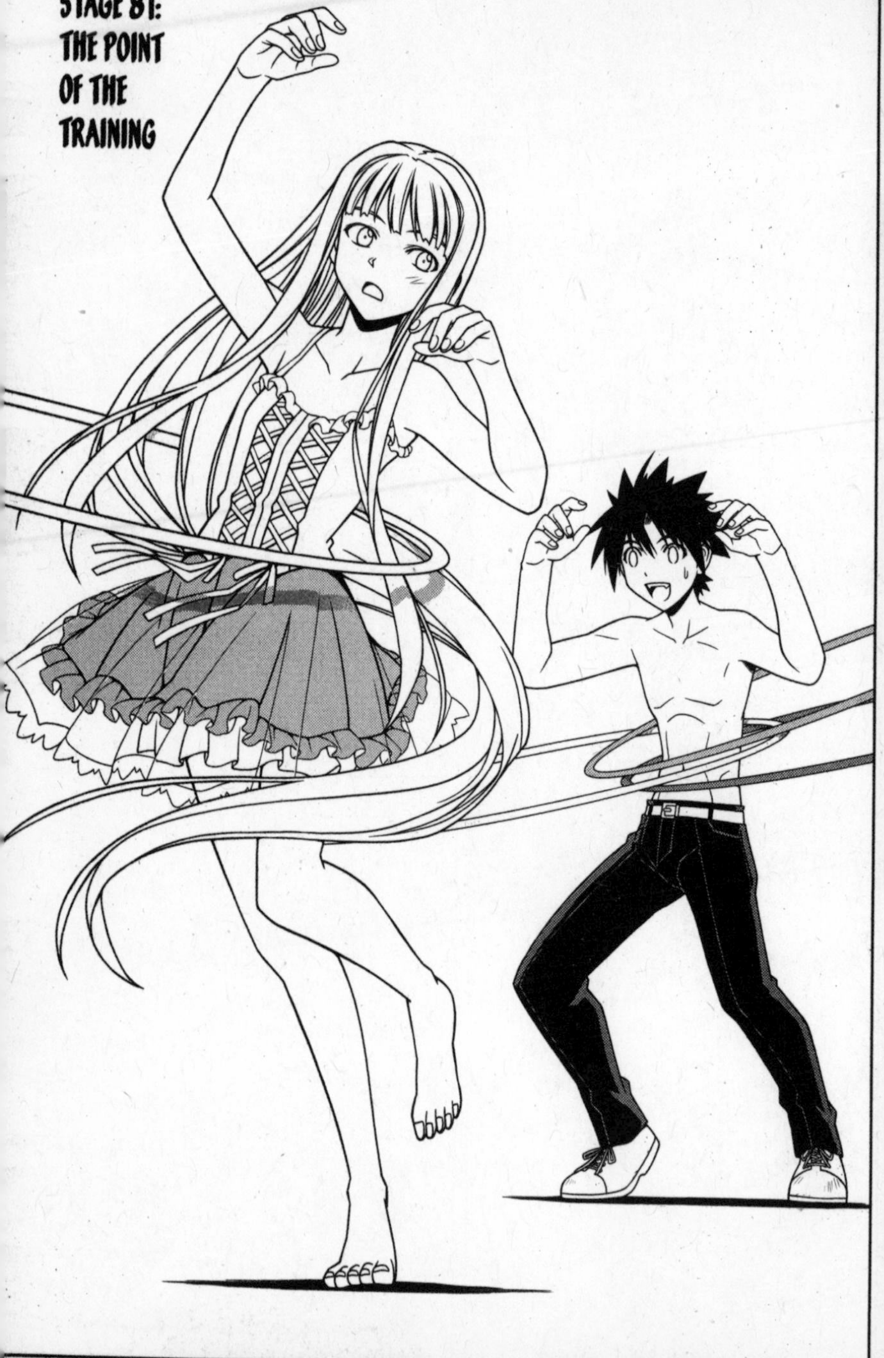
STAGE 81: THE POINT OF THE TRAINING

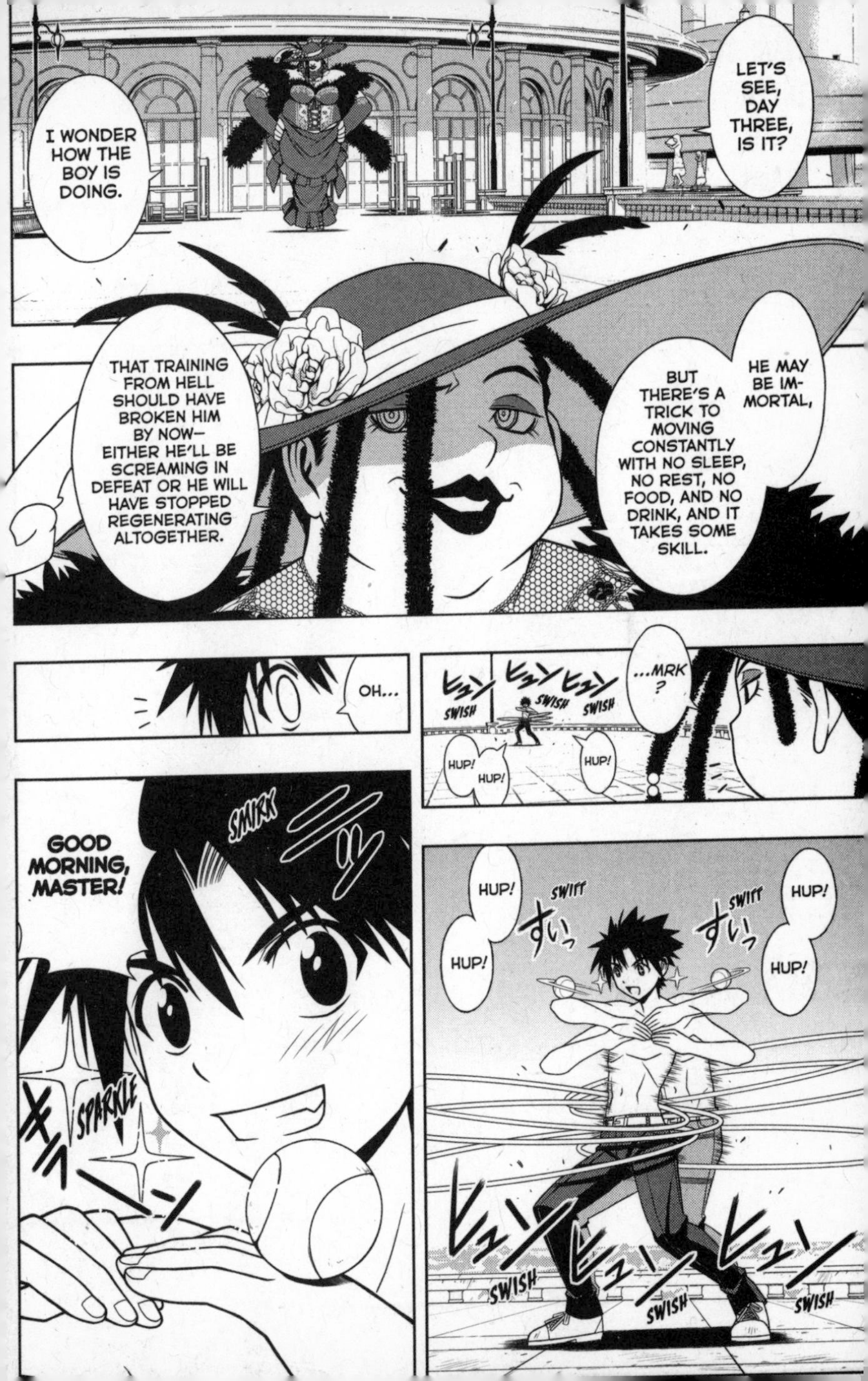
LET'S SEE, DAY THREE, IS IT?
I WONDER HOW THE BOY IS DOING.
HE MAY BE IM-MORTAL,
BUT THERE'S A TRICK TO MOVING CONSTANTLY WITH NO SLEEP, NO REST, NO FOOD, AND NO DRINK, AND IT TAKES SOME SKILL.
THAT TRAINING FROM HELL SHOULD HAVE BROKEN HIM BY NOW— EITHER HE'LL BE SCREAMING IN DEFEAT OR HE WILL HAVE STOPPED REGENERATING ALTOGETHER.
...MRK?
SWISH SWISH SWISH
HUP!
HUP!
HUP!
OH...
HUP!
SWIFT
HUP!
SWIFT
HUP!
HUP!
SWISH SWISH SWISH
SMIRK
GOOD MORNING, MASTER!
SPARKLE

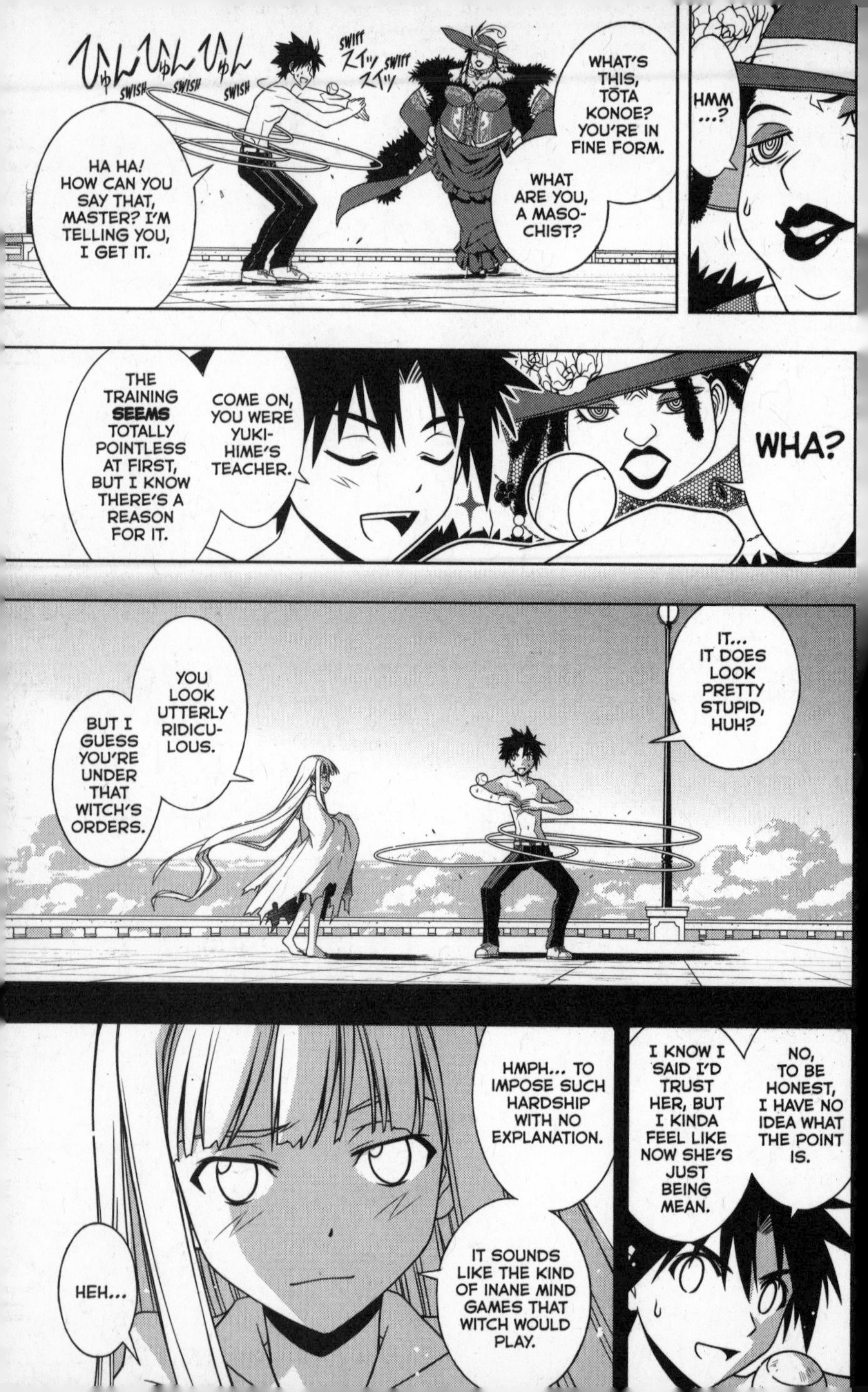
HMM ...?
WHAT'S THIS, TŌTA KONOE? YOU'RE IN FINE FORM.
WHAT ARE YOU, A MASOCHIST?
スイッ SWIFF スイッ SWIFF
ひゅん ひゅん ひゅん SWISH SWISH SWISH
HA HA! HOW CAN YOU SAY THAT, MASTER? I'M TELLING YOU, I GET IT.
WHA?
COME ON, YOU WERE YUKI-HIME'S TEACHER.
THE TRAINING **SEEMS** TOTALLY POINTLESS AT FIRST, BUT I KNOW THERE'S A REASON FOR IT.
IT... IT DOES LOOK PRETTY STUPID, HUH?
YOU LOOK UTTERLY RIDICULOUS.
BUT I GUESS YOU'RE UNDER THAT WITCH'S ORDERS.
NO, TO BE HONEST, I HAVE NO IDEA WHAT THE POINT IS.
I KNOW I SAID I'D TRUST HER, BUT I KINDA FEEL LIKE NOW SHE'S JUST BEING MEAN.
HMPH... TO IMPOSE SUCH HARDSHIP WITH NO EXPLANATION.
IT SOUNDS LIKE THE KIND OF INANE MIND GAMES THAT WITCH WOULD PLAY.
HEH...

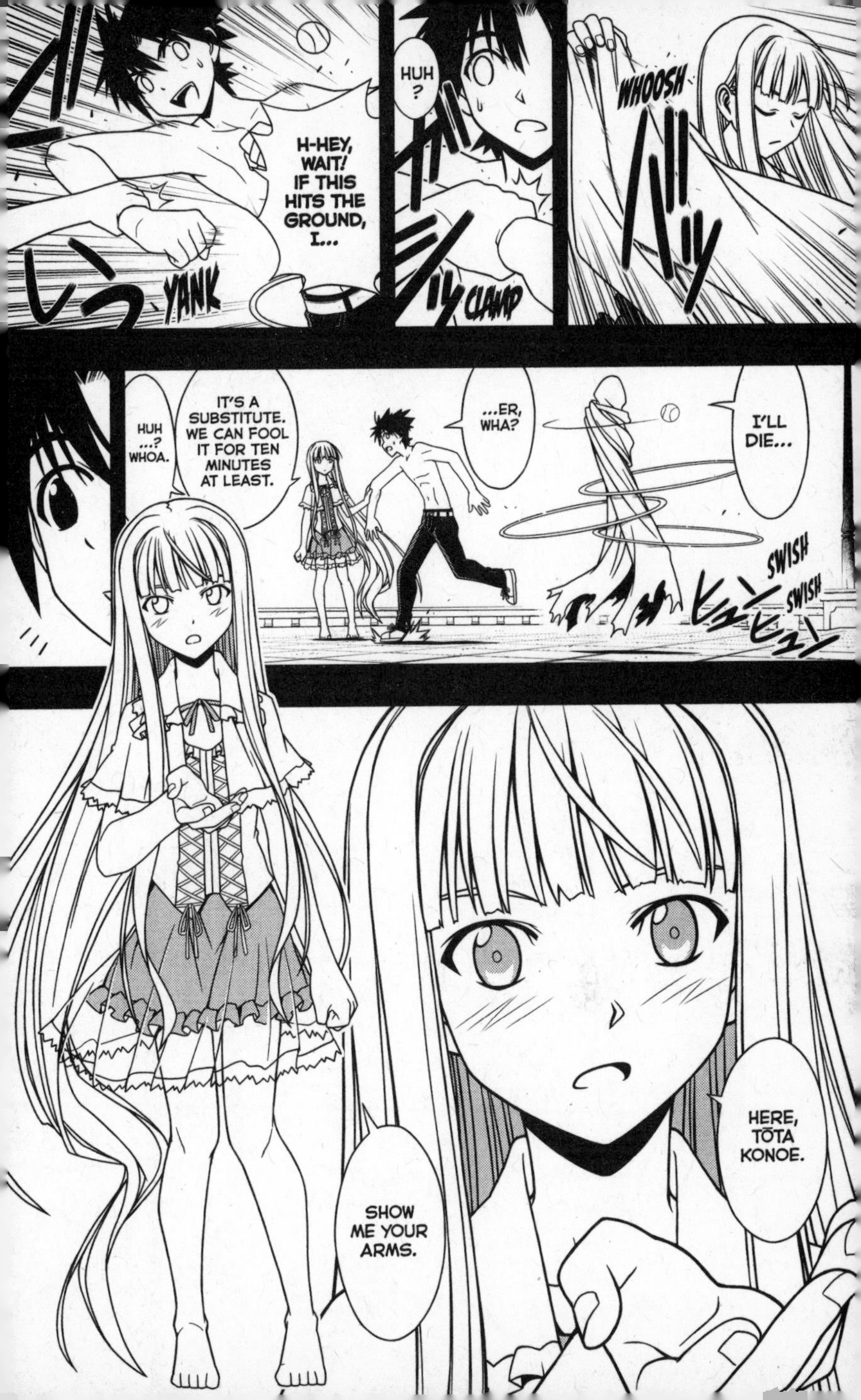
WHOOSH
HUH ?
CLAMP
H-HEY, WAIT! IF THIS HITS THE GROUND, I...
YANK
I'LL DIE...
SWISH
SWISH
...ER, WHA?
IT'S A SUBSTITUTE. WE CAN FOOL IT FOR TEN MINUTES AT LEAST.
HUH ...? WHOA.
HERE, TŌTA KONOE.
SHOW ME YOUR ARMS.

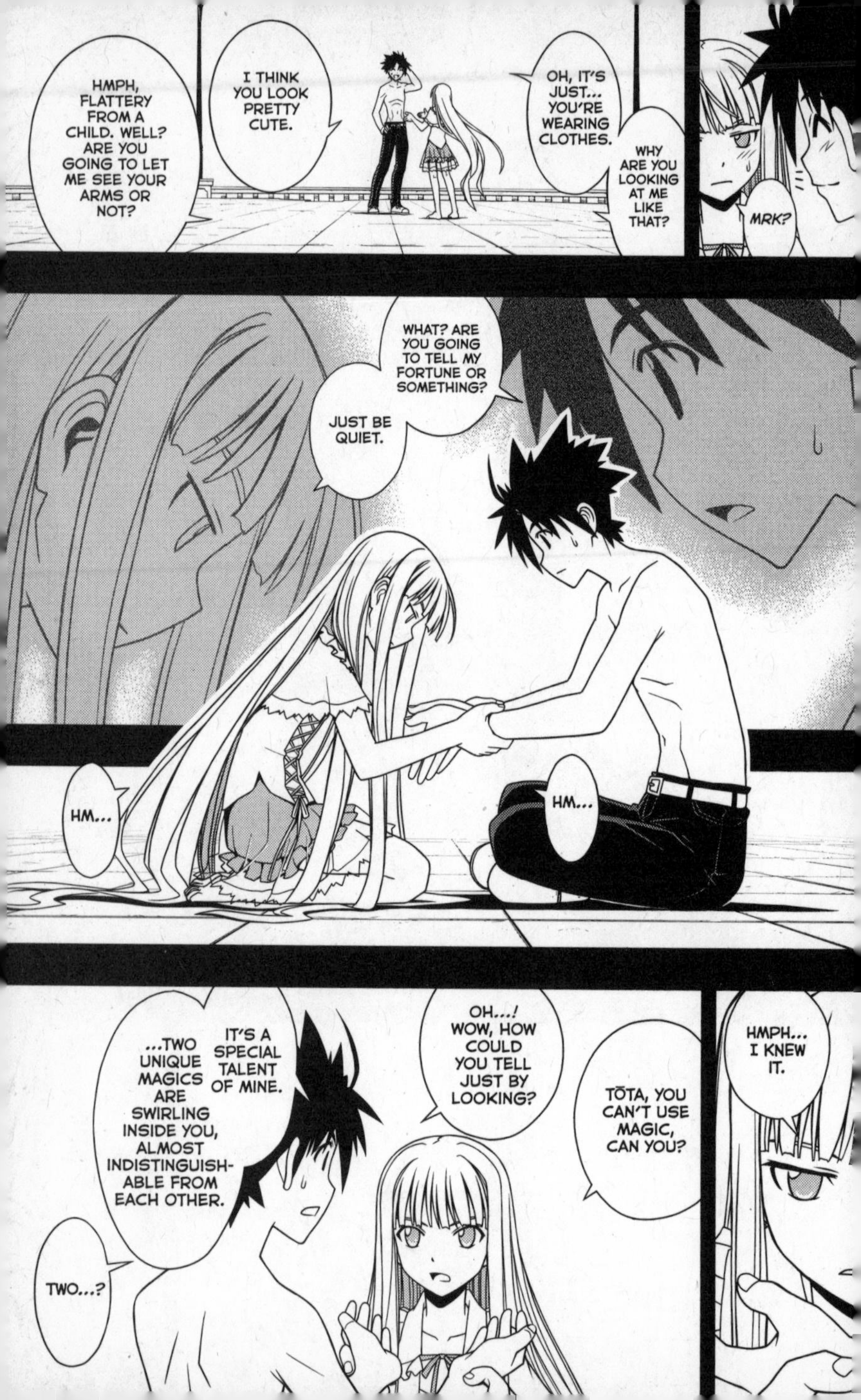
WHY ARE YOU LOOKING AT ME LIKE THAT?
MRK?
OH, IT'S JUST... YOU'RE WEARING CLOTHES.
I THINK YOU LOOK PRETTY CUTE.
HMPH, FLATTERY FROM A CHILD. WELL? ARE YOU GOING TO LET ME SEE YOUR ARMS OR NOT?
WHAT? ARE YOU GOING TO TELL MY FORTUNE OR SOMETHING?
JUST BE QUIET.
HM...
HM...
HMPH... I KNEW IT.
TŌTA, YOU CAN'T USE MAGIC, CAN YOU?
OH...! WOW, HOW COULD YOU TELL JUST BY LOOKING?
IT'S A SPECIAL TALENT OF MINE.
...TWO UNIQUE MAGICS ARE SWIRLING INSIDE YOU, ALMOST INDISTINGUISHABLE FROM EACH OTHER.
TWO...?

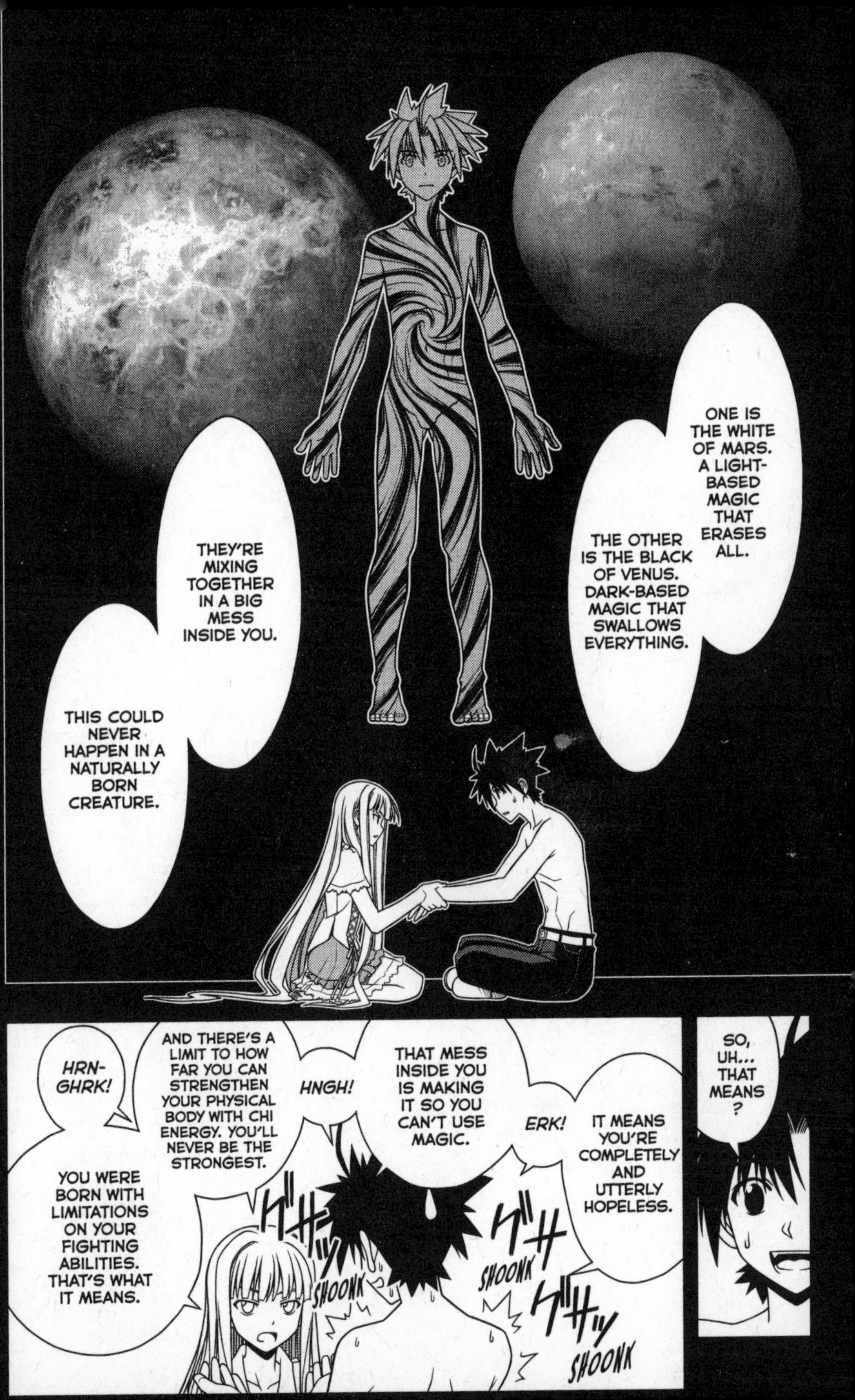
ONE IS THE WHITE OF MARS. A LIGHT-BASED MAGIC THAT ERASES ALL.
THE OTHER IS THE BLACK OF VENUS. DARK-BASED MAGIC THAT SWALLOWS EVERYTHING.
THEY'RE MIXING TOGETHER IN A BIG MESS INSIDE YOU.
THIS COULD NEVER HAPPEN IN A NATURALLY BORN CREATURE.
SO, UH... THAT MEANS?
IT MEANS YOU'RE COMPLETELY AND UTTERLY HOPELESS.
SHOONK
SHOONK
ERK!
THAT MESS INSIDE YOU IS MAKING IT SO YOU CAN'T USE MAGIC.
HNGH!
AND THERE'S A LIMIT TO HOW FAR YOU CAN STRENGTHEN YOUR PHYSICAL BODY WITH CHI ENERGY. YOU'LL NEVER BE THE STRONGEST.
HRN-GHRK!
SHOONK
YOU WERE BORN WITH LIMITATIONS ON YOUR FIGHTING ABILITIES. THAT'S WHAT IT MEANS.

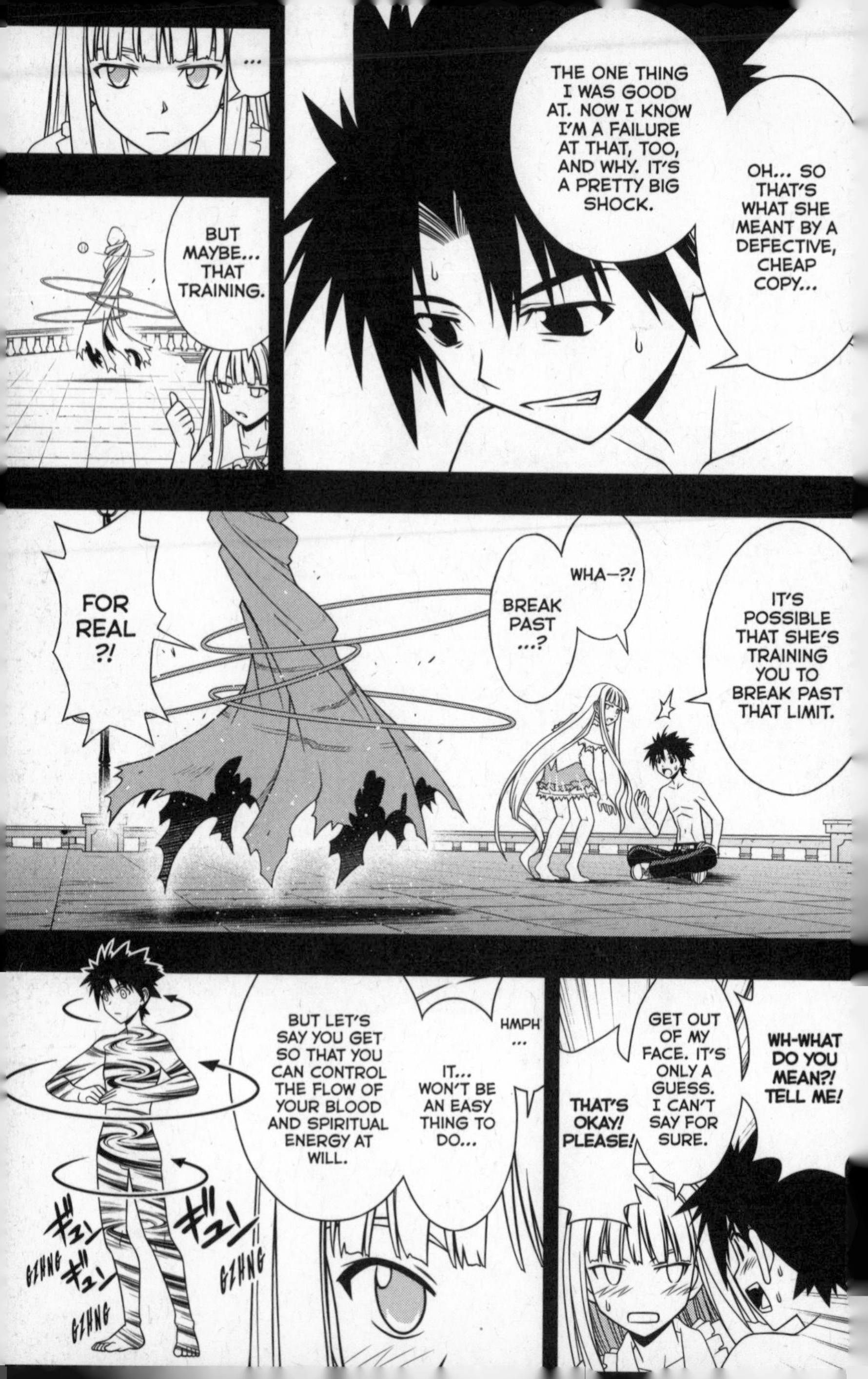
OH... SO THAT'S WHAT SHE MEANT BY A DEFECTIVE, CHEAP COPY...
THE ONE THING I WAS GOOD AT. NOW I KNOW I'M A FAILURE AT THAT, TOO, AND WHY. IT'S A PRETTY BIG SHOCK.
...
BUT MAYBE... THAT TRAINING.
IT'S POSSIBLE THAT SHE'S TRAINING YOU TO BREAK PAST THAT LIMIT.
WHA-?!
BREAK PAST ...?
FOR REAL ?!
WH-WHAT DO YOU MEAN?! TELL ME!
GET OUT OF MY FACE. IT'S ONLY A GUESS. I CAN'T SAY FOR SURE.
THAT'S OKAY! PLEASE!
HMPH ...
IT... WON'T BE AN EASY THING TO DO...
BUT LET'S SAY YOU GET SO THAT YOU CAN CONTROL THE FLOW OF YOUR BLOOD AND SPIRITUAL ENERGY AT WILL.
ギュン
GZHNG
ギュン
GZHNG
ギュン
GZHNG

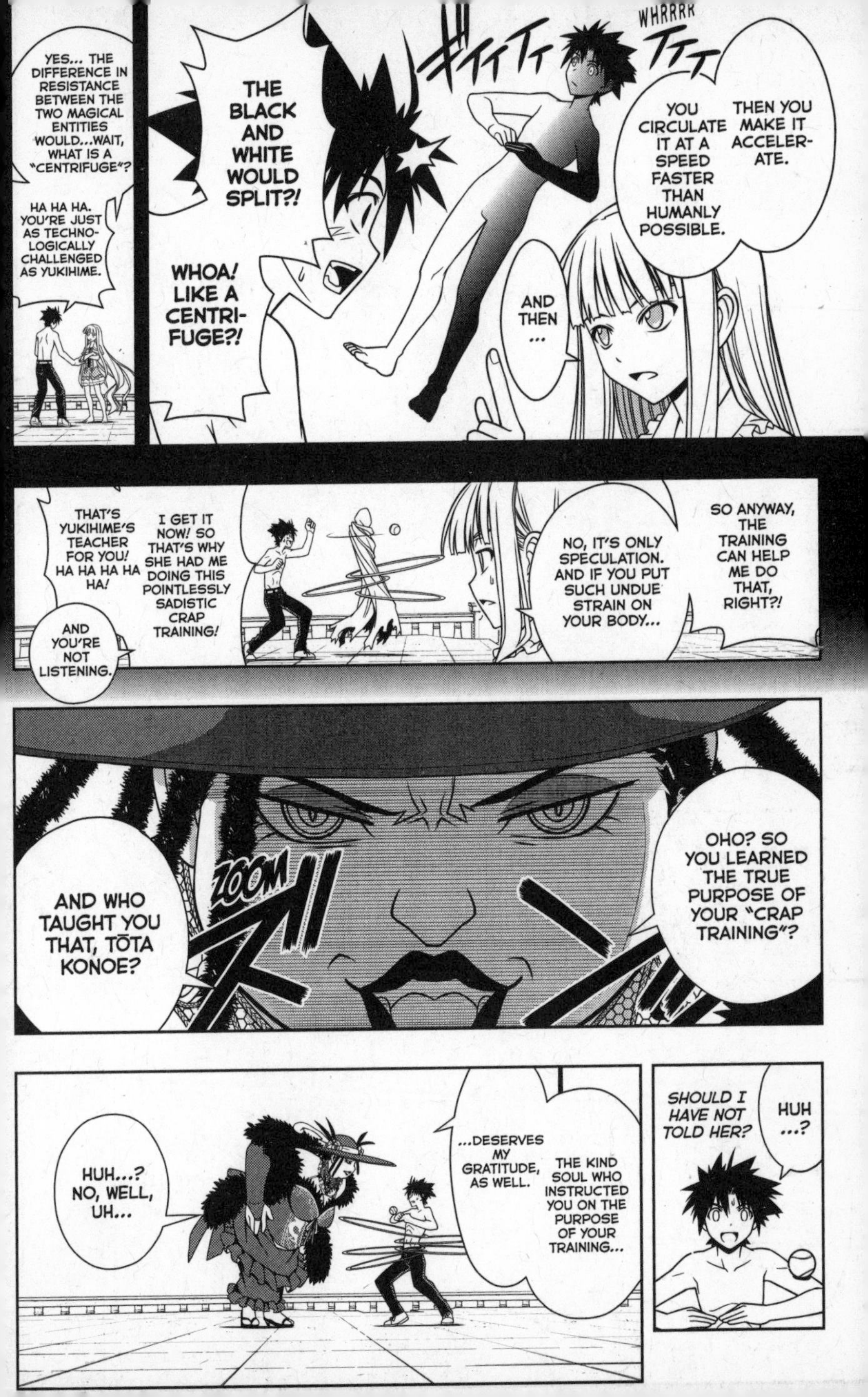
WHRRRR
THEN YOU MAKE IT ACCELERATE.
YOU CIRCULATE IT AT A SPEED FASTER THAN HUMANLY POSSIBLE.
AND THEN ...
THE BLACK AND WHITE WOULD SPLIT?!
WHOA! LIKE A CENTRIFUGE?!
YES... THE DIFFERENCE IN RESISTANCE BETWEEN THE TWO MAGICAL ENTITIES WOULD...WAIT, WHAT IS A "CENTRIFUGE"?
HA HA HA. YOU'RE JUST AS TECHNOLOGICALLY CHALLENGED AS YUKIHIME.
SO ANYWAY, THE TRAINING CAN HELP ME DO THAT, RIGHT?!
NO, IT'S ONLY SPECULATION. AND IF YOU PUT SUCH UNDUE STRAIN ON YOUR BODY...
I GET IT NOW! SO THAT'S WHY SHE HAD ME DOING THIS POINTLESSLY SADISTIC CRAP TRAINING!
THAT'S YUKIHIME'S TEACHER FOR YOU! HA HA HA HA HA!
AND YOU'RE NOT LISTENING.
OHO? SO YOU LEARNED THE TRUE PURPOSE OF YOUR "CRAP TRAINING"?
ZOOM
AND WHO TAUGHT YOU THAT, TŌTA KONOE?
HUH ...?
SHOULD I HAVE NOT TOLD HER?
THE KIND SOUL WHO INSTRUCTED YOU ON THE PURPOSE OF YOUR TRAINING...
...DESERVES MY GRATITUDE, AS WELL.
HUH...? NO, WELL, UH...

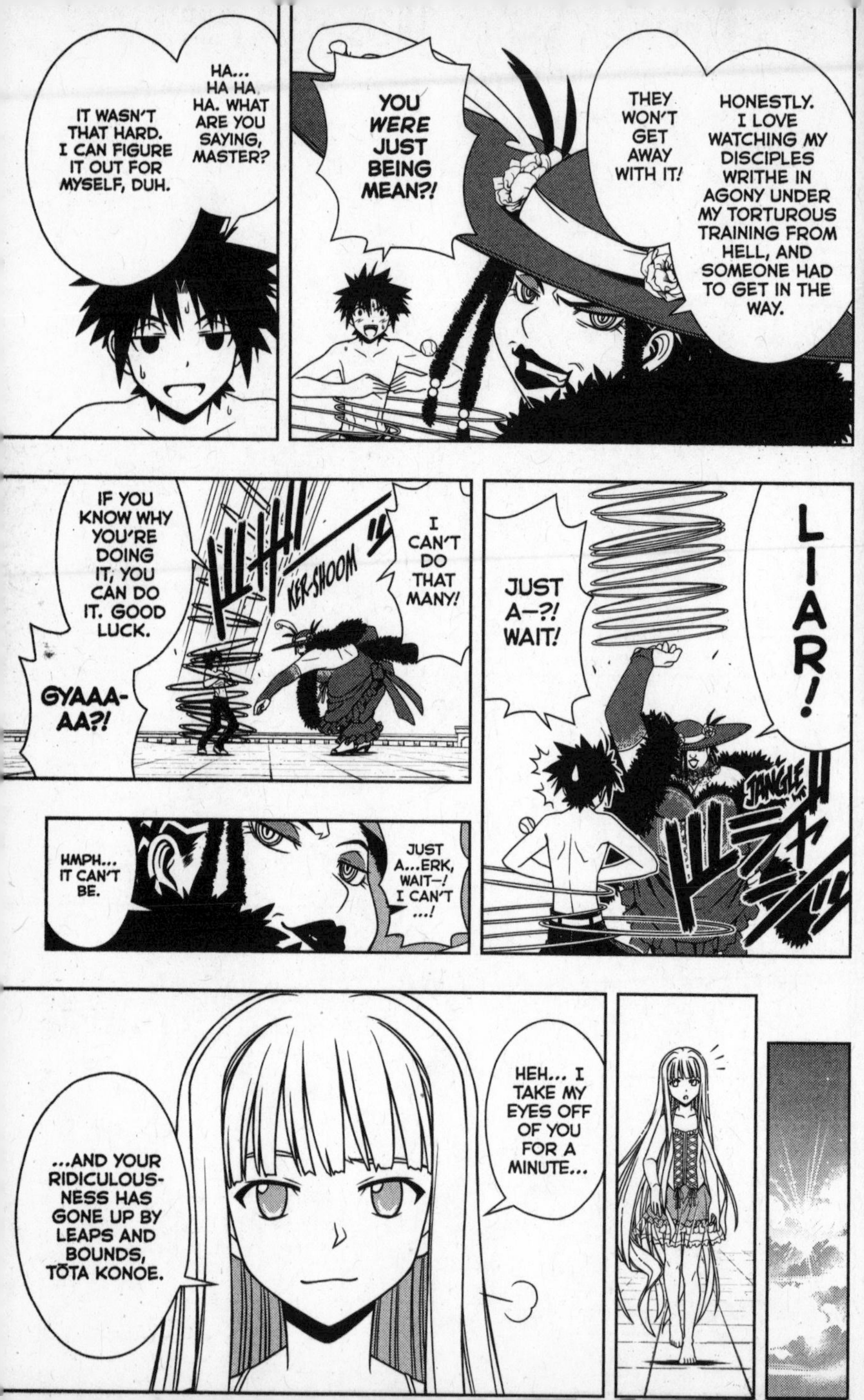
HONESTLY. I LOVE WATCHING MY DISCIPLES WRITHE IN AGONY UNDER MY TORTUROUS TRAINING FROM HELL, AND SOMEONE HAD TO GET IN THE WAY.
THEY WON'T GET AWAY WITH IT!
YOU *WERE* JUST BEING MEAN?!
HA... HA HA HA. WHAT ARE YOU SAYING, MASTER?
IT WASN'T THAT HARD. I CAN FIGURE IT OUT FOR MYSELF, DUH.
LIAR!
JUST A—?! WAIT!
JANGLE
I CAN'T DO THAT MANY!
KER-SHOOM
IF YOU KNOW WHY YOU'RE DOING IT, YOU CAN DO IT. GOOD LUCK.
GYAAA-AA?!
JUST A...ERK, WAIT—! I CAN'T ...!
HMPH... IT CAN'T BE.
HEH... I TAKE MY EYES OFF OF YOU FOR A MINUTE...
...AND YOUR RIDICULOUSNESS HAS GONE UP BY LEAPS AND BOUNDS, TŌTA KONOE.

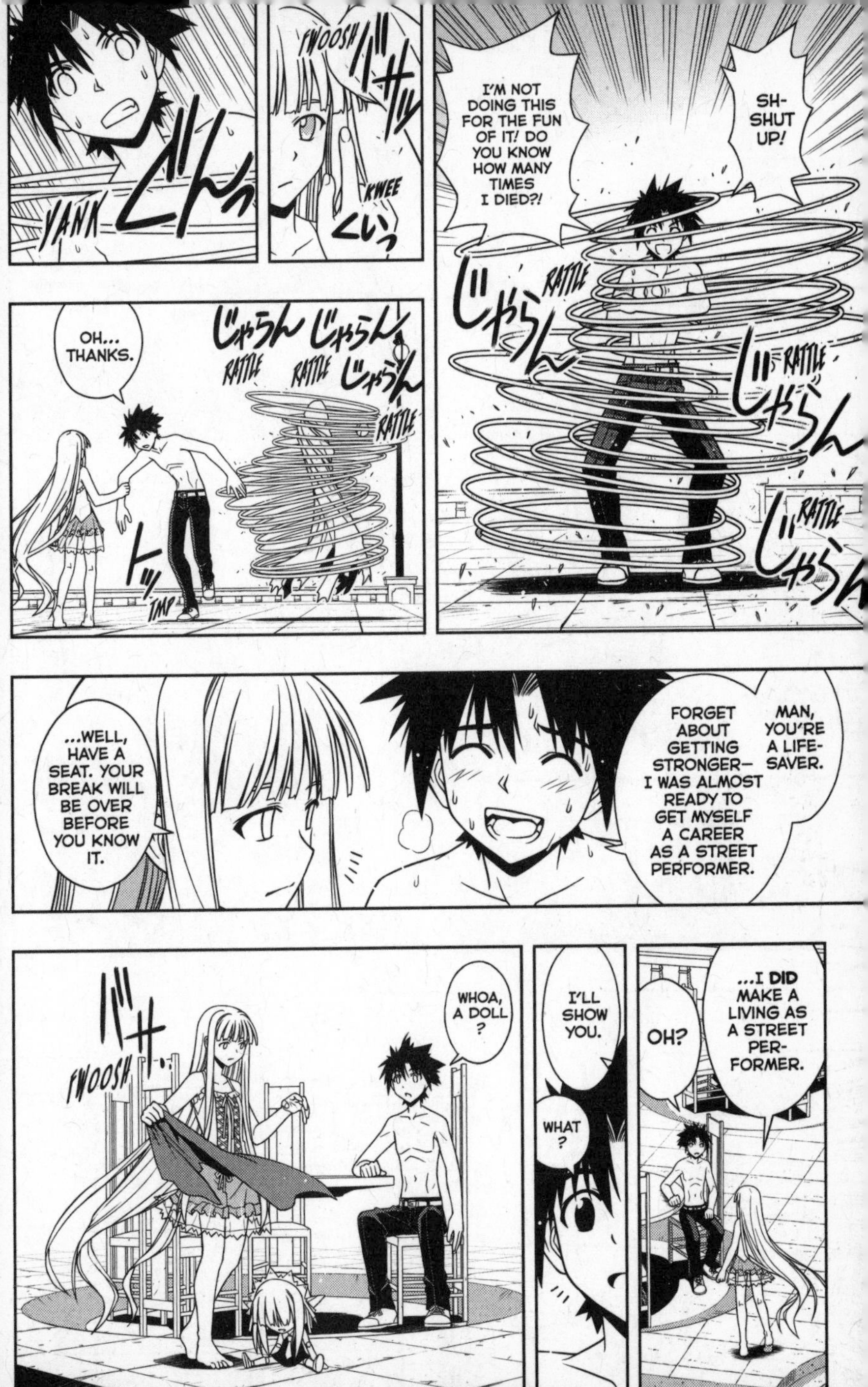
SH- SHUT UP!
I'M NOT DOING THIS FOR THE FUN OF IT! DO YOU KNOW HOW MANY TIMES I DIED?!
RATTLE
RATTLE
RATTLE
FWOOSH
KWEE
YANK
OH... THANKS.
RATTLE
RATTLE
RATTLE
TMP
MAN, YOU'RE A LIFE-SAVER.
FORGET ABOUT GETTING STRONGER— I WAS ALMOST READY TO GET MYSELF A CAREER AS A STREET PERFORMER.
...WELL, HAVE A SEAT. YOUR BREAK WILL BE OVER BEFORE YOU KNOW IT.
...I DID MAKE A LIVING AS A STREET PER-FORMER.
OH?
I'LL SHOW YOU.
WHAT?
WHOA, A DOLL?
FWOOSH

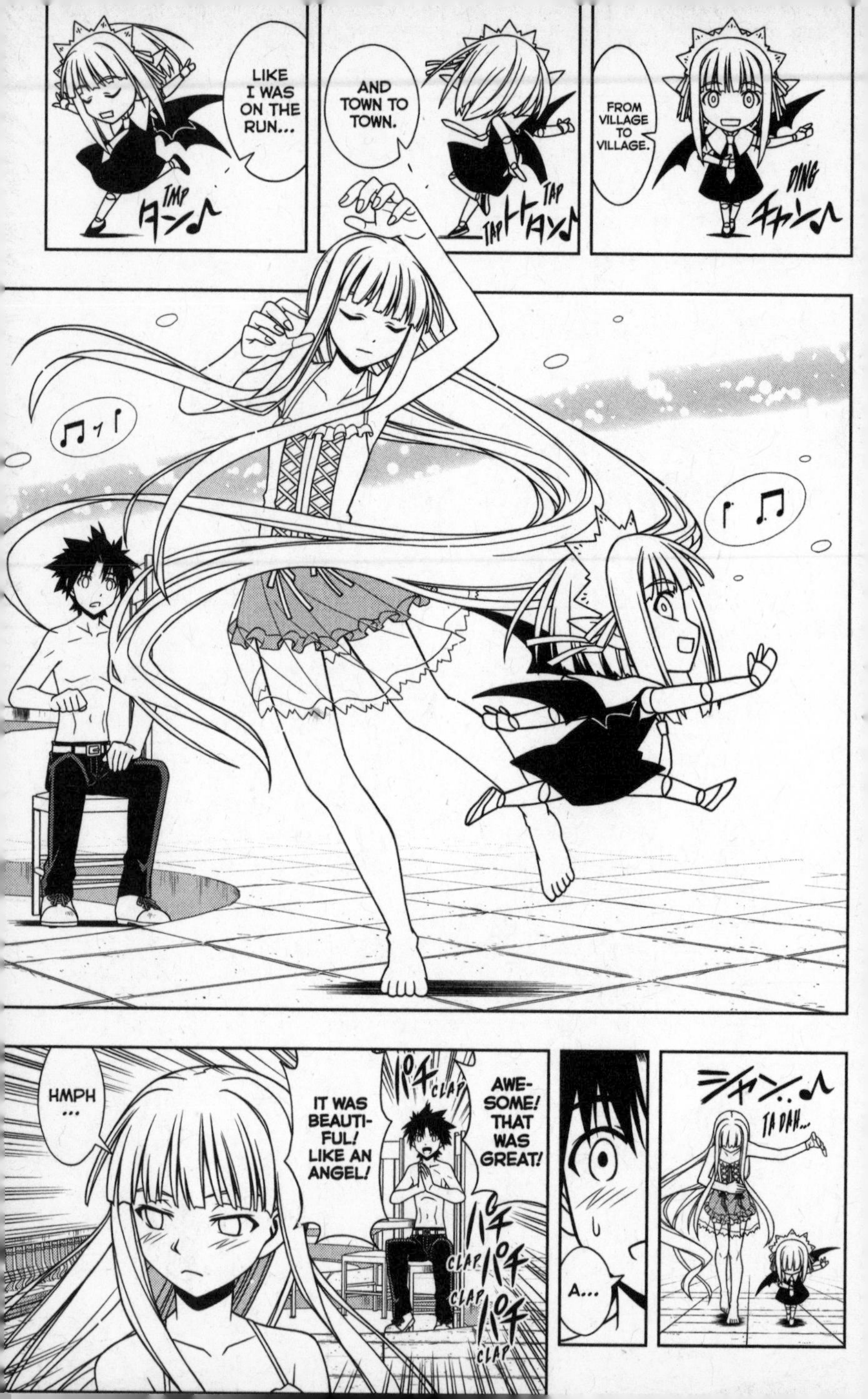
FROM VILLAGE TO VILLAGE.
DING
チャン♪
AND TOWN TO TOWN.
TAP TAP
トトタン♪
LIKE I WAS ON THE RUN...
TMP
タン♪
シャン..♪
TA DAH...
A...
AWE-SOME! THAT WAS GREAT!
パチ
CLAP
IT WAS BEAUTI-FUL! LIKE AN ANGEL!
パチパチパチ
CLAP CLAP CLAP
HMPH...

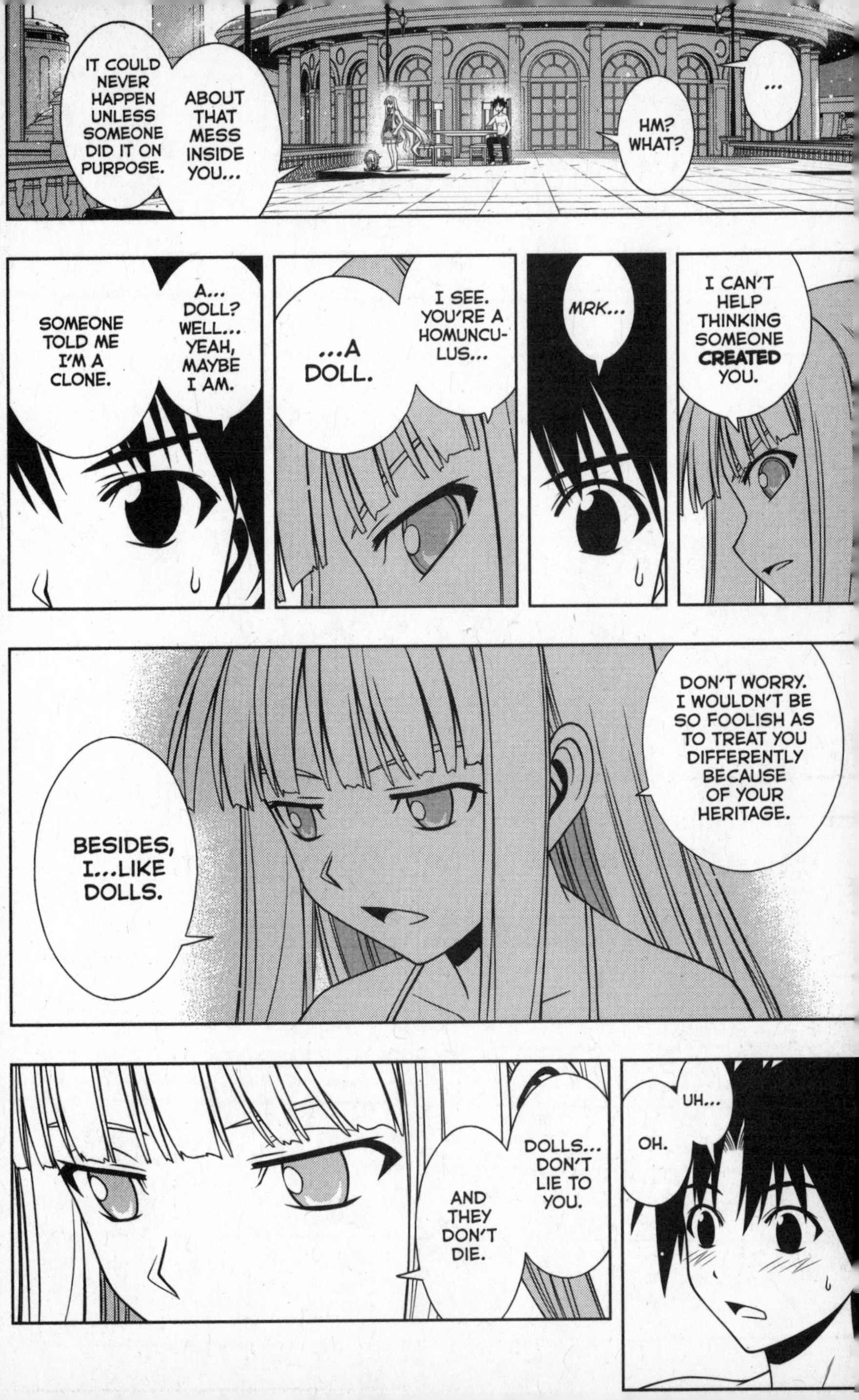
...
HM? WHAT?
ABOUT THAT MESS INSIDE YOU...
IT COULD NEVER HAPPEN UNLESS SOMEONE DID IT ON PURPOSE.
I CAN'T HELP THINKING SOMEONE **CREATED** YOU.
MRK...
I SEE. YOU'RE A HOMUNCU-LUS...
...A DOLL.
A... DOLL? WELL... YEAH, MAYBE I AM.
SOMEONE TOLD ME I'M A CLONE.
DON'T WORRY. I WOULDN'T BE SO FOOLISH AS TO TREAT YOU DIFFERENTLY BECAUSE OF YOUR HERITAGE.
BESIDES, I...LIKE DOLLS.
UH...
OH.
DOLLS... DON'T LIE TO YOU.
AND THEY DON'T DIE.

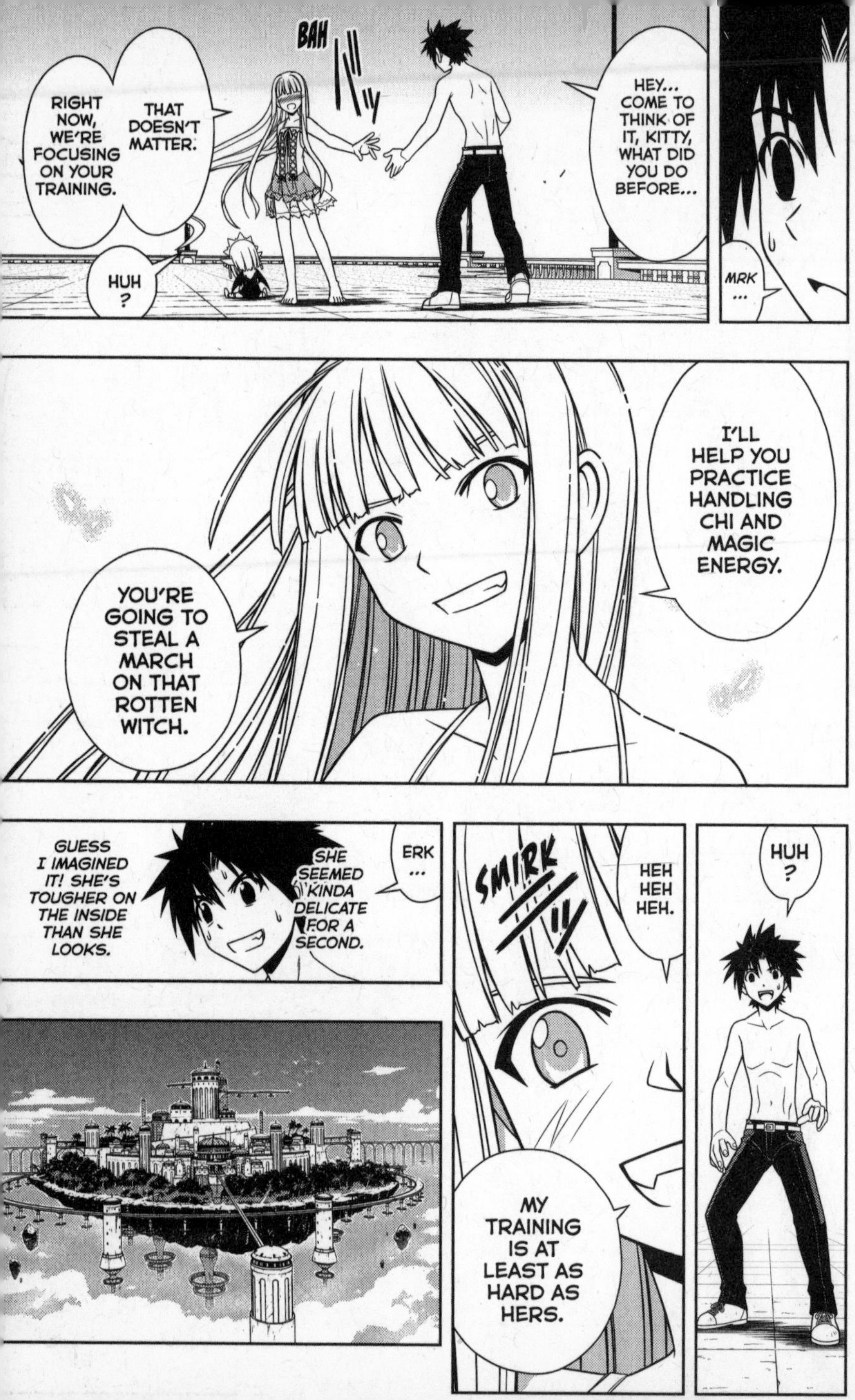
MRK ...
HEY... COME TO THINK OF IT, KITTY, WHAT DID YOU DO BEFORE...
BAH
THAT DOESN'T MATTER.
RIGHT NOW, WE'RE FOCUSING ON YOUR TRAINING.
HUH ?
I'LL HELP YOU PRACTICE HANDLING CHI AND MAGIC ENERGY.
YOU'RE GOING TO STEAL A MARCH ON THAT ROTTEN WITCH.
HUH ?
HEH HEH HEH.
SMIRK
MY TRAINING IS AT LEAST AS HARD AS HERS.
ERK ...
SHE SEEMED KINDA DELICATE FOR A SECOND.
GUESS I IMAGINED IT! SHE'S TOUGHER ON THE INSIDE THAN SHE LOOKS.

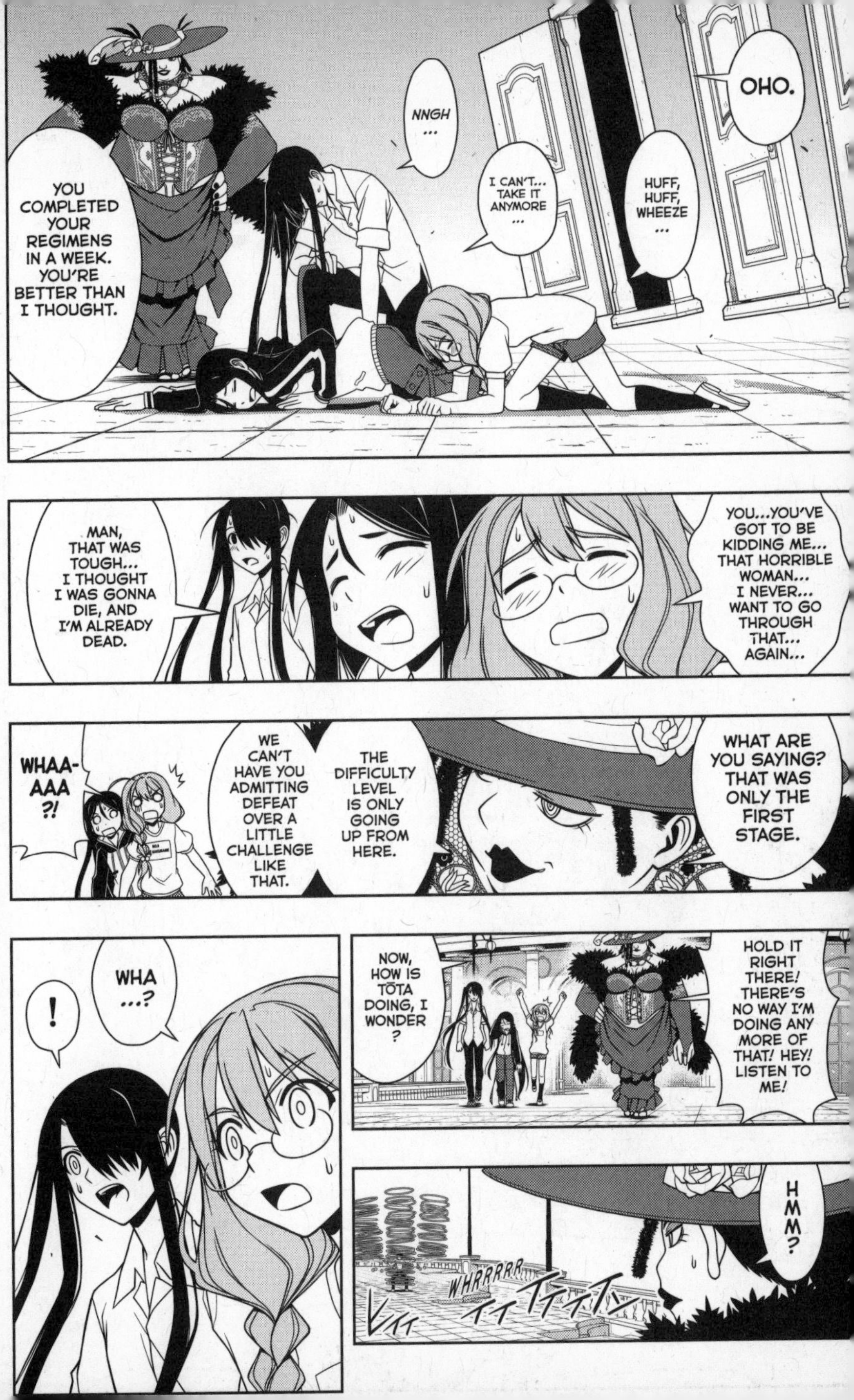
OHO.
HUFF, HUFF, WHEEZE ...
I CAN'T... TAKE IT ANYMORE ...
NNGH ...
YOU COMPLETED YOUR REGIMENS IN A WEEK. YOU'RE BETTER THAN I THOUGHT.
YOU...YOU'VE GOT TO BE KIDDING ME... THAT HORRIBLE WOMAN... I NEVER... WANT TO GO THROUGH THAT... AGAIN...
MAN, THAT WAS TOUGH... I THOUGHT I WAS GONNA DIE, AND I'M ALREADY DEAD.
WHAT ARE YOU SAYING? THAT WAS ONLY THE FIRST STAGE.
THE DIFFICULTY LEVEL IS ONLY GOING UP FROM HERE.
WE CAN'T HAVE YOU ADMITTING DEFEAT OVER A LITTLE CHALLENGE LIKE THAT.
WHAA-AAA ?!
HOLD IT RIGHT THERE! THERE'S NO WAY I'M DOING ANY MORE OF THAT! HEY! LISTEN TO ME!
NOW, HOW IS TŌTA DOING, I WONDER ?
HMM?
WHRRRRR
WHA ...?
!

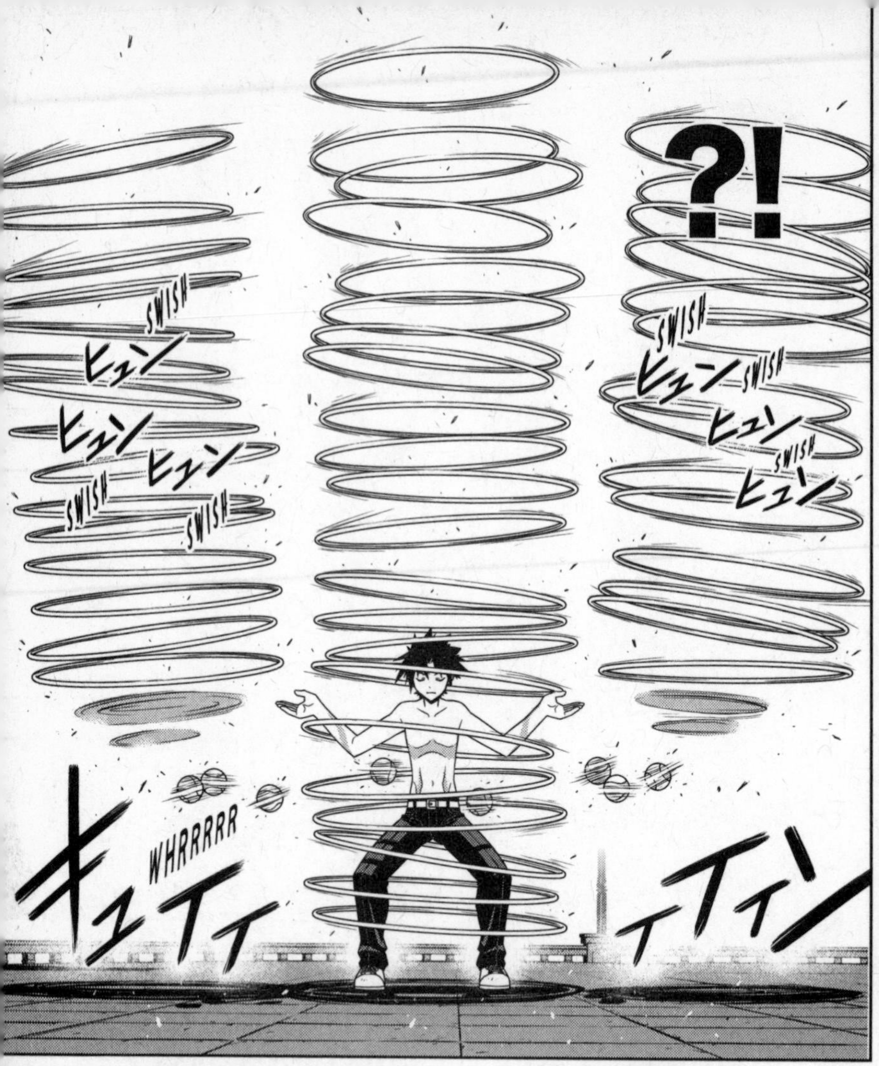
?!
SWISH
ヒュン
SWISH
ヒュン
SWISH
ヒュン
SWISH
ヒュン
ヒュン
SWISH
ヒュン
SWISH
キュイイ
WHRRRRR
イイイン
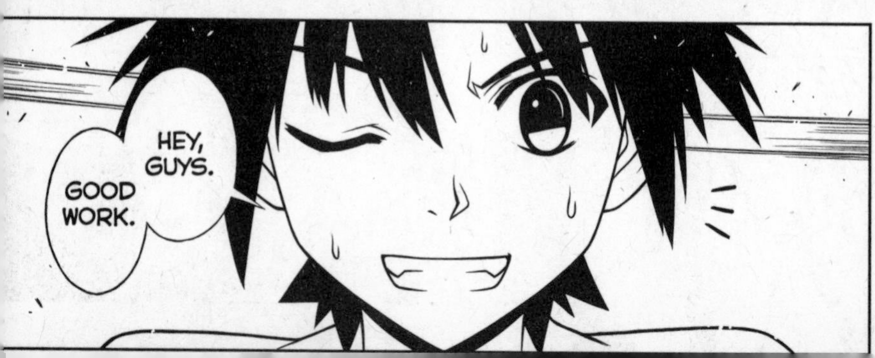
HEY, GUYS. GOOD WORK.

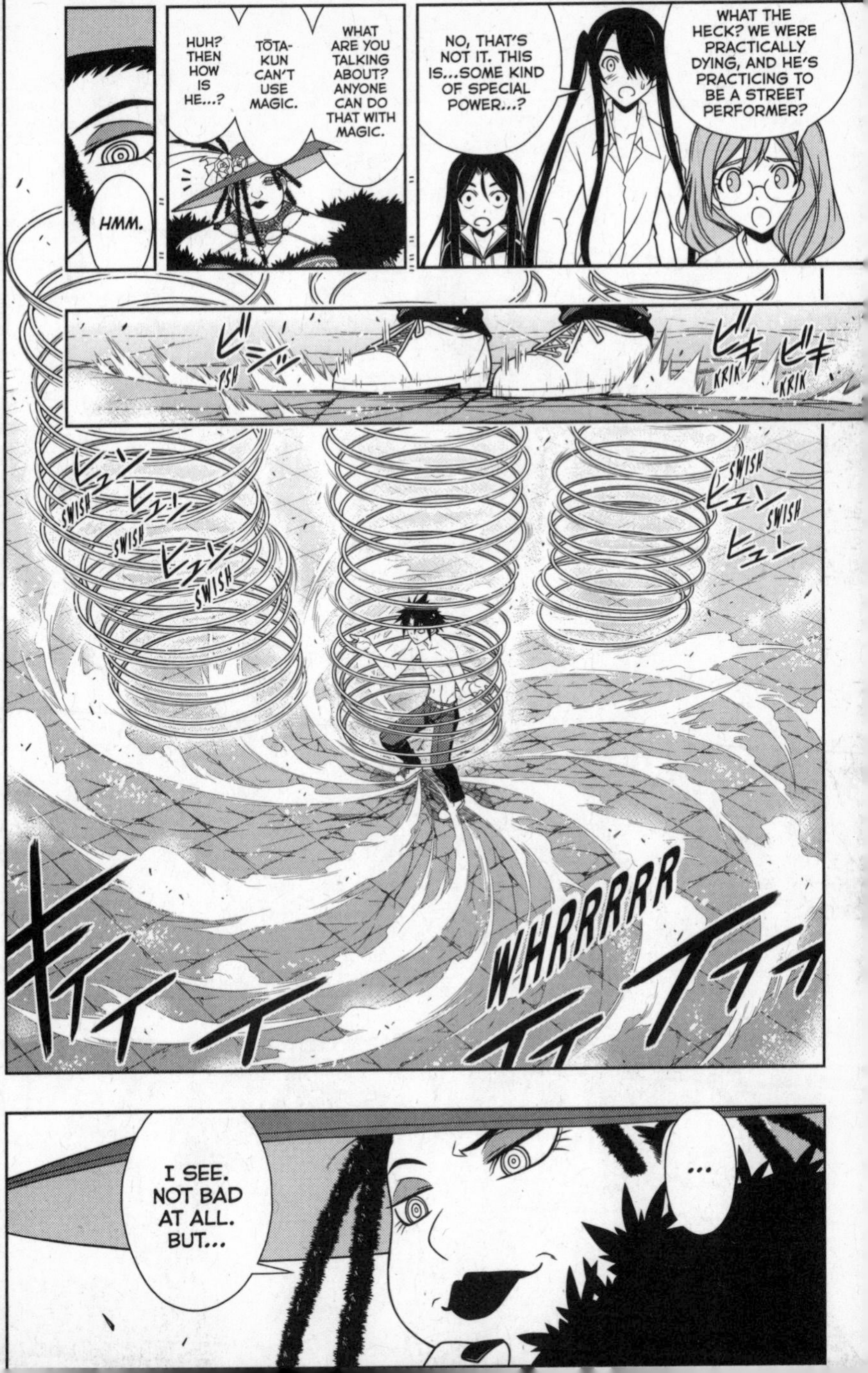

WHAT THE HECK? WE WERE PRACTICALLY DYING, AND HE'S PRACTICING TO BE A STREET PERFORMER?
NO, THAT'S NOT IT. THIS IS...SOME KIND OF SPECIAL POWER...?
WHAT ARE YOU TALKING ABOUT? ANYONE CAN DO THAT WITH MAGIC.
TŌTA-KUN CAN'T USE MAGIC.
HUH? THEN HOW IS HE...?
HMM.
ビキ KRIK
ビキ KRIK
ビシッ PSH
SWISH
SWISH
SWISH
SWISH
SWISH
WHRRRRRR
...
I SEE. NOT BAD AT ALL. BUT...

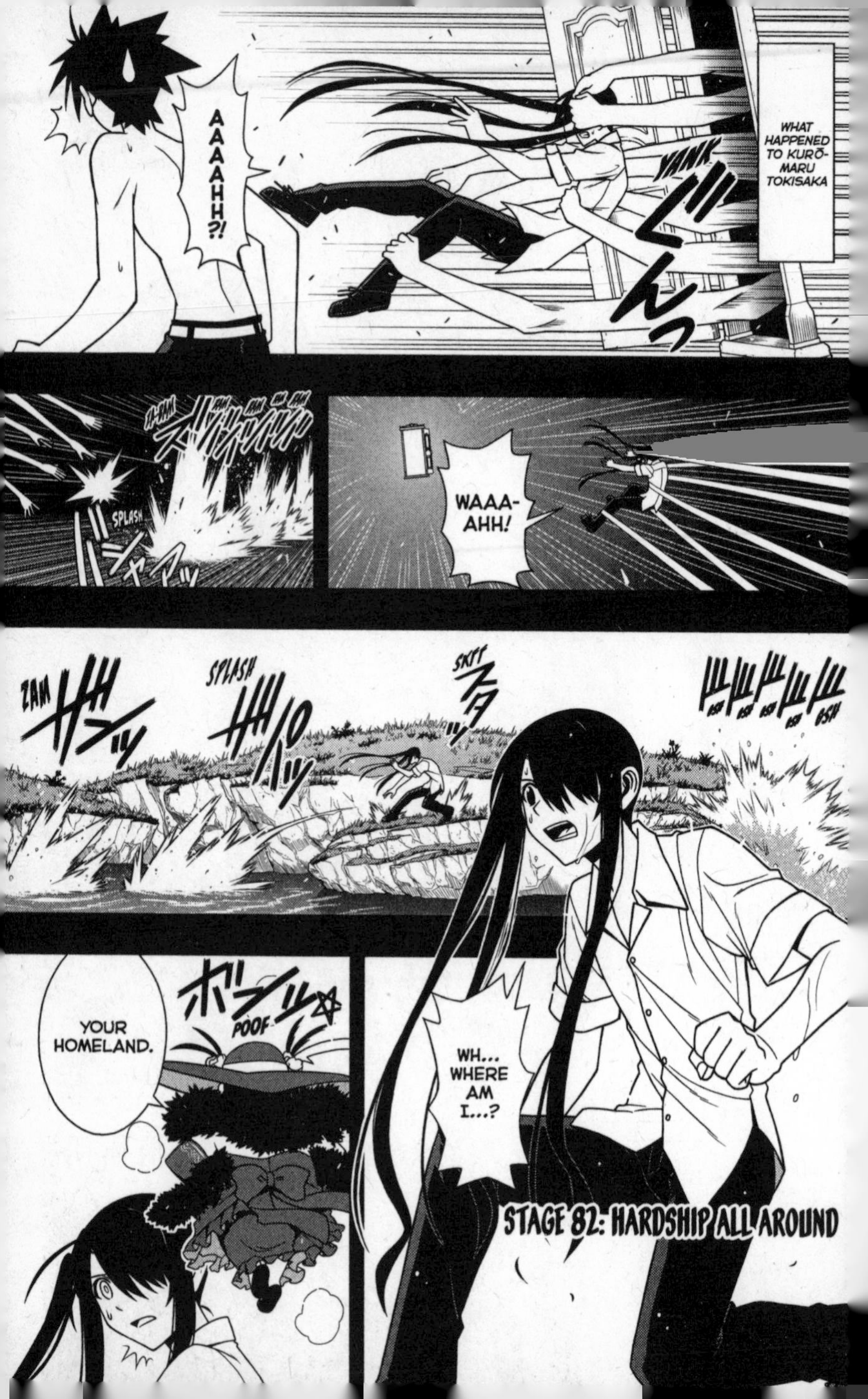
WHAT HAPPENED TO KURŌ-MARU TOKISAKA
YANK
AAAAAHH?!
WAAA-AHH!
SPLASH
SPLASH
ZAM
WH... WHERE AM I...?
STAGE 82: HARDSHIP ALL AROUND
POOF
YOUR HOMELAND.

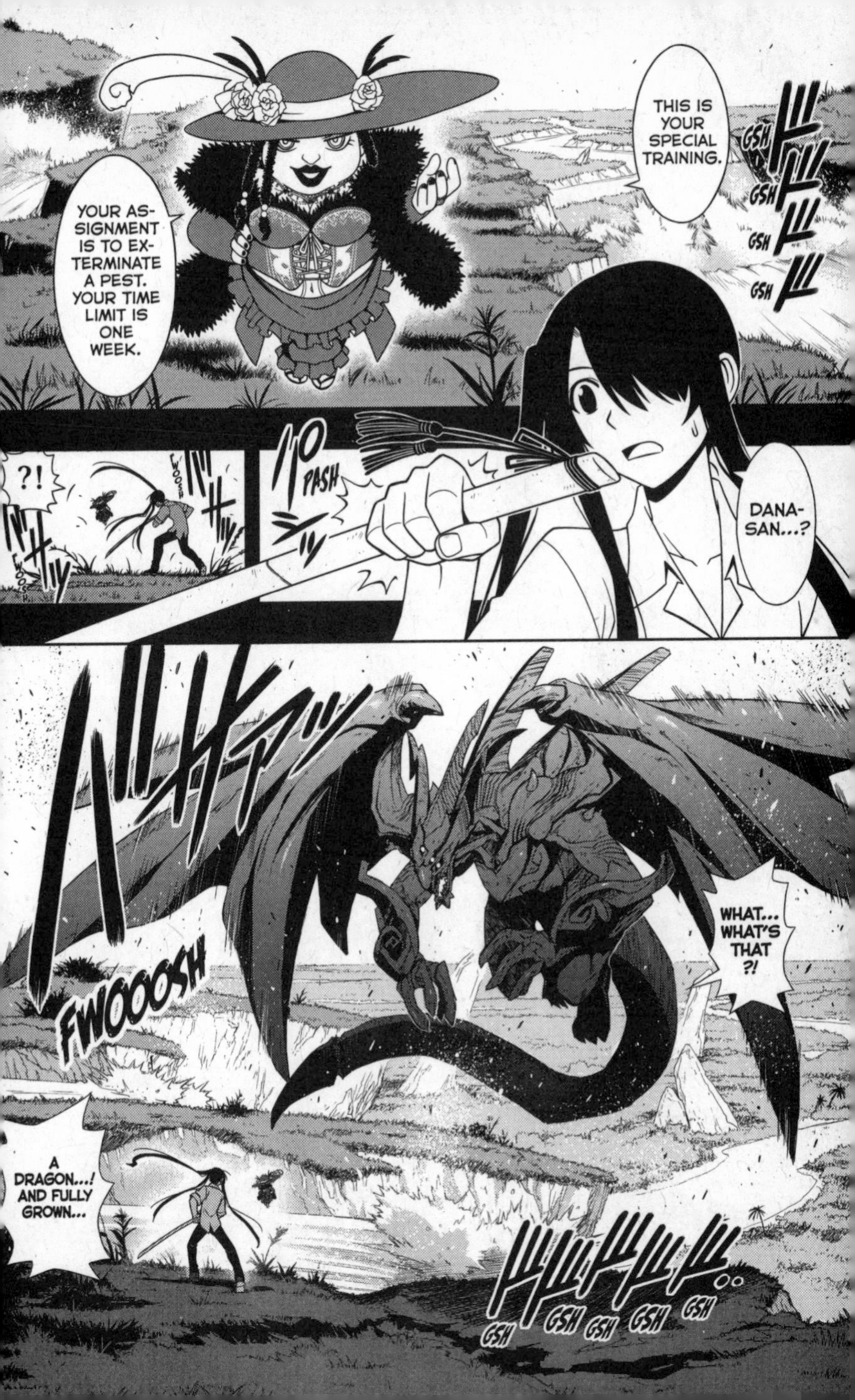
THIS IS YOUR SPECIAL TRAINING.
GSH GSH GSH GSH
YOUR ASSIGNMENT IS TO EXTERMINATE A PEST. YOUR TIME LIMIT IS ONE WEEK.
DANA-SAN...?
PASH
?!
WOOSH
WOOSH
WHAT... WHAT'S THAT ?!
FWOOOSH
A DRAGON...! AND FULLY GROWN...
GSH GSH GSH GSH GSH

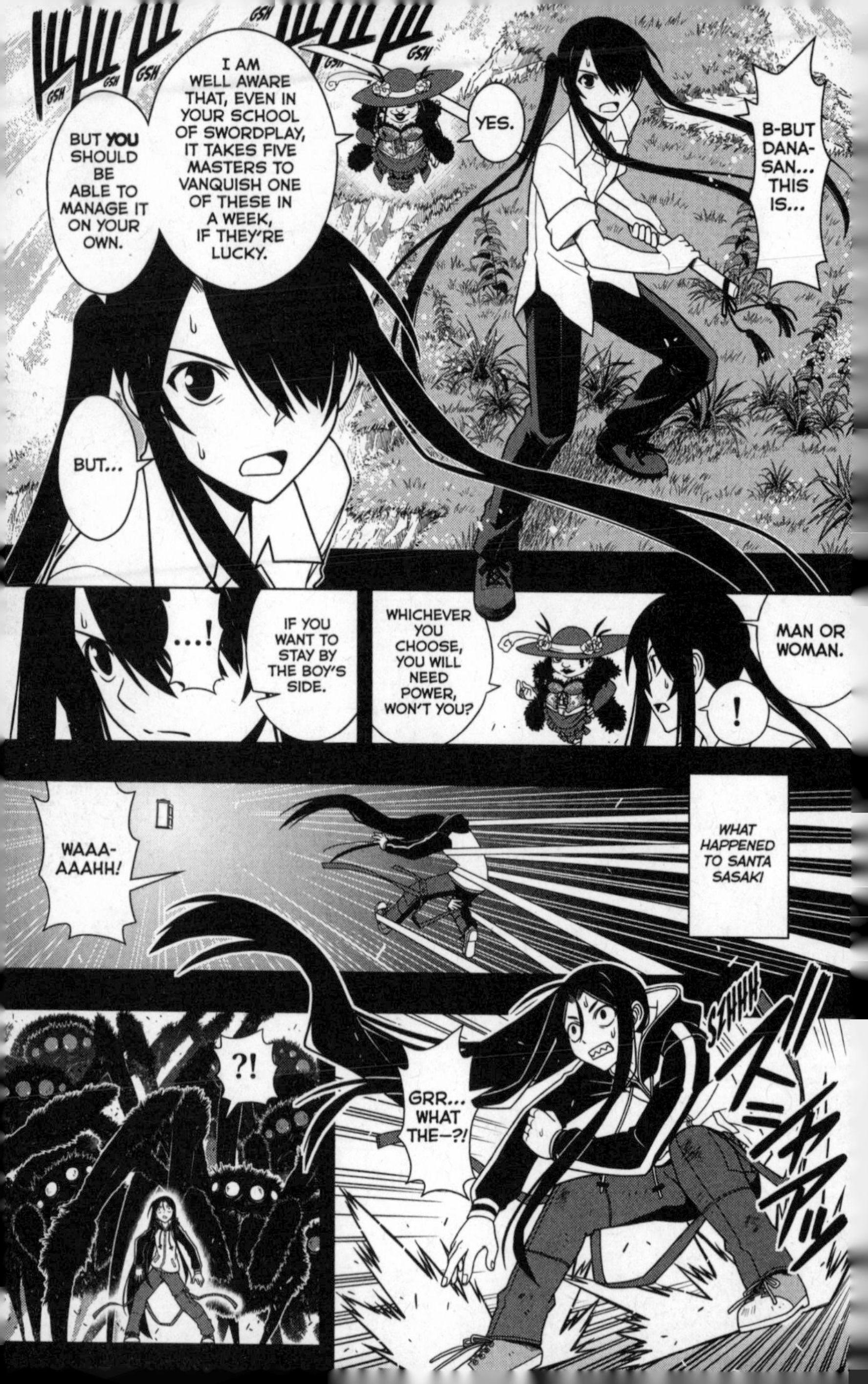
GSH GSH GSH
GSH
B-BUT DANA-SAN... THIS IS...
YES.
I AM WELL AWARE THAT, EVEN IN YOUR SCHOOL OF SWORDPLAY, IT TAKES FIVE MASTERS TO VANQUISH ONE OF THESE IN A WEEK, IF THEY'RE LUCKY.
BUT **YOU** SHOULD BE ABLE TO MANAGE IT ON YOUR OWN.
BUT...
MAN OR WOMAN.
!
WHICHEVER YOU CHOOSE, YOU WILL NEED POWER, WON'T YOU?
IF YOU WANT TO STAY BY THE BOY'S SIDE.
...!
WHAT HAPPENED TO SANTA SASAKI
WAAA-AAAHH!
SZHHH
GRR... WHAT THE-?!
?!

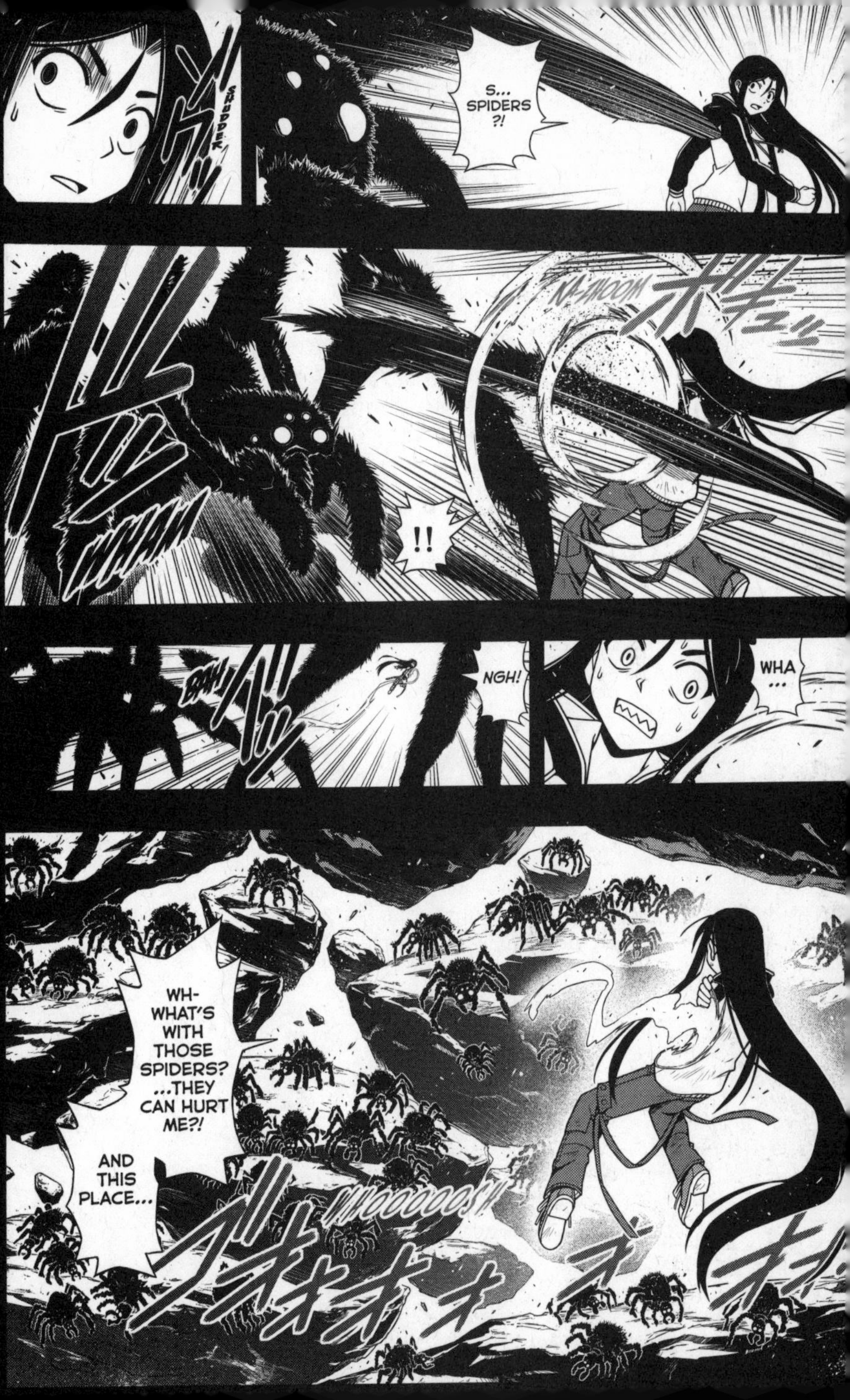
S... SPIDERS?!
SHUDDER
KA-SHOOM
!!
WHAM
WHA...
NGH!
BAM!
WH- WHAT'S WITH THOSE SPIDERS? ...THEY CAN HURT ME?!
AND THIS PLACE...
WHOOOOOSH!

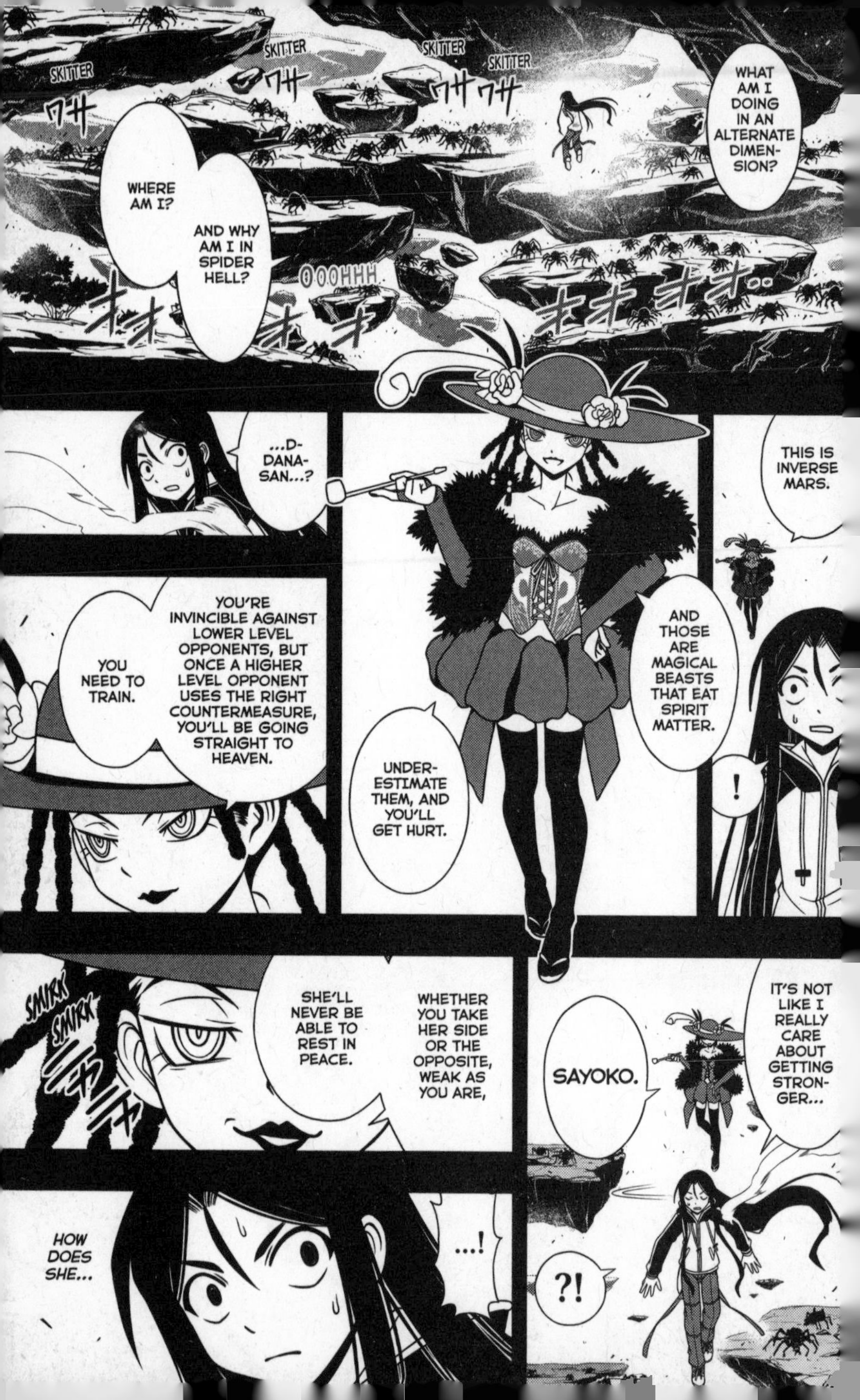
WHAT AM I DOING IN AN ALTERNATE DIMEN-SION?
SKITTER
SKITTER
SKITTER
SKITTER
WHERE AM I?
AND WHY AM I IN SPIDER HELL?
OOOHHH
THIS IS INVERSE MARS.
AND THOSE ARE MAGICAL BEASTS THAT EAT SPIRIT MATTER.
!
UNDER-ESTIMATE THEM, AND YOU'LL GET HURT.
...D-DANA-SAN...?
YOU'RE INVINCIBLE AGAINST LOWER LEVEL OPPONENTS, BUT ONCE A HIGHER LEVEL OPPONENT USES THE RIGHT COUNTERMEASURE, YOU'LL BE GOING STRAIGHT TO HEAVEN.
YOU NEED TO TRAIN.
IT'S NOT LIKE I REALLY CARE ABOUT GETTING STRONG-GER...
SAYOKO.
WHETHER YOU TAKE HER SIDE OR THE OPPOSITE, WEAK AS YOU ARE,
SHE'LL NEVER BE ABLE TO REST IN PEACE.
SMIRK SMIRK
?!
...!
HOW DOES SHE...

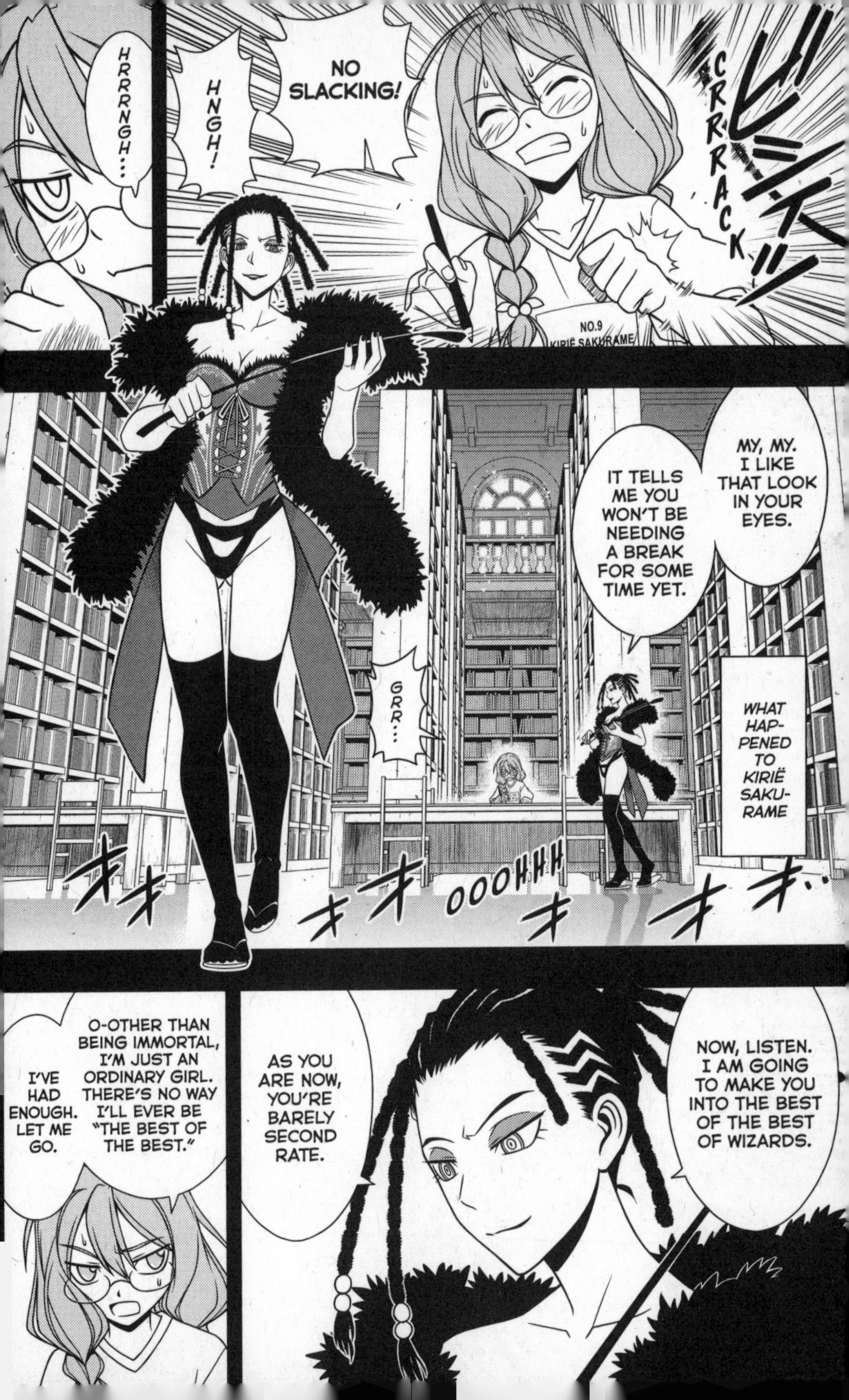
CRRRACK!
NO.9 KIRIË SAKURAME
NO SLACKING!
HNGH!
HRRRNGH...
MY, MY. I LIKE THAT LOOK IN YOUR EYES.
IT TELLS ME YOU WON'T BE NEEDING A BREAK FOR SOME TIME YET.
WHAT HAPPENED TO KIRIË SAKURAME
GRR...
OOOHHHH
NOW, LISTEN. I AM GOING TO MAKE YOU INTO THE BEST OF THE BEST OF WIZARDS.
AS YOU ARE NOW, YOU'RE BARELY SECOND RATE.
O-OTHER THAN BEING IMMORTAL, I'M JUST AN ORDINARY GIRL. THERE'S NO WAY I'LL EVER BE "THE BEST OF THE BEST."
I'VE HAD ENOUGH. LET ME GO.

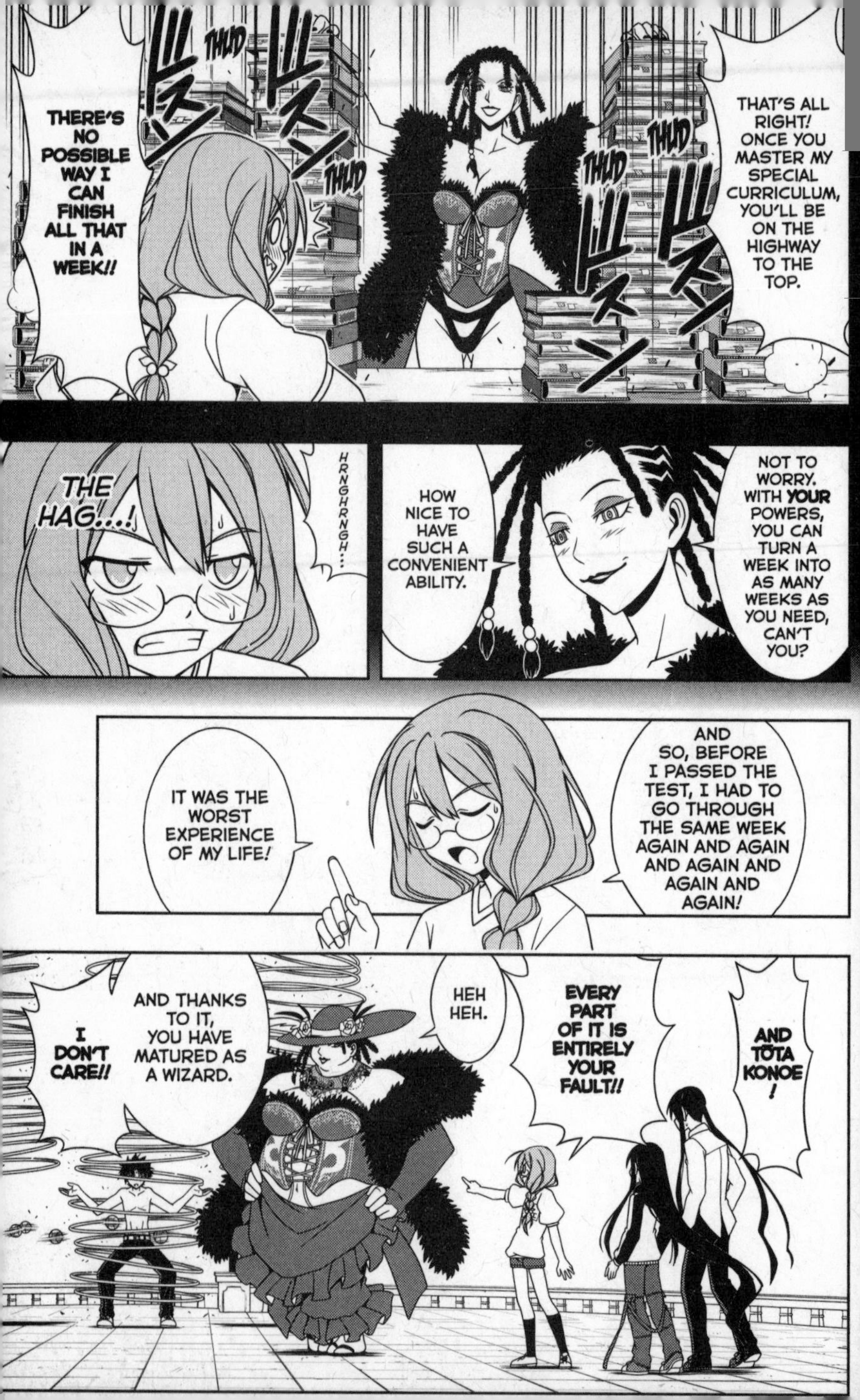
THAT'S ALL RIGHT! ONCE YOU MASTER MY SPECIAL CURRICULUM, YOU'LL BE ON THE HIGHWAY TO THE TOP.
ドスン THUD
ドスン THUD
ドスン THUD
ドスン THUD
THERE'S NO POSSIBLE WAY I CAN FINISH ALL THAT IN A WEEK!!
NOT TO WORRY. WITH **YOUR** POWERS, YOU CAN TURN A WEEK INTO AS MANY WEEKS AS YOU NEED, CAN'T YOU?
HOW NICE TO HAVE SUCH A CONVENIENT ABILITY.
HRNGHRNGH...
THE HAG...!
AND SO, BEFORE I PASSED THE TEST, I HAD TO GO THROUGH THE SAME WEEK AGAIN AND AGAIN AND AGAIN AND AGAIN AND AGAIN!
IT WAS THE WORST EXPERIENCE OF MY LIFE!
AND TŌTA KONOE!
EVERY PART OF IT IS ENTIRELY YOUR FAULT!!
HEH HEH.
AND THANKS TO IT, YOU HAVE MATURED AS A WIZARD.
I DON'T CARE!!

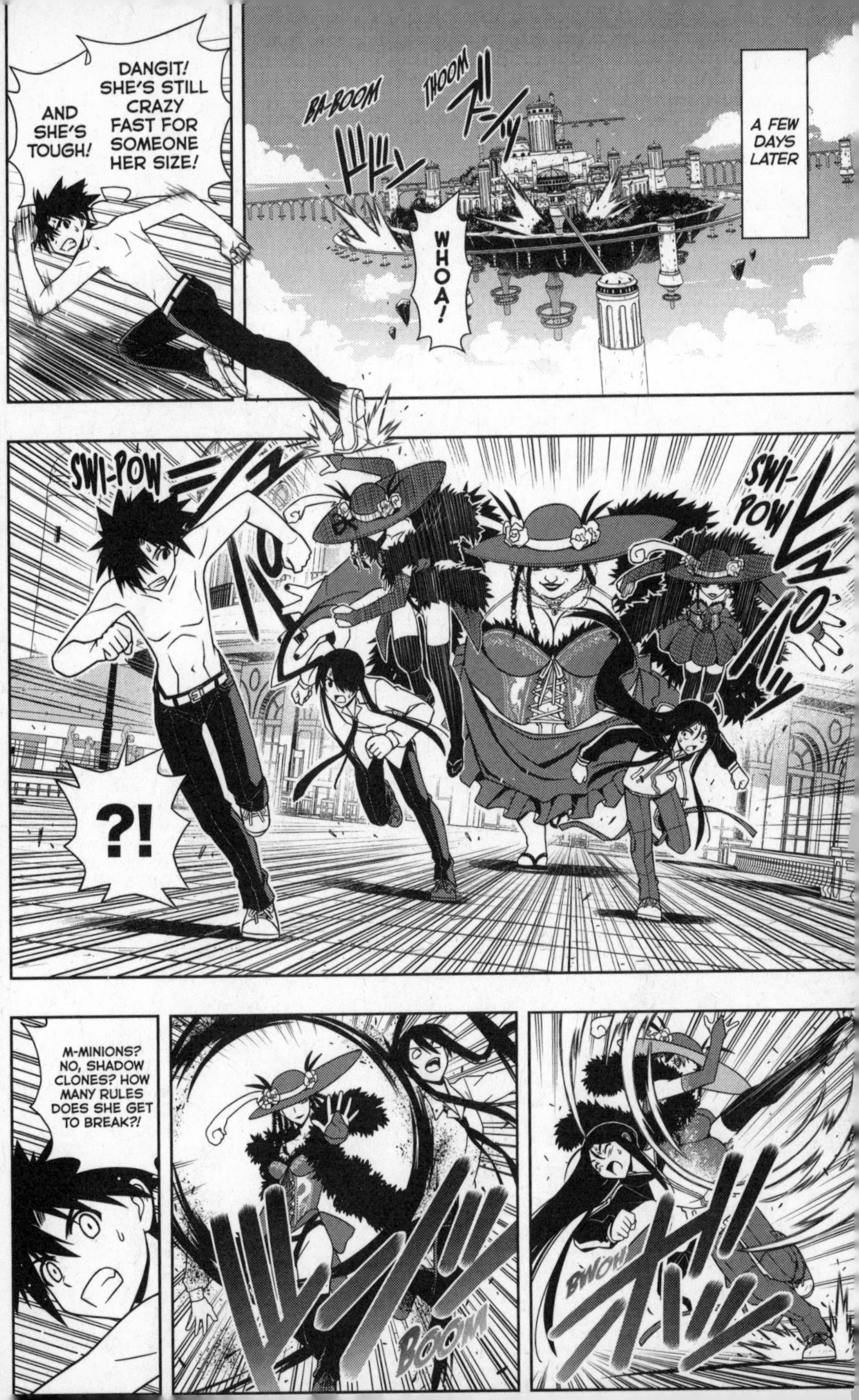

A FEW DAYS LATER
THOOM
BA-BOOM
WHOA!
DANGIT! SHE'S STILL CRAZY FAST FOR SOMEONE HER SIZE!
AND SHE'S TOUGH!
SWI-POW
SWI-POW
?!
BWOH!
BOOM
M-MINIONS? NO, SHADOW CLONES? HOW MANY RULES DOES SHE GET TO BREAK?!

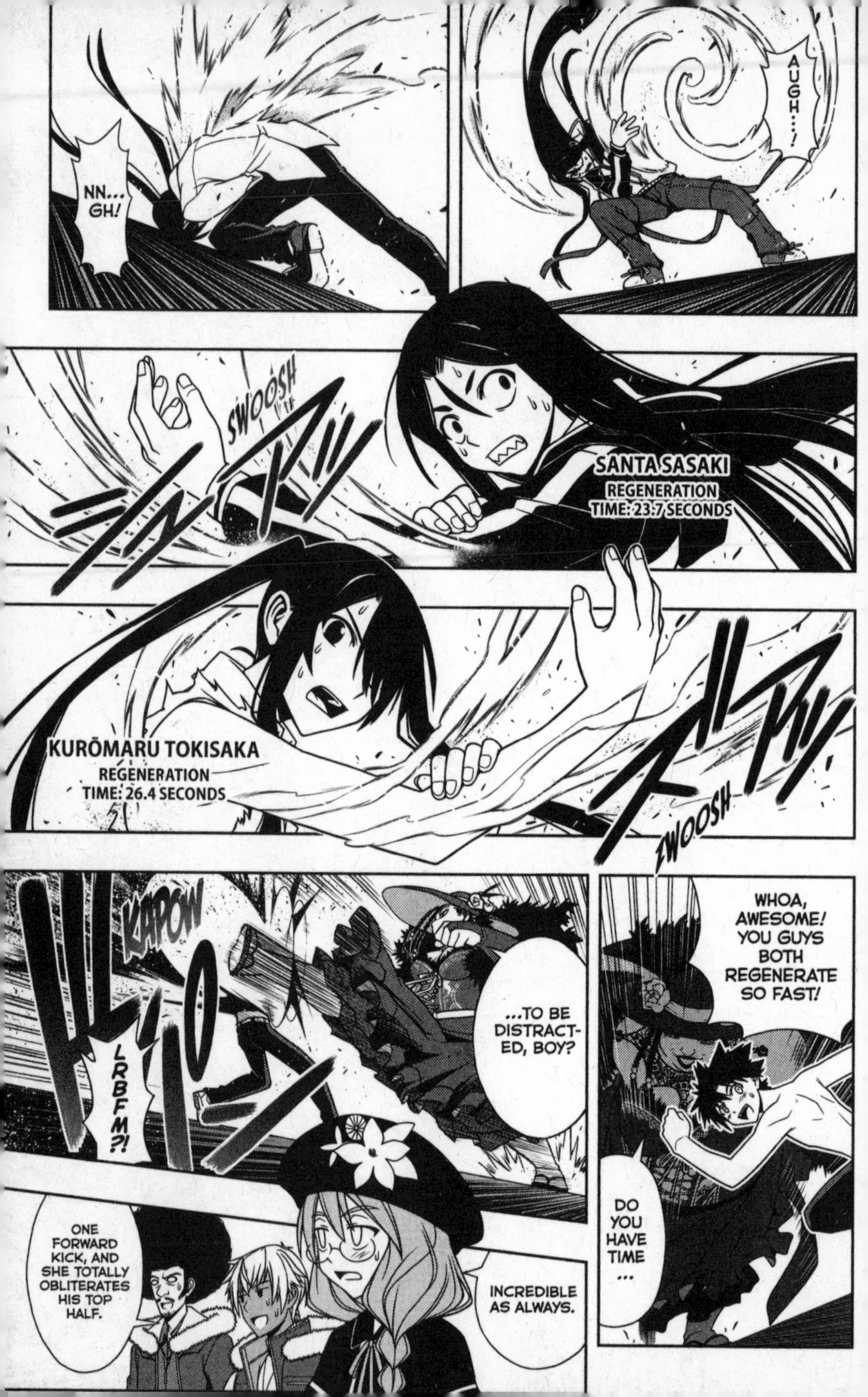
AUGH...!
NN... GH!
SWOOSH
SANTA SASAKI
REGENERATION TIME: 23.7 SECONDS
KURŌMARU TOKISAKA
REGENERATION TIME: 26.4 SECONDS
ZWOOSH
WHOA, AWESOME! YOU GUYS BOTH REGENERATE SO FAST!
DO YOU HAVE TIME ...
...TO BE DISTRACTED, BOY?
KAPOW
LRBFM?!
INCREDIBLE AS ALWAYS.
ONE FORWARD KICK, AND SHE TOTALLY OBLITERATES HIS TOP HALF.

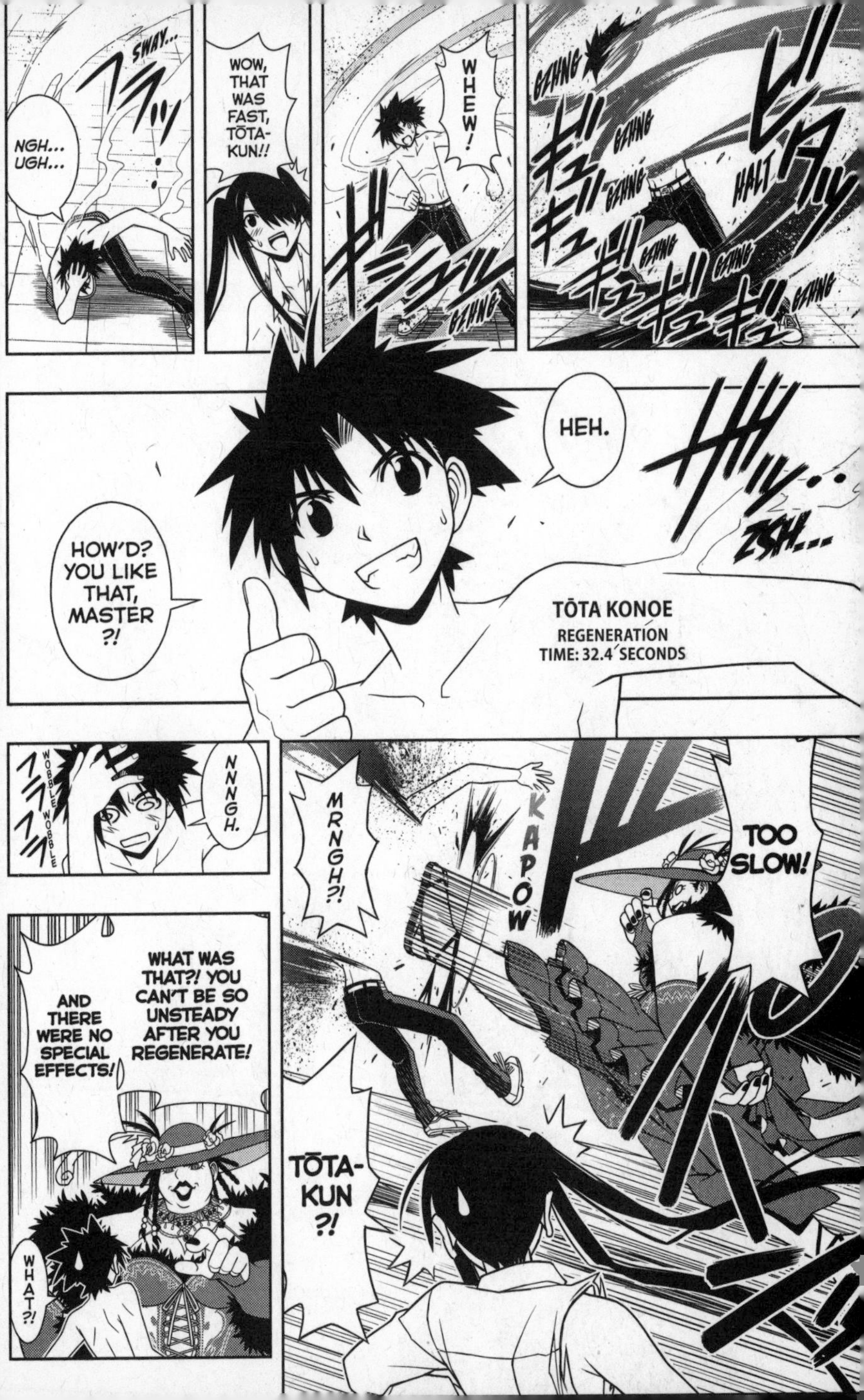
GZHNG
HALT
GZHNG GZHNG GZHNG GZHNG GZHNG GZHNG GZHNG
WHEW!
WOW, THAT WAS FAST, TŌTA-KUN!!
SWAY...
NGH... UGH...
ZSH...
HEH.
HOW'D? YOU LIKE THAT, MASTER?!
TŌTA KONOE
REGENERATION TIME: 32.4 SECONDS
TOO SLOW!
KAPOW
MRNGH?!
TŌTA-KUN?!
NNNGH.
WOBBLE WOBBLE
WHAT WAS THAT?! YOU CAN'T BE SO UNSTEADY AFTER YOU REGENERATE!
AND THERE WERE NO SPECIAL EFFECTS!
WHAT?!

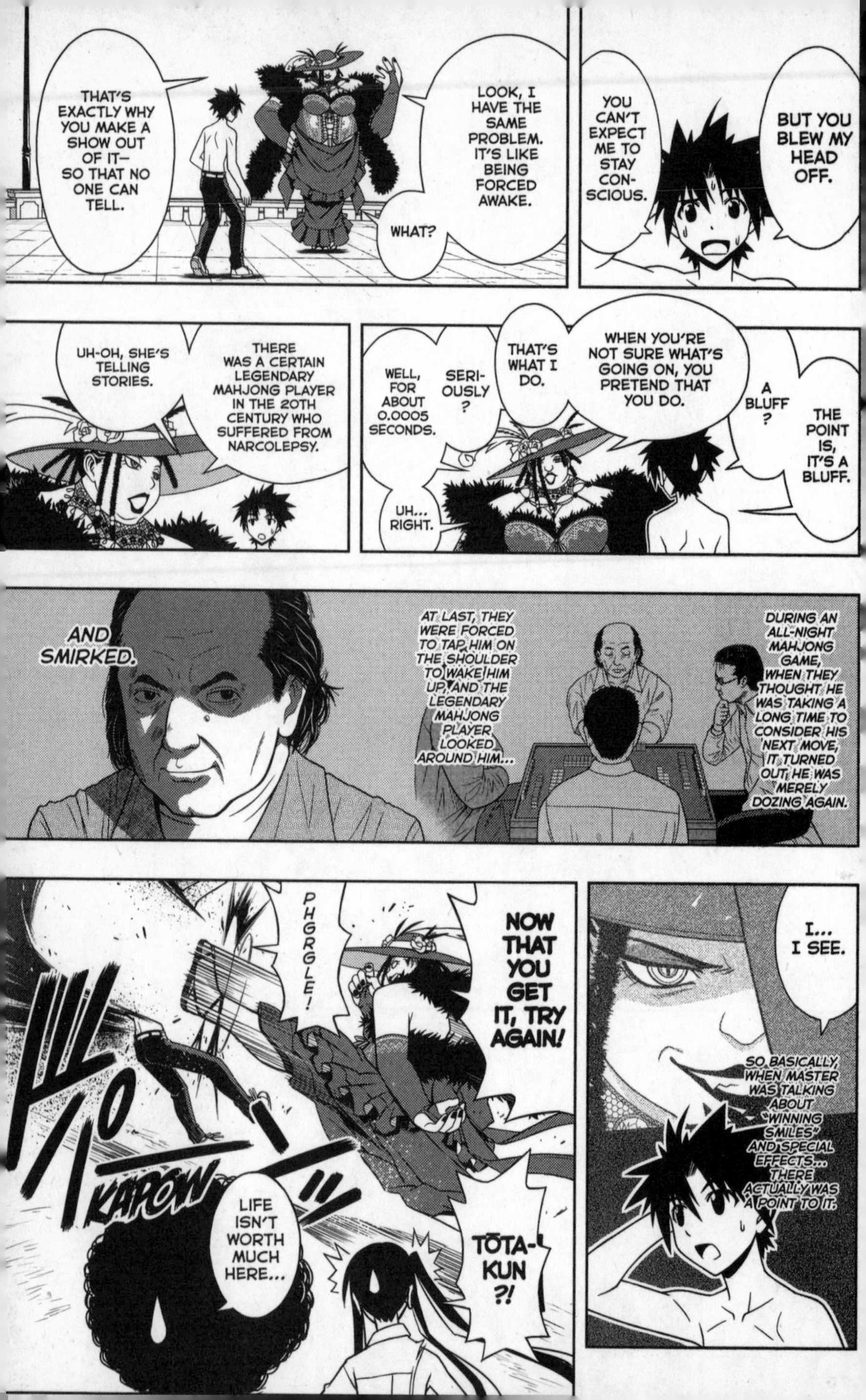
BUT YOU BLEW MY HEAD OFF.
YOU CAN'T EXPECT ME TO STAY CONSCIOUS.
LOOK, I HAVE THE SAME PROBLEM. IT'S LIKE BEING FORCED AWAKE.
WHAT?
THAT'S EXACTLY WHY YOU MAKE A SHOW OUT OF IT— SO THAT NO ONE CAN TELL.
THE POINT IS, IT'S A BLUFF.
A BLUFF?
WHEN YOU'RE NOT SURE WHAT'S GOING ON, YOU PRETEND THAT YOU DO.
THAT'S WHAT I DO.
SERIOUSLY?
WELL, FOR ABOUT 0.0005 SECONDS.
UH... RIGHT.
THERE WAS A CERTAIN LEGENDARY MAHJONG PLAYER IN THE 20TH CENTURY WHO SUFFERED FROM NARCOLEPSY.
UH-OH, SHE'S TELLING STORIES.
DURING AN ALL-NIGHT MAHJONG GAME, WHEN THEY THOUGHT HE WAS TAKING A LONG TIME TO CONSIDER HIS NEXT MOVE, IT TURNED OUT HE WAS MERELY DOZING AGAIN.
AT LAST, THEY WERE FORCED TO TAP HIM ON THE SHOULDER TO WAKE HIM UP, AND THE LEGENDARY MAHJONG PLAYER LOOKED AROUND HIM...
AND SMIRKED.
I... I SEE.
SO BASICALLY, WHEN MASTER WAS TALKING ABOUT "WINNING SMILES" AND SPECIAL EFFECTS... THERE ACTUALLY WAS A POINT TO IT.
NOW THAT YOU GET IT, TRY AGAIN!
PHGRGLE!
KAPOW
TŌTA-KUN?!
LIFE ISN'T WORTH MUCH HERE...

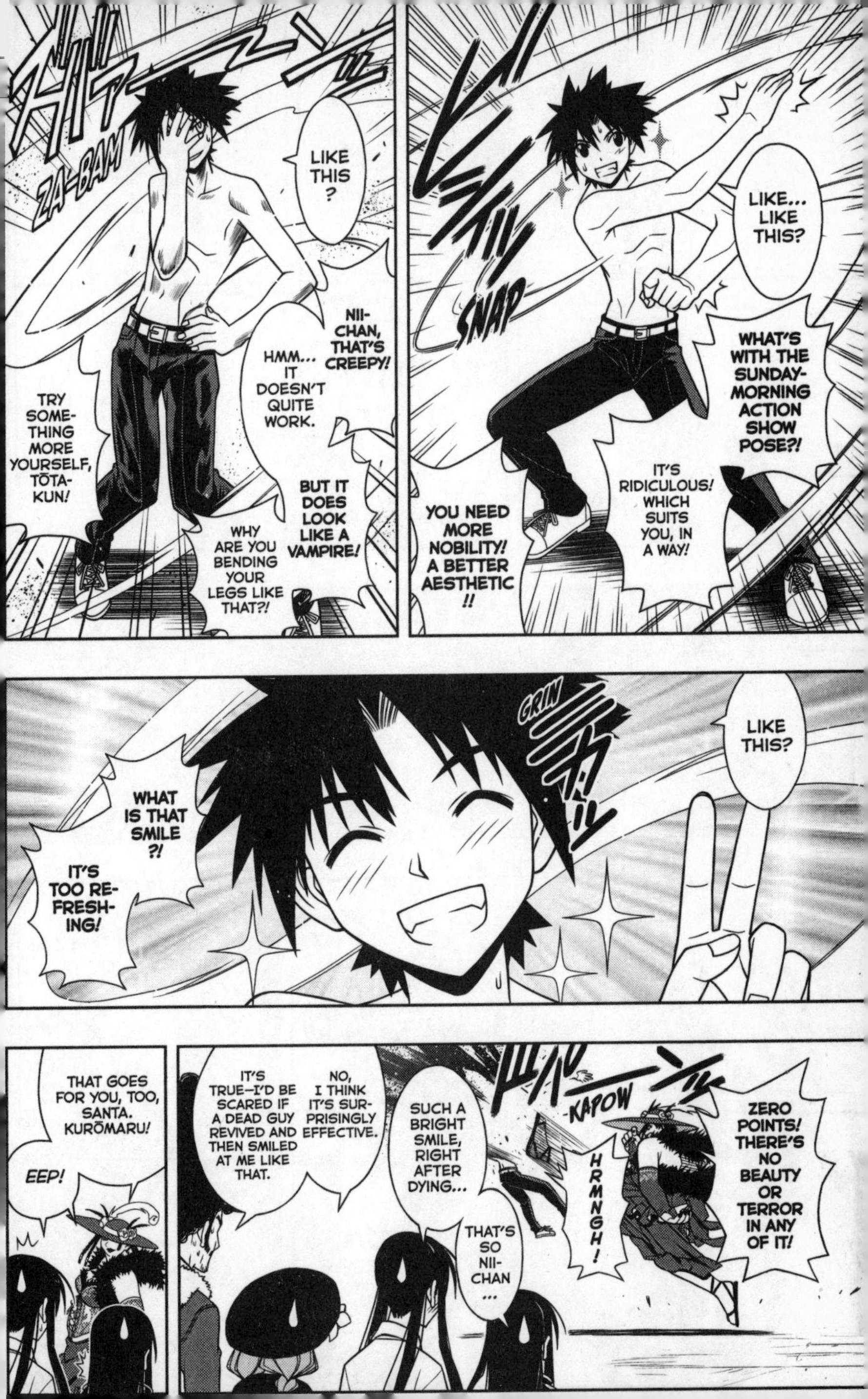
LIKE... LIKE THIS?
SNAP
WHAT'S WITH THE SUNDAY-MORNING ACTION SHOW POSE?!
IT'S RIDICULOUS! WHICH SUITS YOU, IN A WAY!
YOU NEED MORE NOBILITY! A BETTER AESTHETIC!!
LIKE THIS?
ZA-BAM
NII-CHAN, THAT'S CREEPY!
HMM... IT DOESN'T QUITE WORK.
TRY SOME-THING MORE YOURSELF, TŌTA-KUN!
BUT IT DOES LOOK LIKE A VAMPIRE!
WHY ARE YOU BENDING YOUR LEGS LIKE THAT?!
LIKE THIS?
GRIN
WHAT IS THAT SMILE?!
IT'S TOO RE-FRESH-ING!
KAPOW
ZERO POINTS! THERE'S NO BEAUTY OR TERROR IN ANY OF IT!
HRMNGH!
SUCH A BRIGHT SMILE, RIGHT AFTER DYING...
THAT'S SO NII-CHAN...
NO, I THINK IT'S SUR-PRISINGLY EFFECTIVE.
IT'S TRUE—I'D BE SCARED IF A DEAD GUY REVIVED AND THEN SMILED AT ME LIKE THAT.
THAT GOES FOR YOU, TOO, SANTA. KURŌMARU!
EEP!

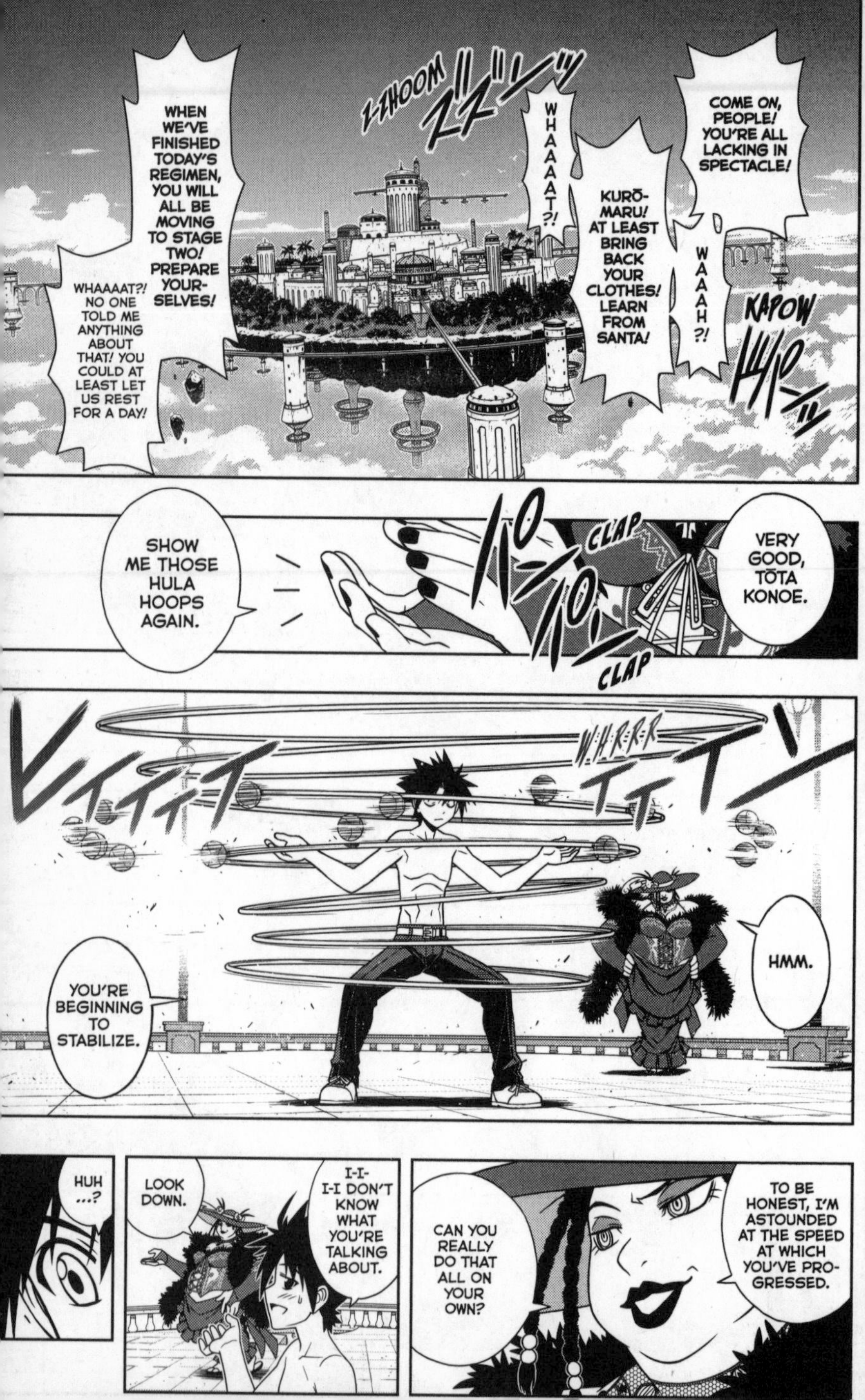
COME ON, PEOPLE! YOU'RE ALL LACKING IN SPECTACLE!
WAAAH?!
KAPOW
KURŌ-MARU! AT LEAST BRING BACK YOUR CLOTHES! LEARN FROM SANTA!
WHAAAAAT?!
Z-ZHOOM
WHEN WE'VE FINISHED TODAY'S REGIMEN, YOU WILL ALL BE MOVING TO STAGE TWO! PREPARE YOUR-SELVES!
WHAAAAT?! NO ONE TOLD ME ANYTHING ABOUT THAT! YOU COULD AT LEAST LET US REST FOR A DAY!
VERY GOOD, TŌTA KONOE.
CLAP
CLAP
SHOW ME THOSE HULA HOOPS AGAIN.
HMM.
W-H-R-R-R
YOU'RE BEGINNING TO STABILIZE.
TO BE HONEST, I'M ASTOUNDED AT THE SPEED AT WHICH YOU'VE PRO-GRESSED.
CAN YOU REALLY DO THAT ALL ON YOUR OWN?
I-I- I-I DON'T KNOW WHAT YOU'RE TALKING ABOUT.
LOOK DOWN.
HUH ...?

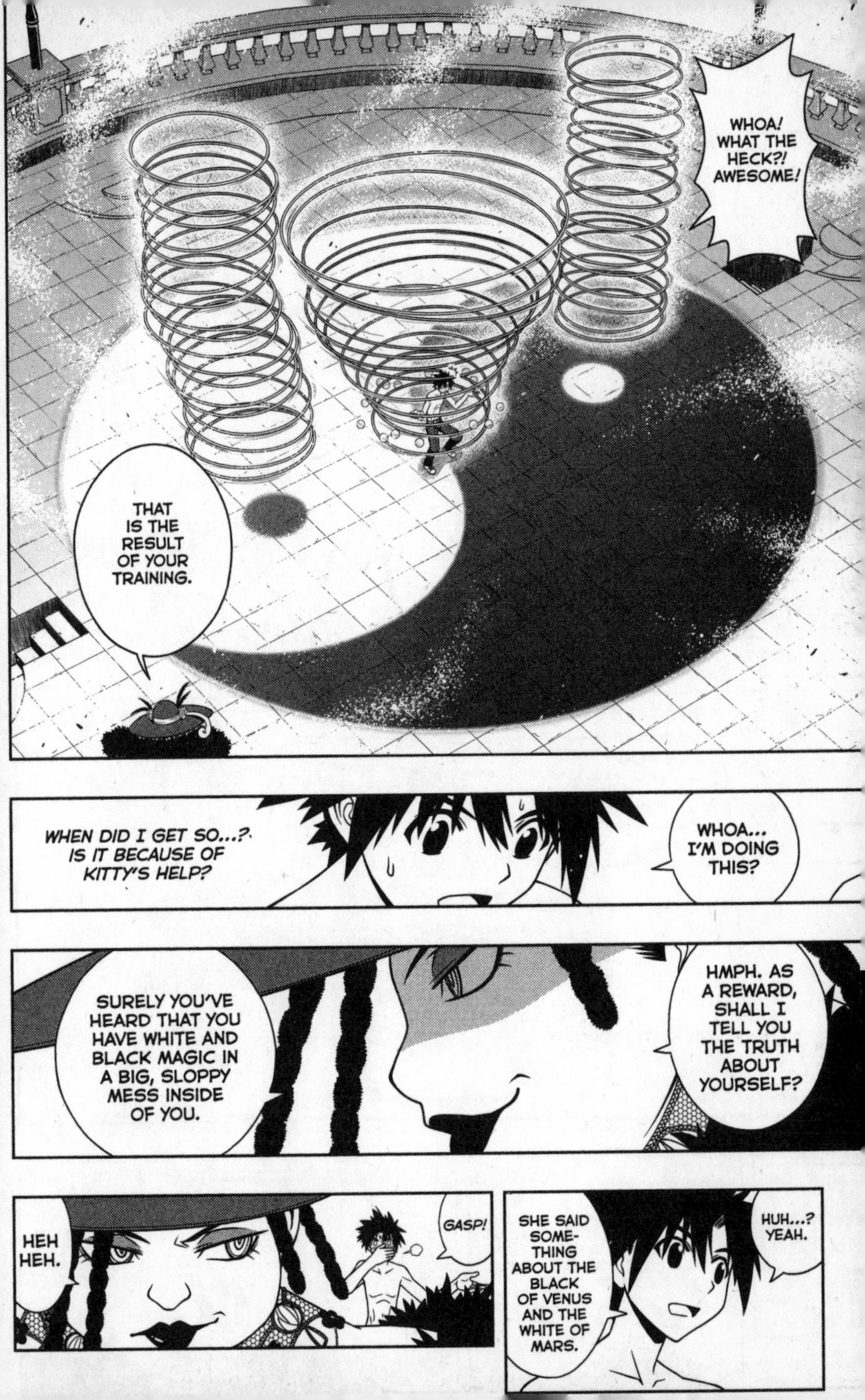
WHOA! WHAT THE HECK?! AWESOME!
THAT IS THE RESULT OF YOUR TRAINING.
WHOA... I'M DOING THIS?
WHEN DID I GET SO...? IS IT BECAUSE OF KITTY'S HELP?
HMPH. AS A REWARD, SHALL I TELL YOU THE TRUTH ABOUT YOURSELF?
SURELY YOU'VE HEARD THAT YOU HAVE WHITE AND BLACK MAGIC IN A BIG, SLOPPY MESS INSIDE OF YOU.
HUH...? YEAH.
SHE SAID SOME-THING ABOUT THE BLACK OF VENUS AND THE WHITE OF MARS.
GASP!
HEH HEH.

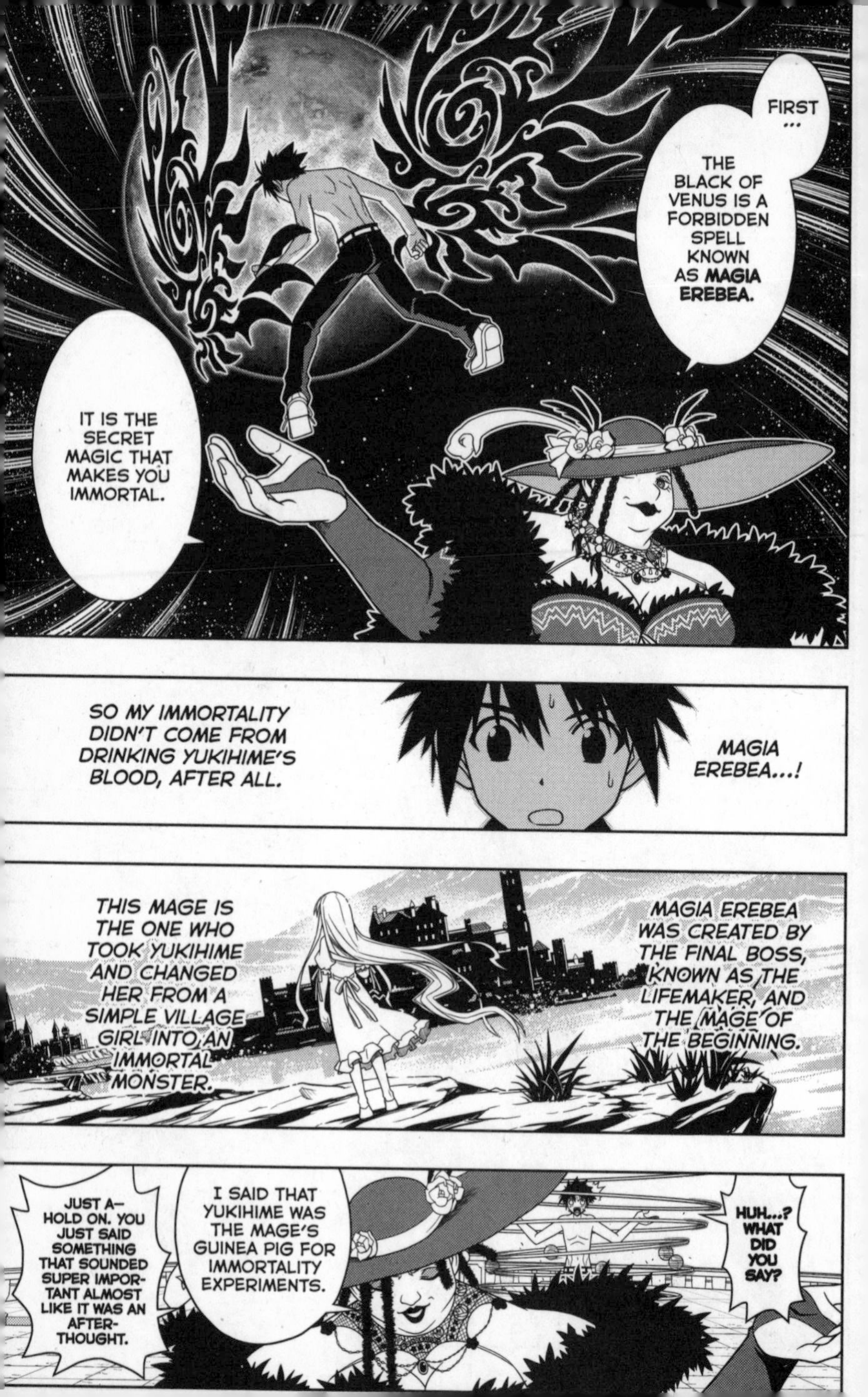
FIRST...
THE BLACK OF VENUS IS A FORBIDDEN SPELL KNOWN AS MAGIA EREBEA.
IT IS THE SECRET MAGIC THAT MAKES YOU IMMORTAL.
MAGIA EREBEA...!
SO MY IMMORTALITY DIDN'T COME FROM DRINKING YUKIHIME'S BLOOD, AFTER ALL.
MAGIA EREBEA WAS CREATED BY THE FINAL BOSS, KNOWN AS THE LIFEMAKER, AND THE MAGE OF THE BEGINNING.
THIS MAGE IS THE ONE WHO TOOK YUKIHIME AND CHANGED HER FROM A SIMPLE VILLAGE GIRL INTO AN IMMORTAL MONSTER.
HUH...? WHAT DID YOU SAY?
I SAID THAT YUKIHIME WAS THE MAGE'S GUINEA PIG FOR IMMORTALITY EXPERIMENTS.
JUST A— HOLD ON. YOU JUST SAID SOMETHING THAT SOUNDED SUPER IMPORTANT ALMOST LIKE IT WAS AN AFTERTHOUGHT.

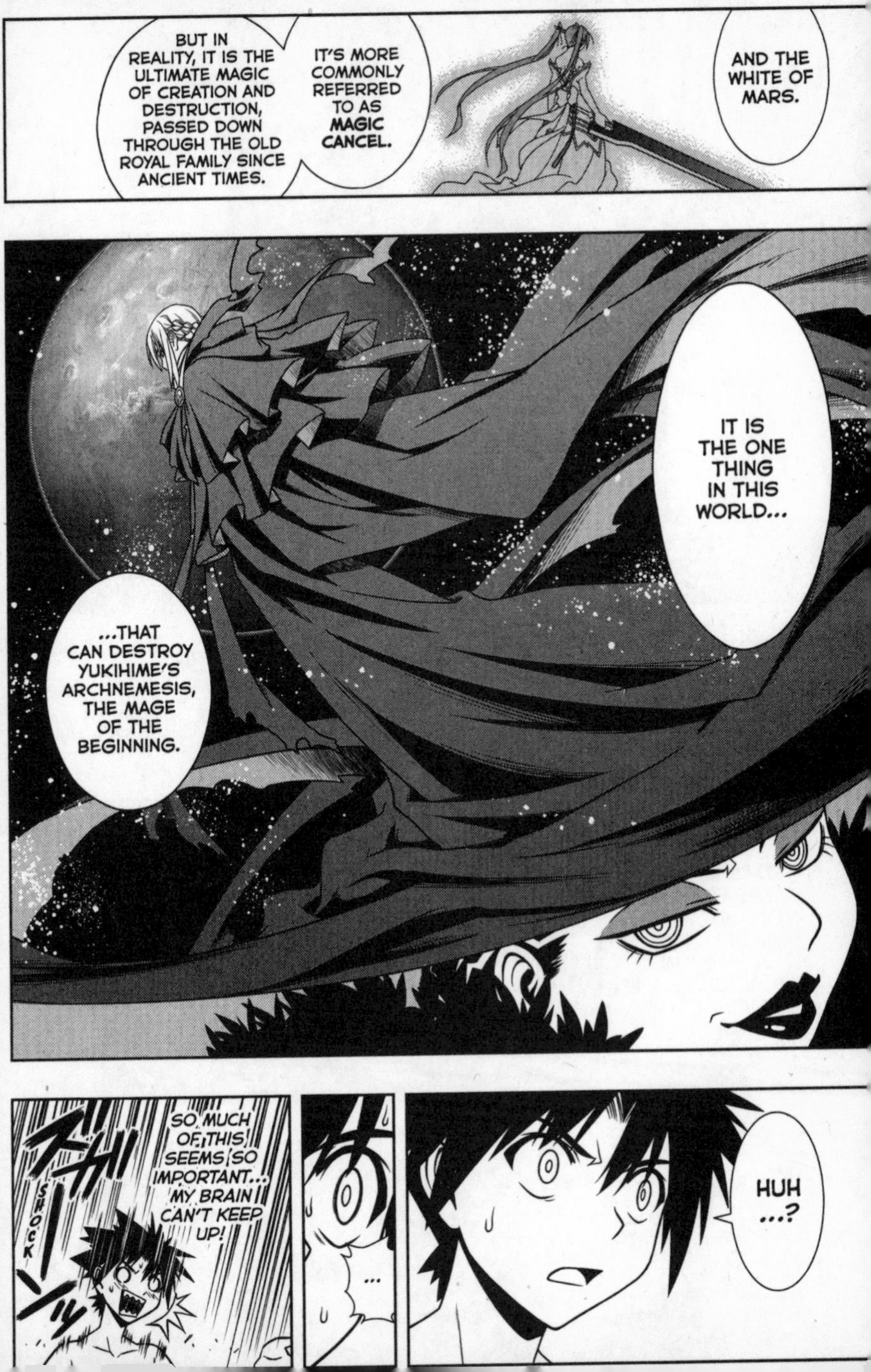
AND THE WHITE OF MARS.
IT'S MORE COMMONLY REFERRED TO AS MAGIC CANCEL.
BUT IN REALITY, IT IS THE ULTIMATE MAGIC OF CREATION AND DESTRUCTION, PASSED DOWN THROUGH THE OLD ROYAL FAMILY SINCE ANCIENT TIMES.
IT IS THE ONE THING IN THIS WORLD...
...THAT CAN DESTROY YUKIHIME'S ARCHNEMESIS, THE MAGE OF THE BEGINNING.
HUH ...?
...
SO MUCH OF THIS SEEMS SO IMPORTANT... MY BRAIN CAN'T KEEP UP!
SHOCK

UQ HOLDER!

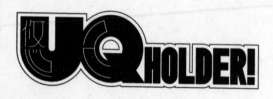

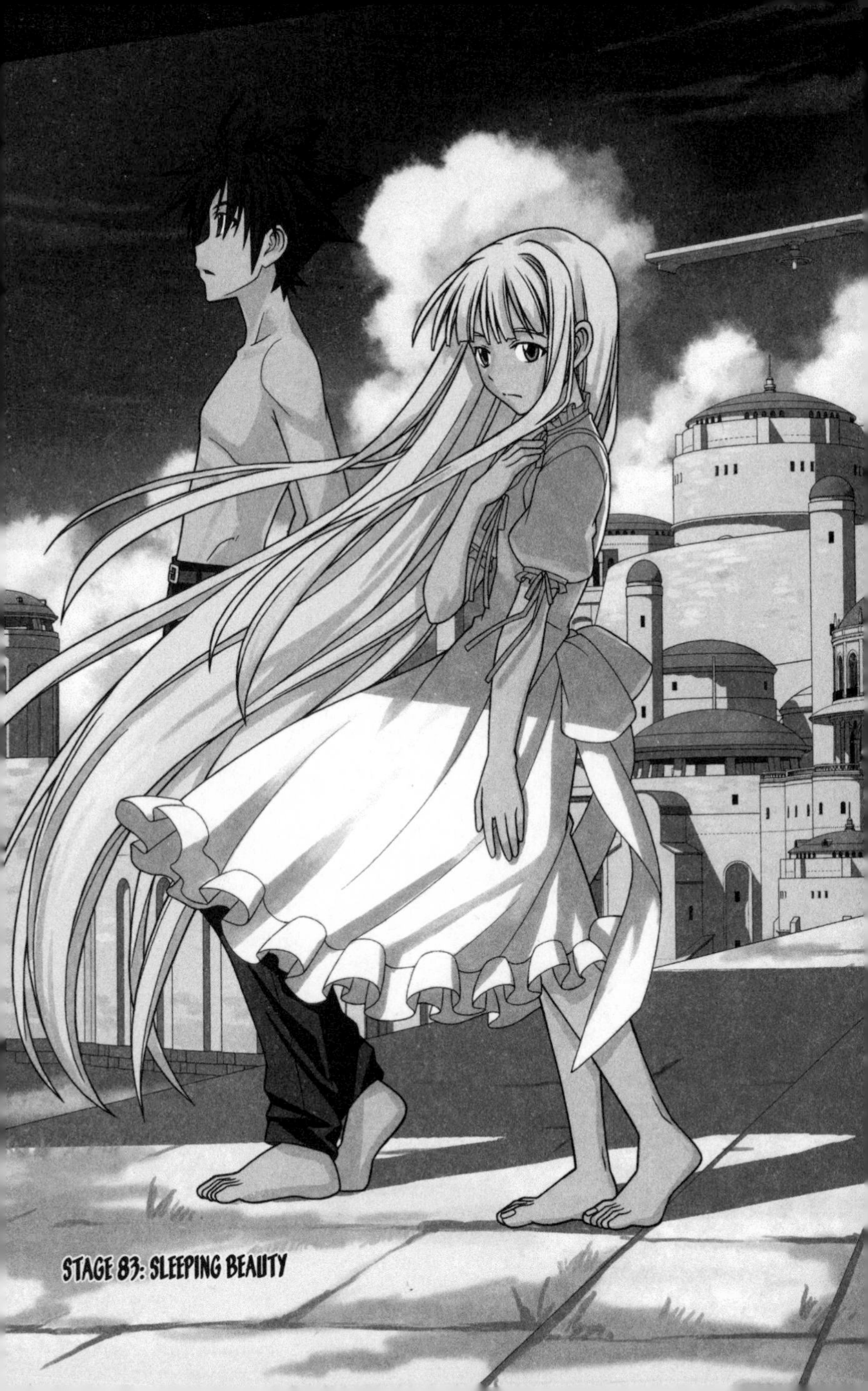
STAGE 83: SLEEPING BEAUTY

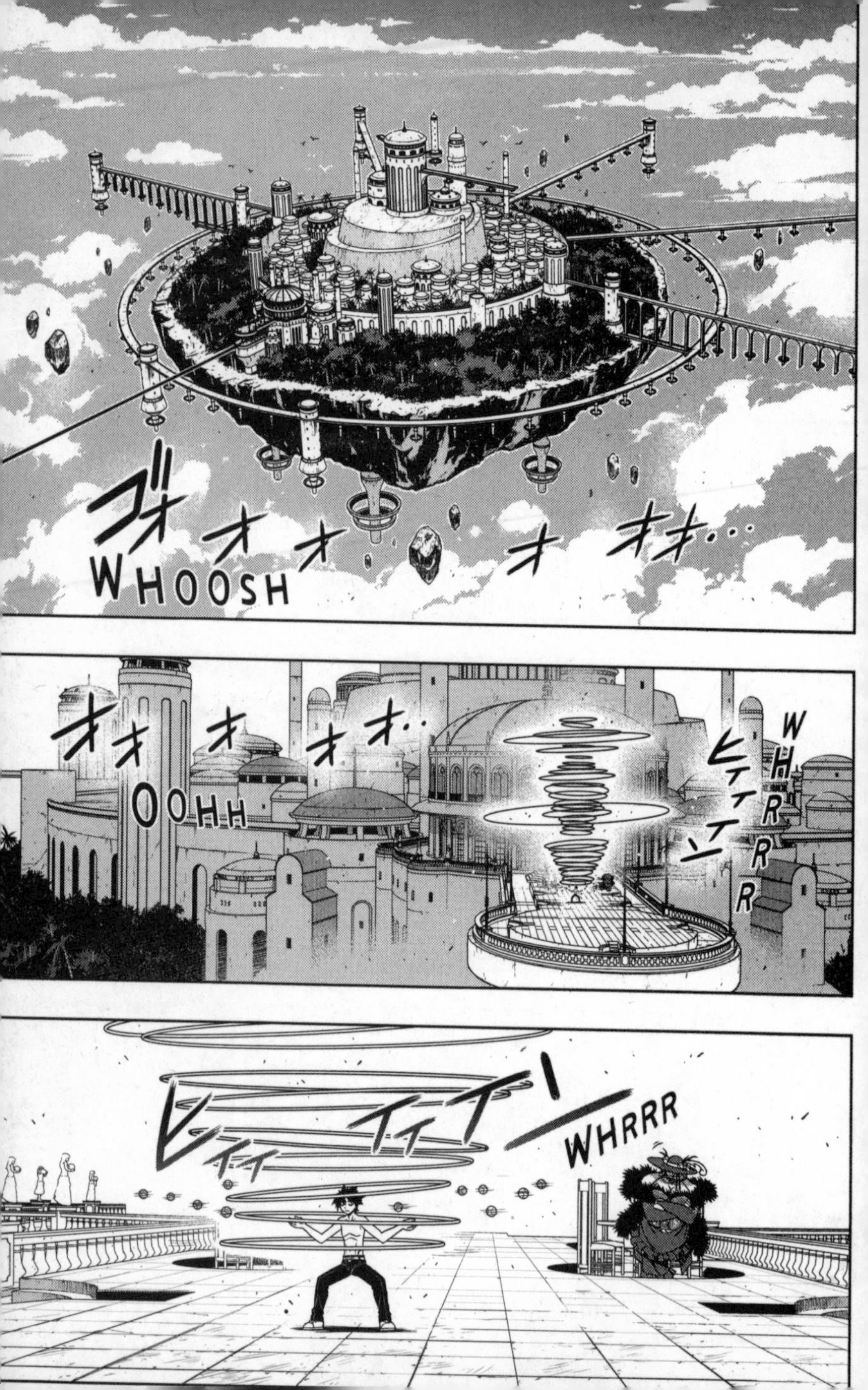
ゴオオオ
オオオ…
WHOOSH
ヒィィィン
WHRRRR
オオオ
オオ…
OOHH
ヒィィィィィー
WHRRR

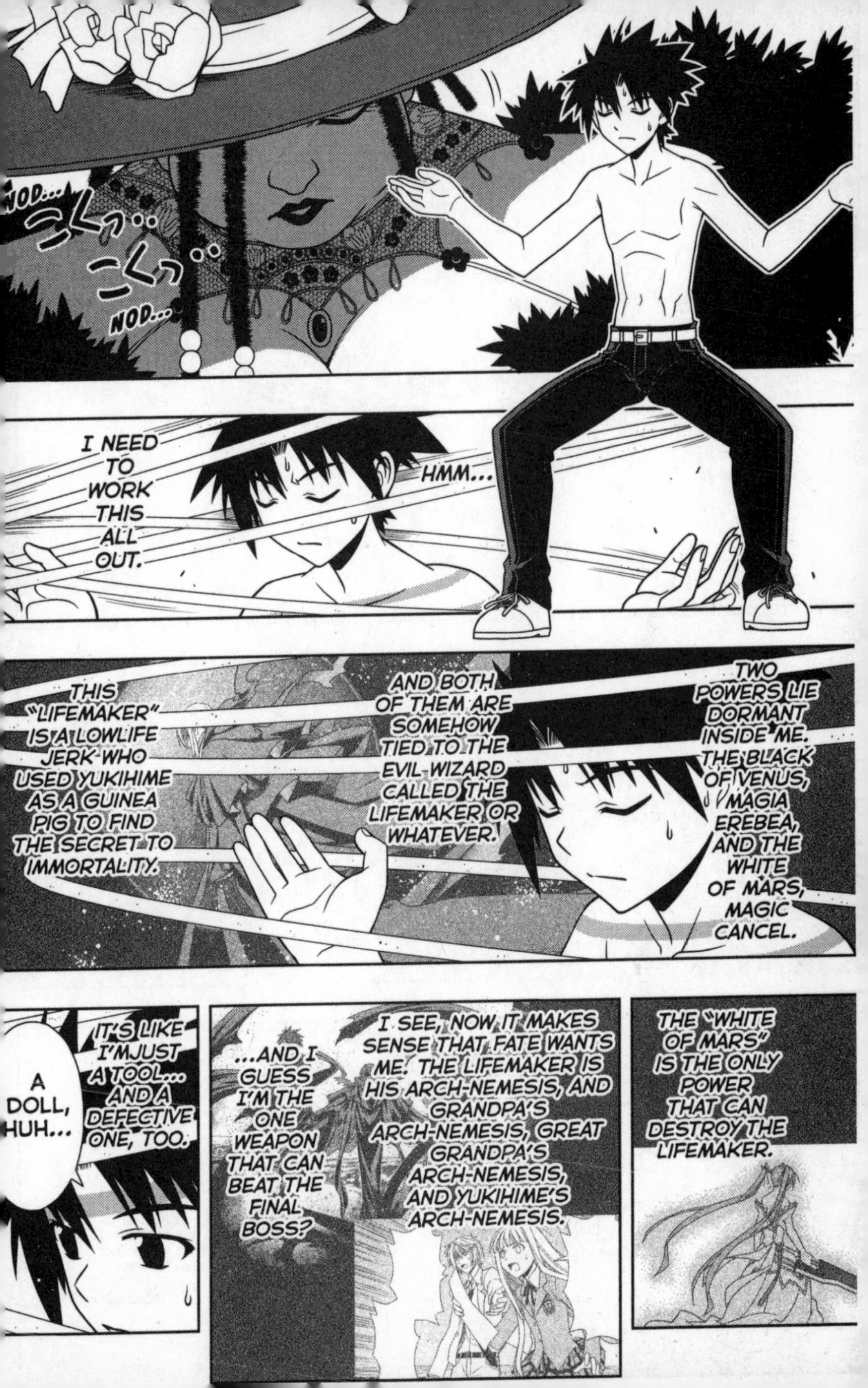
NOD...
NOD...
HMM...
I NEED TO WORK THIS ALL OUT.
TWO POWERS LIE DORMANT INSIDE ME. THE BLACK OF VENUS, MAGIA EREBEA, AND THE WHITE OF MARS, MAGIC CANCEL.
AND BOTH OF THEM ARE SOMEHOW TIED TO THE EVIL WIZARD CALLED THE LIFEMAKER OR WHATEVER.
THIS "LIFEMAKER" IS A LOWLIFE JERK WHO USED YUKIHIME AS A GUINEA PIG TO FIND THE SECRET TO IMMORTALITY.
THE "WHITE OF MARS" IS THE ONLY POWER THAT CAN DESTROY THE LIFEMAKER.
I SEE, NOW IT MAKES SENSE THAT FATE WANTS ME. THE LIFEMAKER IS HIS ARCH-NEMESIS, AND GRANDPA'S ARCH-NEMESIS, GREAT GRANDPA'S ARCH-NEMESIS, AND YUKIHIME'S ARCH-NEMESIS.
...AND I GUESS I'M THE ONE WEAPON THAT CAN BEAT THE FINAL BOSS?
IT'S LIKE I'MJUST A TOOL... AND A DEFECTIVE ONE, TOO.
A DOLL, HUH...

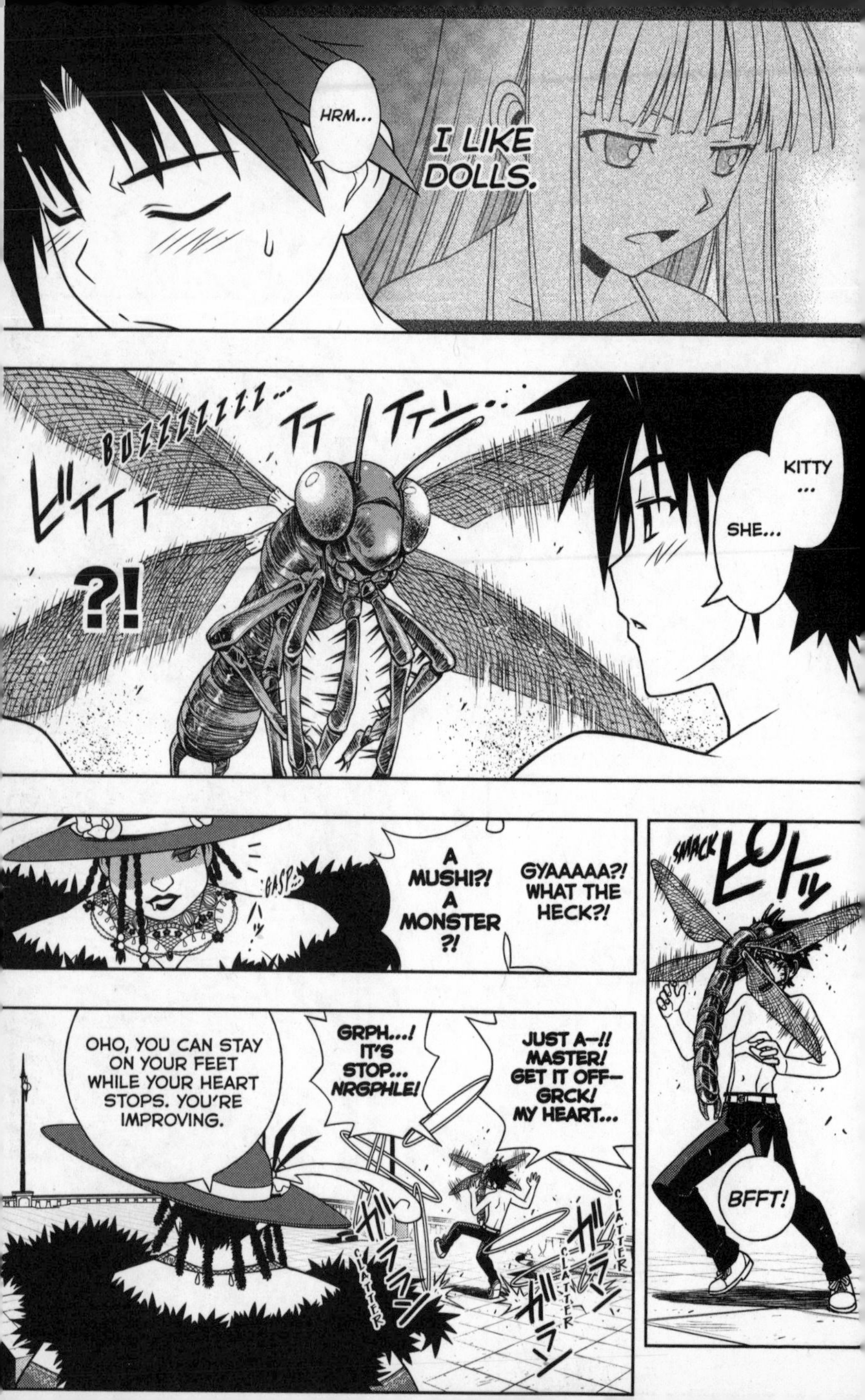
I LIKE DOLLS.
HRM...
KITTY... SHE...
BUZZZZZZZZ...
?!
SMACK
BFFT!
GYAAAAA?! WHAT THE HECK?!
A MUSHI?! A MONSTER?!
GASP
JUST A—!! MASTER! GET IT OFF— GRCK! MY HEART...
GRPH...! IT'S STOP... NRGPHLE!
CLATTER
CLATTER
CLATTER
OHO, YOU CAN STAY ON YOUR FEET WHILE YOUR HEART STOPS. YOU'RE IMPROVING.

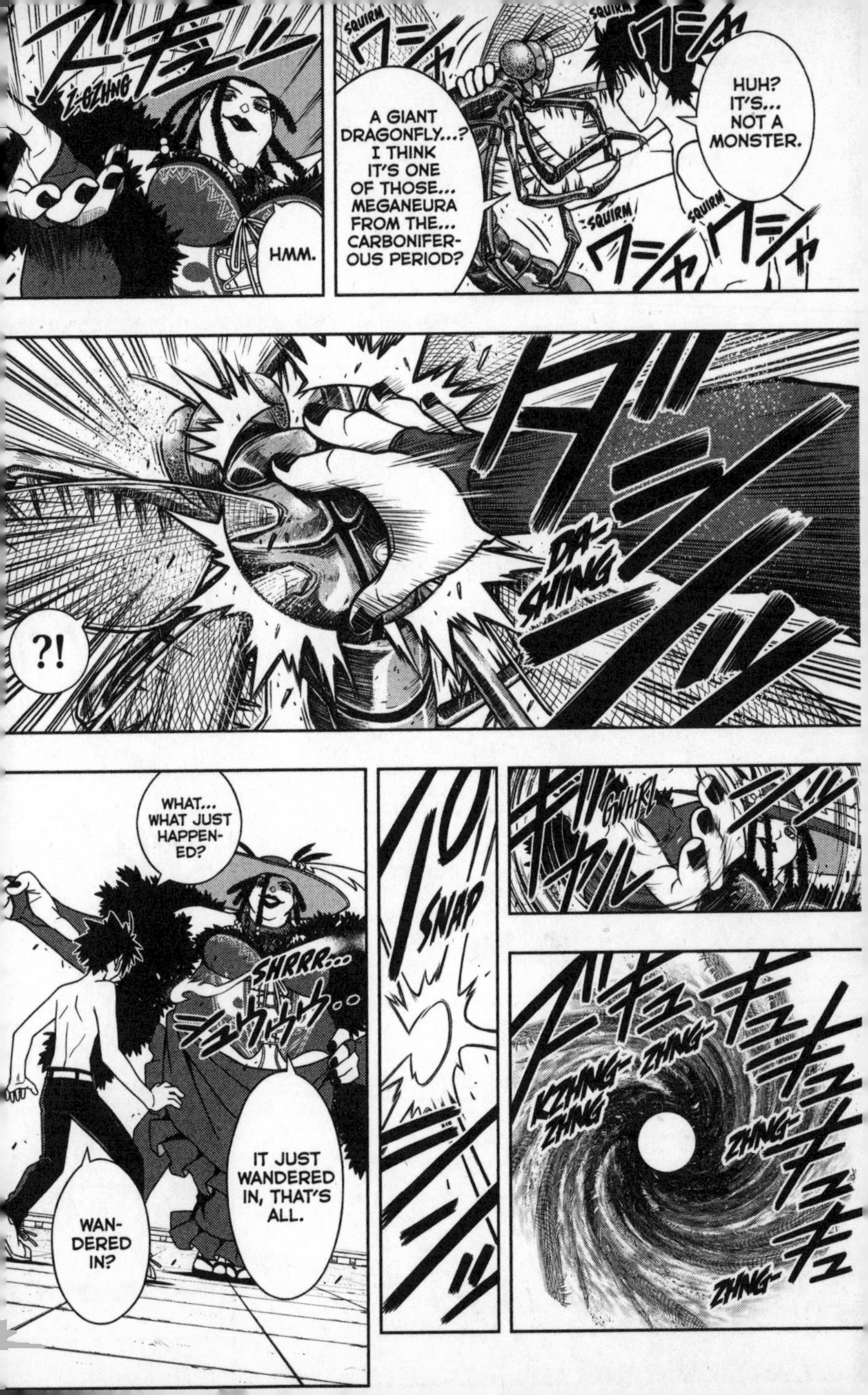
SQUIRM
SQUIRM
HUH? IT'S... NOT A MONSTER.
A GIANT DRAGONFLY...? I THINK IT'S ONE OF THOSE... MEGANEURA FROM THE... CARBONIFEROUS PERIOD?
SQUIRM
SQUIRM
Z-GZHNG
HMM.
DA-SHING
?!
GWHIRL
KZHNG-ZHNG
ZHNG-
ZHNG-
ZHNG-
SNAP
WHAT... WHAT JUST HAPPENED?
SHRRR...
IT JUST WANDERED IN, THAT'S ALL.
WANDERED IN?

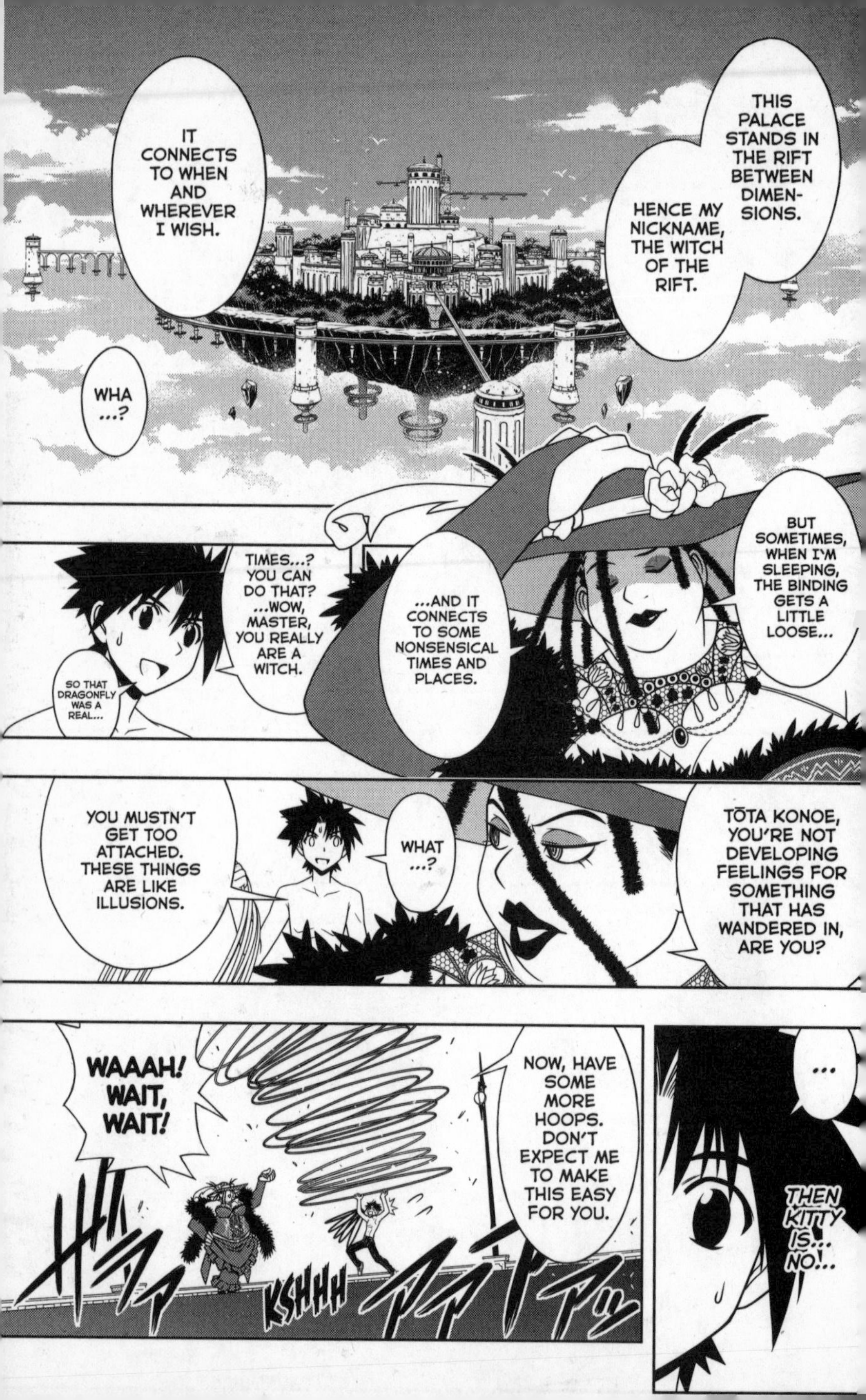
THIS PALACE STANDS IN THE RIFT BETWEEN DIMEN-SIONS.
HENCE MY NICKNAME, THE WITCH OF THE RIFT.
IT CONNECTS TO WHEN AND WHEREVER I WISH.
WHA ...?
BUT SOMETIMES, WHEN I'M SLEEPING, THE BINDING GETS A LITTLE LOOSE...
...AND IT CONNECTS TO SOME NONSENSICAL TIMES AND PLACES.
TIMES...? YOU CAN DO THAT? ...WOW, MASTER, YOU REALLY ARE A WITCH.
SO THAT DRAGONFLY WAS A REAL...
TŌTA KONOE, YOU'RE NOT DEVELOPING FEELINGS FOR SOMETHING THAT HAS WANDERED IN, ARE YOU?
WHAT ...?
YOU MUSTN'T GET TOO ATTACHED. THESE THINGS ARE LIKE ILLUSIONS.
...
THEN KITTY IS... NO!...
NOW, HAVE SOME MORE HOOPS. DON'T EXPECT ME TO MAKE THIS EASY FOR YOU.
WAAAH! WAIT, WAIT!
KSHHH

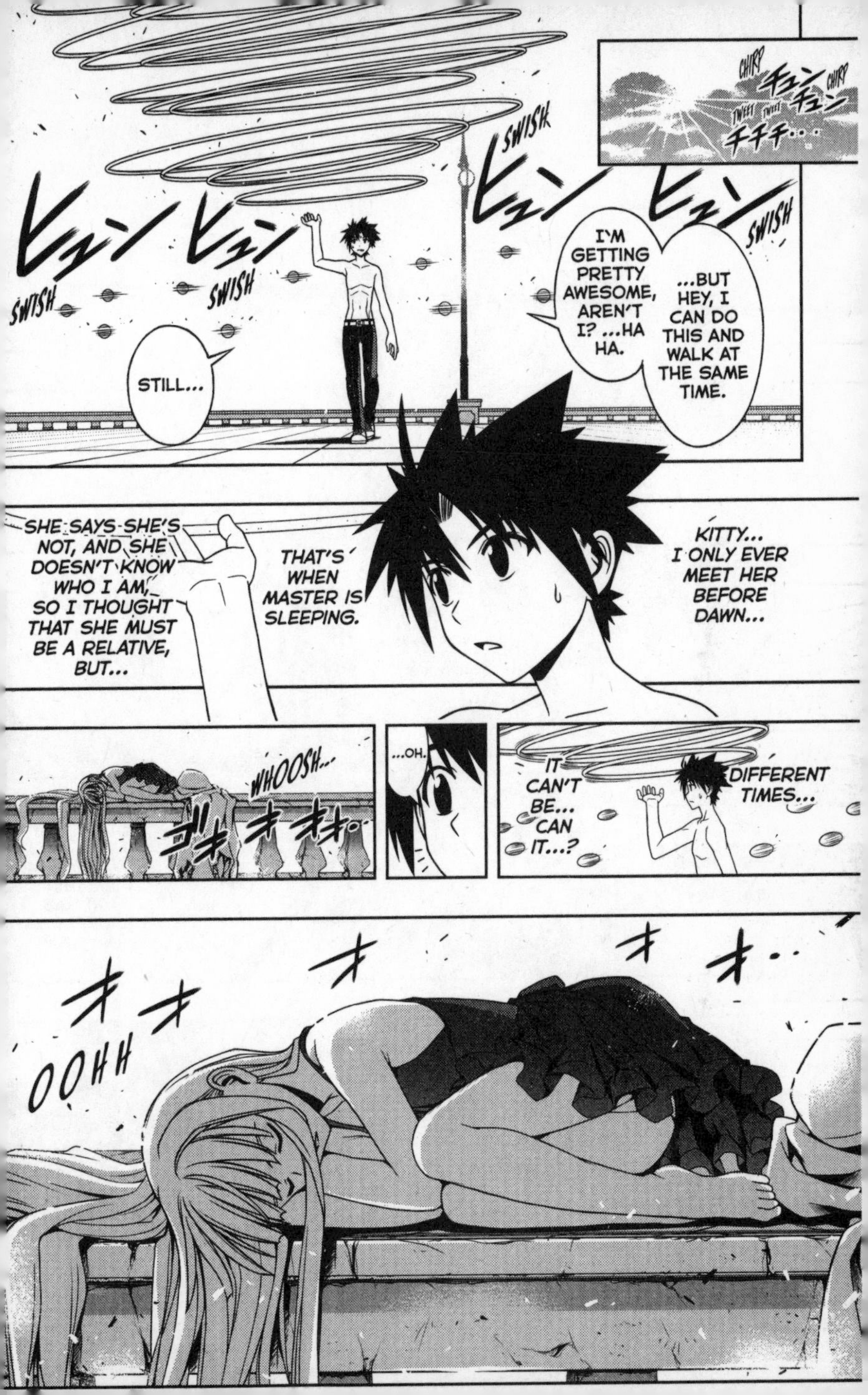
CHIRP
チュン
チュン
CHIRP
TWEET TWEET
チチチ...
SWISH
ヒュン ヒュン
SWISH
...BUT HEY, I CAN DO THIS AND WALK AT THE SAME TIME.
I'M GETTING PRETTY AWESOME, AREN'T I? ...HA HA.
SWISH
ヒュン ヒュン
SWISH
STILL...
KITTY... I ONLY EVER MEET HER BEFORE DAWN...
THAT'S WHEN MASTER IS SLEEPING.
SHE SAYS SHE'S NOT, AND SHE DOESN'T KNOW WHO I AM, SO I THOUGHT THAT SHE MUST BE A RELATIVE, BUT...
DIFFERENT TIMES...
IT CAN'T BE... CAN IT...?
...OH.
WHOOSH...
ゴォォォ
オォォ
OOHH

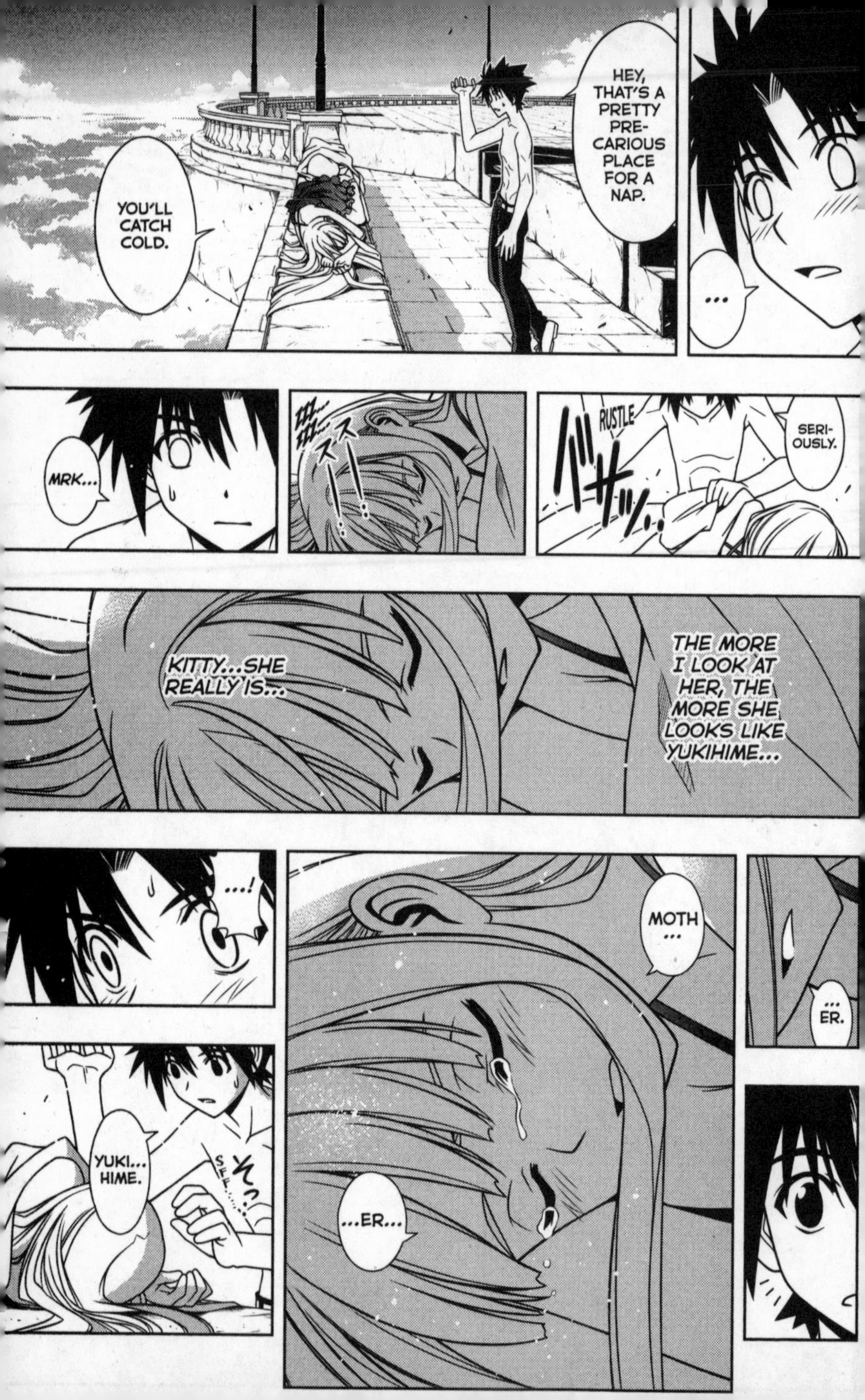
...
HEY, THAT'S A PRETTY PRE-CARIOUS PLACE FOR A NAP.
YOU'LL CATCH COLD.
RUSTLE
SERI-OUSLY.
MRK...
THE MORE I LOOK AT HER, THE MORE SHE LOOKS LIKE YUKIHIME...
KITTY...SHE REALLY IS...
...ER.
MOTH...
...ER...
...!
YUKI... HIME.
SFF...

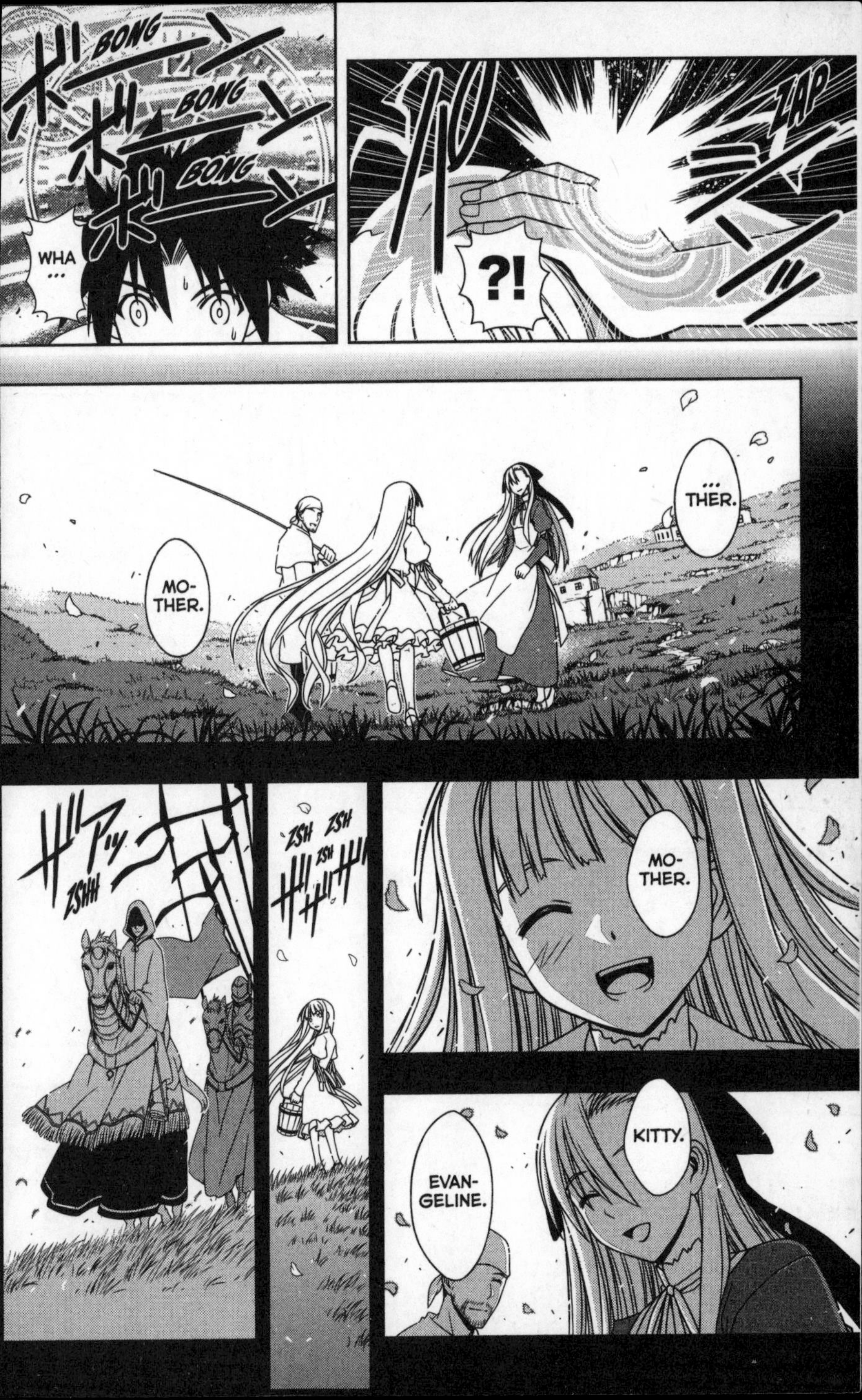
ZAP
?!
BONG
BONG
BONG
WHA ...
... THER.
MO-THER.
MO-THER.
KITTY.
EVAN-GELINE.
ZSH
ZSH
ZSH
ZSHH

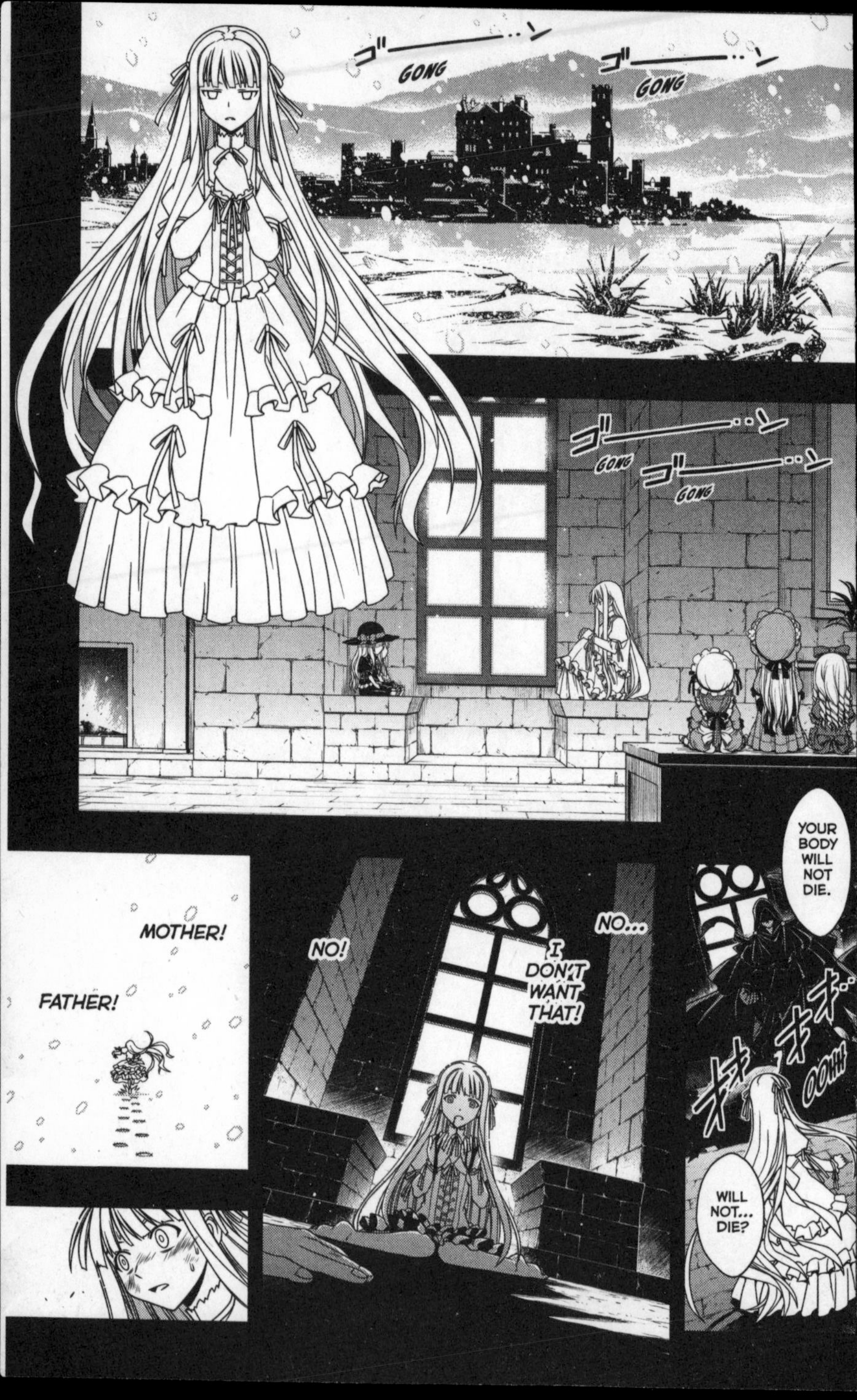
GONG
GONG
GONG
GONG
YOUR BODY WILL NOT DIE.
OOHH
WILL NOT... DIE?
NO...
I DON'T WANT THAT!
NO!
MOTHER!
FATHER!

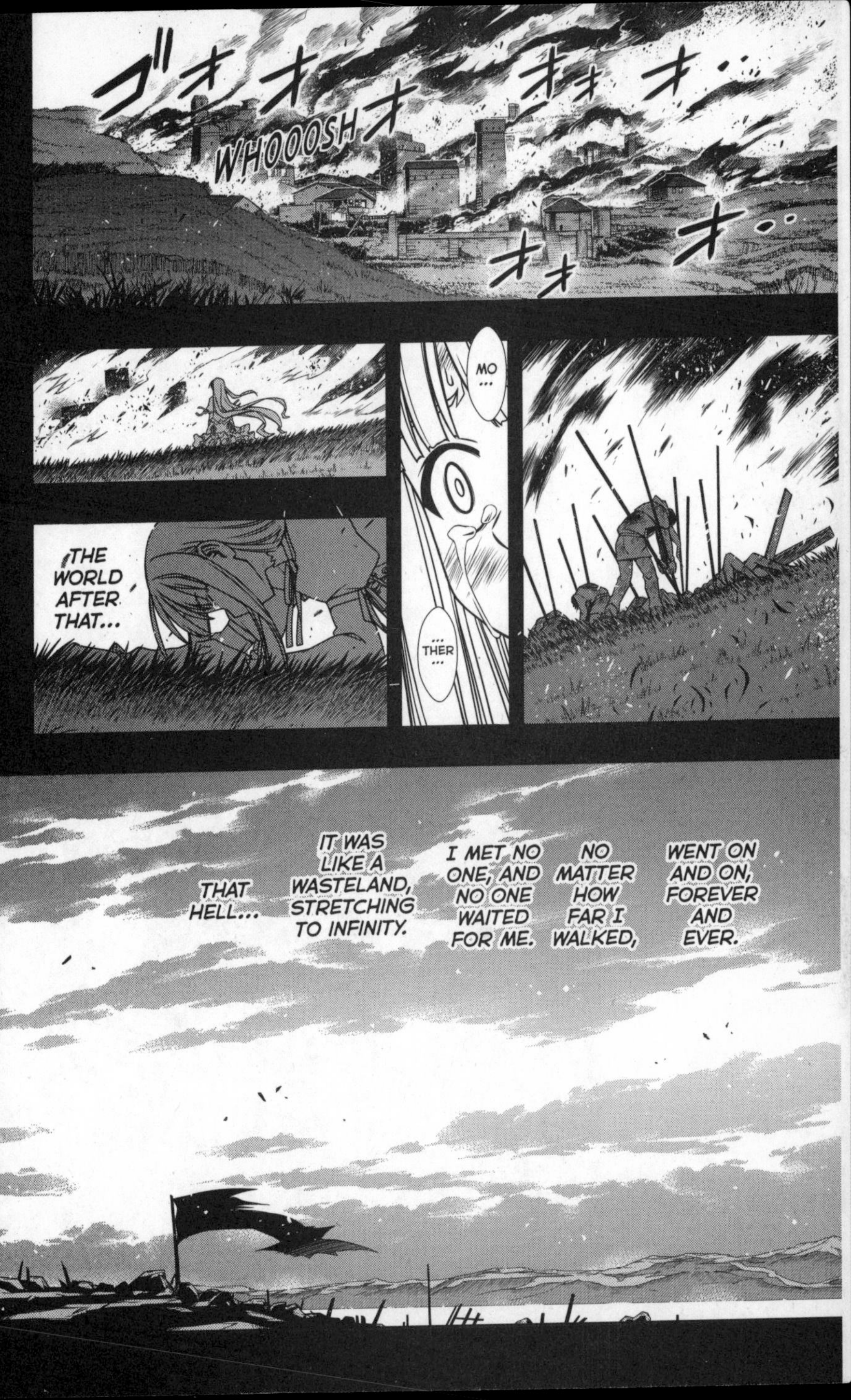
ゴオオオォォオ…
WHOOOSH
ォォオ…
MO ...
... THER ...
THE WORLD AFTER THAT...
THAT HELL...
IT WAS LIKE A WASTELAND, STRETCHING TO INFINITY.
I MET NO ONE, AND NO ONE WAITED FOR ME.
NO MATTER HOW FAR I WALKED,
WENT ON AND ON, FOREVER AND EVER.

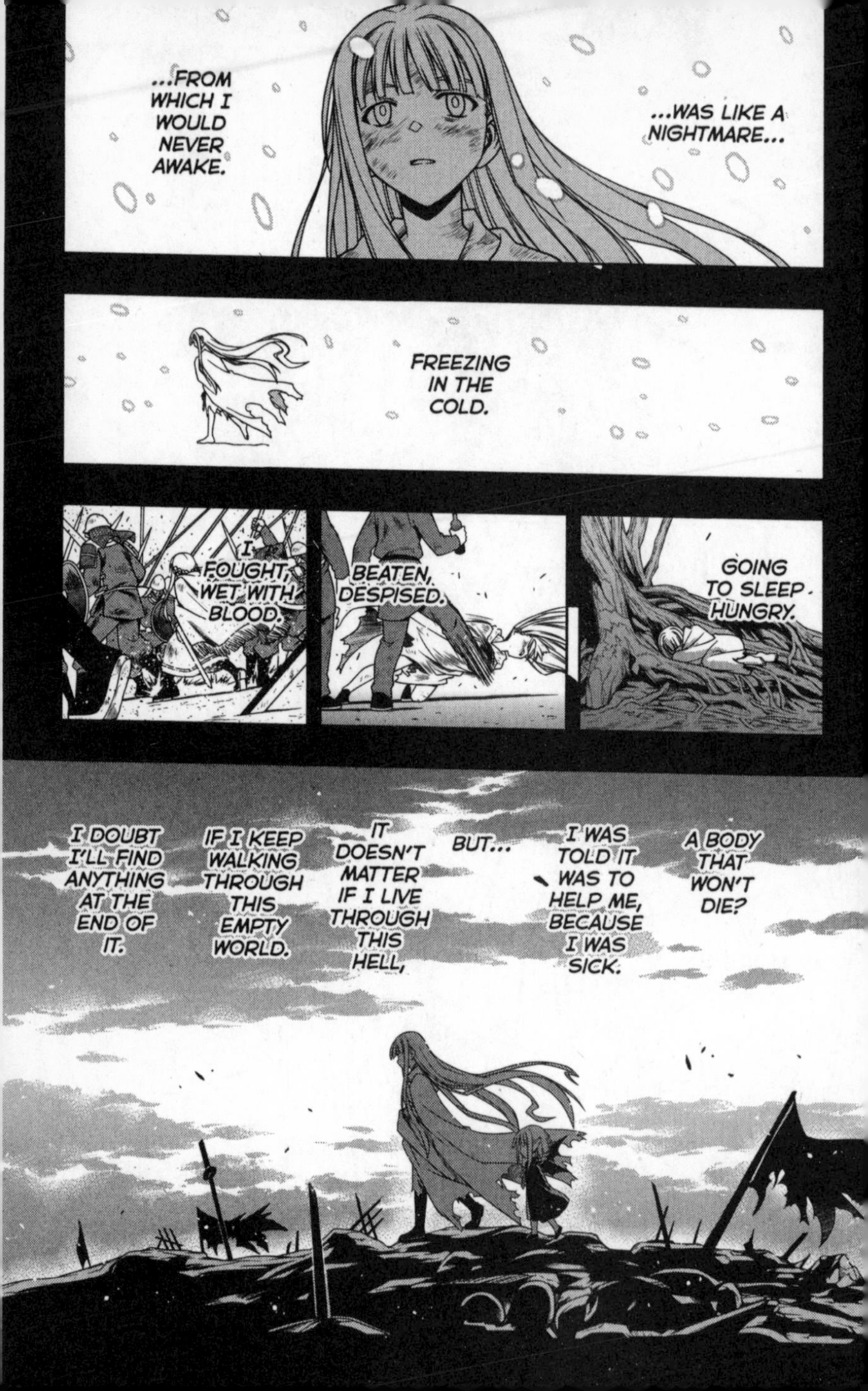
...WAS LIKE A NIGHTMARE...
...FROM WHICH I WOULD NEVER AWAKE.
FREEZING IN THE COLD.
GOING TO SLEEP HUNGRY.
BEATEN, DESPISED.
I FOUGHT, WET WITH BLOOD.
A BODY THAT WON'T DIE?
I WAS TOLD IT WAS TO HELP ME, BECAUSE I WAS SICK.
BUT...
IT DOESN'T MATTER IF I LIVE THROUGH THIS HELL,
IF I KEEP WALKING THROUGH THIS EMPTY WORLD.
I DOUBT I'LL FIND ANYTHING AT THE END OF IT.

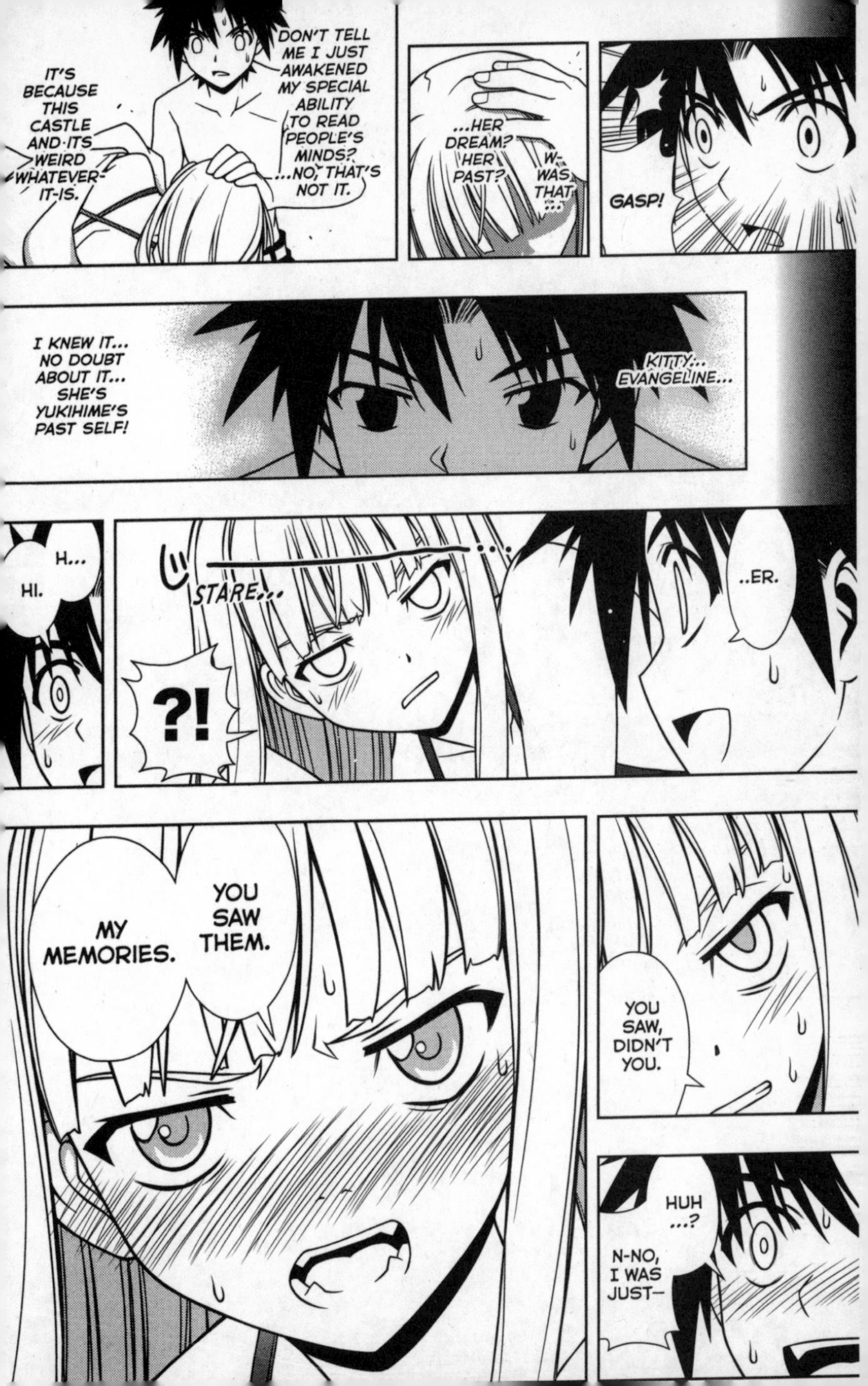
GASP!
W-WAS THAT...
...HER DREAM? HER PAST?
DON'T TELL ME I JUST AWAKENED MY SPECIAL ABILITY TO READ PEOPLE'S MINDS? ...NO, THAT'S NOT IT.
IT'S BECAUSE THIS CASTLE AND ITS WEIRD WHATEVER-IT-IS.
KITTY... EVANGELINE...
I KNEW IT... NO DOUBT ABOUT IT... SHE'S YUKIHIME'S PAST SELF!
..ER.
STARE...
?!
H... HI.
YOU SAW, DIDN'T YOU.
HUH ...?
N-NO, I WAS JUST—
YOU SAW THEM.
MY MEMORIES.

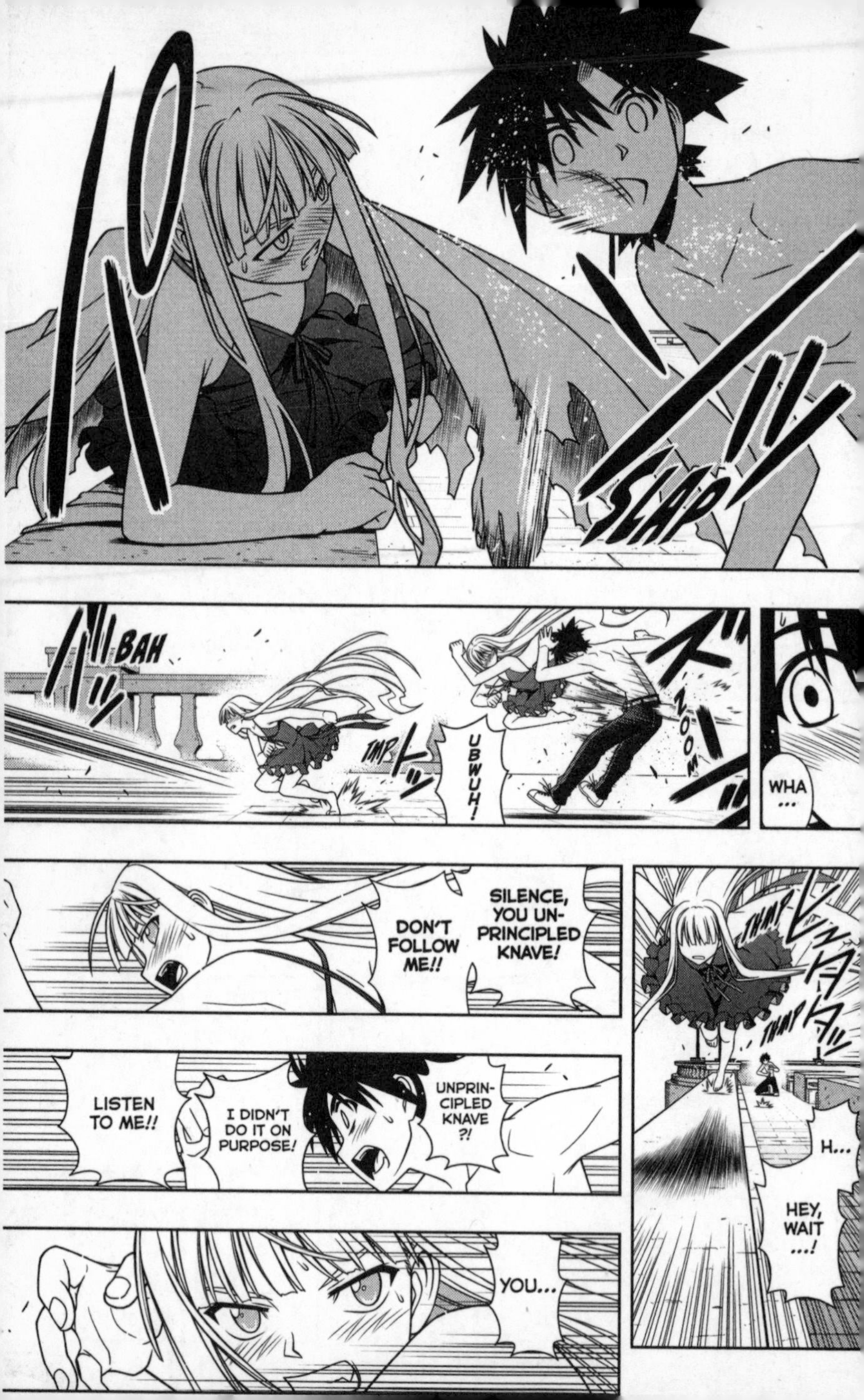
SLAP
WHA...
ZOOM
UBWUH!
BAH
THMP
THMP
THMP
H...
HEY, WAIT...!
SILENCE, YOU UN-PRINCIPLED KNAVE!
DON'T FOLLOW ME!!
UNPRIN-CIPLED KNAVE?!
I DIDN'T DO IT ON PURPOSE!
LISTEN TO ME!!
YOU...

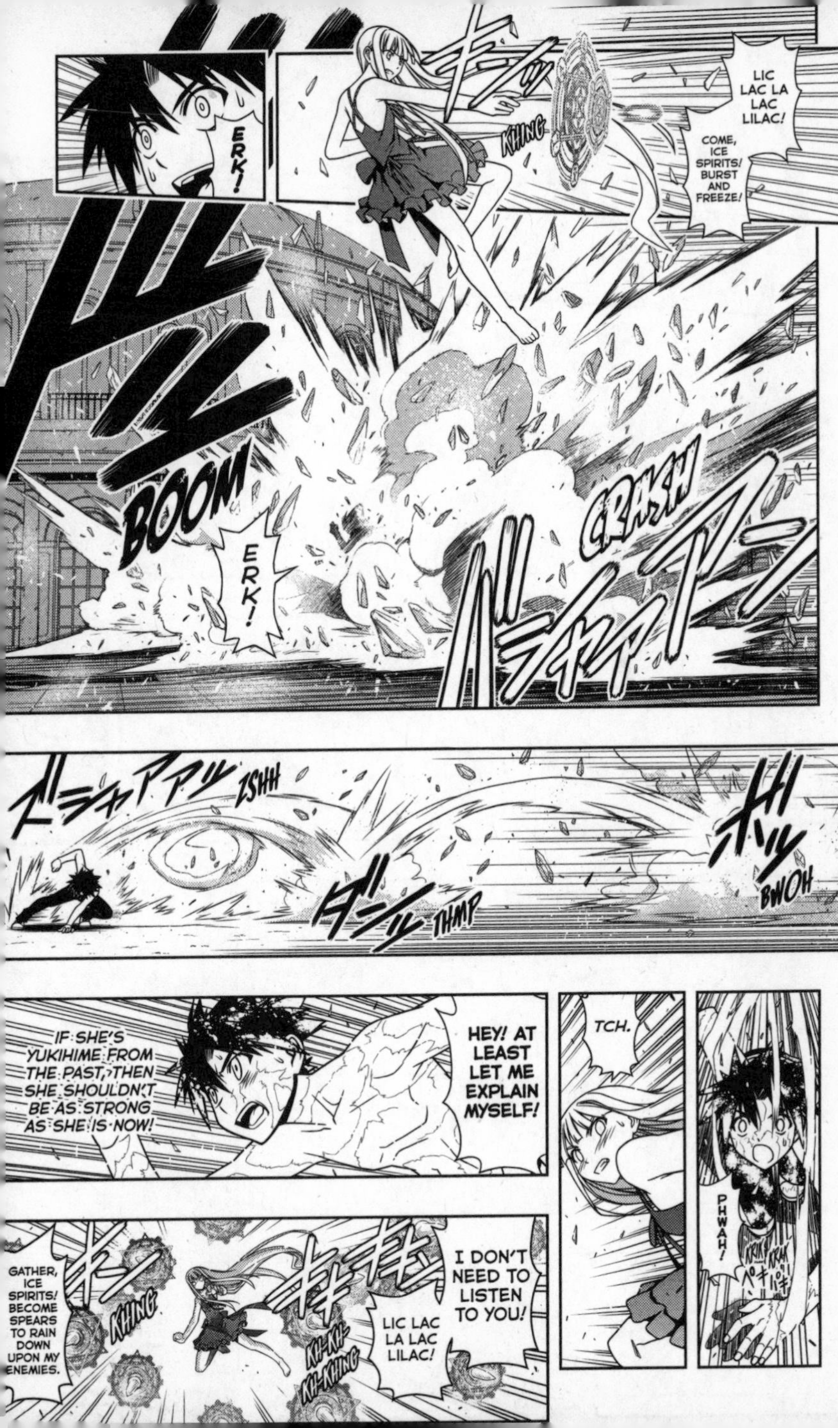
LIC LAC LA LAC LILAC!
COME, ICE SPIRITS! BURST AND FREEZE!
KHING
ERK!
CRASH
BOOM
ERK!
BWOH
THMP
ZSHH
PHWAH!
KRAK KRAK
TCH.
HEY! AT LEAST LET ME EXPLAIN MYSELF!
IF SHE'S YUKIHIME FROM THE PAST, THEN SHE SHOULDN'T BE AS STRONG AS SHE IS NOW!
I DON'T NEED TO LISTEN TO YOU!
LIC LAC LA LAC LILAC!
KH-KH-KH-KHING
KHING
GATHER, ICE SPIRITS! BECOME SPEARS TO RAIN DOWN UPON MY ENEMIES.

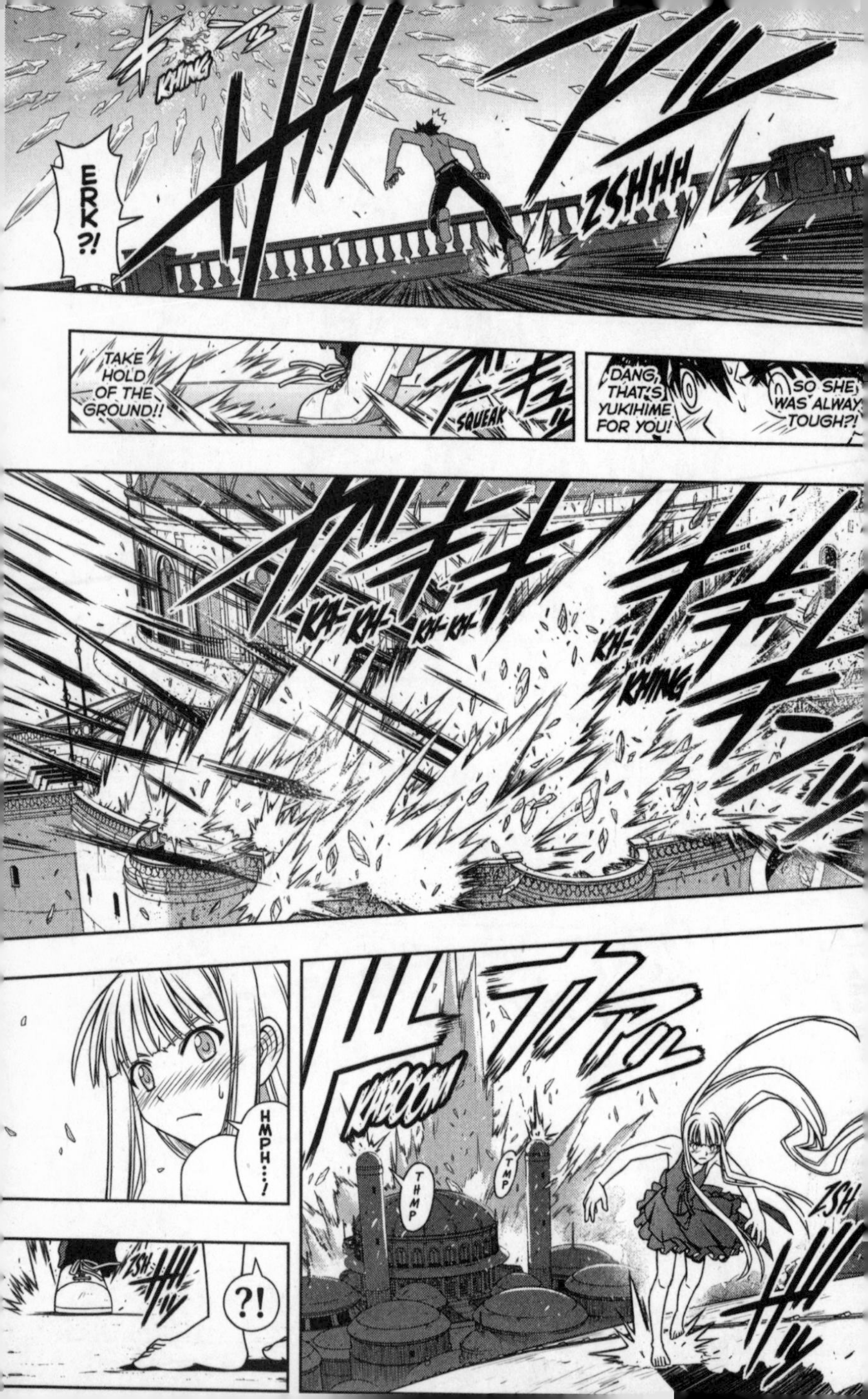

KHING
ERK?!
ZSHHH
SO SHE WAS ALWAY TOUGH?!
DANG, THAT'S YUKIHIME FOR YOU!
TAKE HOLD OF THE GROUND!!
SQUEAK
KH-KH-
KH-KH-
KH-KHING
TMP
THMP
KABOOM
ZSH
HMPH...!
?!
ZSH

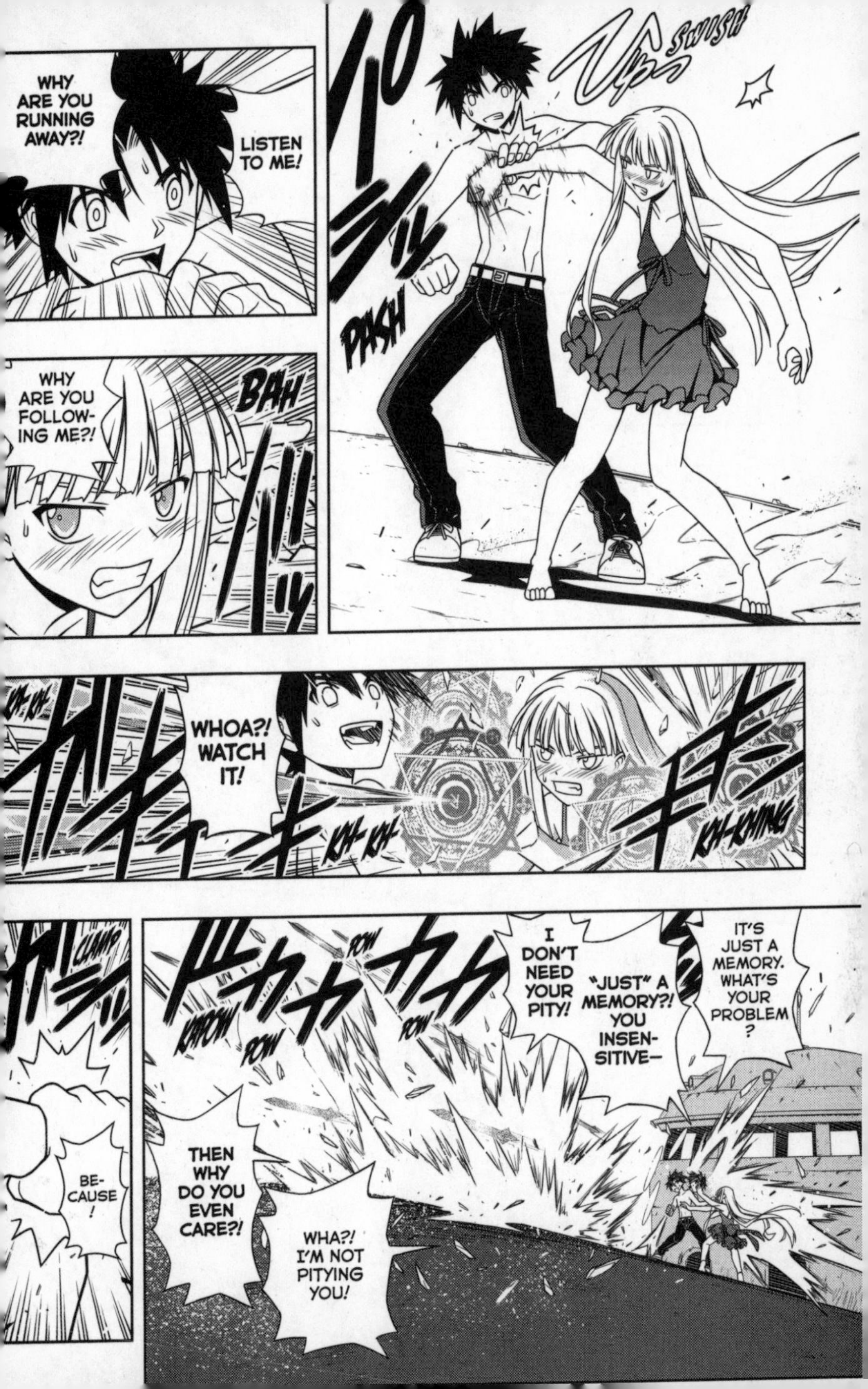
SWISH
PASH
LISTEN TO ME!
WHY ARE YOU RUNNING AWAY?!
BAH
WHY ARE YOU FOLLOWING ME?!
KH-KHING
WHOA?! WATCH IT!
KH-KH
KH-KH
IT'S JUST A MEMORY. WHAT'S YOUR PROBLEM?
"JUST" A MEMORY?! YOU INSEN-SITIVE—
I DON'T NEED YOUR PITY!
POW
POW
KAPOW
POW
WHA?! I'M NOT PITYING YOU!
THEN WHY DO YOU EVEN CARE?!
CLAMP
BE-CAUSE!

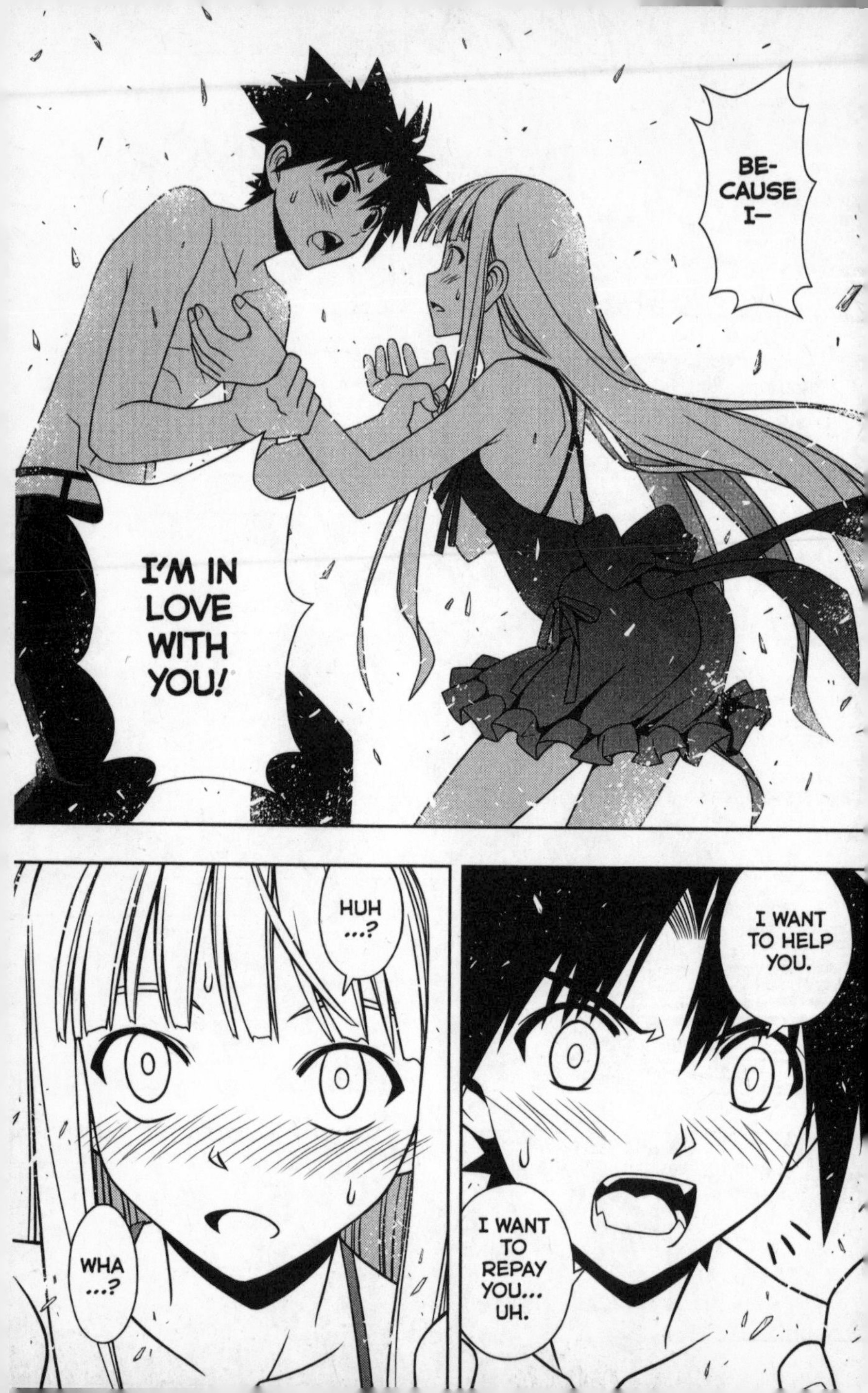
BE-CAUSE I—
I'M IN LOVE WITH YOU!
I WANT TO HELP YOU.
I WANT TO REPAY YOU... UH.
HUH ...?
WHA ...?

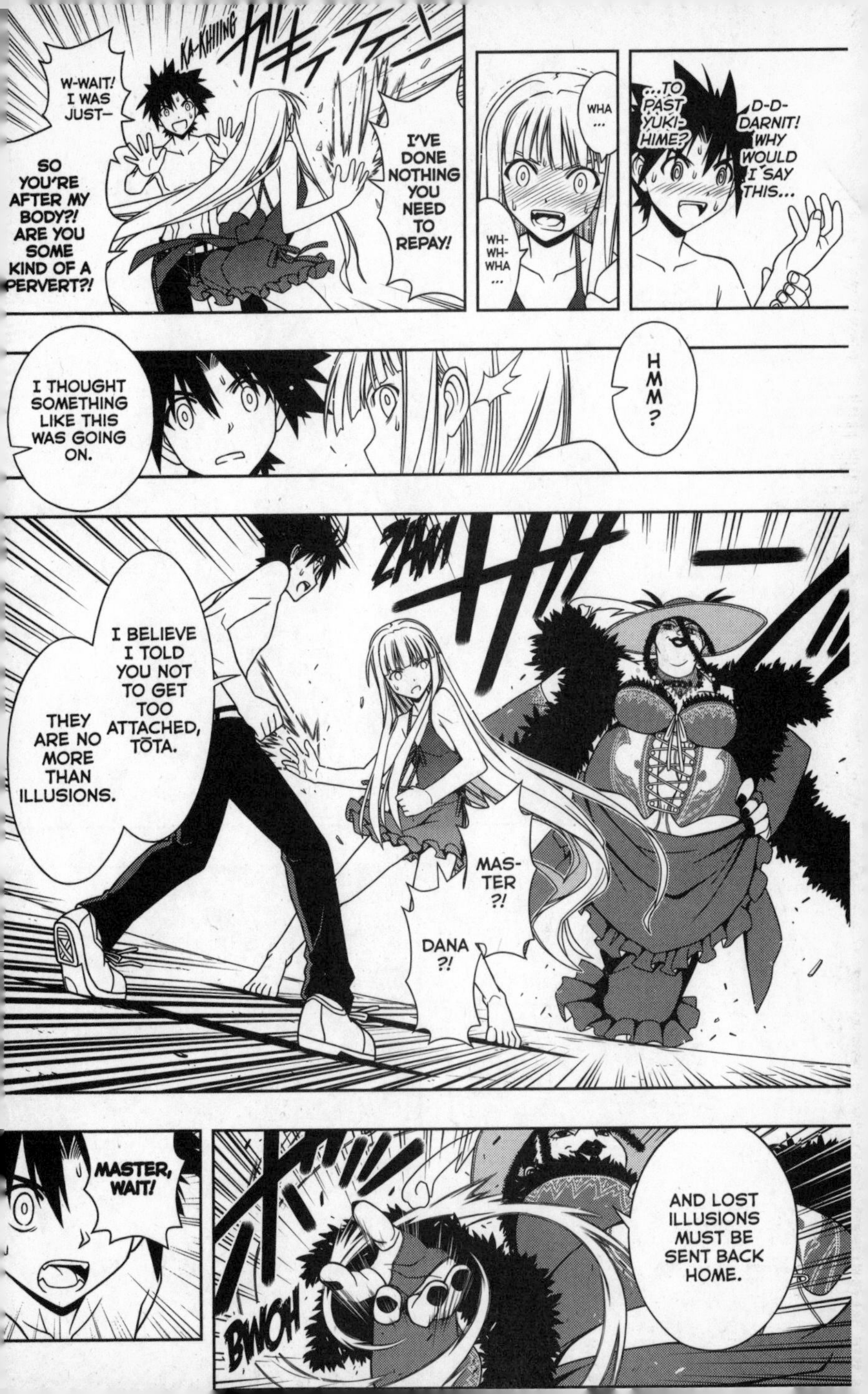
D-D-DARNIT! WHY WOULD I SAY THIS...
...TO PAST YUKI-HIME?
WHA...
WH-WH-WHA...
KA-KHIING
I'VE DONE NOTHING YOU NEED TO REPAY!
W-WAIT! I WAS JUST—
SO YOU'RE AFTER MY BODY?! ARE YOU SOME KIND OF A PERVERT?!
HMM?
I THOUGHT SOMETHING LIKE THIS WAS GOING ON.
ZAAA
I BELIEVE I TOLD YOU NOT TO GET TOO ATTACHED, TŌTA.
THEY ARE NO MORE THAN ILLUSIONS.
MASTER?!
DANA?!
AND LOST ILLUSIONS MUST BE SENT BACK HOME.
BWOH
MASTER, WAIT!

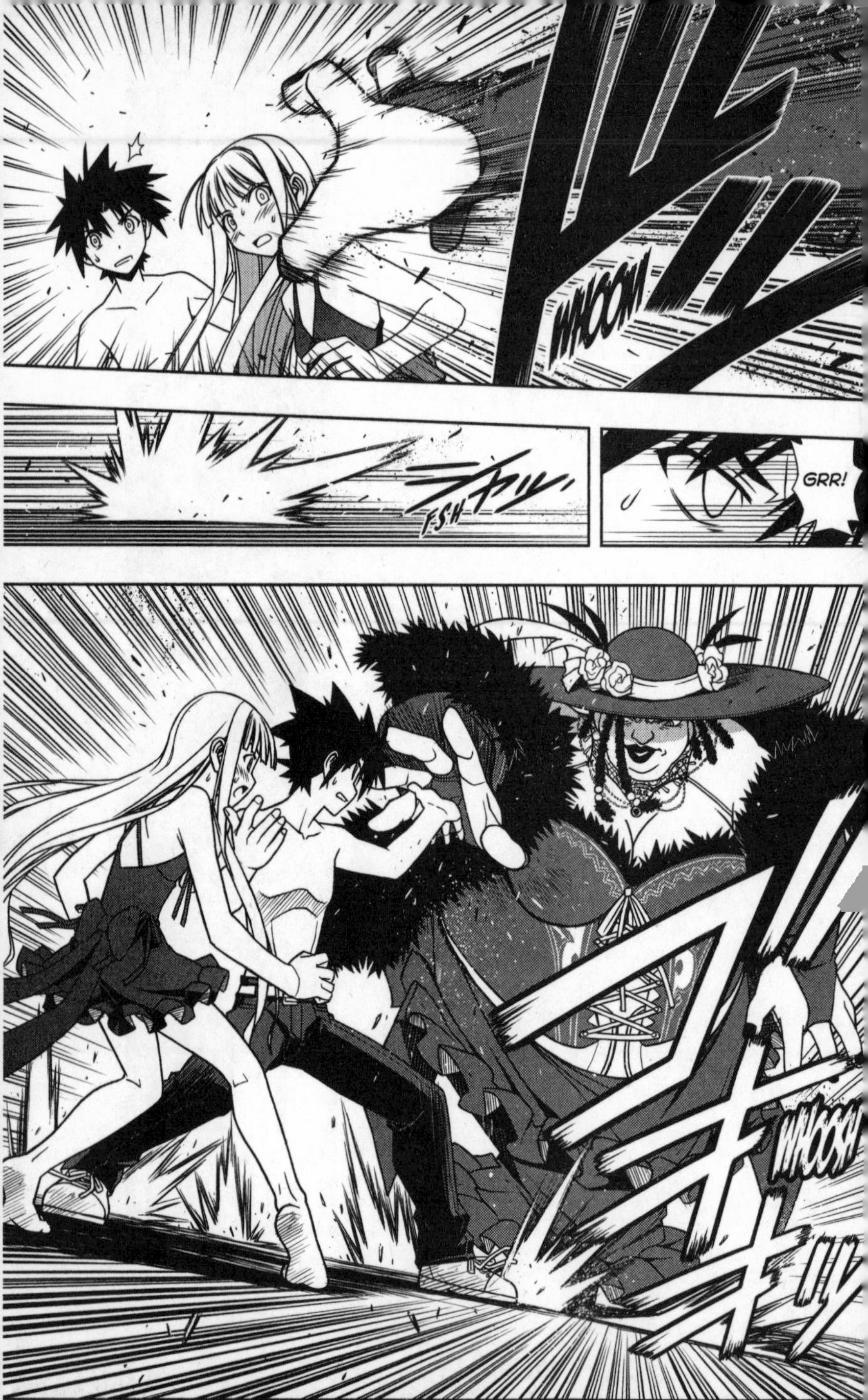
WHOOM
GRR!
F-S-H
WHOOSH

UQ HOLDER!

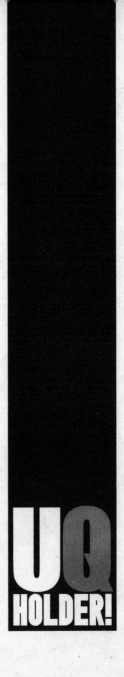

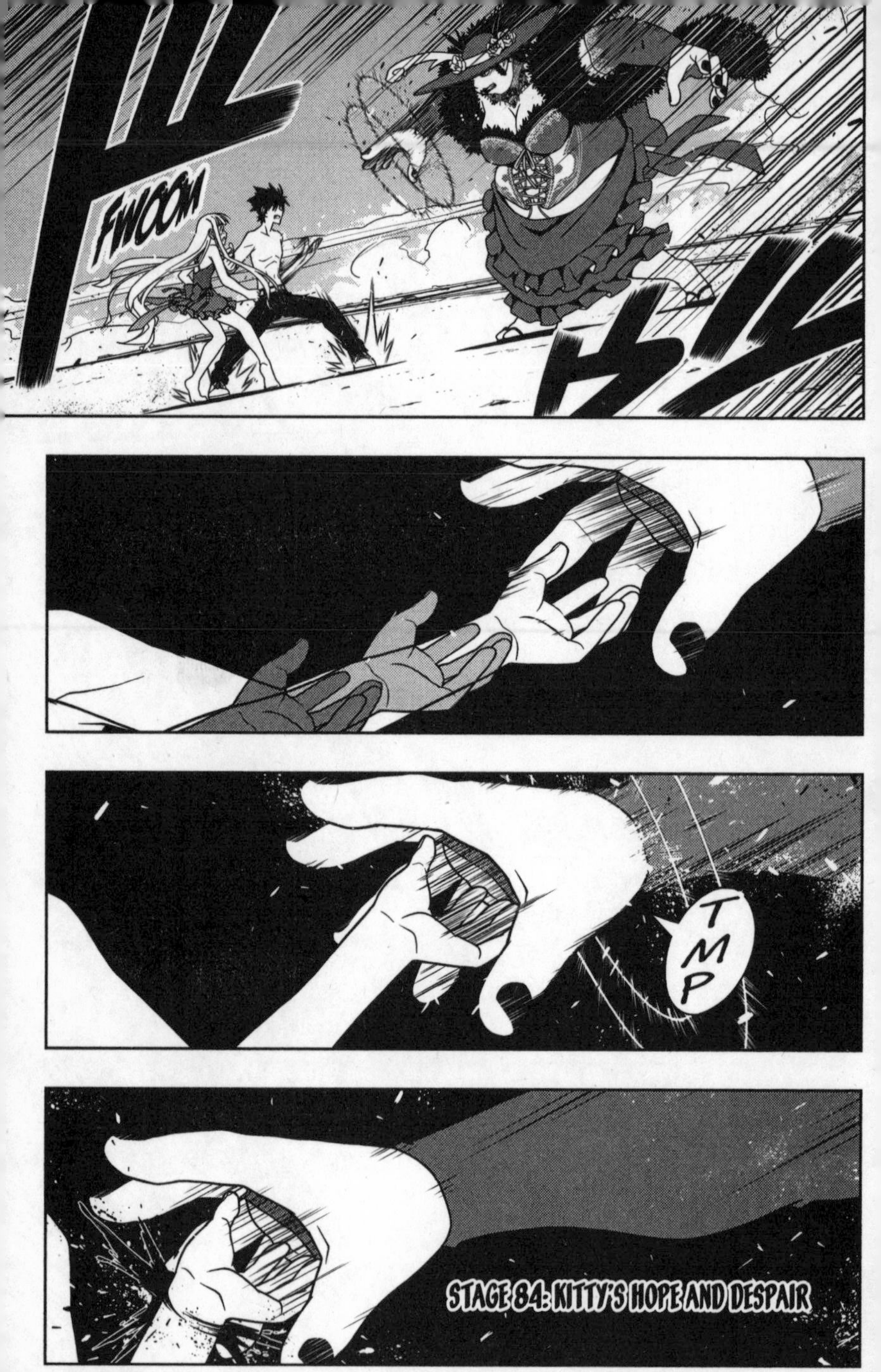
FWOOM
TMP
STAGE 84: KITTY'S HOPE AND DESPAIR

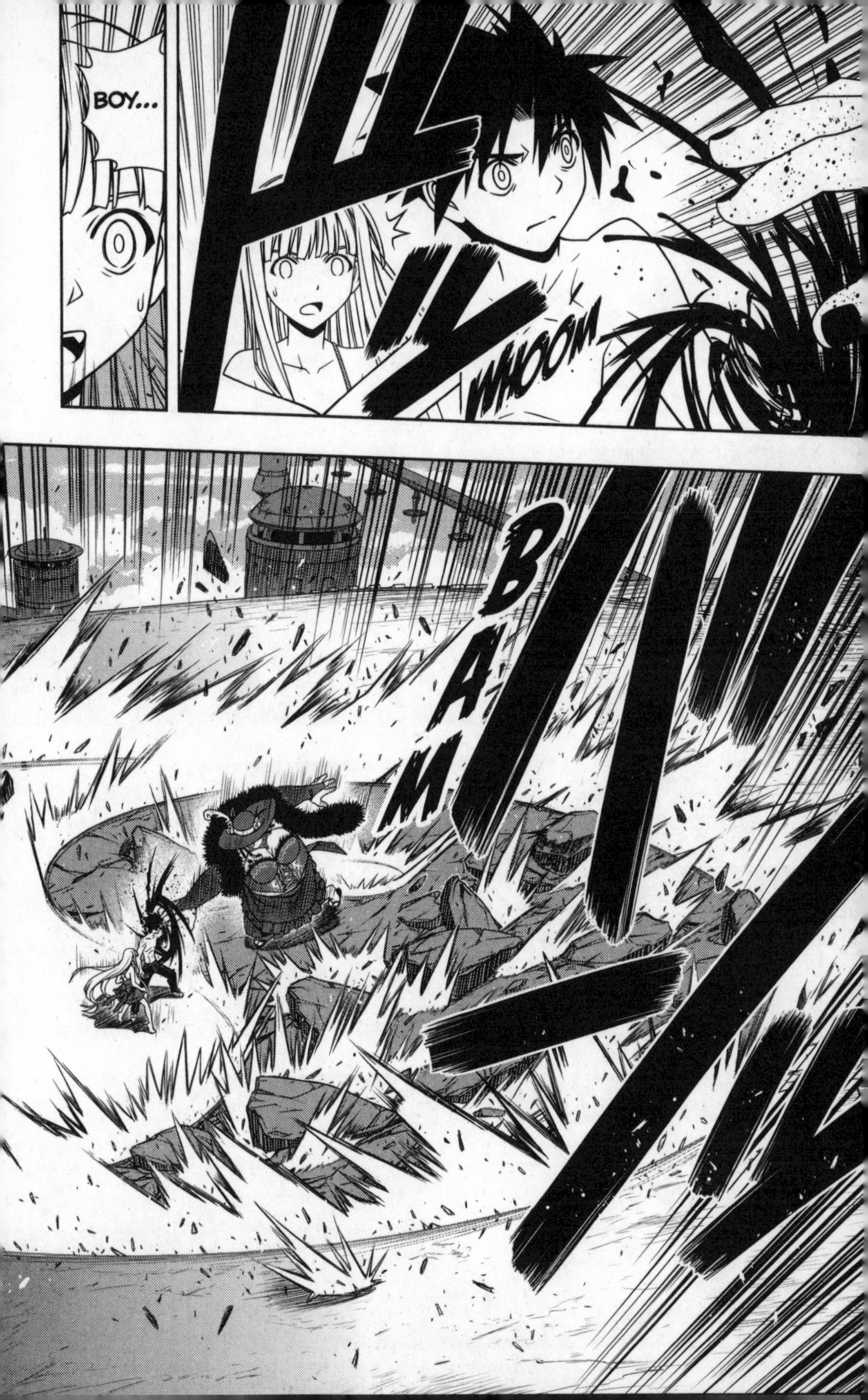
WHOOM
BOY...
BAM

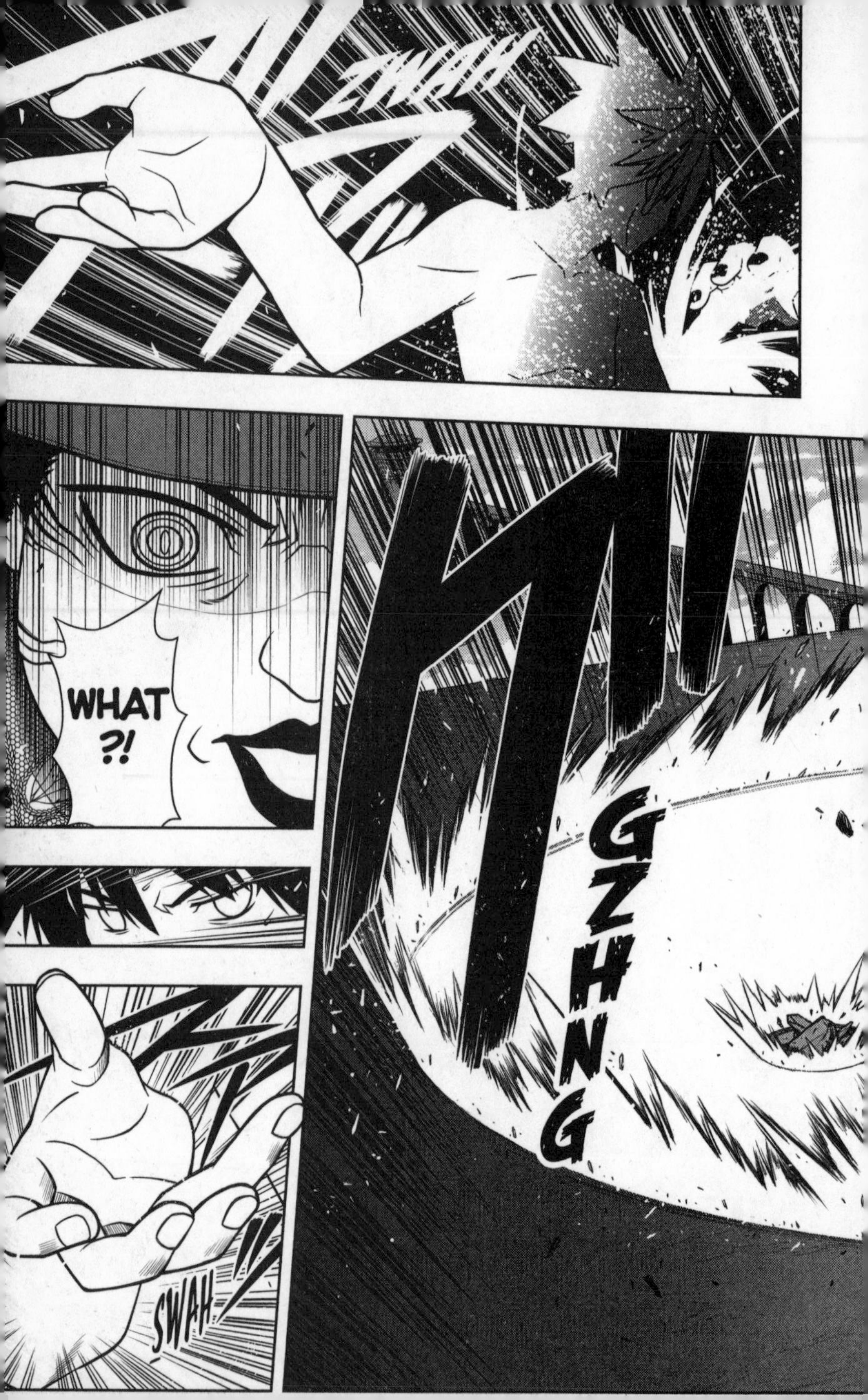
GZHNG
WHAT ?!
SWAH

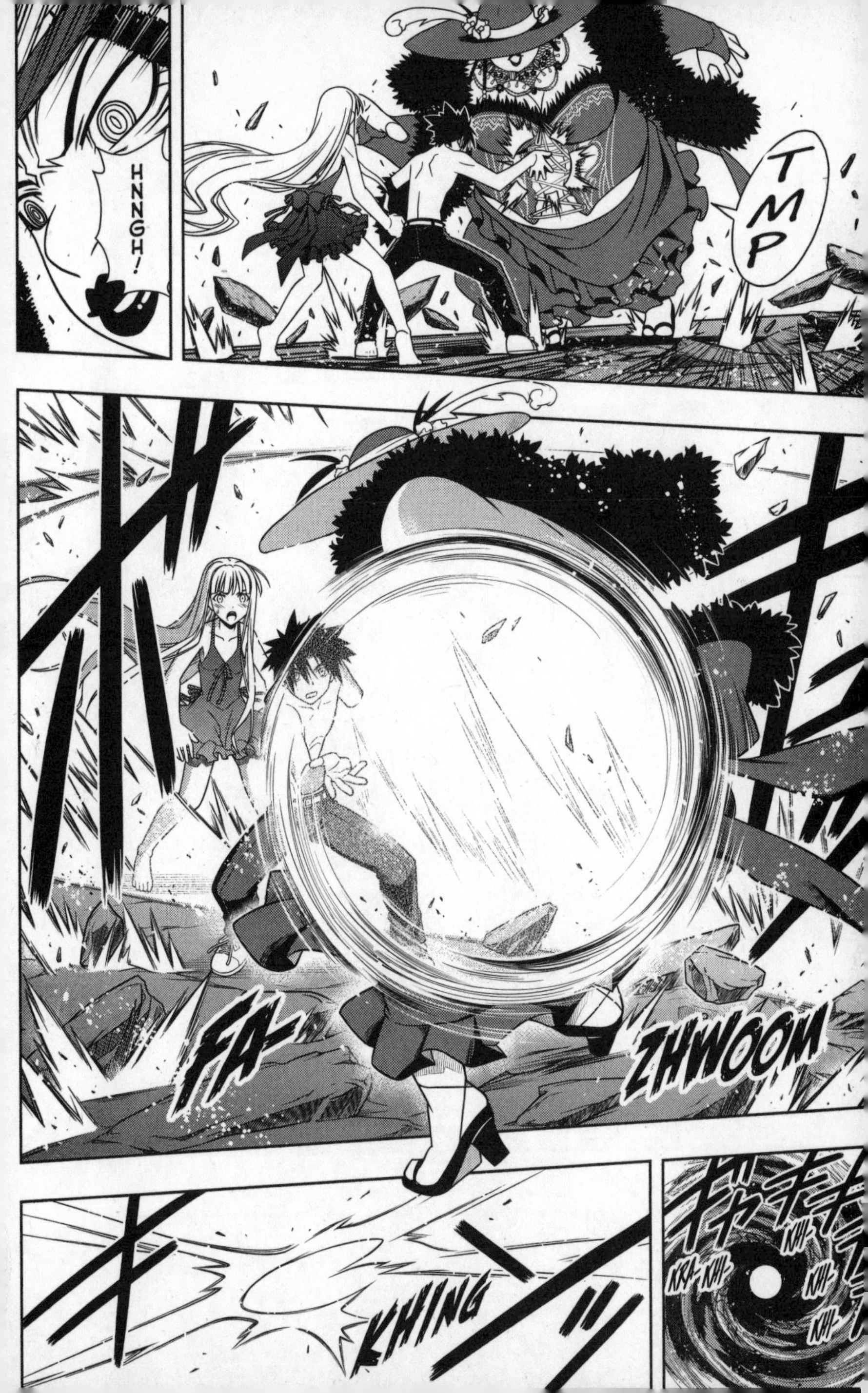
TMP
HNNGH!
FA-
ZHWOOM
KRA-KHI
KHI-
KHI-
KHI-
KHING

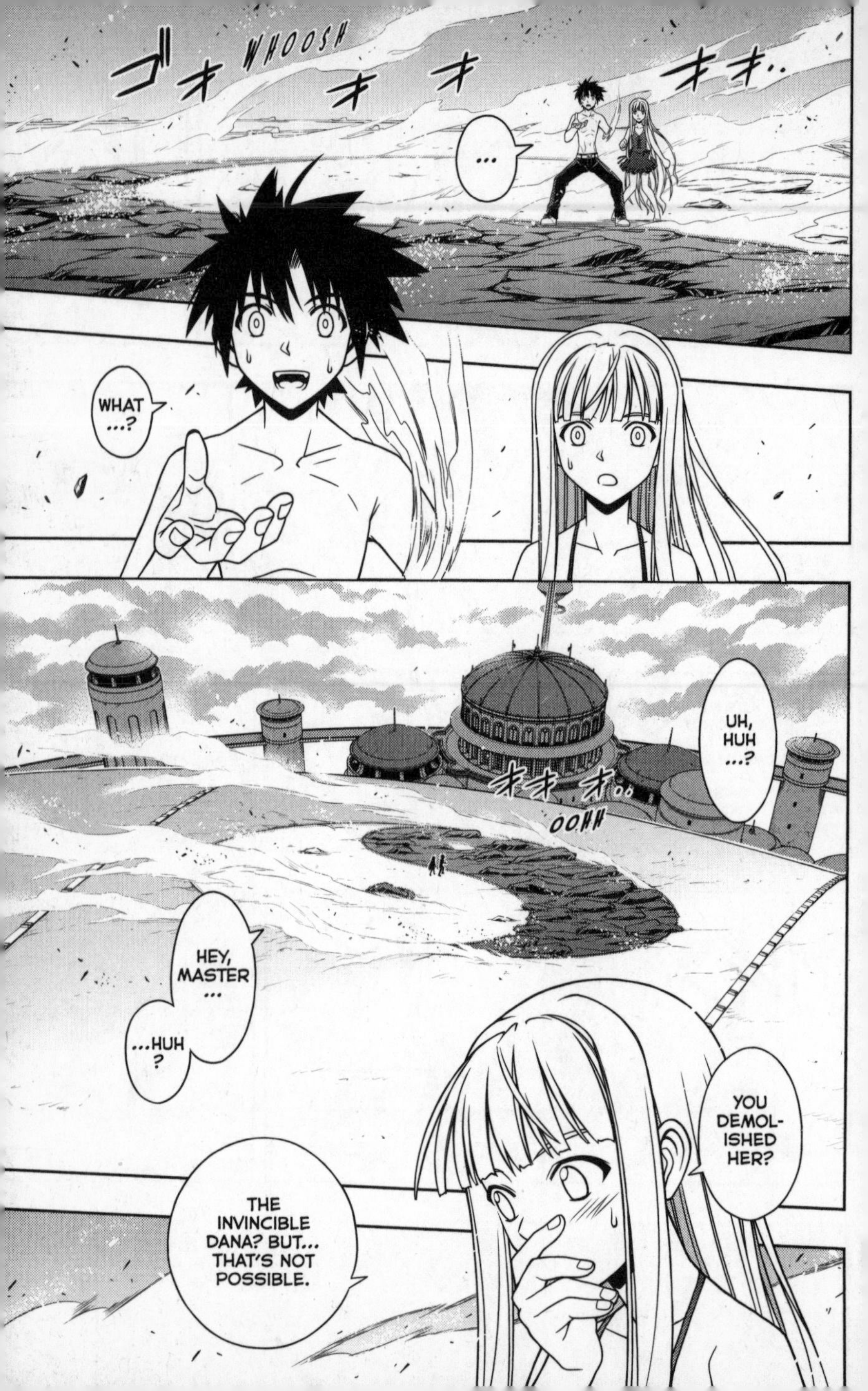
ゴオ WHOOSH オオ オォ..
...
WHAT ...?
UH, HUH ...?
オオオ.. OOHH
HEY, MASTER ...
...HUH ?
YOU DEMOL-ISHED HER?
THE INVINCIBLE DANA? BUT... THAT'S NOT POSSIBLE.

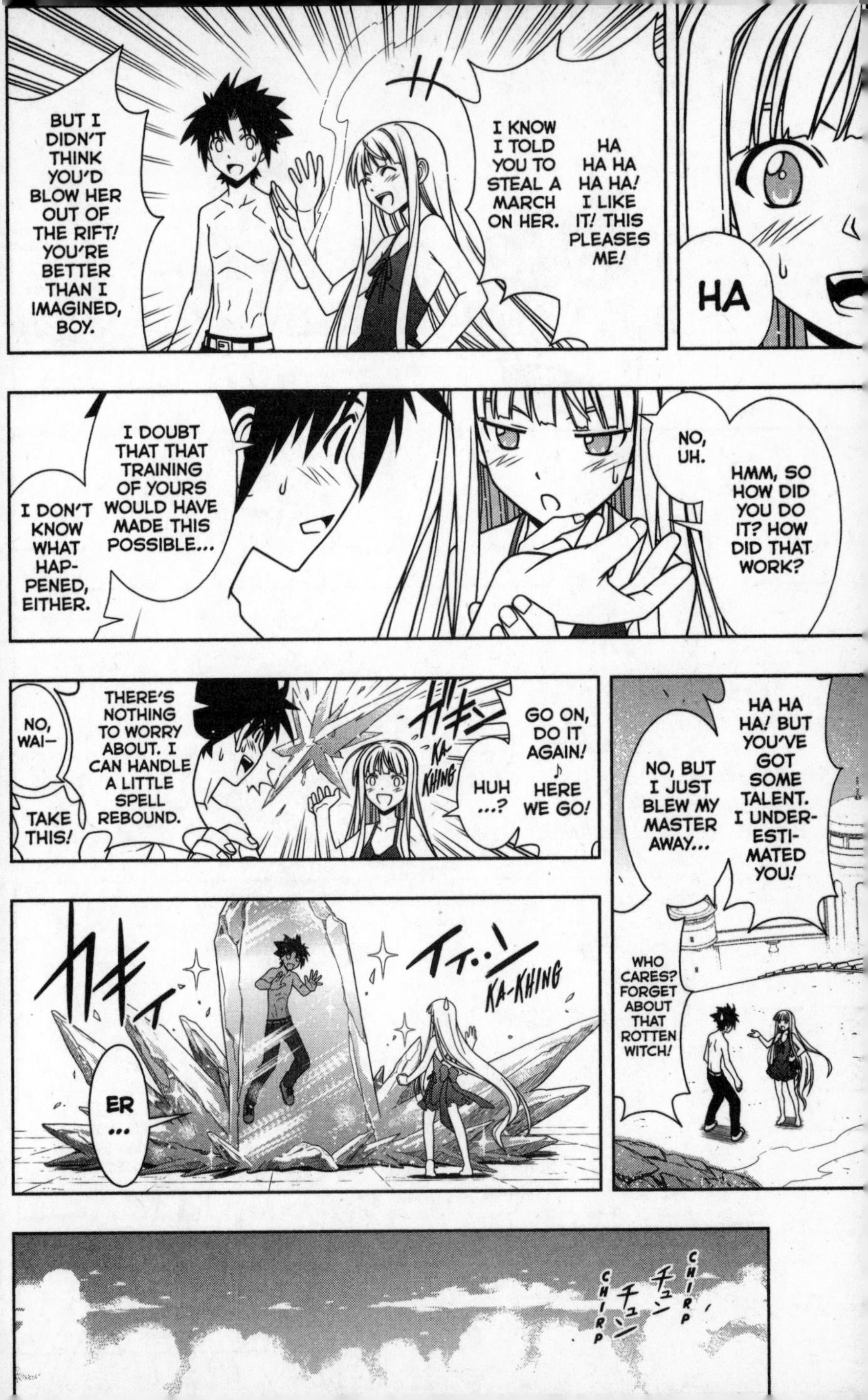
HA
HA HA HA HA! I LIKE IT! THIS PLEASES ME!
I KNOW I TOLD YOU TO STEAL A MARCH ON HER.
BUT I DIDN'T THINK YOU'D BLOW HER OUT OF THE RIFT! YOU'RE BETTER THAN I IMAGINED, BOY.
NO, UH.
HMM, SO HOW DID YOU DO IT? HOW DID THAT WORK?
I DOUBT THAT THAT TRAINING OF YOURS WOULD HAVE MADE THIS POSSIBLE...
I DON'T KNOW WHAT HAPPENED, EITHER.
HA HA HA! BUT YOU'VE GOT SOME TALENT. I UNDERESTIMATED YOU!
NO, BUT I JUST BLEW MY MASTER AWAY...
WHO CARES? FORGET ABOUT THAT ROTTEN WITCH!
GO ON, DO IT AGAIN! ♪ HERE WE GO!
KA-KHING
HUH ...?
THERE'S NOTHING TO WORRY ABOUT. I CAN HANDLE A LITTLE SPELL REBOUND.
NO, WAI—
TAKE THIS!
KA-KHING
ER ...
チュン CHIRP
チュン CHIRP

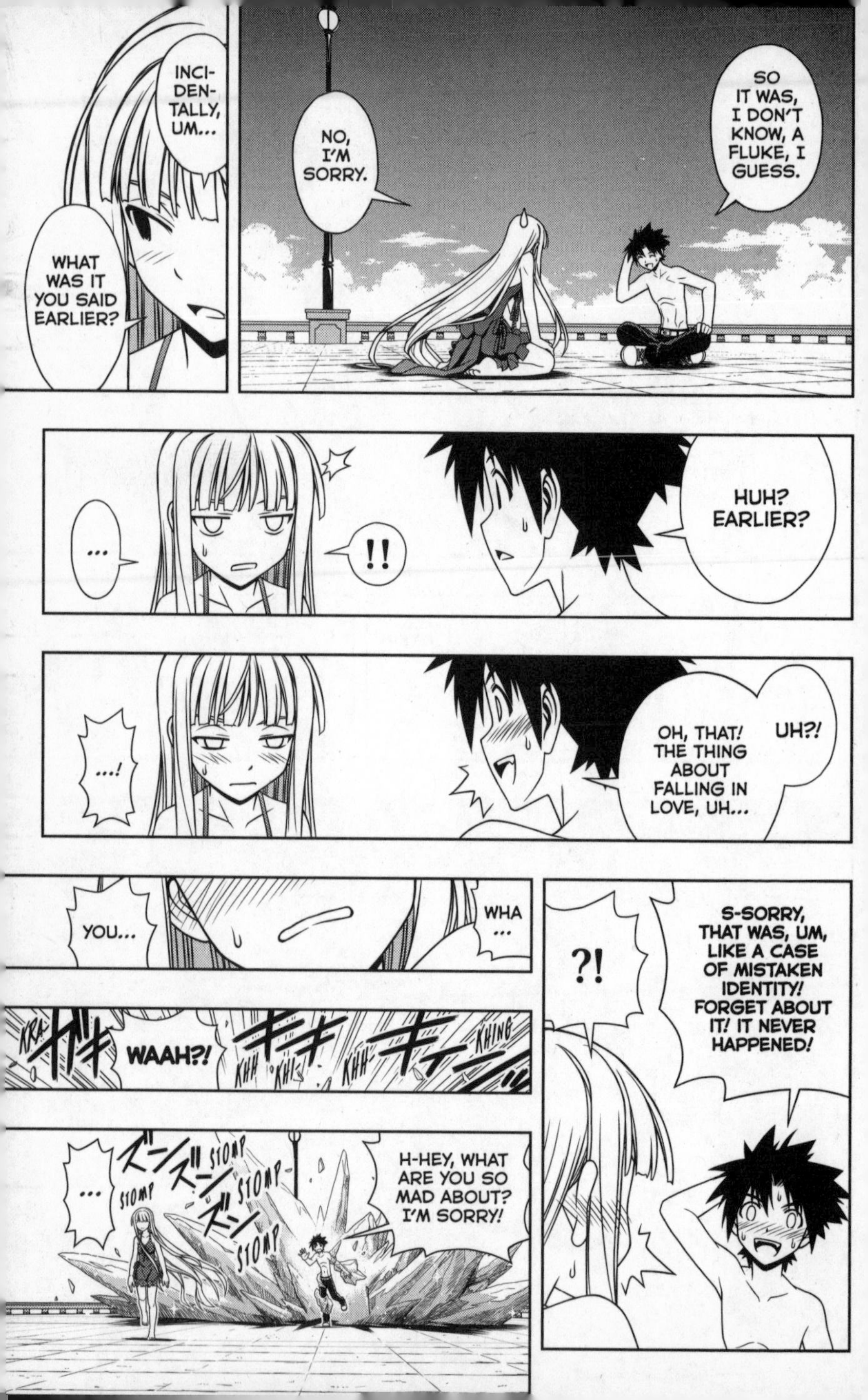

SO IT WAS, I DON'T KNOW, A FLUKE, I GUESS.
NO, I'M SORRY.
INCI-DEN-TALLY, UM...
WHAT WAS IT YOU SAID EARLIER?
HUH? EARLIER?
!!
...
UH?!
OH, THAT! THE THING ABOUT FALLING IN LOVE, UH...
...!
S-SORRY, THAT WAS, UM, LIKE A CASE OF MISTAKEN IDENTITY! FORGET ABOUT IT! IT NEVER HAPPENED!
?!
WHA ...
YOU...
KHING
KHH
KHH
KHH
WAAH?!
KRA
H-HEY, WHAT ARE YOU SO MAD ABOUT? I'M SORRY!
STOMP
STOMP
STOMP
STOMP
...

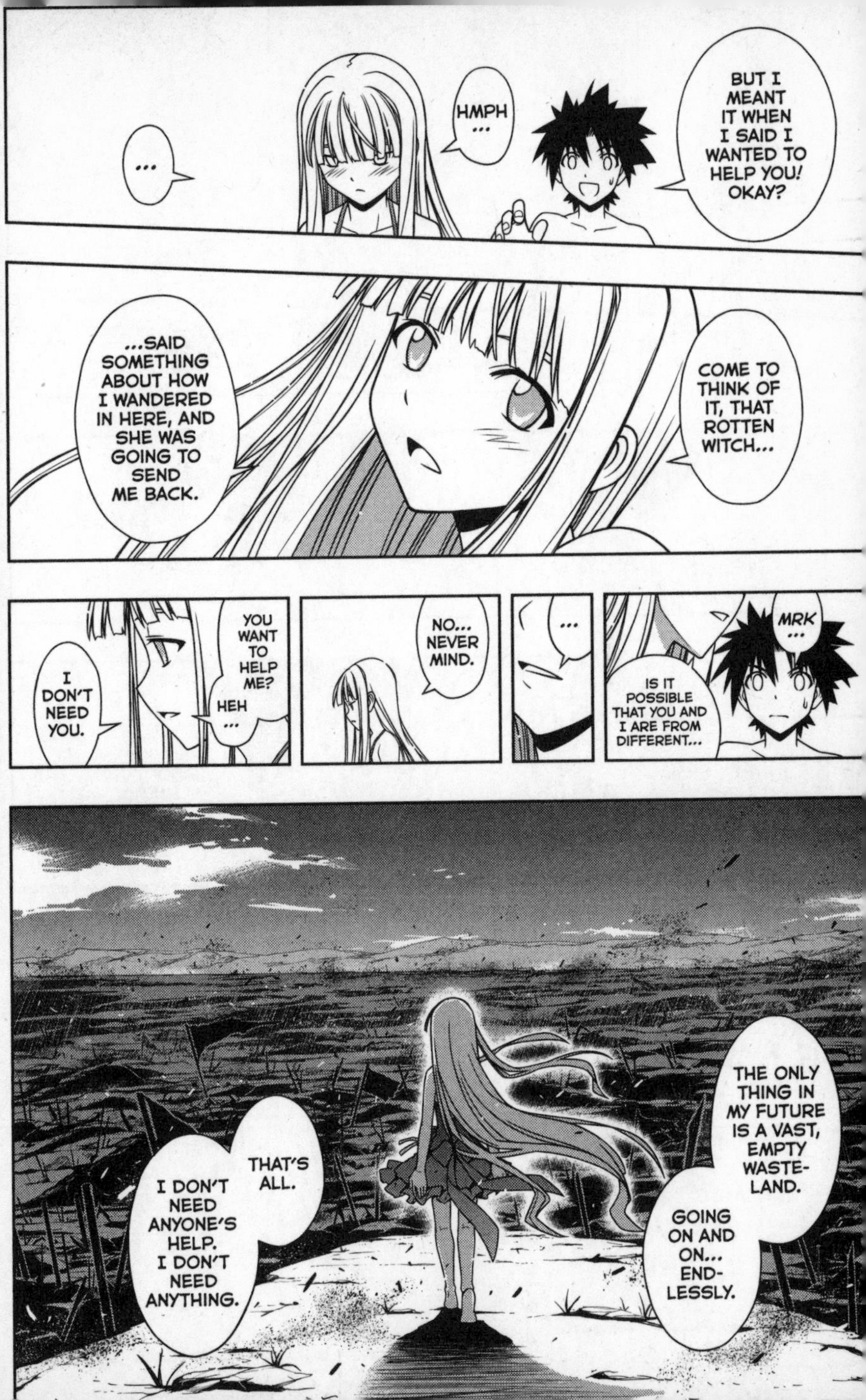
BUT I MEANT IT WHEN I SAID I WANTED TO HELP YOU! OKAY?
HMPH ...
...
COME TO THINK OF IT, THAT ROTTEN WITCH...
...SAID SOMETHING ABOUT HOW I WANDERED IN HERE, AND SHE WAS GOING TO SEND ME BACK.
MRK ...
IS IT POSSIBLE THAT YOU AND I ARE FROM DIFFERENT...
...
NO... NEVER MIND.
YOU WANT TO HELP ME?
HEH ...
I DON'T NEED YOU.
THE ONLY THING IN MY FUTURE IS A VAST, EMPTY WASTE-LAND.
GOING ON AND ON... END-LESSLY.
THAT'S ALL.
I DON'T NEED ANYONE'S HELP. I DON'T NEED ANYTHING.

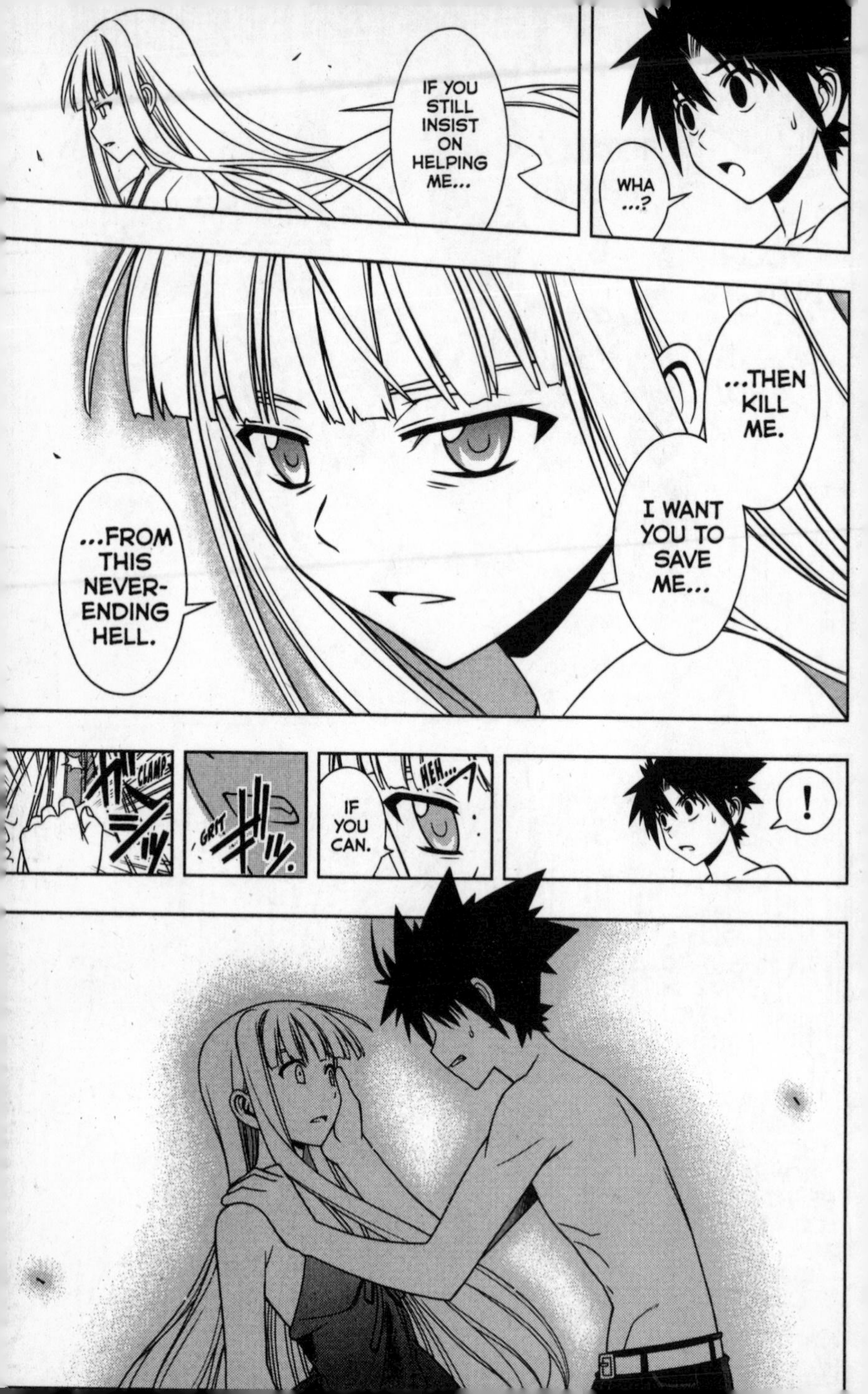
WHA ...?
IF YOU STILL INSIST ON HELPING ME...
...THEN KILL ME.
I WANT YOU TO SAVE ME...
...FROM THIS NEVER-ENDING HELL.
!
HEH...
IF YOU CAN.
GRIT
CLAMP

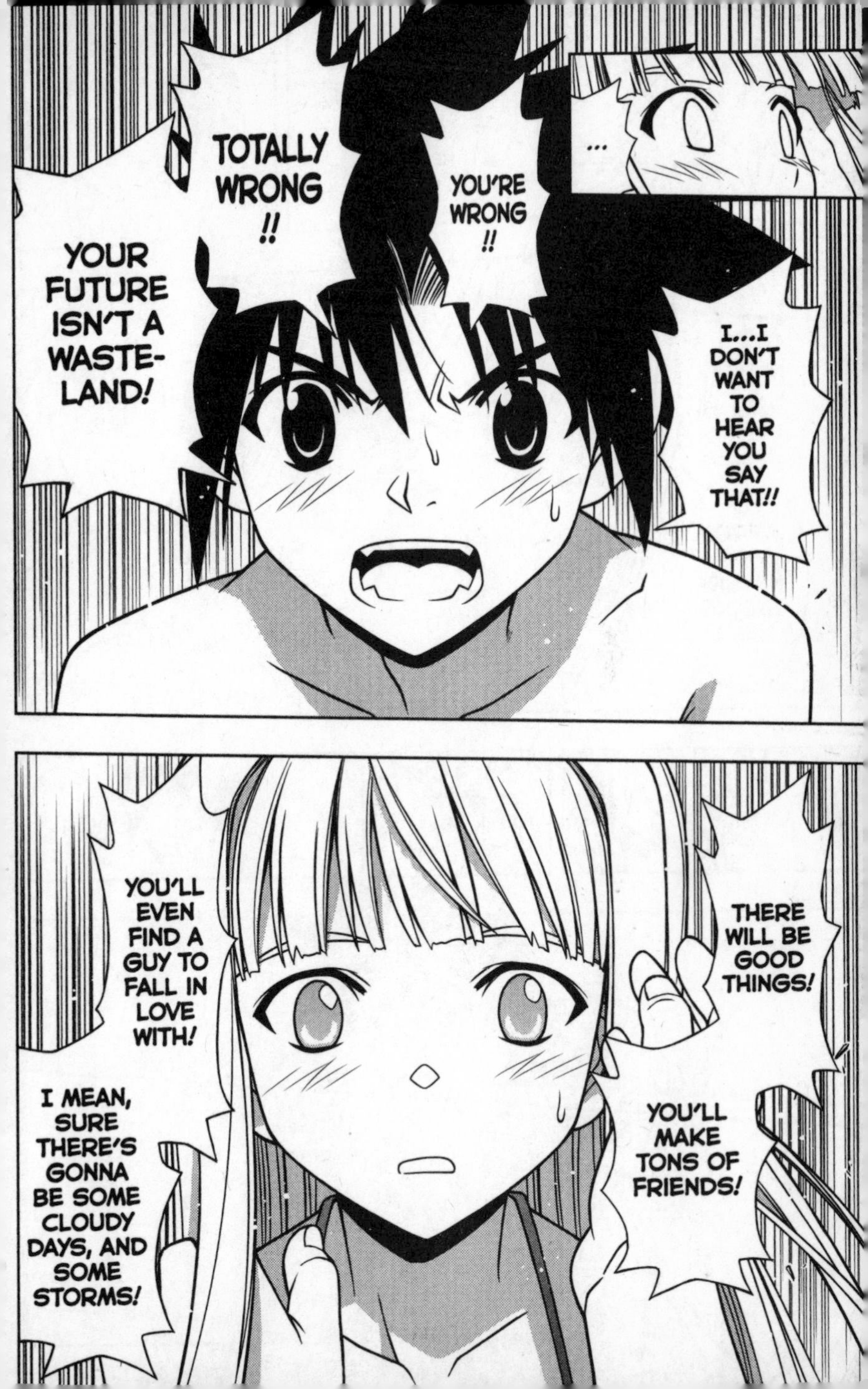
...
YOU'RE WRONG!!
TOTALLY WRONG!!
YOUR FUTURE ISN'T A WASTE-LAND!
I...I DON'T WANT TO HEAR YOU SAY THAT!!
THERE WILL BE GOOD THINGS!
YOU'LL EVEN FIND A GUY TO FALL IN LOVE WITH!
YOU'LL MAKE TONS OF FRIENDS!
I MEAN, SURE THERE'S GONNA BE SOME CLOUDY DAYS, AND SOME STORMS!

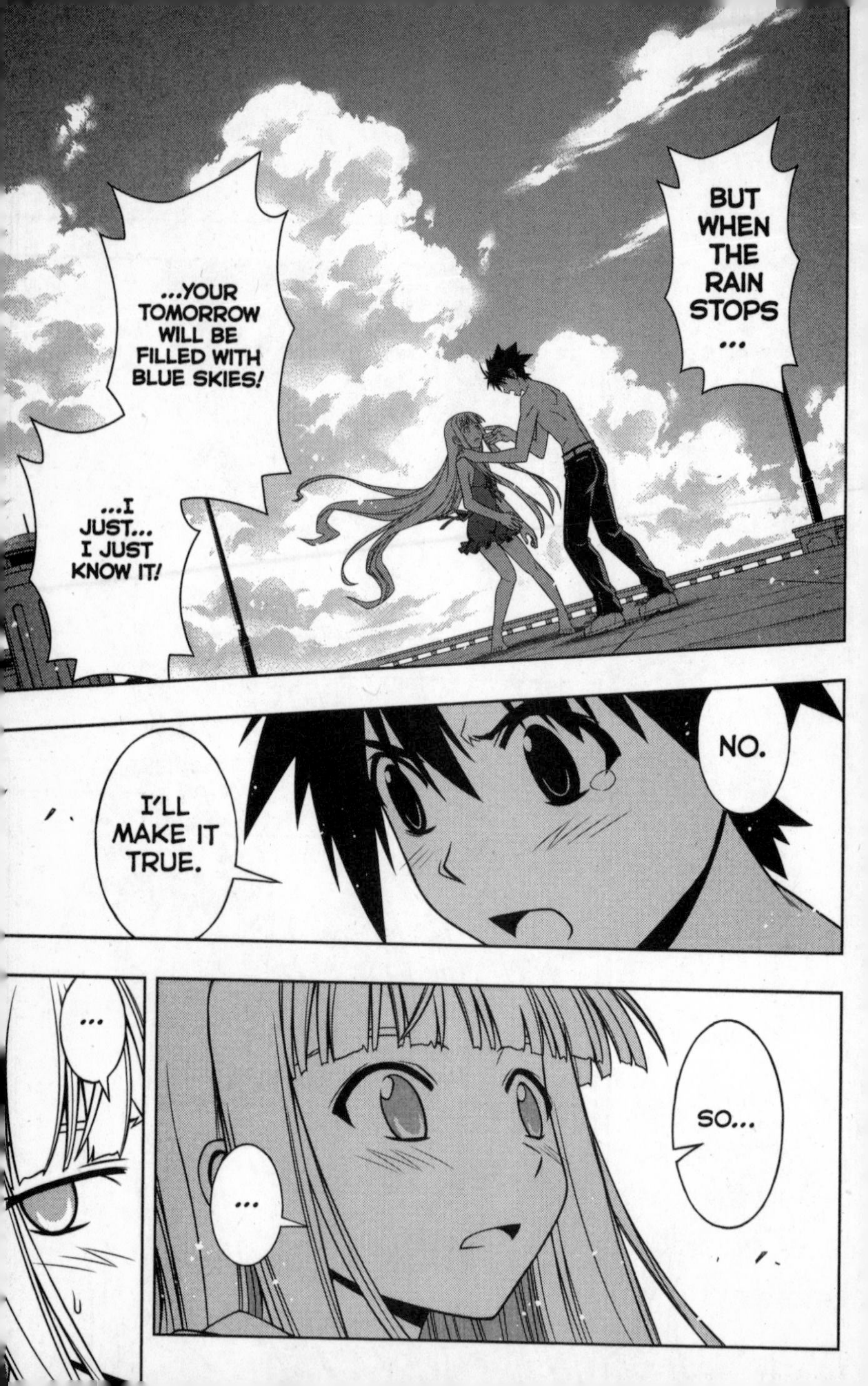
BUT WHEN THE RAIN STOPS...
...YOUR TOMORROW WILL BE FILLED WITH BLUE SKIES!
...I JUST... I JUST KNOW IT!
NO.
I'LL MAKE IT TRUE.
SO...
...
...

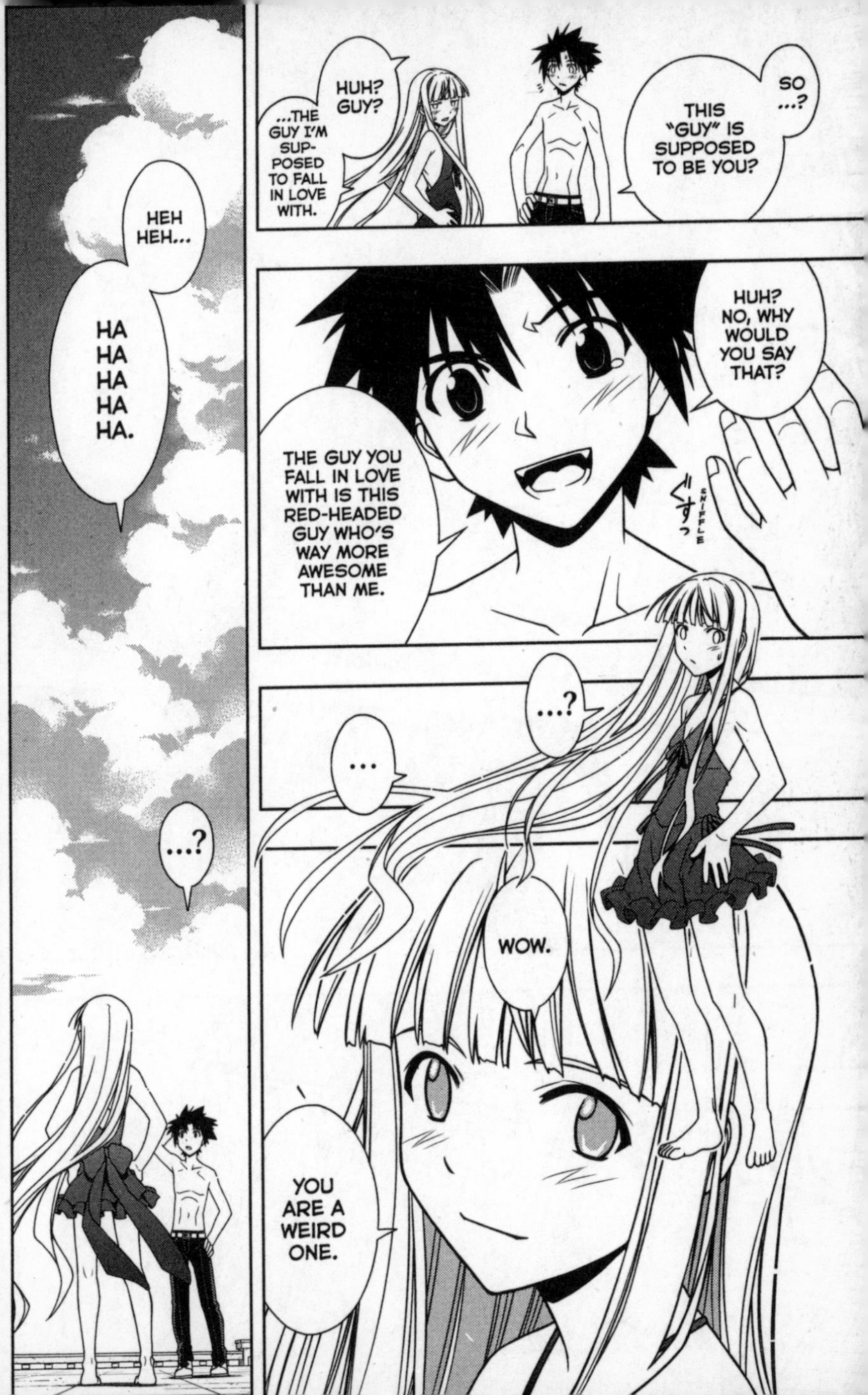
SO ...?
THIS "GUY" IS SUPPOSED TO BE YOU?
HUH? GUY?
...THE GUY I'M SUP-POSED TO FALL IN LOVE WITH.
HUH? NO, WHY WOULD YOU SAY THAT?
ぐすっ
SNIFFLE
THE GUY YOU FALL IN LOVE WITH IS THIS RED-HEADED GUY WHO'S WAY MORE AWESOME THAN ME.
...?
...
WOW.
YOU ARE A WEIRD ONE.
HEH HEH...
HA HA HA HA HA.
...?

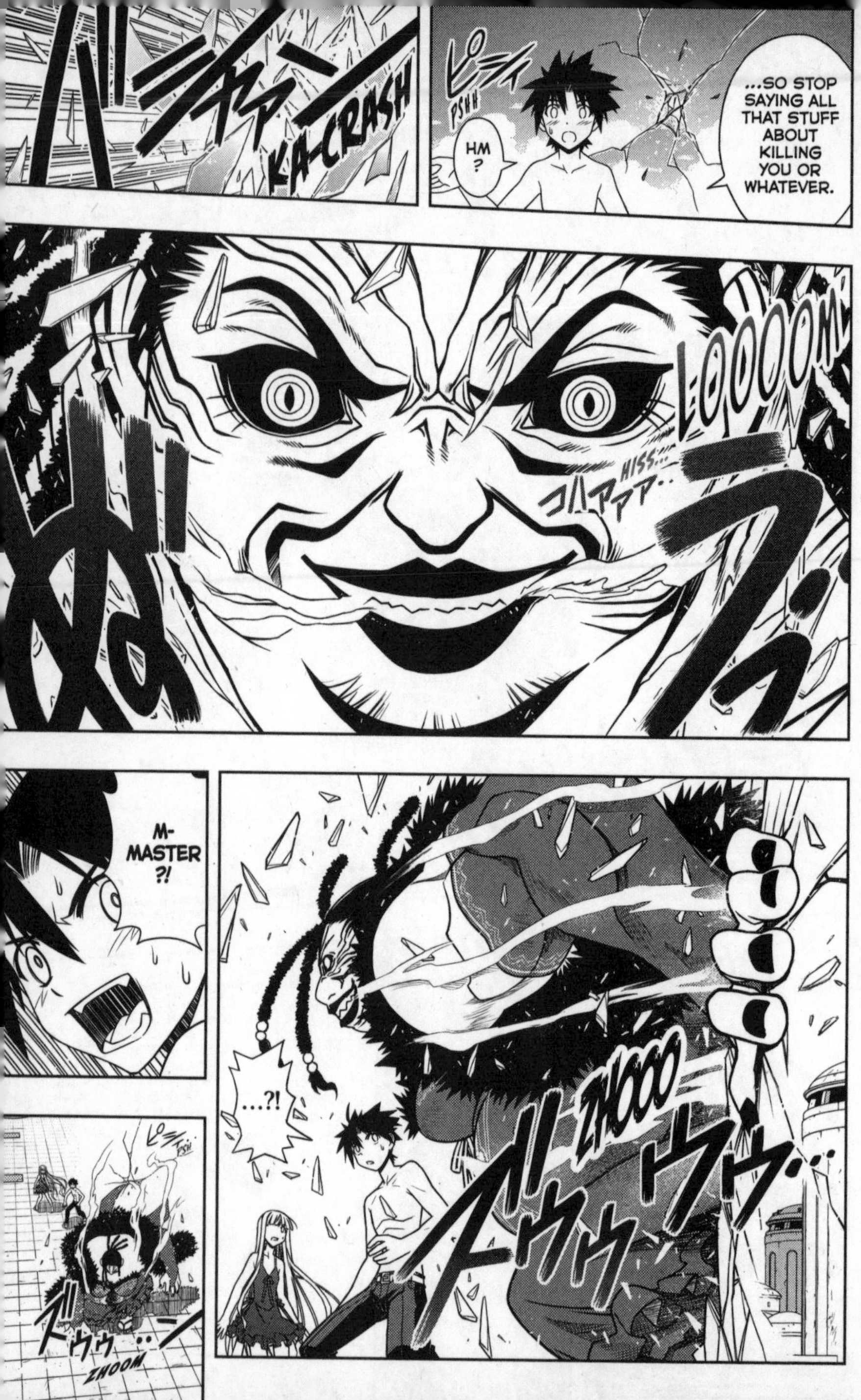
...SO STOP SAYING ALL THAT STUFF ABOUT KILLING YOU OR WHATEVER.
HM ?
PSHH
KA-CRASH
LOOOOM
HISS...
...?!
ZHOOO
M-MASTER ?!
PSH
ZHOOM

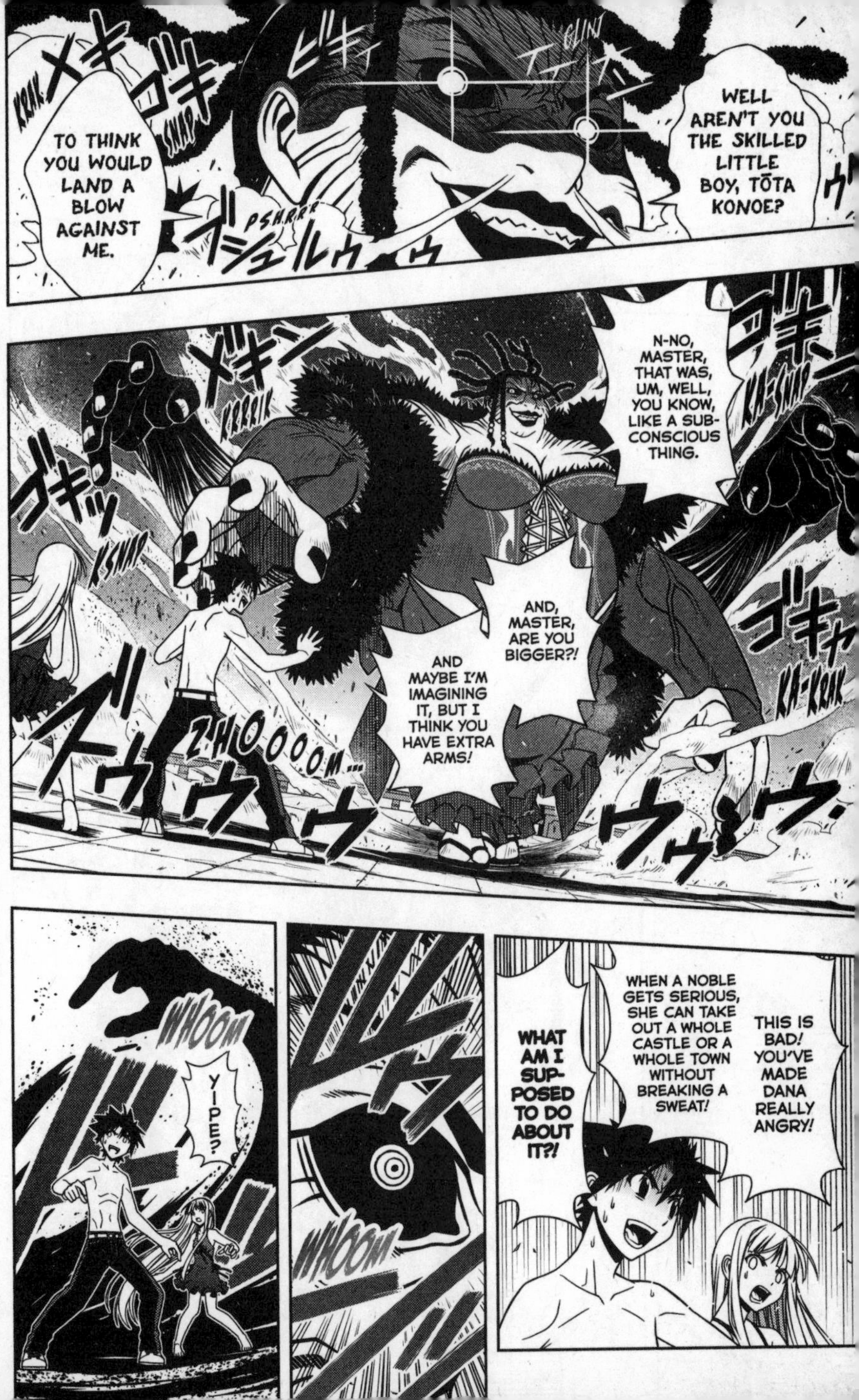
WELL AREN'T YOU THE SKILLED LITTLE BOY, TŌTA KONOE?
GLINT
SNAP
KRAK
TO THINK YOU WOULD LAND A BLOW AGAINST ME.
PSHRRR
N-NO, MASTER, THAT WAS, UM, WELL, YOU KNOW, LIKE A SUB-CONSCIOUS THING.
KA-SNAP
KRRRIK
AND, MASTER, ARE YOU BIGGER?!
AND MAYBE I'M IMAGINING IT, BUT I THINK YOU HAVE EXTRA ARMS!
KSNAP
KA-KRAK
ZHOOOOOM...
THIS IS BAD! YOU'VE MADE DANA REALLY ANGRY!
WHEN A NOBLE GETS SERIOUS, SHE CAN TAKE OUT A WHOLE CASTLE OR A WHOLE TOWN WITHOUT BREAKING A SWEAT!
WHAT AM I SUP-POSED TO DO ABOUT IT?!
WHOOM
WHOOM
YIPE?

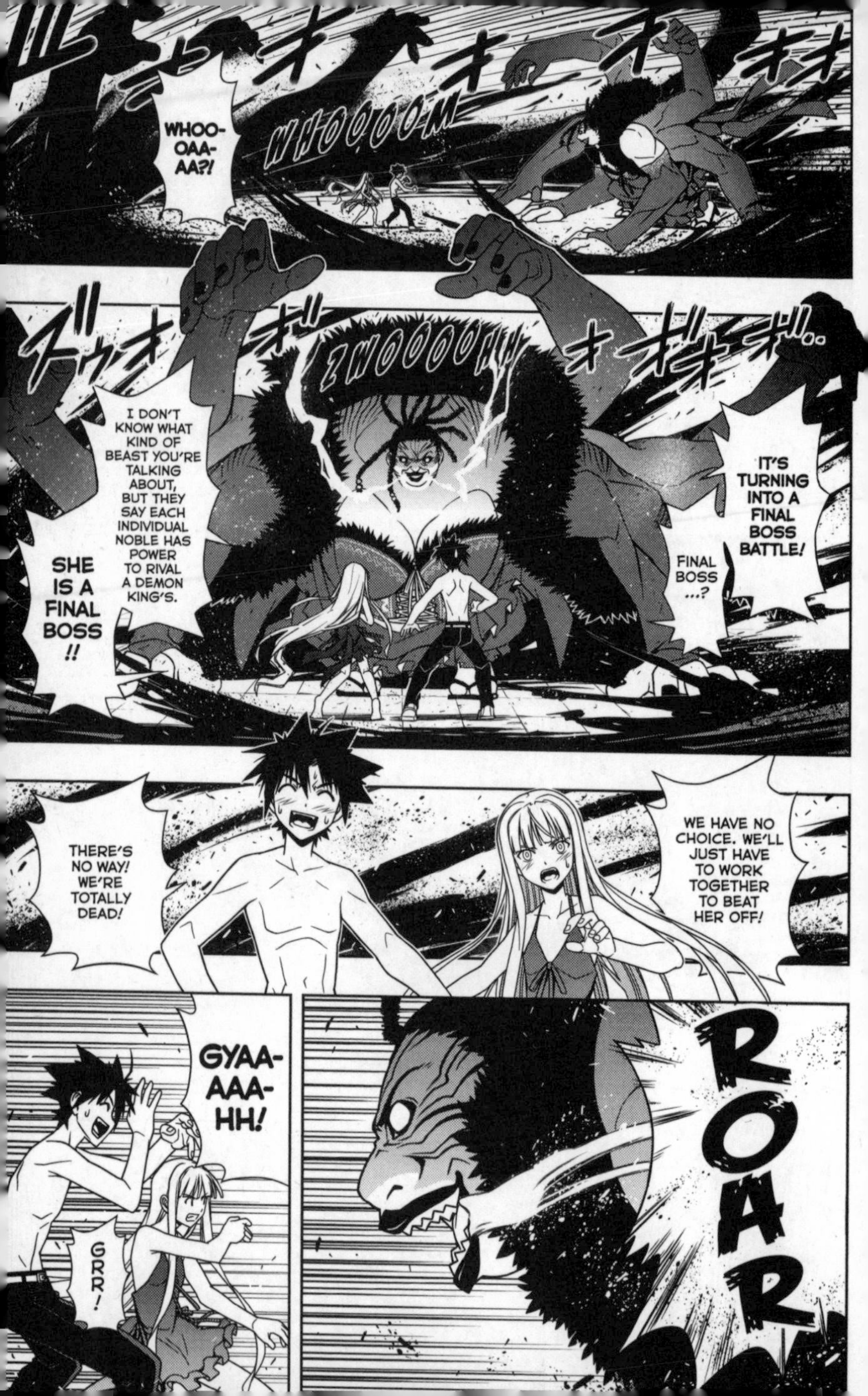
WHOOOOOM
WHOO-OAA-AA?!
ZWOOOOOHH
IT'S TURNING INTO A FINAL BOSS BATTLE!
FINAL BOSS ...?
I DON'T KNOW WHAT KIND OF BEAST YOU'RE TALKING ABOUT, BUT THEY SAY EACH INDIVIDUAL NOBLE HAS POWER TO RIVAL A DEMON KING'S.
SHE IS A FINAL BOSS !!
WE HAVE NO CHOICE. WE'LL JUST HAVE TO WORK TOGETHER TO BEAT HER OFF!
THERE'S NO WAY! WE'RE TOTALLY DEAD!
ROAR
GYAA-AAA-HH!
GRR!

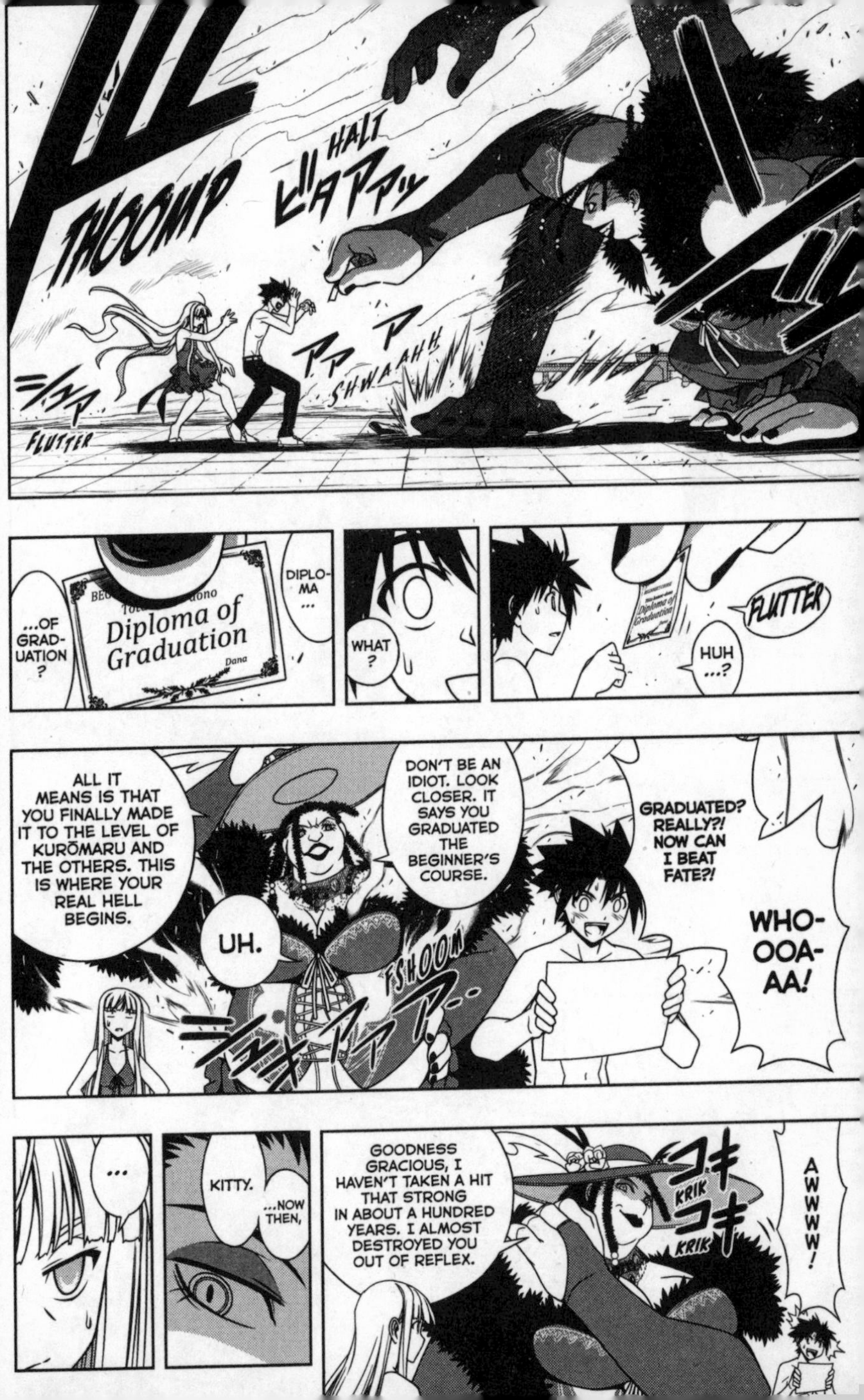
THOOMP
HALT
SHWAAHH
FLUTTER
FLUTTER
HUH ...?
DIPLOMA ...
WHAT ?
Diploma of Graduation
Dana
...OF GRADUATION ?
WHO-OOA-AA!
GRADUATED? REALLY?! NOW CAN I BEAT FATE?!
DON'T BE AN IDIOT. LOOK CLOSER. IT SAYS YOU GRADUATED THE BEGINNER'S COURSE.
ALL IT MEANS IS THAT YOU FINALLY MADE IT TO THE LEVEL OF KURŌMARU AND THE OTHERS. THIS IS WHERE YOUR REAL HELL BEGINS.
UH.
FSHOOM
AWWWW!
KRIK
KRIK
GOODNESS GRACIOUS, I HAVEN'T TAKEN A HIT THAT STRONG IN ABOUT A HUNDRED YEARS. I ALMOST DESTROYED YOU OUT OF REFLEX.
...NOW THEN,
KITTY.
...

STAGE 85: THROUGH ALL THOSE YEARS, I STILL WANTED TO SEE YOU

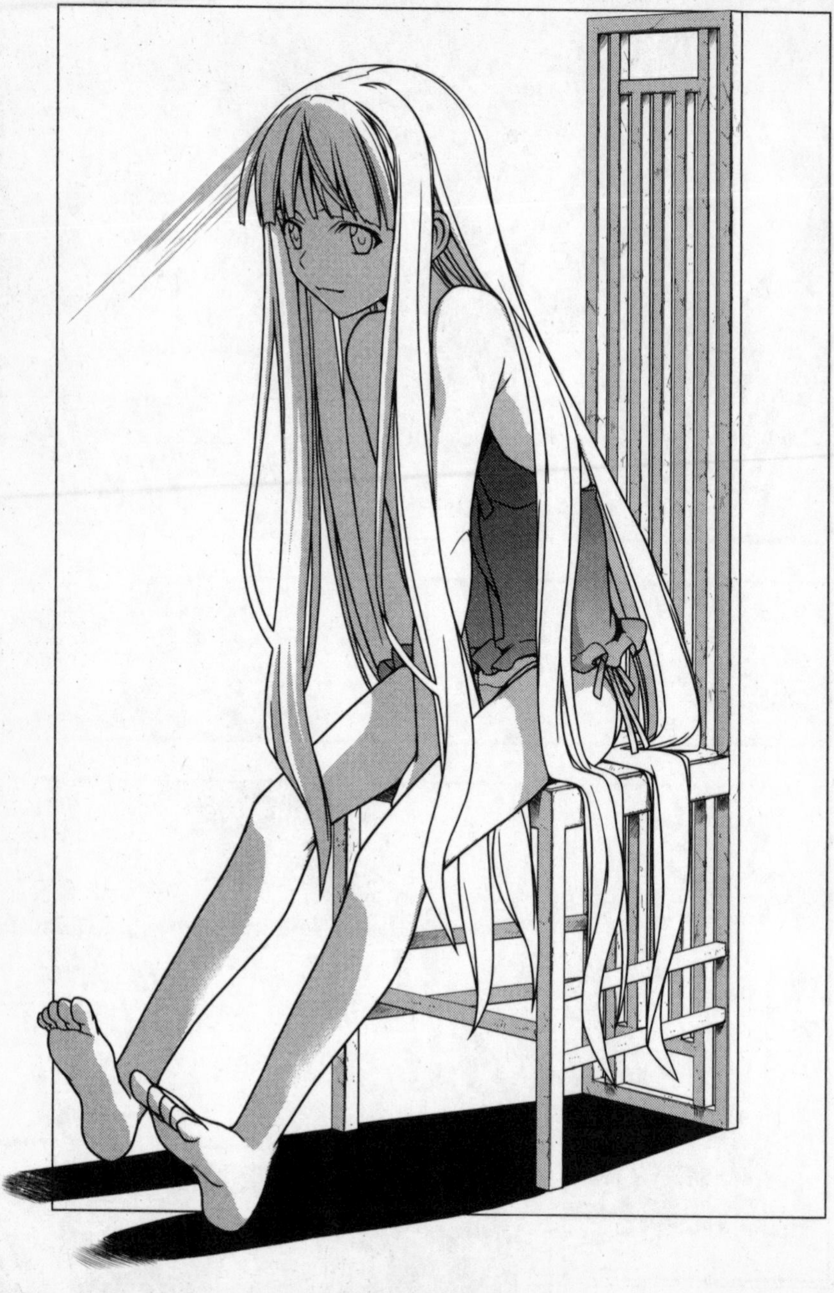

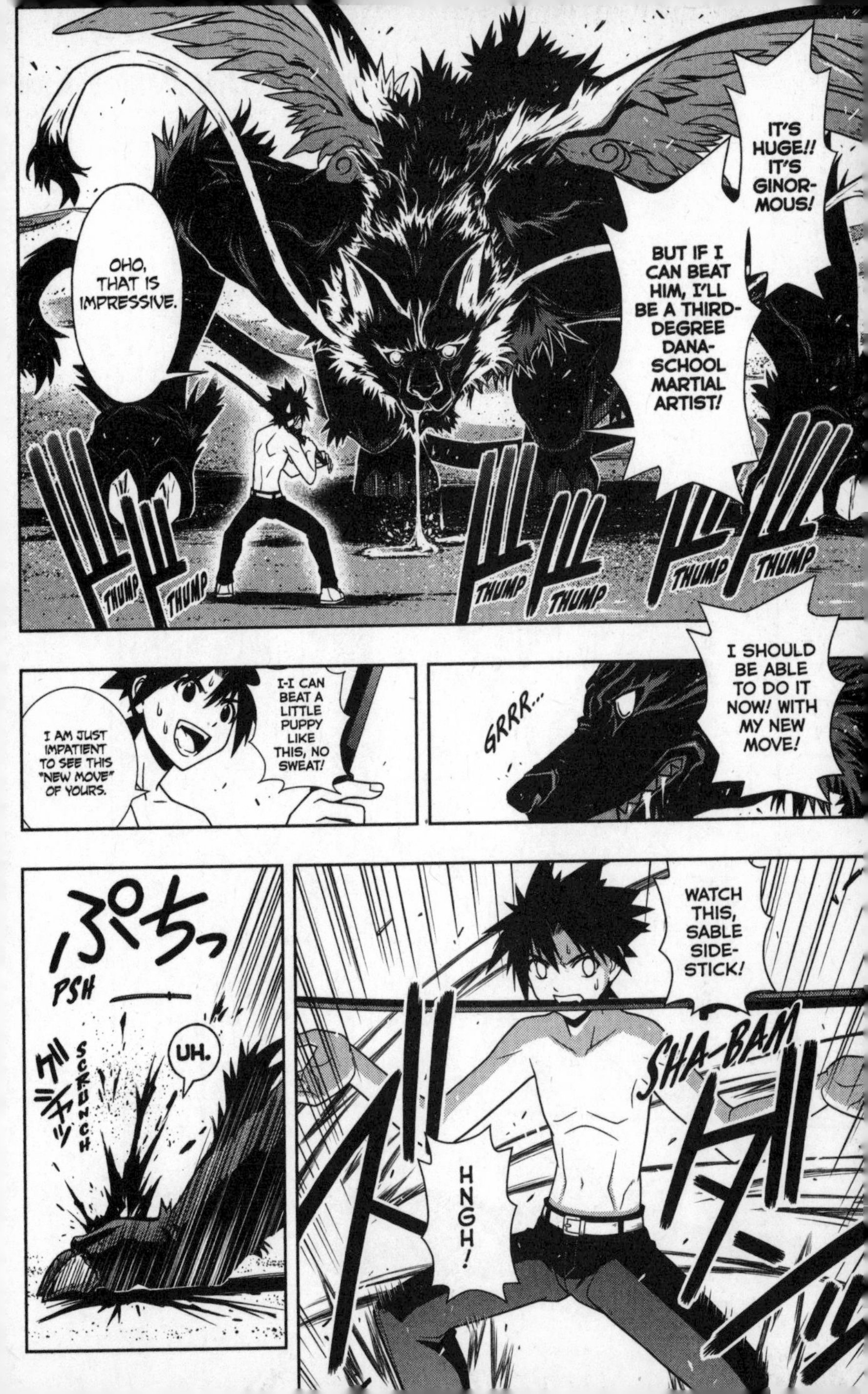
IT'S HUGE!! IT'S GINORMOUS!
BUT IF I CAN BEAT HIM, I'LL BE A THIRD-DEGREE DANA-SCHOOL MARTIAL ARTIST!
OHO, THAT IS IMPRESSIVE.
THUMP
THUMP
THUMP
THUMP
THUMP
THUMP
I SHOULD BE ABLE TO DO IT NOW! WITH MY NEW MOVE!
GRRR...
I-I CAN BEAT A LITTLE PUPPY LIKE THIS, NO SWEAT!
I AM JUST IMPATIENT TO SEE THIS "NEW MOVE" OF YOURS.
WATCH THIS, SABLE SIDE-STICK!
SHA-BAM
HNGH!
ぷちっ
PSH
UH.
SCRUNCH

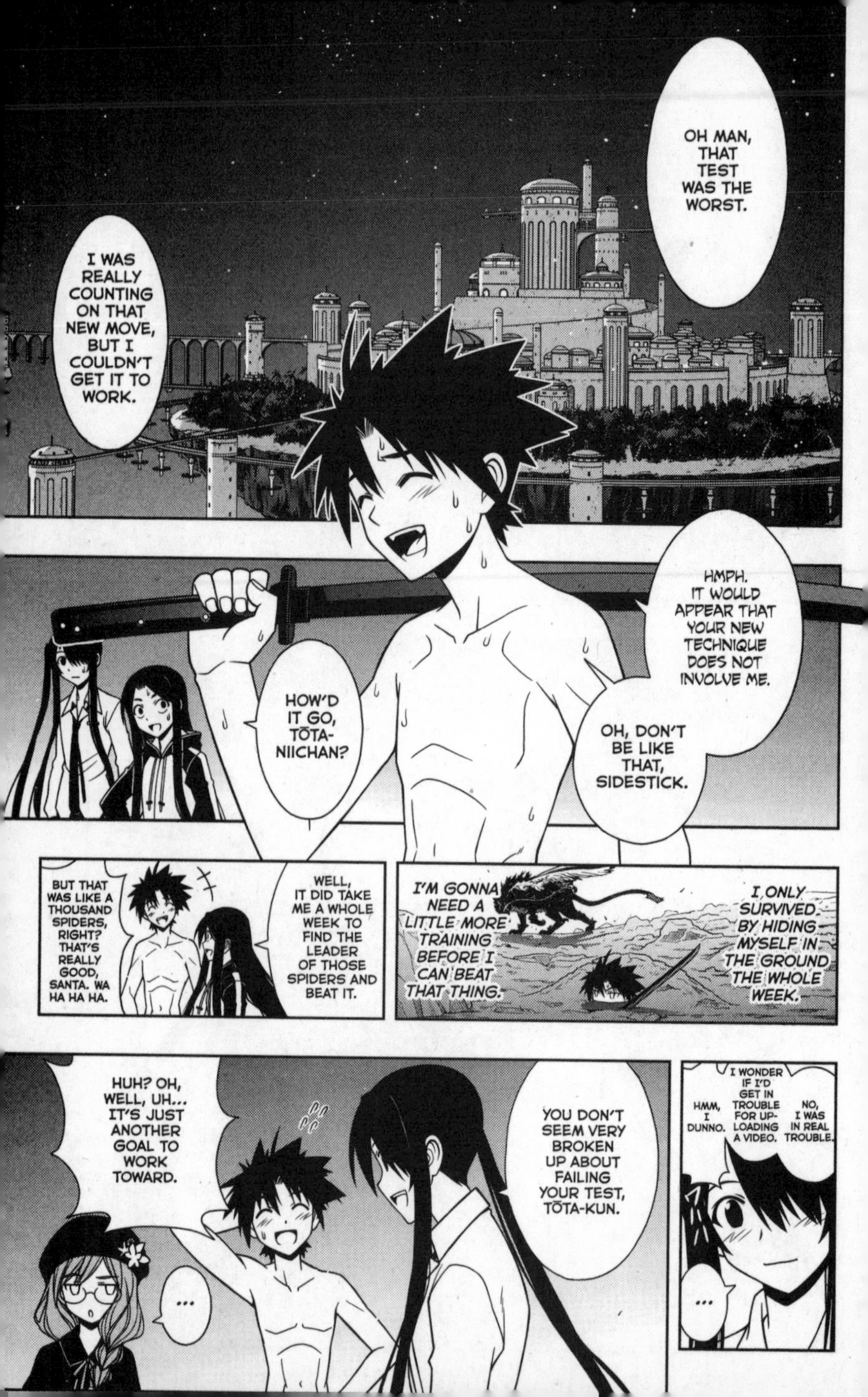
OH MAN, THAT TEST WAS THE WORST.
I WAS REALLY COUNTING ON THAT NEW MOVE, BUT I COULDN'T GET IT TO WORK.
HMPH. IT WOULD APPEAR THAT YOUR NEW TECHNIQUE DOES NOT INVOLVE ME.
HOW'D IT GO, TŌTA-NIICHAN?
OH, DON'T BE LIKE THAT, SIDESTICK.
I ONLY SURVIVED BY HIDING MYSELF IN THE GROUND THE WHOLE WEEK.
I'M GONNA NEED A LITTLE MORE TRAINING BEFORE I CAN BEAT THAT THING.
WELL, IT DID TAKE ME A WHOLE WEEK TO FIND THE LEADER OF THOSE SPIDERS AND BEAT IT.
BUT THAT WAS LIKE A THOUSAND SPIDERS, RIGHT? THAT'S REALLY GOOD, SANTA. WA HA HA HA.
I WONDER IF I'D GET IN TROUBLE FOR UPLOADING A VIDEO.
NO, I WAS IN REAL TROUBLE.
HMM, I DUNNO.
...
YOU DON'T SEEM VERY BROKEN UP ABOUT FAILING YOUR TEST, TŌTA-KUN.
HUH? OH, WELL, UH... IT'S JUST ANOTHER GOAL TO WORK TOWARD.
...

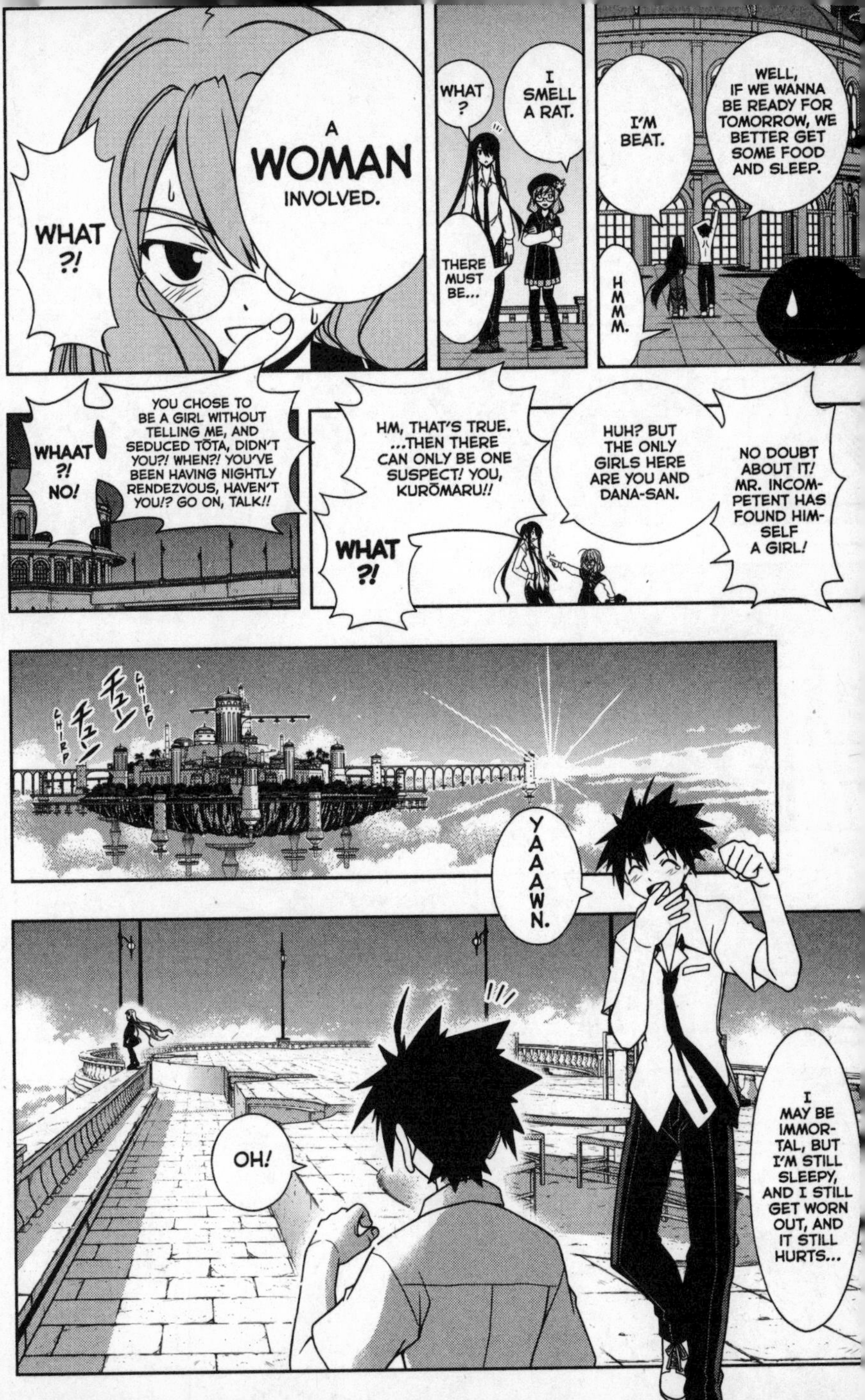
WELL, IF WE WANNA BE READY FOR TOMORROW, WE BETTER GET SOME FOOD AND SLEEP.
I'M BEAT.
HMMM.
I SMELL A RAT.
WHAT?
THERE MUST BE...
A WOMAN INVOLVED.
WHAT?!
NO DOUBT ABOUT IT! MR. INCOMPETENT HAS FOUND HIMSELF A GIRL!
HUH? BUT THE ONLY GIRLS HERE ARE YOU AND DANA-SAN.
HM, THAT'S TRUE. ...THEN THERE CAN ONLY BE ONE SUSPECT! YOU, KURŌMARU!!
WHAT?!
YOU CHOSE TO BE A GIRL WITHOUT TELLING ME, AND SEDUCED TŌTA, DIDN'T YOU?! WHEN?! YOU'VE BEEN HAVING NIGHTLY RENDEZVOUS, HAVEN'T YOU!? GO ON, TALK!!
WHAAT?! NO!
チュン
CHIRP
チュン
CHIRP
YAAAAWN.
I MAY BE IMMORTAL, BUT I'M STILL SLEEPY, AND I STILL GET WORN OUT, AND IT STILL HURTS...
OH!

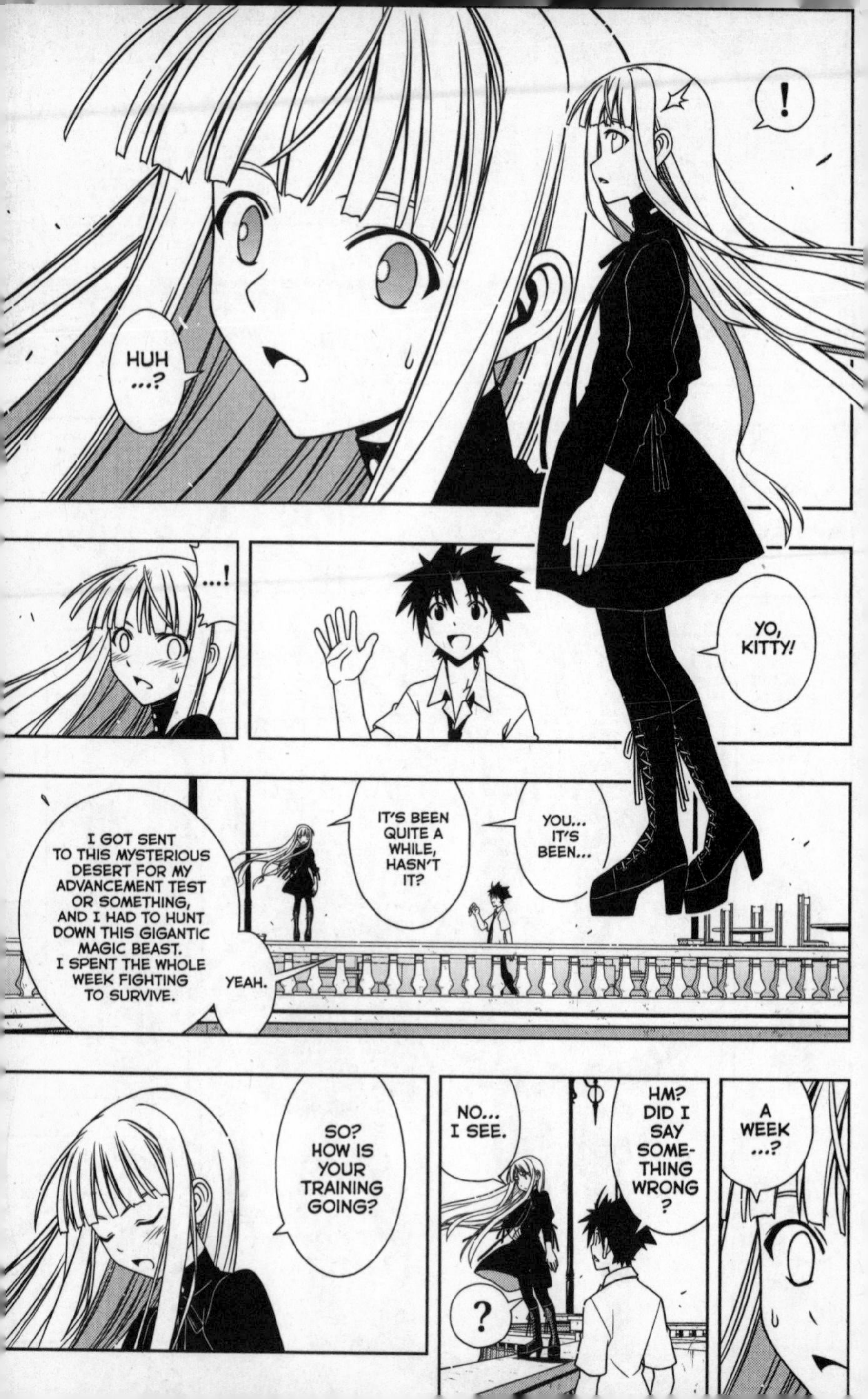
!
HUH...?
YO, KITTY!
...!
YOU... IT'S BEEN...
IT'S BEEN QUITE A WHILE, HASN'T IT?
YEAH.
I GOT SENT TO THIS MYSTERIOUS DESERT FOR MY ADVANCEMENT TEST OR SOMETHING, AND I HAD TO HUNT DOWN THIS GIGANTIC MAGIC BEAST. I SPENT THE WHOLE WEEK FIGHTING TO SURVIVE.
A WEEK...?
HM? DID I SAY SOME-THING WRONG?
NO... I SEE.
?
SO? HOW IS YOUR TRAINING GOING?

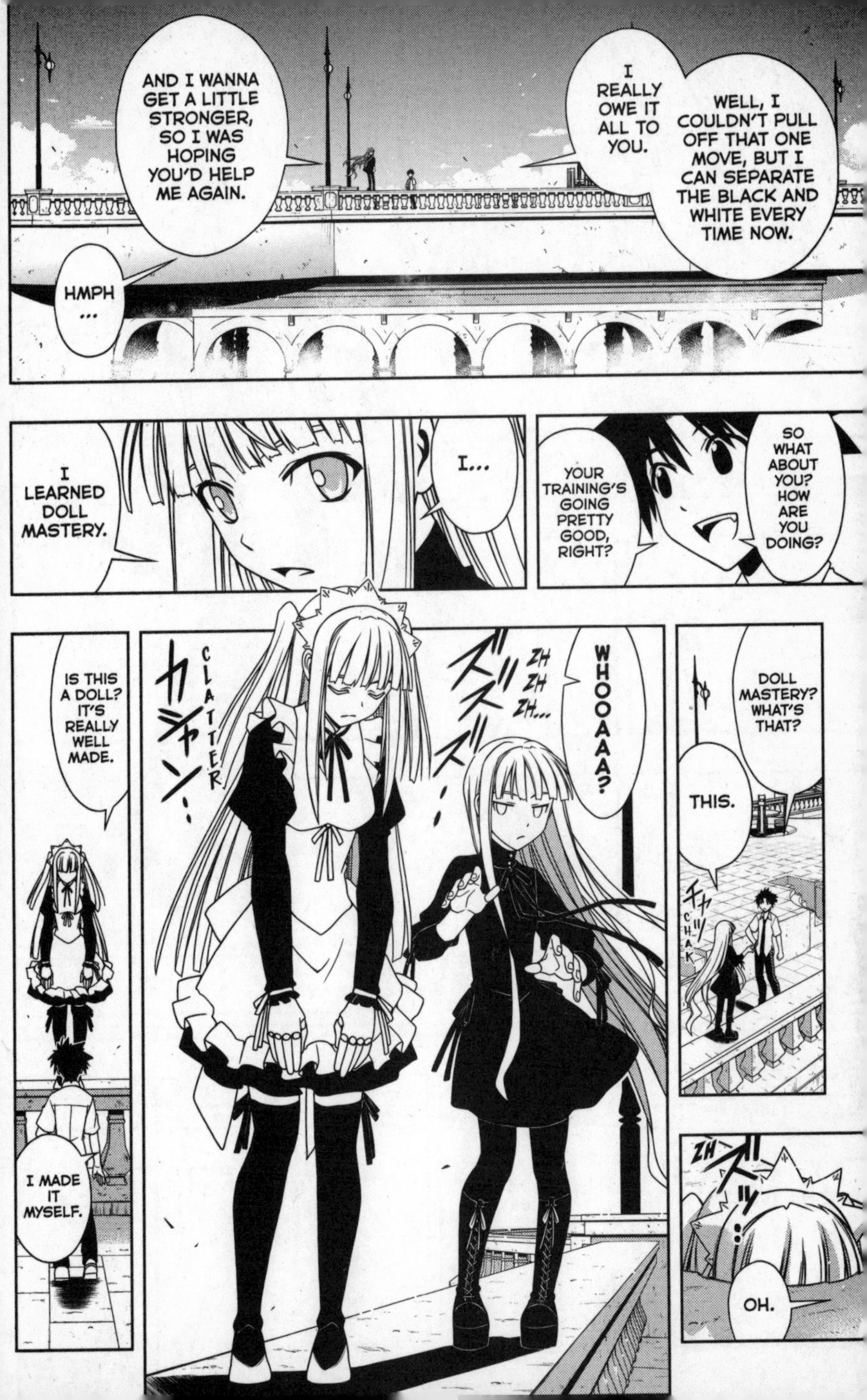

WELL, I COULDN'T PULL OFF THAT ONE MOVE, BUT I CAN SEPARATE THE BLACK AND WHITE EVERY TIME NOW.
I REALLY OWE IT ALL TO YOU.
AND I WANNA GET A LITTLE STRONGER, SO I WAS HOPING YOU'D HELP ME AGAIN.
HMPH ...
SO WHAT ABOUT YOU? HOW ARE YOU DOING?
YOUR TRAINING'S GOING PRETTY GOOD, RIGHT?
I...
I LEARNED DOLL MASTERY.
DOLL MASTERY? WHAT'S THAT?
THIS.
CHAK
ZH
OH.
WHOOAAA?
ZH ZH ZH...
CLATTER
IS THIS A DOLL? IT'S REALLY WELL MADE.
I MADE IT MYSELF.

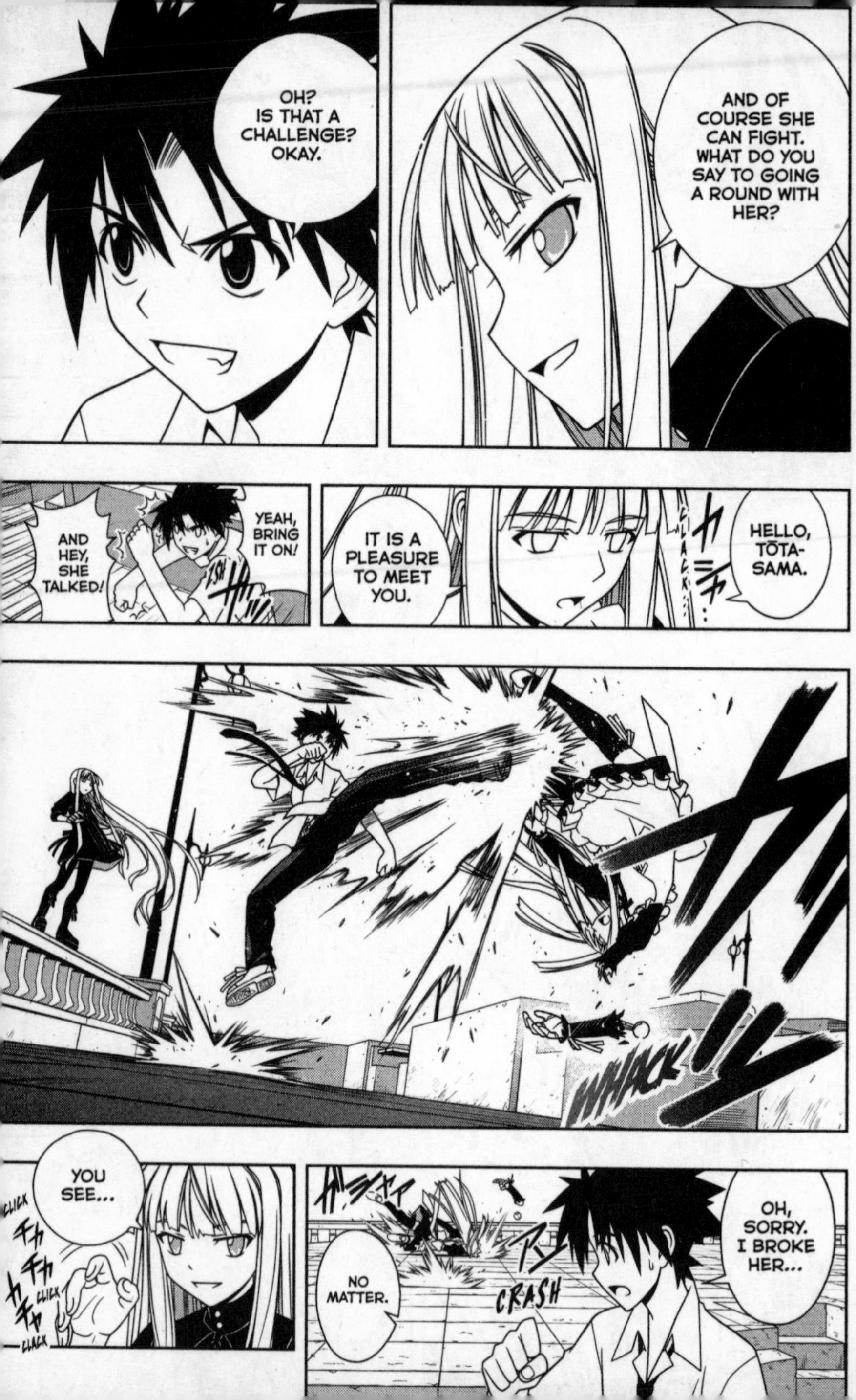
AND OF COURSE SHE CAN FIGHT. WHAT DO YOU SAY TO GOING A ROUND WITH HER?
OH? IS THAT A CHALLENGE? OKAY.
HELLO, TŌTA-SAMA.
CLACK...
IT IS A PLEASURE TO MEET YOU.
YEAH, BRING IT ON!
AND HEY, SHE TALKED!
WHACK
OH, SORRY. I BROKE HER...
CRASH
NO MATTER.
YOU SEE...
CLICK
CLICK
CLACK

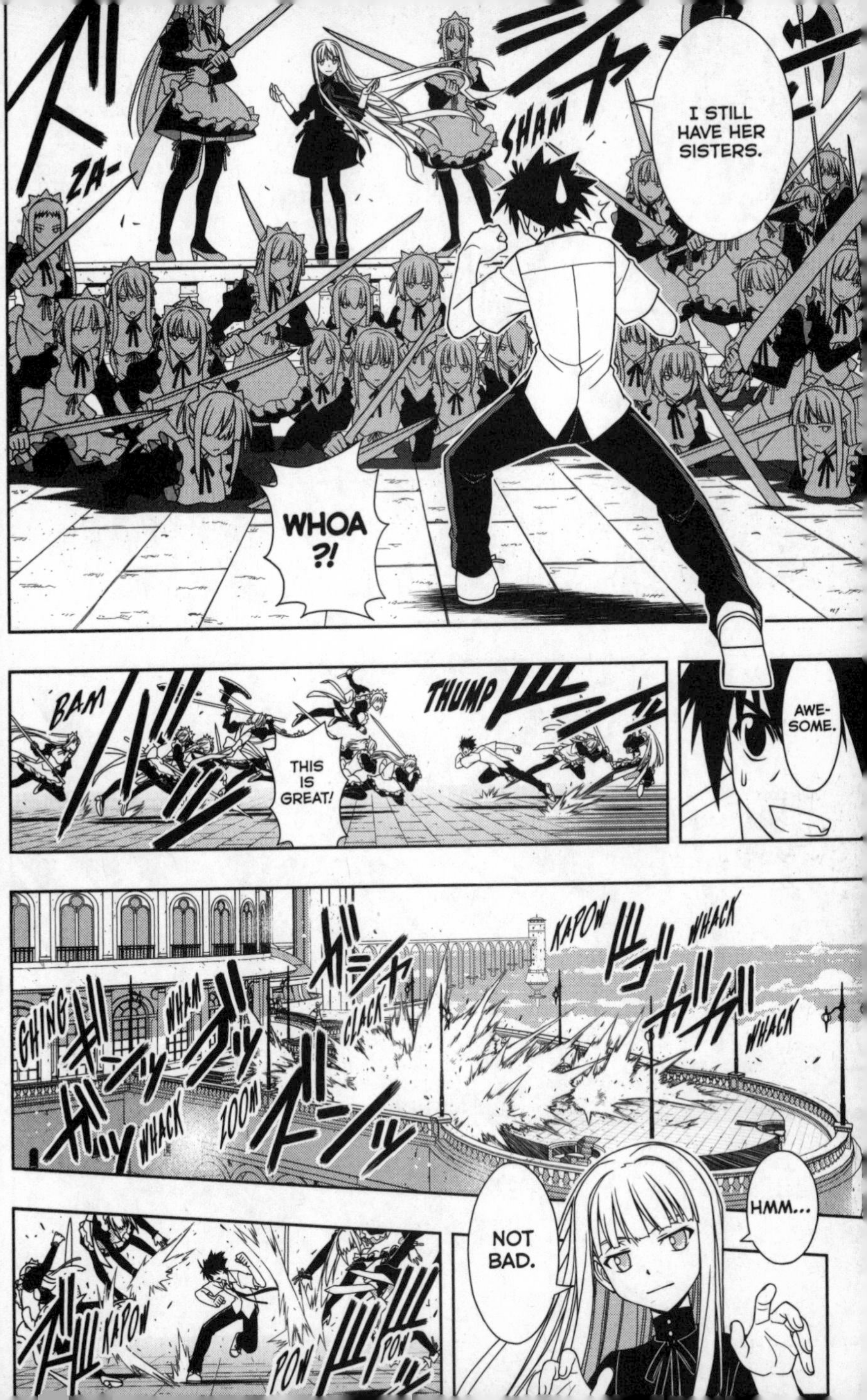
I STILL HAVE HER SISTERS.
SHAM
ZA-
WHOA ?!
AWE-SOME.
THUMP
THIS IS GREAT!
BAM
WHACK
KAPOW
WHACK
CLACK
WHAM
CHING
ZOOM
WHACK
HMM...
NOT BAD.
KAPOW
POW
POW

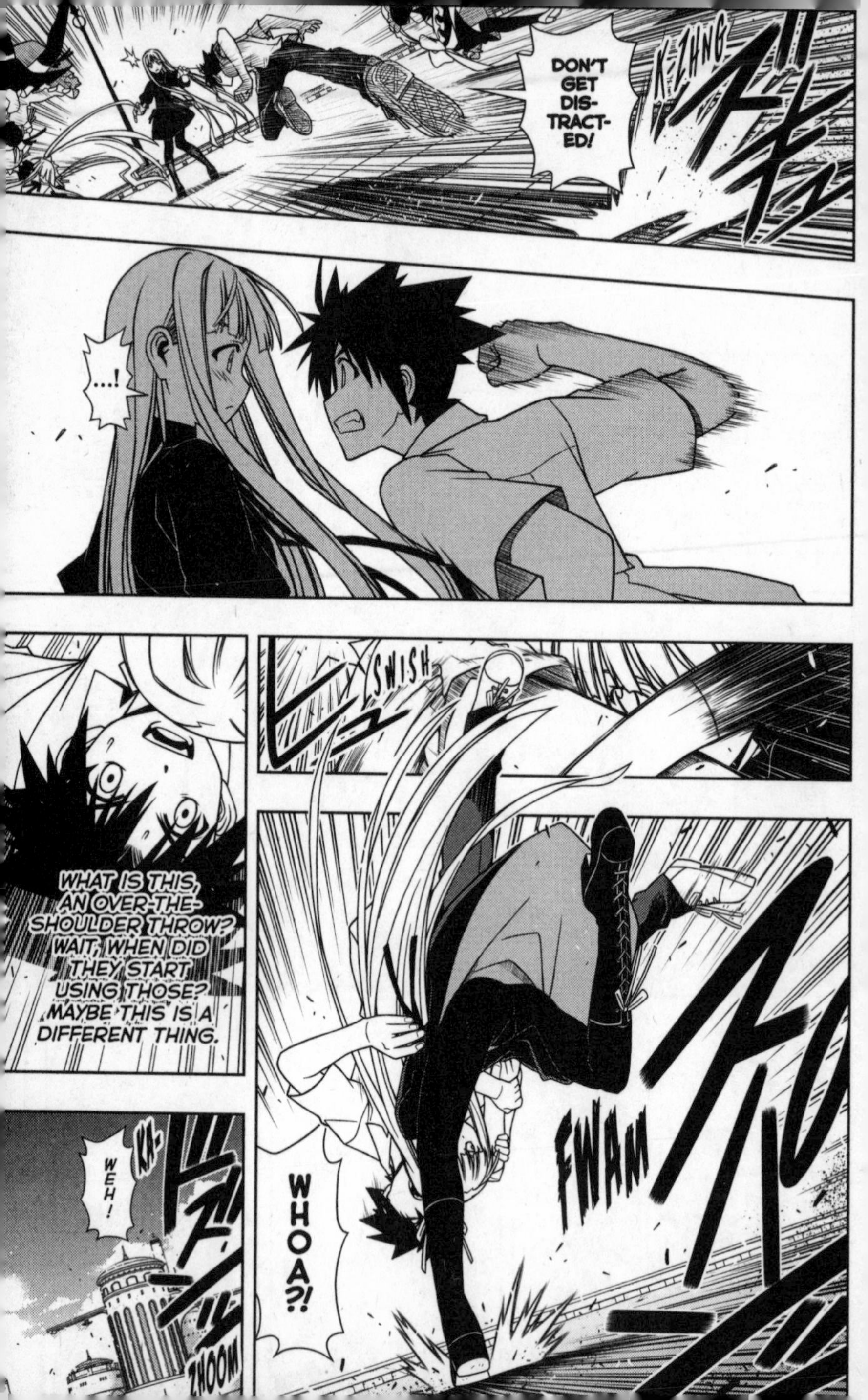
K-ZHNG
DON'T GET DIS-TRACT-ED!
...!
SWISH
FWAM
WHOA?!
WHAT IS THIS, AN OVER-THE-SHOULDER THROW? WAIT, WHEN DID THEY START USING THOSE? MAYBE THIS IS A DIFFERENT THING.
WEH!
KA-
ZHOOM

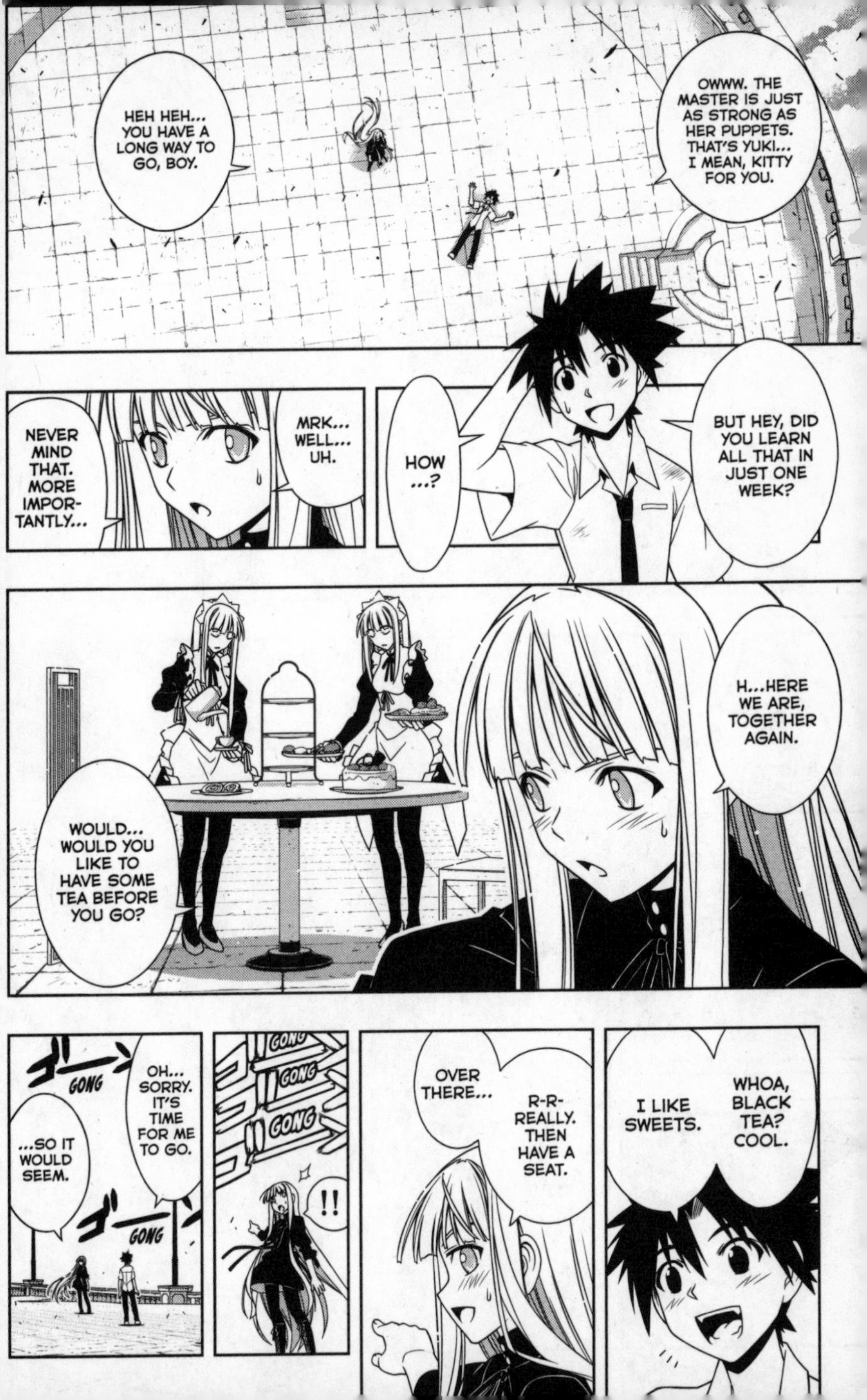
OWWW. THE MASTER IS JUST AS STRONG AS HER PUPPETS. THAT'S YUKI... I MEAN, KITTY FOR YOU.
HEH HEH... YOU HAVE A LONG WAY TO GO, BOY.
BUT HEY, DID YOU LEARN ALL THAT IN JUST ONE WEEK?
HOW ...?
MRK... WELL... UH.
NEVER MIND THAT. MORE IMPORTANTLY...
H...HERE WE ARE, TOGETHER AGAIN.
WOULD... WOULD YOU LIKE TO HAVE SOME TEA BEFORE YOU GO?
WHOA, BLACK TEA? COOL.
I LIKE SWEETS.
R-R-REALLY. THEN HAVE A SEAT.
OVER THERE...
GONG
GONG
GONG
!!
GONG
OH... SORRY. IT'S TIME FOR ME TO GO.
...SO IT WOULD SEEM.
GONG

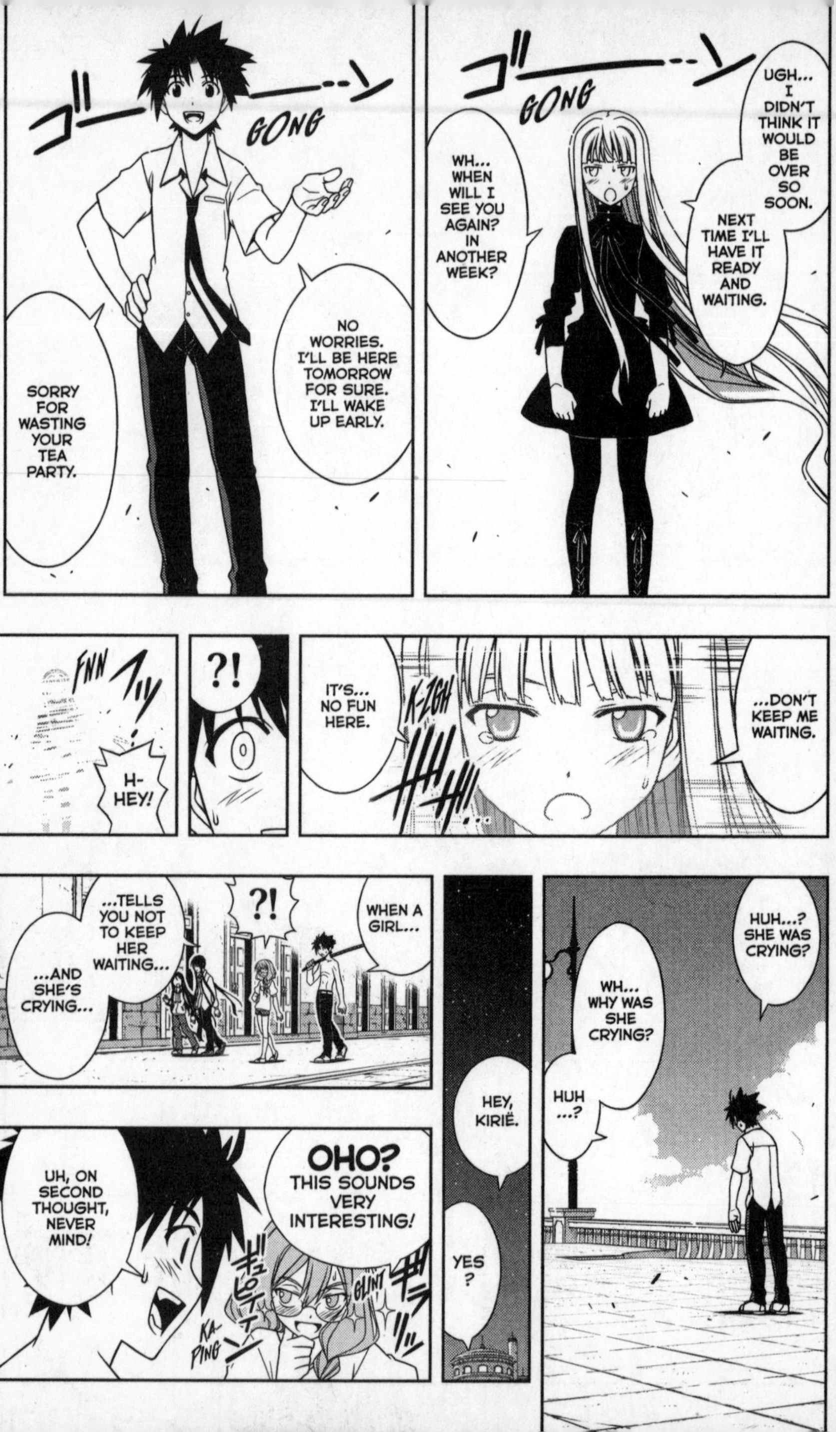
GONG
UGH... I DIDN'T THINK IT WOULD BE OVER SO SOON.
NEXT TIME I'LL HAVE IT READY AND WAITING.
WH... WHEN WILL I SEE YOU AGAIN? IN ANOTHER WEEK?
GONG
NO WORRIES. I'LL BE HERE TOMORROW FOR SURE. I'LL WAKE UP EARLY.
SORRY FOR WASTING YOUR TEA PARTY.
...DON'T KEEP ME WAITING.
K-ZGH
IT'S... NO FUN HERE.
?!
FNN
H-HEY!
HUH...? SHE WAS CRYING?
WH... WHY WAS SHE CRYING?
HUH ...?
HEY, KIRIË.
YES ?
WHEN A GIRL...
?!
...TELLS YOU NOT TO KEEP HER WAITING...
...AND SHE'S CRYING...
OHO? THIS SOUNDS VERY INTERESTING!
GLINT
KA-PING
UH, ON SECOND THOUGHT, NEVER MIND!

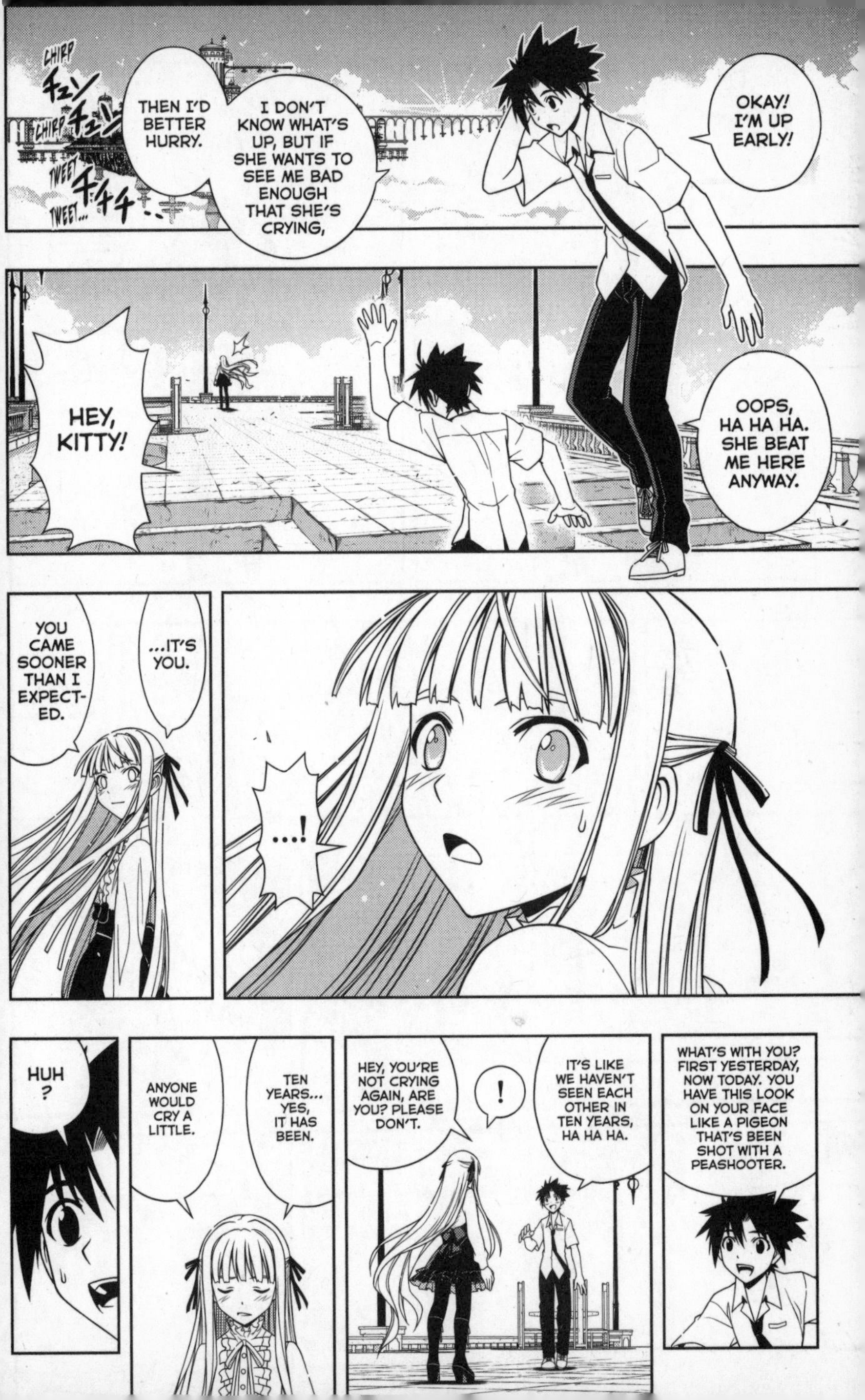
OKAY! I'M UP EARLY!
I DON'T KNOW WHAT'S UP, BUT IF SHE WANTS TO SEE ME BAD ENOUGH THAT SHE'S CRYING,
THEN I'D BETTER HURRY.
CHIRP チュン
CHIRP チュン
TWEET チチチ
TWEET...
OOPS, HA HA HA. SHE BEAT ME HERE ANYWAY.
HEY, KITTY!
...!
...IT'S YOU.
YOU CAME SOONER THAN I EXPECTED.
WHAT'S WITH YOU? FIRST YESTERDAY, NOW TODAY. YOU HAVE THIS LOOK ON YOUR FACE LIKE A PIGEON THAT'S BEEN SHOT WITH A PEASHOOTER.
IT'S LIKE WE HAVEN'T SEEN EACH OTHER IN TEN YEARS, HA HA HA.
!
HEY, YOU'RE NOT CRYING AGAIN, ARE YOU? PLEASE DON'T.
TEN YEARS... YES, IT HAS BEEN.
ANYONE WOULD CRY A LITTLE.
HUH?

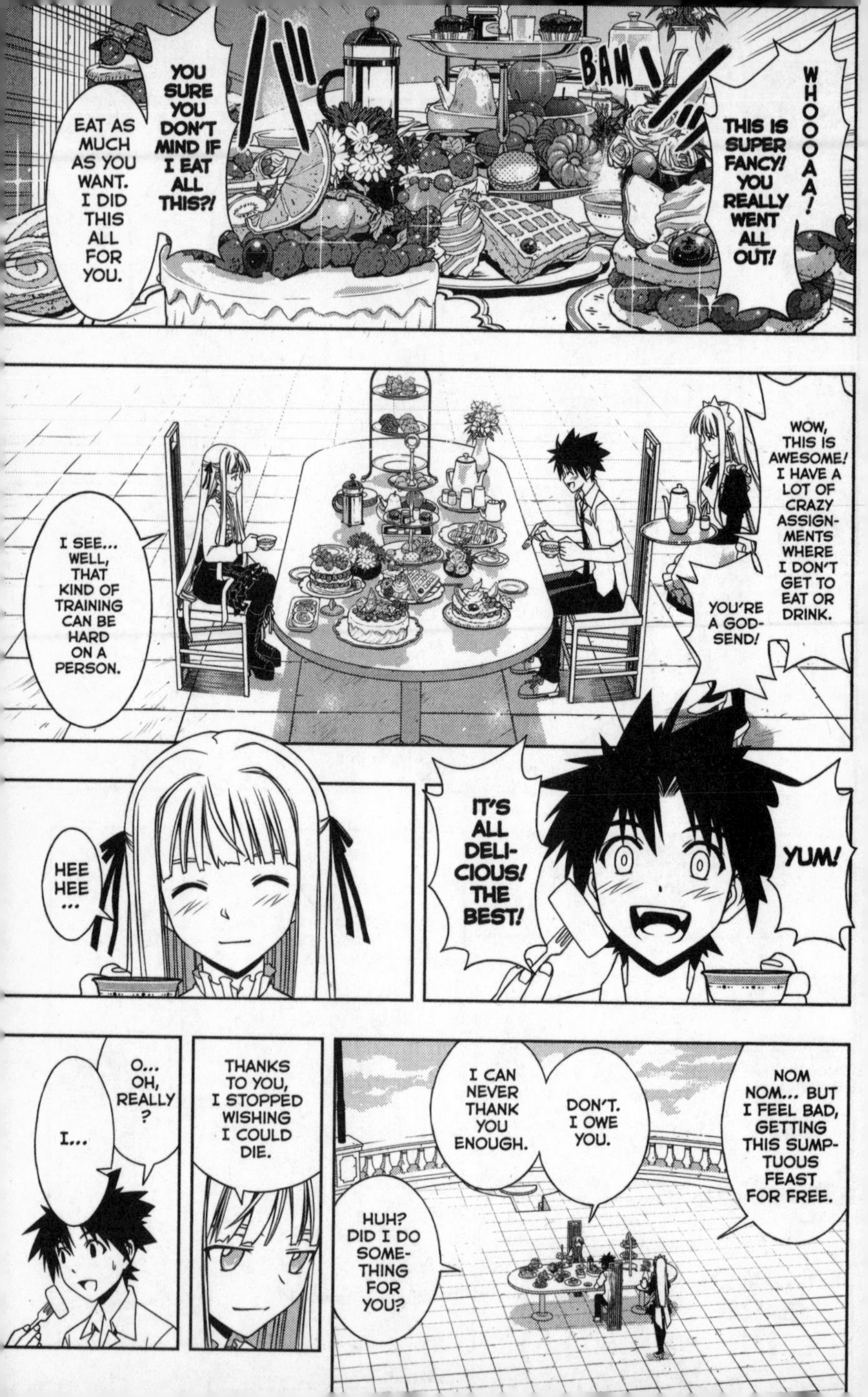
WHOOOAA!
THIS IS SUPER FANCY! YOU REALLY WENT ALL OUT!
BAM
YOU SURE YOU DON'T MIND IF I EAT ALL THIS?!
EAT AS MUCH AS YOU WANT. I DID THIS ALL FOR YOU.
WOW, THIS IS AWESOME! I HAVE A LOT OF CRAZY ASSIGNMENTS WHERE I DON'T GET TO EAT OR DRINK.
YOU'RE A GOD-SEND!
I SEE... WELL, THAT KIND OF TRAINING CAN BE HARD ON A PERSON.
YUM!
IT'S ALL DELICIOUS! THE BEST!
HEE HEE ...
NOM NOM... BUT I FEEL BAD, GETTING THIS SUMPTUOUS FEAST FOR FREE.
DON'T. I OWE YOU.
I CAN NEVER THANK YOU ENOUGH.
HUH? DID I DO SOMETHING FOR YOU?
THANKS TO YOU, I STOPPED WISHING I COULD DIE.
O... OH, REALLY?
I...

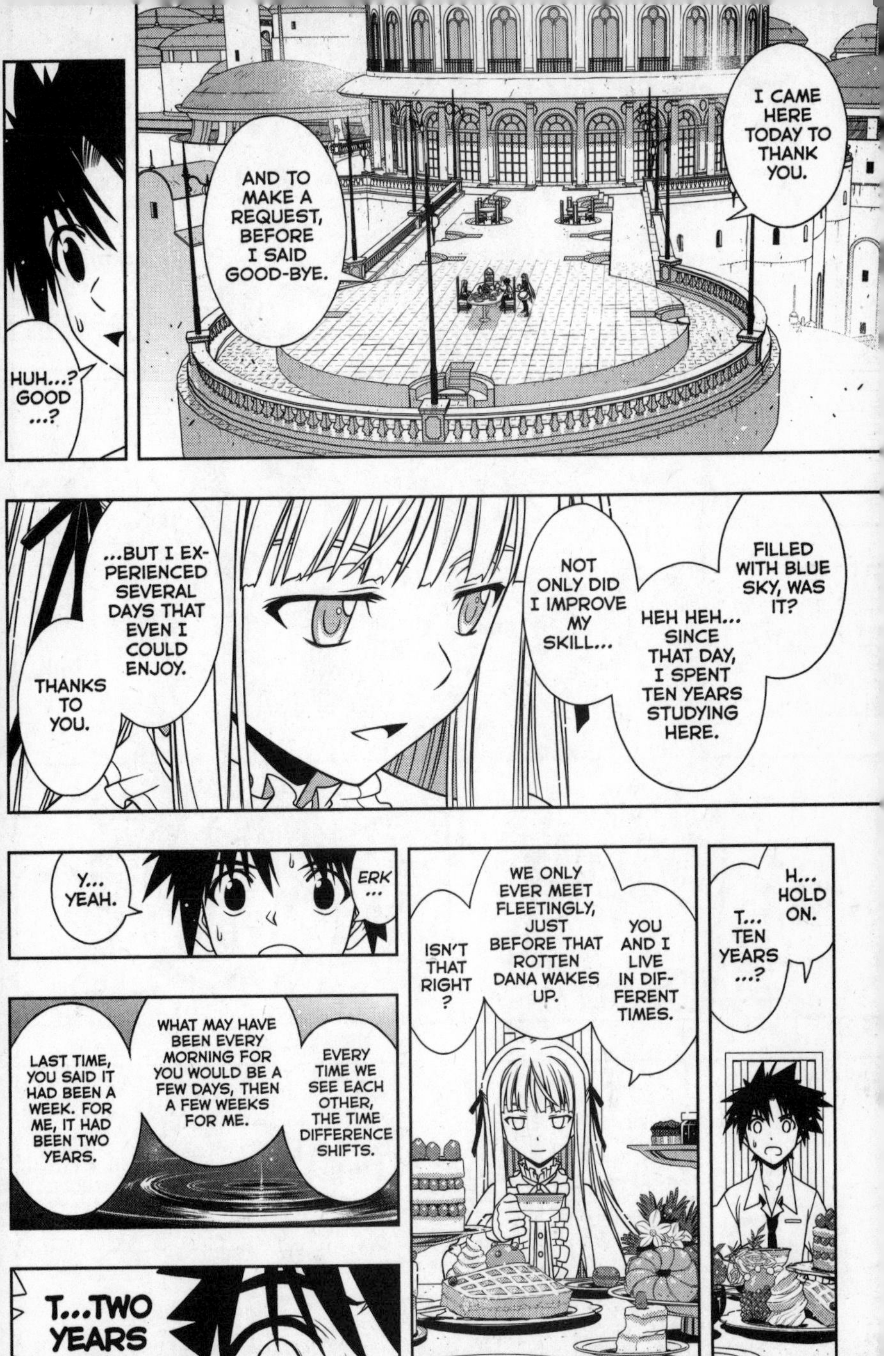
I CAME HERE TODAY TO THANK YOU.
AND TO MAKE A REQUEST, BEFORE I SAID GOOD-BYE.
HUH...? GOOD ...?
FILLED WITH BLUE SKY, WAS IT?
HEH HEH... SINCE THAT DAY, I SPENT TEN YEARS STUDYING HERE.
NOT ONLY DID I IMPROVE MY SKILL...
...BUT I EXPERIENCED SEVERAL DAYS THAT EVEN I COULD ENJOY.
THANKS TO YOU.
H... HOLD ON.
T... TEN YEARS ...?
YOU AND I LIVE IN DIFFERENT TIMES.
WE ONLY EVER MEET FLEETINGLY, JUST BEFORE THAT ROTTEN DANA WAKES UP.
ISN'T THAT RIGHT?
ERK ...
Y... YEAH.
EVERY TIME WE SEE EACH OTHER, THE TIME DIFFERENCE SHIFTS.
WHAT MAY HAVE BEEN EVERY MORNING FOR YOU WOULD BE A FEW DAYS, THEN A FEW WEEKS FOR ME.
LAST TIME, YOU SAID IT HAD BEEN A WEEK. FOR ME, IT HAD BEEN TWO YEARS.
T...TWO YEARS ?!

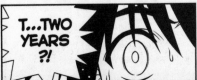

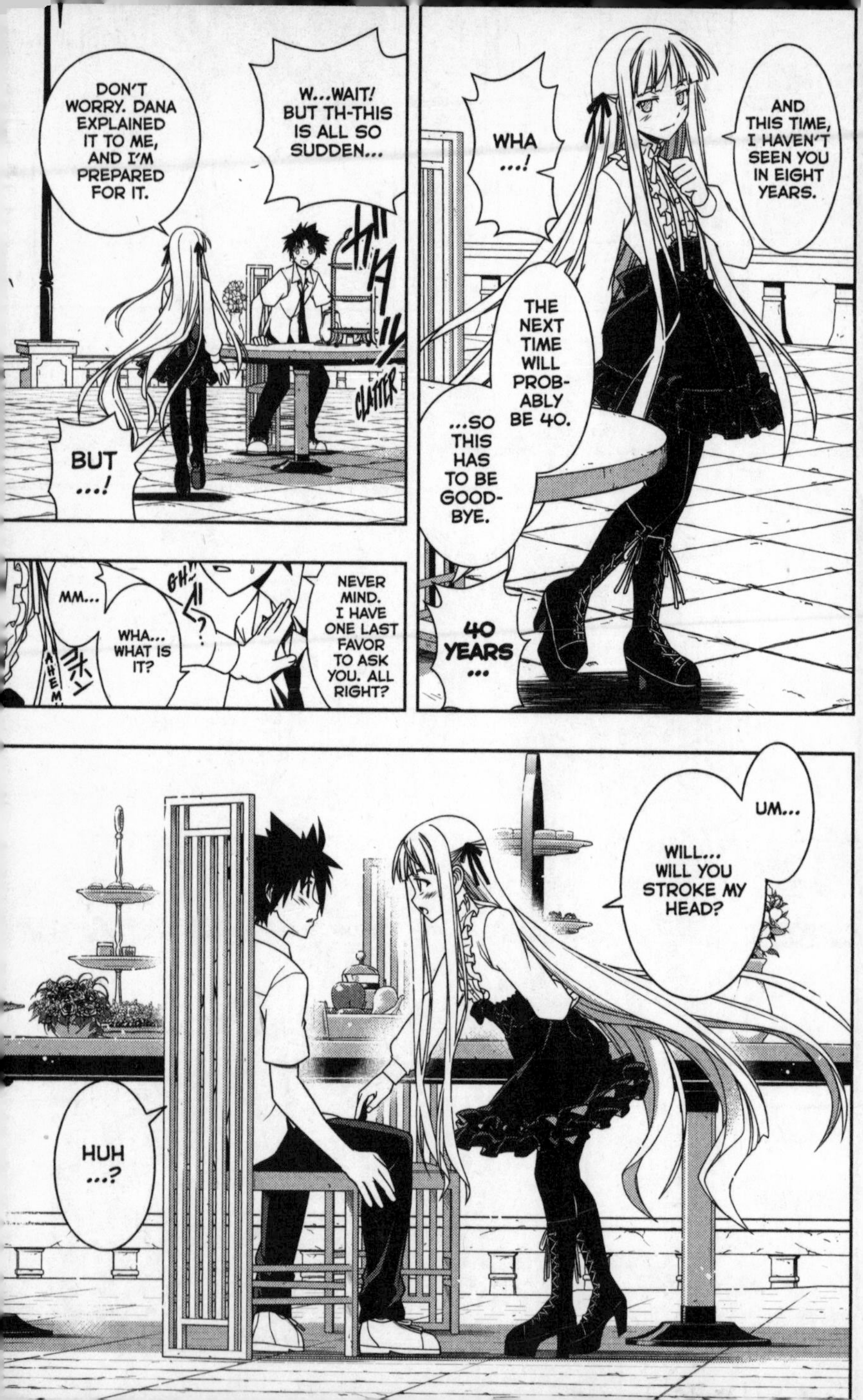

AND THIS TIME, I HAVEN'T SEEN YOU IN EIGHT YEARS.
WHA ...!
THE NEXT TIME WILL PROBABLY BE 40.
...SO THIS HAS TO BE GOOD-BYE.
40 YEARS ...
W...WAIT! BUT TH-THIS IS ALL SO SUDDEN...
DON'T WORRY. DANA EXPLAINED IT TO ME, AND I'M PREPARED FOR IT.
CLATTER
BUT ...!
NEVER MIND. I HAVE ONE LAST FAVOR TO ASK YOU. ALL RIGHT?
WHA... WHAT IS IT?
MM...
AHEM
UM...
WILL... WILL YOU STROKE MY HEAD?
HUH ...?

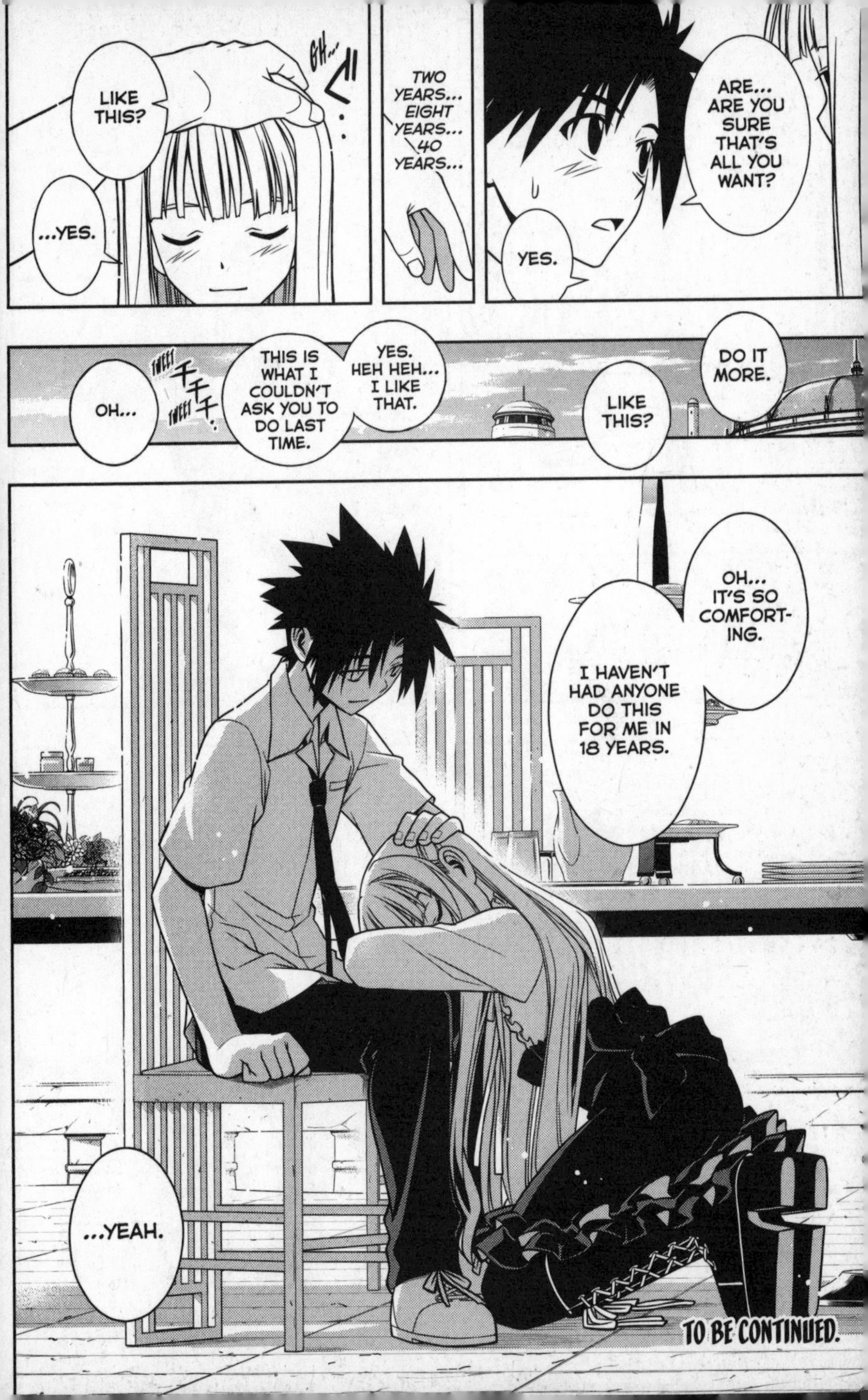
ARE... ARE YOU SURE THAT'S ALL YOU WANT?
YES.
TWO YEARS... EIGHT YEARS... 40 YEARS...
LIKE THIS?
...YES.
DO IT MORE.
LIKE THIS?
YES. HEH HEH... I LIKE THAT.
THIS IS WHAT I COULDN'T ASK YOU TO DO LAST TIME.
OH...
OH... IT'S SO COMFORT-ING.
I HAVEN'T HAD ANYONE DO THIS FOR ME IN 18 YEARS.
...YEAH.
TO BE CONTINUED.

UQ HOLDER!

STAFF

Ken Akamatsu
Takashi Takemoto
Kenichi Nakamura
Keiichi Yamashita
Tohru Mitsuhashi
Susumu Kuwabara
Yuri Sasaki

Thanks to Ran Ayanaga

TRANSLATORS NOTES

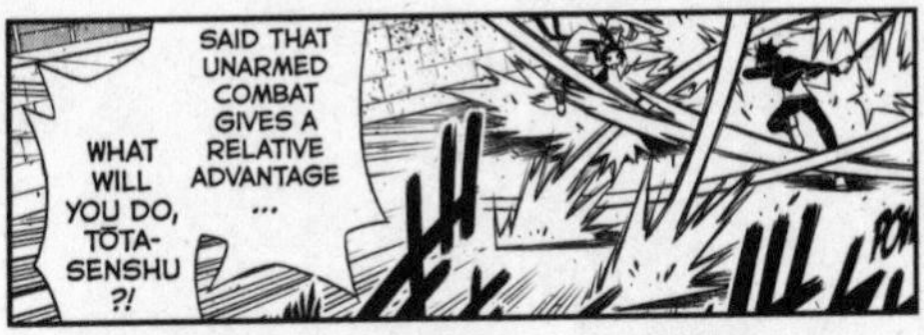
SAID THAT UNARMED COMBAT GIVES A RELATIVE ADVANTAGE ...
WHAT WILL YOU DO, TŌTA-SENSHU ?!

TŌTA-SENSHU, PAGE 17

The word *senshu* is a name honorific that indicates someone is an athlete, similar to *sensei* for doctors and teachers.

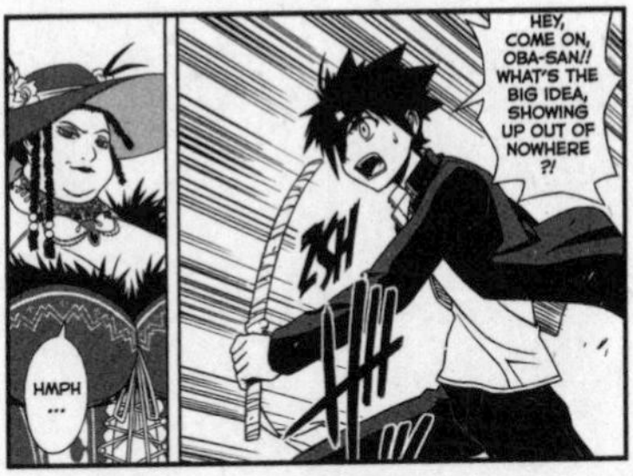
HEY, COME ON, OBA-SAN!! WHAT'S THE BIG IDEA, SHOWING UP OUT OF NOWHERE ?!
ZSH
HMPH ...

OBA-SAN, PAGE 39

While *oba-san* can refer to one's aunt, it is commonly used as a term of respect for middle-aged women to whom one is not necessarily related. A similar term for young women is *onee-san*, which Dana would likely prefer.

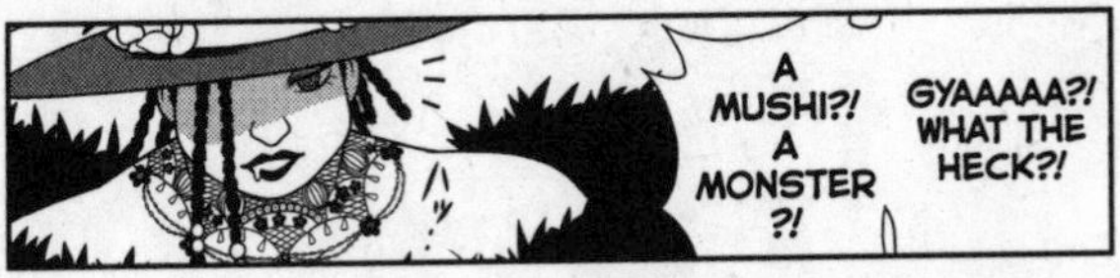
GYAAAAA?! WHAT THE HECK?!
A MUSHI?! A MONSTER ?!

MUSHI, PAGE 139

Although *mushi* generally means "insect," in this case, it refers to a supernatural insect creature.